MA

The Life and Times of "Ma" Barker and Her Boys

"Ma"

The Life and Times of "Ma" Barker and Her Boys

John Koblas

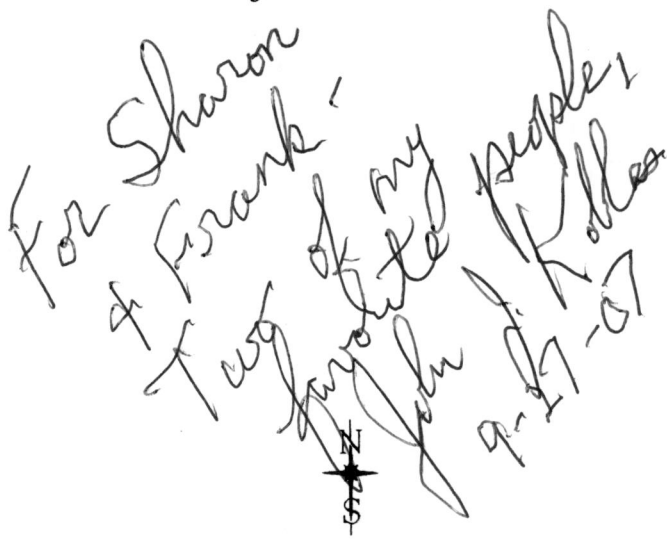

North Star Press of St. Cloud, Inc.
St. Cloud, Minnesota

Copyright © 2007 John Koblas

ISBN: 0-87839-264-5

First Edition: September 2007
First Printing: September 2007

All rights reserved.

Printed in the United States of America

Published by
North Star Press of St. Cloud, Inc.
P.O. Box 451
St. Cloud, Minnesota 56302
northstarpress.com

Contents

Introduction		vii
Chapter One	Born to Be Bad	1
Chapter Two	The Barker-Karpis Gang	44
Chapter Three	Robbery and Murder	85
Chapter Four	Larry Devol & Earl Christman	117
Chapter Five	Hamm Kidnapping	144
Chapter Six	Bremer Kidnapping	180
Chapter Seven	Crackdown	220
Chapter Eight	Assassinations	246
Chapter Nine	The Death of Ma Barker	272
Chapter Ten	Life Imprisonment	303
Chapter Eleven	The End of an Era	334
Chapter Twelve	The Great Escape	363
Chapter Thirteen	The Rock	388
Bibliography		423

Introduction

Ma Barker and her boys. It's the stuff of legend. A criminal mother and her four sons. The aging matriarch dying side-by-side with her youngest boy in a Tommy gunduel with "G-men" at a Florida bungalow. It's a haunting, somewhat Oedipal, image of family-style crime that must have captivated Americans in a vein similar to the "romantic" boy-and-girl bandit team of Bonnie and Clyde.

Most people had never heard of Ma Barker before her death in January 1935 and contradictory images of her survive to this day. Was she a larcenous matriarch andmastermind of a family of killers? Or simply a gullible old hillbilly woman, to whom blood was thicker than law, who knew little of her sons' activities, forgave what she knew, and allowed herself to be dragged around the country by them as camouflage. Did she die with a chattering machine gun in her hand or was this a convenient smokescreen for the FBI after accidentally gunning down an old woman?

Two of her sons and their informally adopted buddy Alvin Karpis led a crew of associates in blazing a bloody trail across the Midwest Depression landscape—robbing banks, kidnapping millionaires, and ruthlessly gunning down anyone who got in their way.

"Ma"—The Life and Times of "Ma" Barker and Her Boys

Her oldest son had shot himself in the Twenties to avoid capture after a Southwestern crime spree that produced some regional headlines and another son missed out on the action entirely by earning early a long sentence for mail robbery. But, despite the later grotesque imagery of comic books and absurd movies like Ma Barker's Killer Brood and Bloody Mama, the simple truth is that Ma was never seen at the scene of a crime, never charged with a crime, never fingered by alleged accomplices Her status as a headlined "public enemy" began entirely with her gruesome demise.

Of the existence of the Barker-Karpis Gang there can be no doubt. Their known crimes are numerous and difficult to catalog. They were the first and the last of the major Depression bandit gangs and practically a crime wave in themselves. Even John Dillinger was a piker by comparison. Arrie Barker, on the other hand, may have been as much a victim as Zerelda Samuel, who lost an arm to an attack by Pinkerton detectives out to get sons Jesse and Frank at any cost. But even the Pinkertons never claimed Zerelda to be the brains behind the James Gang.

Ma's role may forever be conjecture but I've got to hand it to any historian willing to tackle the convoluted exploits of the Barkers. Aside from bits and pieces in various books on Thirties crime and the tape-recorded and edited memoirs of Alvin Karpis, very little has been published on this gang, probably the most professional and dangerous of their era. It's a difficult trail to follow, and the literature is sparse on the Barkers in comparison to their headline-grabbing contemporaries such as Dillinger, "Pretty Boy" Floyd, "Baby Face" Nelson, and Bonnie and Clyde.

Jack Koblas has my respect in this department. An outlaw historian with over fifty books to his credit, many dealing with other outlaw brotherhood clans such as the Jameses and Youngers, I can understand his enthusiasm with this project. As his early chapters illustrate, it's not such a broad step from the Jameses to the Barkers, both products of a bygone period of rural Missouri. Arrie married George Barker just a month before the Daltons died at Coffeeville and her boys carried on an outlaw tradition—modernized with cars and machine guns. It just might be that the "Old West" really ended not at Coffeeville but with that Tommy gun battle at Ocklawaha.

—Rick Mattix, author of
The Complete Public Enemy Almanac

Movie poster. (Author's collection)

Chapter One

Born to Be Bad

"God alone knows what my brother and I suffered. We starved almost to death with our pockets stuffed with money. Many times we had to lie badly wounded for weeks in the woods without medical attention. Always we were hunted like the wolves of the prairie."
—Frank James[1]

ollowing breakfast, on April 3, 1882, thirteen days after Bob Ford boasted that he'd kill Jesse James, the opportunity finally presented itself. Bob and his older brother Charlie had been watching Jesse and had anxiously been awaiting the right opportunity to murder him. Jesse, however, was always heavily armed and ever watchful. They had discarded any plan of taking him alive, considering the attempt suicidal.[2]

Charlie Ford and Jesse had been out in the stable preparing the

Robert Ford. (Courtesy Library of Congress)

Jesse James. (Courtesy Library of Congress)

horses for that evening's intended Platte City, Missouri, robbery. Returning inside the house, Jesse said to Bob, who was seated in the room, "It's an awfully hot day." Jesse pulled off his coat and vest, and placed them on his bed. Then he said, "I guess I'll take off my pistols, for fear somebody will see them if I walk in the yard" and unbuckled his gun belt. Placing his two 45s—a Smith & Wesson and a Colt—on the bed, he picked up a brush to dust some pictures on the wall.[3]

When Jesse turned his back to his friends, they stepped between him and his revolvers, and at a motion from Charlie, both drew their pistols. Robert drew quicker than his brother and fired at the back of Jesse's head from a distance of only two to four feet. Jesse heard the slight motion and had began to turn his head, but he fell to the floor with no outcry. The fatal bullet had entered the back of the skull, and America's most feared outlaw was dead.

Little ten-year-old Arizona Clark had never forgotten the day she had seen Jesse James ride through Carthage, Missouri, near her family's Ozark foothills home. Learning of her hero's death at the hands of a man he had trusted, she wept bitterly. Her childhood infatuation with the outlaw mystique would never diminish.[4]

The citizens of the Midwestern part of the United States had, for a number of years, known and feared many notorious criminals who lived by outside the law—outlaws, such as the James-Younger Gang, who on galloping steeds ravaged Missouri, Arkansas, Oklahoma, and Kansas at will.

Train robbers, bank robbers, and other gun-toting outlaw gangs plagued the citizens of Oklahoma and bordering states, and often took refuge in the Cookson Hills. The daring exploits of men on both sides of the law often were the subject of sensational news stories. But the grim reality was that law and order in the early days of Oklahoma was a deadly business, and shootouts between outlaws and lawmen were commonplace.[5]

Infamous gangs such as Frank and Jesse James, the Youngers, and the Daltons all sought refuge at one time or another in the Indian Territory. The federal court for the Western District of Arkansas had been established in Fort Smith by Congress. The court had jurisdiction over all lands between Kansas and the Red River, the largest jurisdiction in the world.

In 1875, Isaac C. Parker was appointed judge. Parker, the "Hanging Judge," took exception to outlaws who hid out in the Indian Territory, hiring almost two hundred deputy marshals to track down lawbreakers who robbed and killed in both Oklahoma and the surrounding states.

The Indian Territory was a favorite hiding place for outlaws wanted elsewhere because there was no law to extradite bad men for their crimes in another state or territory. During the years of Judge Parker's court, 160 offenders were sentenced to death by orders of the "Hanging Judge." Seventy-nine of them were hanged in Fort Smith, Arkansas. But the cost for bringing them in had been high. More than one hundred deputy marshals died at the hands of these outlaws during this period of outlawry.

The land run of 1889 opened Oklahoma to settlement. Oklahoma Territory was organized in 1890, and the territorial capital was established at Guthrie. In

Judge Isaac Parker, the "Hanging Judge." (Author's collection)

1892, the notorious Dalton Gang was gunned down just across the border in Coffeyville, Kansas, while attempting a double bank robbery.

Bill Doolin. (Author's collection)

Gang member Bill Doolin escaped and returned to start a new reign of bloodshed with his own gang. Deputy United States marshals riding out of Guthrie followed the Doolin Gang to the small community of Ingalls in 1893. In what became known as the "Ingalls Raid," more than a dozen lawmen surrounded the tiny town east of Stillwater where the Doolin Gang was holed up. A fierce gun battle were killed in the process, but Bill Doolin escaped again.

With the coming of the new century, the role of a fast horse was greatly diminished, giving way to a new, more effective, suddenly necessary mode of transportation—the automobile. Along with this technological change, law breakers morphed as well. Representative of the new criminal element was an outlaw band which originated in the Ozark Mountains of Missouri and Arkansas and the Cookson Hills of Oklahoma. The infamous Karpis-Barker Gang, which, except for its mobility and modern equipment—machine guns and fast automobiles—was made up of fairly typical southwestern bandits.[6]

The mother of the Barker brothers—Herman, Lloyd, Fred, and Arthur—was Arizona Donnie Clark Barker, commonly known as Kate Barker. Many of her friends called her Arrie Barker, but to her sons and their associates she was affectionately known as "Ma" or "Mother."

Kate Barker was born in 1872 near Ash Grove, Boone Township, Greene County, Missouri, some eighteen miles from Springfield. Her parents

Ma Barker (Mrs. Arrie Barker, also known as Mrs. George Anderson) (Photographer: Bureau of Criminal Apprehension, Photograph Collection 1931 Location no. por 16552 r1, Negative no. 91502)

were Scotch-Irish, although it was sometimes rumored that she also had some Indian blood in her veins too. She came from an ordinary family and, during her early life, was reared near Springfield.[7]

Arrie was the third of four children born to John and Emeline (Parker) Clark, who had been married in Greene County, Missouri, on December 8, 1864. Her father apparently died in the late 1870s, for by 1880, her mother had married Reuben J. Reynolds also known as James J. Reynolds of 419 South Wheeling Avenue, Tulsa, Missouri. They had another daughter, Buetta Reynolds.

It appears that the family moved to Lawrence County by 1889. The oldest daughter, Electa A. Clark, of Aurora, was married to A.J. Watesburg of Aurora, at Mt. Vernon on April 6, 1889. No record has been found for Jessie

Clark, born circa 1869, only son of John and Emeline Clark. According to an FBI file on "Ma" Barker, all Kate's siblings remained in Oklahoma except for one sister who became a Mrs. Vosburg and moved to Long Beach, California.[8]

Kate's stepfather was employed as a watchman and director of traffic at the Oil Exposition at Tulsa. Kate had asked her stepfather for a loan, and when he refused, they had little to do with each other after that. Reynolds, in fact, had little respect for any of Kate's children in later years, characterizing Fred and Arthur Barker as being mean and no good; neither having done any work since they were released from the penitentiary the first time. He told an FBI agent that he was surprised that Governor Murray would parole such a man as Doc Barker.[9]

Growing up on a poor but tidy farm, Arrie's childhood was not unusual. Her parents were hard-working, church-going people, who raised her to be a law-abiding, church-going Presbyterian. It is unclear as to why her parents bestowed the name Arizona on her, but because she despised it, she went by Arrie, and soon Kate. And Kate it would stay.[10]

Despite her being mesmerized by the abundance of outlaw lore when and where she was growing up, Ash Grove offered her a strong pioneer heritage. In 1781, Nathan Boone was born in Kentucky, the youngest son of Daniel Boone. Boone grew up to be similar to his famous father in character, temperament, and achievement. As a captain of the Missouri Rangers during the War of 1812, Boone established himself as a capable leader and demonstrated abilities quite equal to his legendary father. In 1833, he was made a captain of dragoons, a military regiment at the time, and was stationed at Fort Gibson in Oklahoma. He was assigned the task of surveying the boundaries between the Creek and Cherokee Indian nations. Ten years later, he conducted an expedition into the unsettled area of what is now Oklahoma and Kansas. On February 16, 1847, Boone was made major of the First Dragoons. In 1850, he was given a commission as lieutenant colonel of the Second Dragoons. He resigned from military service on July 15, 1853, because of failing health.

As early as 1834, Boone's sons, James, Benjamin Howard, and John Colter were acquiring land on which to build the family home near Ash Grove.

Boone and his wife, Olive, left their stone mansion in what is now Defiance, Missouri, in 1837 and moved into the newly built house in Ash Grove, which began as a "double-pen log cabin with an open dogtrot through the center." It was a story and a half with a sleeping loft on the second floor and was built primarily of locally harvested ash logs with walnut being used for the sills and much of the trim work. As time went on, the cabin evolved with the dogtrot being closed in and the exterior being covered in walnut weatherboarding. The interior was finished with plaster and lathe. Boone lived here until his death in 1856, and both he and Olive were buried in the nearby family cemetery. From the pioneering-rich Boones to the infamous Jameses, Kate's imagination knew no bounds, and the majestic Cookson Hills comprised her playground where the ghosts of these rebels still lurked behind every tree.[11]

North of the Ouachitas, set apart from them by the valley of the Arkansas River, the Cookson Hills make up the Ozark Plateau, with its broad, flat-topped hills separating one from another by narrow, V-shaped river valleys. Elevations here range from 600 to 1,200 feet. There were cabins all over the hills when Jesse James had spent a night, and in nearby Carthage lived a man who had ridden with the James boys. In Carthage also was the old farm where Myra Belle Shirley had been born, and by the time Arrie Clark was a young girl, Myra Belle had become Belle Starr, "the notorious bandit and outlaw woman of Arkansas and the Indian Territory." But back in the Ozarks, Belle was a heroine and idol of most of the inhabitants.[12]

When Arrie reached her teens, she became "Kate," atypical of other hill folk, though still tough, fierce in her affections and loyalties, and always suspicious of outsiders. The God-fearing, short, dark-haired girl with the penetrating eyes never missed church, and like everyone else in the hills, was devoted to the Bible and the fiddle.[13]

She considered herself deeply religious and was a true believer in fundamentalist Christianity. She knew scores of hymns and loved to sing them constantly while cooking in the kitchen. As a cook, she was remarkably good and very vain about it.[14]

She was in no way an attractive girl, and her pointed nose and chin gave her a witch-like appearance, especially as she grew older. As for her temperament, she presented contrary impressions to all who knew her. To many she appeared amiable, easy-going, and quite ordinary, but to those who knew her best, few escaped her violent, explosive temper.

On September 14, 1892, Arrie "Kate" Clark and her boyfriend, George D. Barker, a farm laborer from Lebanon, Missouri, appeared before Lawrence County Recorder W.C. Trimble and applied for a marriage license at Aurora, Missouri.[15] They were married the same day by Reverend W.B. Cochran, pastor of the First Christian Church of Aurora. She gave her address as Mt. Vernon.[16]

George Barker was a somewhat pathetic figure. Shy and weak, he was the opposite of his wife and later their children. He was a frail, wispy little man with a long face and deep-set blue eyes; ignorant and uneducated, he bore the appearance and personality of a life-long nobody. But he was also mild and patient, an honest man who loved his children dearly and even his unpredictable wife until he could take no more.[17]

Kate's youngest sister, Eva M. Clark, of Miller, was married to Elmer B. Hays, of Miller on December 31, 1895.[18]

Cole Younger. (Courtesy Library of Congress)

The early married life of George and Kate was spent at Aurora, Missouri, where their four sons—Herman, Lloyd, Arthur "Doc," and Freddie were born, and Kate became known as "a good wife, devoted to the Presbyterian Church, a fair housekeeper, and averse to back-fence gossip."

The prospects for the future looked good for Kate and George Barker. The legendary outlaws of the 1870s and 1880s were mostly dead, in prison, or keeping a low profile. Cole Younger was serving a twenty-five-year sentence for his part in a bank robbery attempt in Northfield, Minnesota. From his prison cell, he warned young people against a life of violence and crime, but men like the Dalton brothers had not yet learned their lessons.

These former Coffeyville, Kansas, residents were interested in the new bank there for reasons quite different from those of Luther Perkins, who had erected his shiny new bank two years earlier. Bob Dalton planned to outdo the James boys by using Coffeyville as the setting for a spectacular double bank robbery.

Early in the morning on October 5, 1892, less than a month after the Barker's were married, five members of the Dalton Gang—Bob, Grat, and Emmett Dalton, Bill Powers, and Dick Broadwell—rode into Coffeyville. They tied their horses in the alley across from the banks, then strolled across the street and divided into two groups, one entering Condon National Bank and the other going into First National Bank.[19]

However, not unlike Northfield, Minnesota, they were recognized by citizens, and the alarm was given. Townsmen quickly armed themselves with weapons from the local hardware stores and took up positions to defend the town and its banks. As the bandits tried to make good their escape, a fierce gun battle took place in which four citizens and four members of the gang lost their lives. Emmett, the sole surviving member of the gang, was seriously wounded.

Dalton Gang. (Courtesy Library of Congress)

Emmett Dalton later wrote: "Then came darkness and quiet. The popping of the guns died away. The brightness of the sun ceased and all was still. I sank back on the ground. The Dalton Gang was no more."[20]

Two months later, Ned Christie, a former blacksmith, gunsmith, and Cherokee senator, continued to stand up for the sovereignty of the Cherokee Nation and vowed never to speak English again—instead, he'd only use his own native tongue, Cherokee. During this time, Christie became known as a hunted outlaw and was accused of every unsolved crime in the Cherokee Nation and in the vicinity of the Cherokee Nation/Arkansas border. On December 14, 1892, a posse attempted to fire a canon to blow him out of the house. Being unsuccessful, as the home was high above a creek, the deputies resorted to dynamiting the house. The setting of the dynamite prompted Christie to run from the house in front of the officers, only to be shot to death. Ned Christie became a Cherokee martyr and another of Ma Barker's fallen heroes.[21]

A boy (maybe over fourteen) at heavy work, shoveling ore at Daisy Bell Mine, Aurora, Missouri, in 1910. (Courtesy Library of Congress)

"MA"—THE LIFE AND TIMES OF "MA" BARKER AND HER BOYS

Ma Barker was undoubtedly moved by the demise of the Daltons and heroes like Ned Christie, just as she had been with the death of Jesse James, even though she and her new husband had more than enough troubles of their own. George and Arrie purchased a lot at Aurora on September 5, 1898 (lot 202, block 21, Linzee's Second Addition; Book 79, page 178). The property was located at 108 Jasper.[22]

"Heck" Thomas. (Author's collection)

The couple lived in a tumbled-down miner's shack and initially had a tough go of it. George did some farming to raise a limited crop and some vegetables for the table.

On October 30, 1893, their first son, Herman, was born, followed by Lloyd in 1896, Arthur (nicknamed "Dock" but later trimmed to "Doc") in 1899, and finally Fred in 1901. With each new arrival, George Barker had to work a little harder both on the farm and in the mines. Even so, he could barely eek out a living to feed his growing family.[23]

Kate's world of Old West outlaws shrank even more in 1896, the year Lloyd was born. Leading the fight for law and order in the Oklahoma Territory were Deputy United States Marshals Bill Tilghman, "Heck" Thomas, and Chris Madsen, known as the "Three Guardsmen."[24] Tilghman went after outlaw Bill Doolin, reportedly tracked him down in Eureka Springs, Arkansas, on January 12, 1896, and captured him single-handedly without firing a shot.[25]

Given the reality of train schedules and layout, Tilghman, however, could not have made the trip to Arkansas in the time frame he claimed. Doolin apparently surrendered to Tilghman in Wichita in a pre-arranged agreement with U.S. Marshal E.D. Nix, who was about to be fired for being a crooked law officer. Tilghman's "capture" of Doolin was set up in an effort to save Nix's job.[26]

"MA"—THE LIFE AND TIMES OF "MA" BARKER AND HER BOYS

Bill Tilghman. (Author's collection)

Doolin was returned to the federal jail in Guthrie, but later led a daring jailbreak and escaped. Heck Thomas took to the trail of the outlaw and, in 1896, found Doolin in Lawson on the Payne/Pawnee County line east of Stillwater. Doolin fired on the lawmen and was killed in a hail of bullets. The language of the posted reward read: "Five thousand dollars will be paid for the arrest and conviction of William Doolin." Since he was never convicted, the reward was never paid.

The next year, 1897, Deputy United States Marshal James Franklin (Bud) Ledbetter captured outlaws Al and Frank Jennings. Ledbetter was a former deputy sheriff in Johnson County, Arkansas, where he was known to thieves and killers as one of "the Invincibles." He also served as city marshal, chief of police, and sheriff. Marshal Ledbetter and his posse cornered the brothers and their gang in a ranch near Claremore, Oklahoma.[27]

The Barkers sold their house and property on September 16, 1899. According to local businessman, Jack Turner, the Barkers moved east of Riverdale, in Christian County, for a while. The older sons attended school at Aurora, albeit briefly.[28]

About 1903 or 1904 the family moved from Aurora to Webb City, a small village just north of Joplin, where Herman and Lloyd, the elder sons, attended grade schools. Webb City was a rough and wild mining town and perhaps not the best environment for raising four boys. But George was still head of the family, and "Ma" and the kids dutifully went along with whatever he said.[29]

John C. Webb had platted the town in July 1875 when miners began to flood the area. Soon mines surrounded the town, and between the years

1894 and 1904, they produced twenty-three million dollars in lead and zinc. While most of the miners made their homes in nearby Joplin, with its gambling halls, saloons, and brothels, many mine owners made their living quarters in Webb City.

Ma Barker was probably aware that Jesse and Frank James and Cole Younger had at least once ridden through Webb City. The trio had once departed from Eureka Springs, Arkansas, rather hastily down the old "pig trail" wagon road after being recognized by a Baptist preacher and two other men. The old road took them through Huntsville in Madison County, across the War Eagle and White rivers to Brashiers.[30]

From Brashiers, they rode south over the mountain pass to Franklin County where they forded the Mulberry River just below the Cass Post Office at Turner Bend. About a mile and a half south of the Mulberry, at the foot of Black Mountain, they stopped at a farmer's house before moving south to Ozark, Arkansas, on the Arkansas River's north bluff bank. When the outlaws crossed the Arkansas River at Ozark, they rode into Webb City.

Early on, George Barker and his sons enjoyed a good relationship, and Herman and Lloyd, as soon as they were old enough, went hunting with their father in the solitude and splendor of the Ozark hills. The woods were teeming with wildlife, and it wasn't long before the boys had an expert knowledge of rifles and shotguns.

Ma Barker, as she was already called, did her best as a good wife, devoted mother, and avid churchgoer. During services, whenever the church organist played, "Oh Promise Me," and the congregation sang, Ma's booming voice could be heard over all the others. Seated beside her every Sunday were her four sons, who sang hymns as well.

George Barker worked very hard in Webb City's lead and zinc mines, but per always, his wages were meager. Ma, meanwhile, had one good friend in the area—a Mrs. Farmer, who had a young boy named Herbert. The Farmer boy became one of the Barker children's best pals and later played a significant role in their criminal history. The Farmers and the Barkers were both dirt poor, and this brought them close together. Mrs. Farmer and Ma Barker were both described by the neighbors as kind of strange and standoffish.

"Ma"—The Life and Times of "Ma" Barker and Her Boys

Doc and Fred Barker were just infants when the family moved to Webb City, but Herman and Lloyd lost little time getting acquainted with the local police through acts of petty theft and vandalism. Their timid father, George, tried his best to keep his sons on the right track, but he finally gave up. While George had, up to this time, enjoyed his shaky role as head of the household, Ma turned on him suddenly and ordered him to keep his mouth shut. She informed George that she would raise her boys and didn't need any help from him.

From that day on, George Barker adopted a hands-off role in the bringing up of his sons. Whenever a neighbor would come to him to complain about one of his boys, he would merely shrug his shoulders and relate, "You'll have to talk to their mother. She handles the boys."[31]

When Herman was arrested for petty thievery, Ma descended on the police station ranting and raving. When she saw that this technique got her nowhere, she switched gears and tearfully pleaded for mercy. This trick worked much better, and she was allowed to take him home. Back in the little shack, she gave Herman the chewing out of his life—not, however, for stealing, but for getting caught. She went on to explain what he should have done, and this became the beginning of her "motherly chats" with each of her sons.

Old ideas mingled with new ones as people in America welcomed the twentieth century. While most Americans were awed by the wonders of the developing machine age, the problems and dangers it posed also intimidated them. The new century was a time of enterprise, invention, and industrial concentration, but it was also one of trust busting, added public control, and a regression from old-time faith in laissez faire.[32]

In November, President McKinley won re-election on the slogan, "The dinner pail is full." America was emerging as a nation of great opportunity. People all over the world abandoned dire futures in old countries, often facing persecution or desperate poverty. Here, expectations flourished. Even the most underpaid immigrant was doing better than he ever hoped to do, and some could even send money home to those who stayed behind.[33]

National and world fairs dominated the first decade of the new century, and in 1901, President William McKinley was assassinated at the Pan

American Exposition in Buffalo, New York. Americans became involved in the new fad of jujitsu.[34] Campaigns were launched against "deleterious" patent medicines and adulterated foods, while Lincoln Steffens, Ida Tarbell, and others led a fight against contemporary evils.

Americans in 1904 sang, "Meet Me in St. Louis" and "In the Good Old Summertime," while reading such bestsellers as *Rebecca of Sunnybrook Farm*, *Beverly of Graustark*, the latest adventures of Sherlock Holmes, and Churchill's *The Crossing*. *Raffles* was a big hit on stage, but on a more sophisticated front, Arnold Daly was performing Shaw's *Candida*, and Minnie Maddern Fiske was tantalizing in Ibsen's *Hedda Gabler*. Fads swept the country, including jujitsu and Charles Wagner's "Simple Life," as well as Theodore Roosevelt's contribution to support simplified spelling. Popular magazines, taking advantage of wood pulp, photography, and sensationalism, multiplied.[35]

By 1900, the pattern of America's rail system had been worked out, while iron ore, lumber, grain, and coal were carried on large fleets of ships over the Great Lakes. As the larger cities grew, streetcar systems were developed. Steam power had replaced the horse, but by 1890, electric-powered streetcars rattled along city streets. During the 1890s, the automobile passed its experimental period, and by 1900, a dozen motor companies turned out 4,000 cars.

As early as 1910, each of Kate's four sons had been arrested at least once. On March 5, 1915, Herman Barker was arrested at Joplin, Missouri, on a charge of highway robbery. With his crime partners Lee Flournoy and Lyman Ford, they had hijacked a high stakes gambling operation in Joplin. Herman's mother, of course, came to his rescue and got him released. She told neighbors she had had it with the police persecuting her boys and planned to move out of the area where they could be treated fairly.[36]

That same year a wave of bank robberies swept across Oklahoma and neighboring states. The man behind them, Henry Starr, a relative of the infamous Belle Starr; he had begun a life of crime in 1890 which lasted for thirty years.

On March 27, 1915, Henry Starr and six members of his gang attempted to rob two banks at the same time in Stroud, Oklahoma—the Stroud State Bank and the First National Bank. During the gunfight which

Belle Starr with Blue Dick. (Author's collection) Duck?

Henry Starr. (Author's collection)

followed in the street, seventeen-year-old Paul Curry shot Starr in the left thigh below the hip, shattering the leg bone and knocking him down. Like the Daltons in their earlier attempt at two banks, the robbery was a failure.[37]

The *Chandler News-Publicist* later reported: "Even while the banks were being robbed, news was phoned to Chandler, and in just eleven minutes from the time the word came, Sheriff George Arnold, Deputy Sheriff Hi Frisbie and several citizens were en route to the scene in automobiles. . . . Bill Tilghman did not hear of the robbery in time to leave his home at Chandler with the others, but went to Stroud later. . . . Arriving at Stroud, a posse was organized and the chase after the fleeing bandits began."[38]

Henry Starr was sentenced to twenty-five years in the Oklahoma State Penitentiary at McAlester. He was forty-three years old. It was the year that author Henry James died, and the United States Supreme Court decided that an Indian could still be treated as a ward of the United States Government, and Congress could still regulate his affairs for him.[39]

Starr was paroled after serving four years. He was killed in Arkansas in 1921, attempting another bank robbery. Starr did, however, illustrate the changing style of the outlaws. Starr had ridden into Stroud on horseback armed with a six-shooter, but when he was killed in 1921 he had driven into town in a high-powered automobile.[40]

Ma Barker, meanwhile, moved the family to Tulsa, Oklahoma, where they settled into a two-room shack near the Santa Fe Railroad tracks. The old clapboard house they called home had two tiny rooms. The floor was comprised of bare boards laid on the ground. The bathroom was a fly infested shed behind the house, and when the flies finished their breeding there, they swarmed into Ma's house through the unscreened windows. The house was so crowded and they were so poor that the boys had to sleep on the bare floor.[41]

By then Tulsa had changed from a small Indian town to a boomtown with the discovery of oil. Wildcatters and investors flooded into the area and the town began to take shape. Neighborhoods were established in Tulsa on the north side of the Arkansas River, away from the drilling sites, and began to spread out from downtown Tulsa in all directions. In 1904, Tulsans constructed a bridge across the river, allowing oil-field workers, supplies, food and equipment to cross the river more easily, reaffirming Tulsa's position as the center of the oil field. In 1905, the Glenn Pool oil field was discovered. This strike created such a large supply of crude oil that it forced Tulsans to develop storage tanks for the excess oil and gas and, later, pipelines.

By the time Oklahoma achieved statehood in 1907, Tulsa had a population of 7,298. By 1920 the population boomed to 72,000. "Tulsey Town" had become a free-wheeling, wide open city submerged in oil, mud, and trouble, and it didn't take the Barker boys long to get their hands dirty.

In Tulsa, the Barker shack became an underworld post office and meeting place. After Freddie visited ex-con Herb Farmer at his hideout in Joplin, he invited several fugitives to stay at Ma's in Tulsa. They began showing up in 1915—shadowy characters such as Al Spencer, Frank Nash, Ray Terrill, and Earl Thayer. Chicago-bred hoods such as Francis Keating and Tommy Holden layed low at the Barker house while the heat was on.[42]

"Ma ruled the roost with an iron hand and took nothing off of nobody," recalled Harry Stege, who founded the police identification bureau in town. He remembered the Barker boys as "slippery young hoodlums."[43]

"Ma"—The Life and Times of "Ma" Barker and Her Boys

Fred and Arthur associated with other boys in the vicinity of the Lynch-Forsythe School at East First Street and Rockford Avenue, Tulsa, Oklahoma, and hung out with the boys around the section known as Central Park. All of Ma's sons were, at one time or another, members of the Central Park mob, which at one time had twenty-two "hijackers, bandits, and thugs" enlisted in their ranks.[44]

Many of the boys who associated with the sons of Kate Barker later became associates of these boys and entered into criminal activities with them. Harry Campbell and Volney Davis matured and grew up with the sons of Kate Barker; in later years they became prominent members of the Karpis-Barker Gang.

Another young man who ran with the Barker boys in the Central Park neighborhood was Ray Terrill, who later wrote of his association with the brothers: "I had decided to go to Texas and pull a few jobs down there, but I ran into some of the boys who had been casing the town of Coweta and thought it was ripe for a bank job. A short time before this, I had robbed the bank of Tyron. Ordinarily, I never undertook a job unless I had cased the town myself, but I let Doc Barker, who is now at Alcatraz, persuade me to go over to Coweta. There were four of us.

Ray Terrill, November 1936. (Courtesy of *Oklahoma News*)

"One of the boys had been rooming at Coweta for some time and I went out to his room to get some sleep. We had all our tools, shotguns, rifles, and other equipment in a big touring car, which we left parked in the back yard. While I was asleep, Doc and one of the other boys decided to go downtown and give the situation a final once over, which turned out to be a grave mistake. Someone had been passing hot checks there, and the town was pretty hot, so the law picked up Doc and his companion and began to ask them a lot of questions.

"As a result of Doc's arrest, they found our car and our layout of artillery and tools, so they brought us up to Wagoner and booked us for conspiracy. A few days later, we were taken to Chandler. My parents had moved to Los Angeles, but when they heard I was under arrest, my mother hurried back to Oklahoma to try to help me. She made me promise to plead guilty and take my medicine. . . .

"Anyway, I went ahead and agreed to plead guilty. In the meantime, we had been taken to McAlester for safekeeping and were there for five months before they took us back to Chandler. I was chained to Doc Barker on the train, and Harry Campbell and Roland Williams were chained together. On the way over to Chandler, Harry and Roland managed to break their chains. Doc and I knew they were ready to make a break and by this time; we had determined to see it through and get a fresh start in life, so we didn't want to go with them. There were some tense moments on that train. But finally, Harry and Roland managed to jump out the window and make a getaway. The case against Doc was dismissed, and I was sentenced to three years when I admitted the Tyron bank job was mine."[45]

Lloyd "Red" Barker, according to FBI records, was not a member of Ma Barker's Gang at the height of his operations. At the time he was spending twenty-five years in the federal penitentiary at Leavenworth for mail robbery in Baxter Springs, Kansas.[46]

The *St. Paul Pioneer Press* for Christmas Day 1887 remarked that the "five prominent institutions in every new born Western town are the school, the church, the general store, the newspaper, and the saloon."[47] Thirty-two years later, however, not everybody saw it quite that way. Among the groups fighting to ban consumption of alcohol were the Women's Christian Temperance Union (WCTU) and the Anti-Saloon League. Their success and anti-German sentiment after World War I led to the passage of the National Prohibition Act. It put legal brewers out of business and opened the nation's door to unintended consequences: bootlegging, gambling, prostitution, rackets, gangsters, and organized crime.

Despite consequences, the Volstead Act (National Prohibition Enforcement Act) passed on October 28, 1919, through the work, in large part, of Wayne Wheeler, the legislative lawyer of the Anti-Saloon League. Authored by Andrew Volstead, a leading Republican member of the House of Representatives, the act provided for enforcement of the recently ratified Eighteenth Amendment, which prohibited the manufacture, sale, or transportation of alcoholic beverages in the United States.

The act, passed over President Woodrow Wilson's veto, affirmed and further specified the provisions of the Eighteenth Amendment, delineated fines and prison terms for violation of the law, empowered the Bureau of Internal Revenue to administer prohibition, and classified as alcoholic all beverages containing more than one-half of one percent alcohol by volume. The act was condemned by a large number of the American population, who considered it a violation of their constitutional rights.

One of the consequences of the National Prohibition Act was the sharp increase in crime. Enforcement of prohibition was a difficult task, and a growth in illegal drinking establishments took place. "Moon-shiners" distilled alcohol illegally, while bootleggers sold the alcohol and also imported it from abroad.

Because liquor was no longer legally available, people had to deal with gangsters, who readily took on the bootlegging industry and supplied them with liquor. Because the industry was so profitable, more gangsters became involved. Crime became so organized because "criminal groups organize around the steady source of income provided by laws against victimless crimes such as consuming alcohol"[48]

As a result of the money involved in the bootlegging industry, there was a great deal of rivalry between gangs. The profit motive caused over four hundred gang-related murders a year in Chicago alone.[49] Although there were over a half dozen powerful gangs in New York, Chicago was the capital of racketeers, with the likes of Johnny Torrio, "Bugs Moran," the Gennas, and the O'Banions well in control.[50]

Prohibition officers raiding the Lunch Room of 922 Pennsylvania Avenue Washington, D.C. (Courtesy Library of Congress)

The most powerful and infamous bootlegger operating out of Chicago, however, was Al Capone. Alphonse Capone was not a native of Chicago. He had been a twenty-one-year-old dishwasher in a Brooklyn cabaret when the Eighteenth Amendment took effect in 1920. His cousin, John Torrio, had gone to Chicago to run the illegal enterprises of his uncle, Big Jim Colosimo, and he brought Capone along as his assistant. Torrio was dubbed the "father of American gangsterdom" by a U.S. Treasury official, and a British newspaper referred to Capone as the "Nineteenth Amendment."[51]

Following a stint with the U.S. Army in France during World War I, Capone enjoyed an income of thirty-million dollars per year by the late 1920s. Within a few short years he consolidated his hold on

Al Capone. (Courtesy Library of Congress)

Lieutenant O.T. Davis, Sergeant J.D. McQuade, George Fowler of the Internal Revenue Service, and H.G. Bauer with the largest still ever taken in the national capitol and bottles of liquor. (Courtesy Library of Congress)

the city of Chicago and controlled virtually every illegal activity. One of the most gruesome and remembered gangster shoot-outs of all time occurred on Valentine's Day 1929. Because of business differences, Capone had his henchman, "Machine Gun" Jack McGurn, plotted the murder of the O'Banions, led by Bugs Moran.

McGurn staged a delivery of alcohol to Moran at a warehouse and had his gang members impersonate police officers and pretend to raid the transaction. With a sweep of machine gun fire, McGurn killed all who were inside. Capone had a solid alibi, being in Miami at the time, and no convictions were ever made. This event is an example of how prohibition fueled gang warfare and increased the crime rate in America. "Seldom has law been more flagrantly violated. Not only did Americans continue to manufacture, barter and possess alcohol, they drank more of it," concluded one writer.[52]

"I was one of the women who favored prohibition when I heard it discussed in the abstract, but I am now convinced it has proved a failure," stated Pauline Sabin in a 1928 issue of *Outlook Magazine*. "It is true we no longer see the corner saloon, but in many cases has it not merely moved to the back of a store, or up or down one flight of stairs under the name of a speakeasy? It is not true that they are making their own gin and drinking it furtively in their own rooms?"[53]

Halting the illegal traffic of alcohol seemed impossible. Few political leaders had realistic plans for funding a naval blockade of the coasts or for closing the thousands of miles of borders along Canada and Mexico. Nor were elected officials inclined to pay for the huge police forces necessary to restrict the bootlegging that became pandemic or to monitor the distillation of medical alcohol, which flowed easily into illicit outlets, or to track the production of sacramental wines, which so often found secular markets.

Token raids on speakeasies by federal agents usually encouraged colorful newspaper stories rather than respect for federal law. In fact, after 1925, more and more citizens seemed to resent the cynicism with which the federal government was so inconsistently pursuing an intrusive interest in whatever it was they might be tempted to drink.

"I loved speak-easies," recalled New York songwriter Alec Wilder. "If you knew the right ones, you never worried about being poisoned by bad whisky. I'd kept hearing about a friend of a friend who had been blinded by bad gin. I guess I was lucky. The 'speaks' were so romantic. [They] had that marvelous movie-like quality, unreality. And the food was great. Although some pretty dreadful things did occur in them."

Congress had placed the matter within the jurisdiction of the Treasury Department, whose untrained Prohibition officers faced insurmountable challenges. They operated with ineffective budgets—if any at all could have been effective—and only slight approval by the public.

Journalist H.L. Mencken was a fierce critic of alcohol prohibition. He wrote in 1925: "Five years of prohibition have had, at least, this one benign effect: they have completely disposed of all the favorite arguments of the Prohibitionists. None of the great boons and usufructs that were to follow the

Latest thing in flasks. Mlle. Rhea, dainty dancer who was in Washington, D.C., as part of the Keiths program inaugurated the garter flask fad. (Courtesy Library of Congress)

passage of the Eighteenth Amendment has come to pass. There is not less drunkenness in the Republic, but more. There is not less crime, but more. There is not less insanity, but more. The cost of government is not smaller, but vastly greater. Respect for law has not increased, but diminished."

In 1924, U.S. Attorney General Harry M. Daugherty appointed J. Edgar Hoover the acting director of the Federal Bureau of Investigation. He became the permanent director of the Bureau the following year. When Hoover took over the Bureau of Investigation, it had approximately 650 employees, including 441 special agents.[54] By the end of the decade, there were approximately thirty field offices, with divisional headquarters in nine key cities: New York, Baltimore, Atlanta, Cincinnati, Chicago, Kansas City, San Antonio, San Francisco, and Portland.

Hoover immediately fired agents he considered unqualified and proceeded to professionalize the organization. For example, he abolished the seniority rule of promotion and introduced uniform performance appraisals. He scheduled regular inspections of the operations in all his field offices. Then, in January 1928, Hoover established a formal training course for new agents, including the requirement that new agents had to be in the twenty-five-to-thirty-year range to apply. He also returned to the earlier preference for special agents with law or accounting experience.[55]

J. Edgar Hoover, 1924. (Courtesy Library of Congress)

The new director was also keenly aware that the Federal Bureau of Investigation could not fight crime without public support. In remarks prepared for the attorney general in 1925, he wrote, "The agents of the Bureau of Investigation have been impressed with the fact that the real problem of law enforcement is in trying to obtain the cooperation and sympathy of the public and that they cannot hope to get such cooperation until they themselves merit the respect of the public." Also in 1925, Agent Edwin C. Shanahan became the first agent to be killed in the line of duty when he was murdered by a car thief.

Hoover had been born in Washington, D. C., but details of his early life are sketchy; a birth certificate for him was not filed until 1938. He was educated at George Washington University, graduating in 1917 with a law degree. Rather than enlisting for military service during World War I, Hoover had found work with the Justice Department. He soon proved himself capable and was promoted to head the Enemy Aliens Registration

Section. In 1919, he became head of the new General Intelligence Division of the Justice Department. Two years later, he joined the Bureau of Investigation as deputy head. He served as FBI director from 1925 to 1972.[56]

Hoover's personal life has always been a mystery. Speculation and rumors that Hoover was homosexual have circulated for decades. However, there is no concrete evidence for these claims, so they are mostly based upon speculation. The allegation that he was also a crossdresser is generally considered to be an urban legend. Hoover's right-hand man, Clyde Tolson, was a constant companion for more than forty years, and they often vacationed together. Hoover and Tolson were both lifelong bachelors, and Hoover lived with his mother until her death in 1938, when he was forty-three years old.

Hoover was raised a devout Presbyterian, and he had considered the ministry as a career. Some critics said he used this to try to render his personal conduct (sexual or otherwise) above reproach during his tenure at the FBI. But even within Hoover's own lifetime, journalists and other observers made observations that hinted at a hidden personal life. Walter Winchell, the famed gossip columnist, once wrote an article that superficially extolled Hoover, while at the same time included many of the aforementioned peculiarities. A female journalist who managed to talk her way into an interview with Hoover wrote an article sarcastically entitled, "Hoover: He Always Gets his Man, But he Never Found a Woman."

It has long been rumored that the New Orleans and Chicago Mafia blackmailed Hoover with photos of him in drag and performing homosexual acts, which may partially explain why he allegedly never went after them, but according to sources in the Mafia, no such photos existed. True or untrue, the FBI became pre-eminent in the field of domestic intelligence under Hoover's leadership. He made changes such as expanding and combining fingerprint files in the Identification Division to compile the largest collection of fingerprints ever made. Hoover also helped greatly to expand the FBI's recruitment and create the FBI Laboratory.

Ma Barker and her brood probably paid little attention to FBI appointments in the mid-1920s. The Barkers were poor and received little financial support from Ma's husband, George Barker, who later profited from the criminal earnings of his wife and sons, but did not put himself into such a position that he could be termed a member of the gang. During the time his wife and sons, with other members of their gang, were roving the country perpetrating bank robberies and kidnappings, George Barker was content to remain in the vicinity of Joplin, Missouri, and operate a small filling station.

The early religious training of the Barkers, as is the case in families of this particular section, was influenced by evangelism and sporadic revivals. The parents of the Barkers and the other boys with whom they were associated did not reflect any special interest in educational training. As a result their sons were more or less illiterate.

But when it came to committing crimes, the boys had graduated from petty crooks to big-time hoods. Kate Barker was very fond of her sons—especially Arthur, and it was reciprocated. According to the FBI, Kate was of a criminal disposition and condoned the acts of her sons.[57] J. Edgar Hoover once remarked, "The eyes of Arizona Clark Barker . . . always fascinated me. They were queerly direct, penetrating, hot with some strangely smoldering flame, yet withal as hypnotically cold as a muzzle of a gun."[58]

In June 1926, Herman Barker and an accomplice were apprehended by police in Fort Scott, Kansas, for stealing a Paige coupe from Henry Ward of Fairfax, Oklahoma. They were turned over to Oklahoma State Police and returned to Miami, Oklahoma, to face charges of bank robbery and grand larceny. The two suspects gave their names as Al Ayers and C.L. White.[59]

Agent D.H. Graham filed a report on August 27, 1926, and stated that he had been advised by Chief of Police J.W. Ball that on June 11, the prisoners were turned over to the justice of the peace in Ketchum, Oklahoma, and Deputy Sheriff Frank Barker of Miami, Oklahoma. Sheriff Barker held a warrant for Ayers, for robbery of the county attorney in Miami of valuables and money to the amount of $600, and for White, for robbery of the bank and post office at Ketchum, Oklahoma.

On September 27, the Oklahoma Bureau received the following letter from Chief of Police Ball, Fort Scott, Kansas: "Your letter and card Re: Ayers and White. All the officers identify White [sic] most of them think it is Ayers. Ayers wore his hair different when here, also cleaned collar and tie.

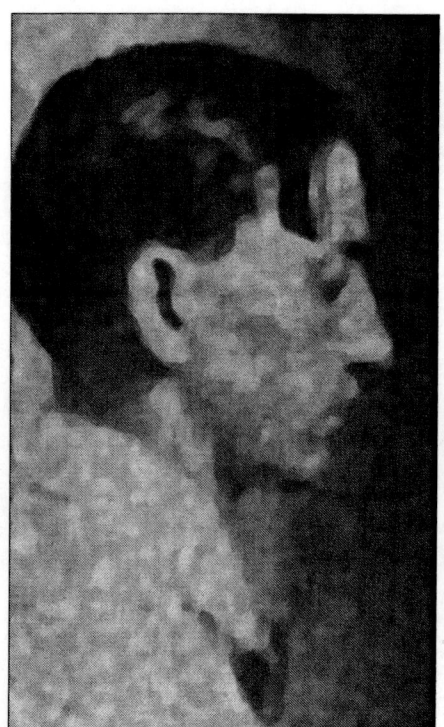

Herman Barker. (Courtesy Library of Congress)

"Subject Barker, alias Ayers, returned to Ottawa County, Oklahoma, on charge of robbery; released under bond on June 22, 1926. Subject Inman, alias C.L. White returned to Ketchum, Oklahoma, but not held on a charge in Ketchum. Inman a parole violator of Kansas State Penitentiary was arrested in Claremore, Oklahoma, on July 25, 1926, while in act of robbing a store. The men who received subjects at Fort Scott, Kansas, were not interested in the car in question. Information received that subjects would not be prosecuted effectively in the Oklahoma state courts. Kansas City Bureau office requested to present this case to the United States Attorney of Kansas District per prosecution."[60]

On September 27, 1926, Elmer A. Inman and Ray Terrill broke jail by overpowering the jailer and making their escape. Authorities were confident that the escapees had been assisted by Mrs. Ray Terrill and others, all

Kansas State Prison. (Courtesy Kansas State Historical Society)

of whom simply disappeared. Inman and Terrill were next heard of in Springfield, Missouri, where they robbed a bank and proceeded to Wichita, Kansas. From Wichita they planned to winter in Arizona, where agents would be unable to locate them. Inman, however, was arrested in Oklahoma City on December 30th.[61]

Herman Barker, meanwhile, was delivered on January 21, 1927, to the sheriff of Washington County, Arkansas, to answer for a bank robbery offense. Sheriff Henry Walker, Fayetteville, Arkansas, announced on February second that Herman Barker would be tried at the term of court to be convened April 25, 1927, for the robbery of the West Fork Bank, West Fork, Arkansas. Barker was to remain in jail until that time in default of a $10,000 bond.[62]

Elmer A. Inman was convicted in the state court at Oklahoma City for burglary on February 9, 1927, and was sentenced to serve seven years in the state penitentiary. A retainer had been placed at the penitentiary.

Inman, however, escaped from state officials on March 17th while en route to the Oklahoma State Prison in McAllister.

Sheriff Henry Walker of Fayetteville dispatched a memo to federal officers stating that during the night of March 30, 1927, Herman Barker escaped from the county jail at Fayetteville. Claude Cooper, who was being held on a forgery charge, escaped with him. The two men sawed their way out of the jail through the roof with saws provided by Cooper, who was a native of Fayetteville. Walker noted that he had compiled complete descriptions and names of persons who wrote and visited them while in jail, and the addresses of Ma Barker and Herman Barker's sweetheart.

The day after the jail break, Harry Bowman, a Muskogee, Oklahoma, Dodge-automobile salesman, saw Herman Barker with his sweetheart, Carol Hamilton, in a Dodge sedan headed towards Radium Springs with spotlights on the windshield. Bowman was reported to have recognized the car as one he sold to Carol Hamilton a few months earlier.

Herman Barker was seen again on April 10th in Tulsa. Deputy Sheriff Sid Jackson of Tulsa was a relative of Barker, and speculation was that the criminal would show up at the Jackson house. Jackson was interviewed but had seen nothing of Barker. Records of the Tulsa Police Department revealed that Herman Barker had served time in the Minnesota State Penitentiary, Stillwater, for grand larceny.

His brother, Fred Barker, was committed to the Kansas State Penitentiary on March 12, 1927, while police were still searching for Herman. Upon entering the penitentiary, Fred stated that he was from Missouri, he was American, he had no religion, his occupation was laundryman, he had a sixth-grade education, that he had been married to Billie Orr, had no children from the union, and that his parents were living at 401 Cincinnati Avenue, Tulsa.

On May 21st, police officers in the Pacific Northwest were on the lookout for Herman Barker after Seattle police received information that the suspect was in the Seattle area. According to Detective Belland of the Seattle Police Department, Barker was believed to be hiding with Ace Pendleton, alias Edgar Murphy.

"Ma"—The Life and Times of "Ma" Barker and Her Boys

On Monday, August 1, 1927, a man using the name of R.D. Snodgrass walked into the American National Bank in Cheyenne, Wyoming, and cashed three American Express Traveler's Checks. As "Snodgrass" left the bank, the teller glanced at his memorandum on stolen American Express checks and noted that the checks he had just cashed were listed as taken in a bank robbery at Buffalo, Kansas, in December 1926.

The teller followed Snodgrass across the street to his automobile and informed him the checks were no good and asked him to return the money. Snodgrass was backing his car away from the curb as the teller approached. He told the bank teller that he would drive his car around the block and stop at the bank. The teller returned to the bank but the other man did not. The sheriff's office was notified and all nearby officers were given a description of Snodgrass and his female companion, as well as a description of the car they were driving.

Arthur E. Osborn, deputy to Sheriff George Carroll of Laramie County, was one of the officers who had received the message to be on the lookout for Snodgrass. Osborn proceeded to a point on the Lincoln Highway about five miles west of Pine Bluffs. He flagged the suspect's vehicle down. When he approached it on foot, Snodgrass picked up a gun from the seat beside him and shot Osborn twice. The information on the Osborn shooting came from a woman who was with Barker and later arrested.[63]

About thirty minutes later, Osborn was found on the road by a deputy sheriff from Nebraska, who happened along the highway. He was unconscious and died a few minutes later. A doctor's examination revealed that he had been shot through the body twice with a .32 automatic pistol. Osborn's revolver was in his holster. He had apparently been shot down when approaching the car just after he had signaled the driver of the car to stop.[64]

All officers within a radius of two hundred miles were notified by telephone of the murder and requested that all roads be covered. No trace was found of Barker's Chrysler Coach until August 5th, when a report was received by Sheriff Carroll that the suspect's car had stalled in a mud hole Monday afternoon on the road leading from Bushnell, Nebraska, to Sterling, Colorado.

"Ma"—The Life and Times of "Ma" Barker and Her Boys

The Barker boys had always had a way of influencing crime-oriented friends from the Central Park neighborhood. "And so once more, I resumed my life in crime," recalled Ray Terrill. "This time I hooked up with Herman Barker, Doc's brother. There were four of the Barker boys, Herman, Lloyd, Doc, and Freddy. Herman and Freddy are dead, Lloyd is at Leavenworth, and Doc, as I have said before is at Alcatraz. Herman was one of the fastest men I ever worked with, and I went with him to Texas, where we planned to punch several boxes in banks.

"We were stopping at Wichita Falls, but drove almost one hundred miles south of there to punch a box. On this job, we were almost caught in the act, and I had to jump through a plate-glass window to get away. This was no easy matter, and I had to rush at the window twice. The second time I went through, but I cut my leg and was bleeding profusely until we got out into the country, and I fashioned a tourniquet to stop the flow.

"Freddy met us in Wichita Falls, and we decided to go to Ardmore because Wichita Falls was getting hot, due to a series of burglaries in which I had no part. It was Mother's Day when we drove there, and I ordered some flowers sent to her. That night by coincidence, the florist's shop was robbed, although I had no knowledge of it. The next day they checked back to my address at Wichita Falls, and when we decided to go back there they were lying in wait for us. I made bond on this charge but was taken to Pawnee again, and after being held there awhile I was again transferred to the jail at Ardmore, where another of my escapes took place. I was arraigned at Ardmore, but I broke jail that night. I had succeeded in getting hold of some files, and so I contrived to crack the bars and get down into the jail office. There I overpowered the jailer and left him tied up.

"Then Herman Barker and I got together and undertook a wild career of robbing stores. For a while, we got more money than we could make hauling "nigger-heads" out of the banks. We'd go into a town and get several big stores cased and then pull the jobs in rapid succession and get out of town. Some of these jobs yielded more that $2,000. Our method was to work either early in the night or along toward morning when the traffic was beginning to stir again. There was too much danger attracting attention by some chance noise if we worked in the dead of the night when everything was quiet. We'd figured when the police were changing shifts and all the other angles. Herman was one of the slickest hands getting through transoms or skylights I ever saw, and we were doing well in our sordid business. We did a number of Sunday morning jobs on drug stores, which had enjoyed their Saturday receipts.

"Early in 1927, Herman [Barker] and Danny Daniels sent for me to come to Carterville, Missouri, near Joplin where Herman and his wife had taken a house. Herman and Danny had rigged up a truck for hauling "niggerheads" out of banks and had got a safe down in Arkansas they couldn't open up. I went up there and opened it for them after they had hauled it around for four days, but they were disappointed in the loot, which was only $1,600....

"Danny and Herman split over something at this time, and I went to Herman's and lived. We had hauled off one safe and were staying pretty close around the house there in Carterville, taking things sort of easy. One day about 4:00 A.M., a gang of peace officers surrounded the house and ordered us to come out. Herman ran out the back door, and they shot him."[65]

The report that Herman Barker died on August 29, 1927, was verified by the Kansas City Bureau office. According to the report, a furious gun battle broke out and Police Officer J.E. Marshall was killed. Barker, rather than face arrest and prison, committed suicide. Elmer Inman once more escaped, and a third member of the gang, Charles Stalcup, was held in Wichita by police.[66]

Herman's death came as quite a blow to Ma Barker and the rest of her family. According to Ma, Herman, the oldest, had always been a good son, sending home part of his earnings as a minor holdup man and petty swindler.[67]

Herman's widow, Carol, who came from Batesville, Arkansas, and who was wanted in Cheyenne, Wyoming, as an accessory in the killing of Deputy Sheriff Art Osborn near Pine Bluffs, was returned to Cheyenne from Neosho, Missouri. Learning of Herman's demise, she collapsed. She admitted that Herman was guilty but that she was just as guilty as well.[68]

"All I want now," she cried, "is for the state of Wyoming to end me—and I don't mean life imprisonment." She was, however, imprisoned and not executed.

"Ma"—The Life and Times of "Ma" Barker and Her Boys

On October 6, 1927, Sheriff George Carroll, Cheyenne, Wyoming, stated that Mrs. Herman Barker made a confession to him that her husband, "a notorious bandit," was the one who killed deputy sheriff Art Osborn at Pine Bluffs, Wyoming, and that Elmer A. Inman was not the party that killed the officer. Mrs. Barker was sentenced to four years in the Canon City, Colorado, penitentiary for being an accessory.[69]

Several years prior to Kate Barker's separation from George Barker, which occurred in 1928, and which was subsequent to the time that Herman, Lloyd, and Arthur received prison sentences, Kate began to show signs of turning her back on morality. She was seen with a male neighbor of hers upon several occasions and was known to have been in the company of other men in the vicinity of Tulsa, Oklahoma. This double life led to Kate's separation from her husband.

Things had, after all, gone very badly for her sons by this time. Arthur "Doc" Barker had stolen a government car in 1918, and although he escaped, he was later captured and tried for the murder of a night watchman in Tulsa, and was sent to the Oklahoma State Penitentiary in 1927. Ma claimed he was innocent. Another man is said to have confessed to the killing many years later. Doc was paroled September 17, 1932.[70]

Lloyd Barker was caught robbing a bank in Kansas in 1922 and was sentenced to twenty-five years in Leavenworth Federal Penitentiary.

Herman had been involved in robbing several banks, and after killing a policeman and getting wounded himself, had killed himself September 1927. Ma Barker never accepted this explanation, insisting it was a police execution.

Fred had been arrested for robbing a bank in Winfield, Kansas, in 1926 and was sentenced to five to ten years in the Kansas State Penitentiary at Lansing. He was paroled March 20, 1931.

Ma Barker lived with her sons at such periods when they were released from their penitentiary sentences and cast her lot with their lawlessness and criminal activities. Inasmuch as she was more intelligent than any of her sons, she ruled them with an iron will and found this expression of dominance easily exerted because of the submission of her sons Fred and Arthur.

"Ma"—The Life and Times of "Ma" Barker and Her Boys

Maybe because of the dirt-poor years she had endured, Ma liked to live well and purchased expensive clothing, furniture, and other necessities from the spoils of her sons' depredations. At the same time, she was very jealous of her boys and did not wish to have them associate with any girlfriends. She would disclose the conversations she'd had with various women members of the gang to her sons, particularly stressing the women's statements with reference to them. This procedure on her part caused frequent evidence of dissension among the other women of the gang who, in most instances made every effort to avoid her.

Although Kate Barker gave most of her attention to her boys, she met and took up with Arthur W. Dunlop, alias George Anderson. Dunlop, late in the year 1931, rented a cottage one and one-half miles from Thayer, Missouri, where he lived with Ma Barker. The couple was soon joined by Ma's son Fred, who had been released from the Kansas State Penitentiary on March 20, 1931.

During the time that Fred Barker was in the penitentiary, where he had served a sentence for burglary, he had befriended Alvin "Creepy" Karpis, who not unlike the Barker brothers, came from a poor and uneducated family. The parents of Alvin Karpis, Mr. and Mrs. John Karpavicz, had migrated to the United States from Lithuania. Upon first arriving in America, Mr. and Mrs. Karpavicz lived in New York City, thence moved to Grand Rapids, Michigan, and then to Montreal, Canada, where they remained for two years. Alvin Karpis was born in Montreal on August 10, 1907. He was christened Francis Alvin Karpavicz.[72]

The eldest child, Mihalin, had been born in London, England. Alvin's sister Emily was born later in Grand Rapids, Michigan, and his youngest sister, Clara, in Topeka, Kansas.

The Karpis family moved into an old house on Second Street in Topeka, Kansas, when Alvin was two years old. They remained there until 1923, before moving to Chicago, Illinois. The old house was two stories high, and out back was a barn with milking cows and a chicken coop. Alvin lived with his parents, his two older sisters, and a younger sister. His father not only ran the farm but also worked a full-time job as a design painter for the Santa Fe Railroad. His dad was the disciplinarian of the family and had a bullwhip to keep Alvin in line, although his mother was much easier on him.[73]

In Topeka, a schoolteacher at Branner Elementary shortened his name to Alvin Karpis, because she claimed it was "easier to manage." The boy was soon given an examination by a physician, which disclosed that he suffered from a leakage of the heart, and he was advised to take an extended vacation.

"What a laugh that was when I think about it now," Karpis recalled many years later. "I had to quit my honest job because it was too much of a strain for my heart, and I went right back to my criminal ways, which, putting it mildly, can create some light strain on the heart."[74]

Alvin then went to live with his sister, Mrs. Bert Grooms, at 1234 Monroe Street, Topeka, Kansas. It was at Topeka, that Alvin Karpis, at age ten, began an active criminal career that was to lead him eventually to Ma Barker at Thayer, Missouri.

Alvin hung out around Kansas Avenue and Fourth Street in Topeka where he ran errands for whores, pimps, and petty gamblers to earn a buck or two. These excursions were much to his liking until the day he met his first hero, someone he wished to emulate. Eighteen-year-old Arthur Witchey, who had served time in the state reformatory, taught the ten-year-old Karpis that he could have what he wanted by tossing a brick through a store window, scooping up the loot, and running down the nearest alley. Young Alvin considered him a "big shot" and tagged along after the older boy whenever he could. Alvin stole his first gun at the age of ten, and when Witchey asked him if he wanted to rob a grocery store with him, the younger boy was sure he had hit the major leagues. The pair burgled the store of all its cash as well as easily disposable merchandise. For five years, Karpis made a tough living through his petty thievery.[75]

Karpis accompanied his parents when they moved to Chicago and accepted honest work as a shipping clerk and a baker. But when he was seventeen, Karpis and his family returned to Topeka where Alvin and a friend operated a shabby roadhouse, fencing stolen goods, and selling rotgut booze under the table. Tired of these activities, he took to hopping freight trains and rode the rails from Iowa south through Missouri, Kansas, Oklahoma, and Arkansas into Louisiana and Mississippi, and from Ohio west through Michigan, Illinois, Wisconsin, and Minnesota and into the Dakotas. As he traveled through the South and the Midwest, he familiarized himself with small town businesses he later planned to rob.

It was on a train in Van Buren, Arkansas, that Karpis ran into his first serious trouble with the law. A railroad "bull," known to be the toughest, meanest bull in that part of the country, was probing boxcars with a flashlight, hoping to shake down hoboes catching a free ride. Young Karpis leaped from the box car and dashed down the track, blasting away with a pistol as he ran. His riding the rails adventures ended in Florida where he was caught riding on the roof of the Pan American. He was arrested for vagrancy and sentenced to thirty days on a chain gang.[76]

Upon serving his sentence, Karpis returned to Kansas and quickly became involved in a warehouse burglary and was sentenced to serve ten years in the State Industrial Reformatory at Hutchinson, Kansas, where he was received in February 1924. The reformatory was structured to handle inmates between the ages of sixteen and thirty years of age. They had to be new commits having never served time in prison before.

The reformatory concept divided the inmates into classes. When an inmate entered the reformatory he was placed into the Intermediate Grade where he remained for six months. If he exhibited good behavior, good working habits, and went to school, at the end of the six months period he was promoted to what was called the First Grade. The inmate was in the First Grade for a period of six months, and if he had no problems he was eligible for parole at the end of this period of time. If, however, the inmate became a disciplinary problem, refused to work or did not meet the criteria of parole, he was reduced to the Third Grade another six months, then promoted to the Intermediate Grade for six months and finally once again to the First Grade for an additional six months. All inmates at the reformatory went to school two hours every night after a regular eight-hour work day. Many also went to school all day on stormy days and on Saturdays.[77]

At the reformatory, Karpis was assigned as a baker's helper. This required long hours of work starting very early in the morning, seven days a week, which was not in accordance with his desires. As a result, he violated many rules of the institution and served many days in solitary confinement.[78]

He struck up a friendship with Larry Devol, who slept in a neighboring cell, and the two spent hours talking. Even though Devol was only twenty-five years old, Karpis let him do most of the talking, because he had been around, and Alvin looked up to him. Karpis was young and a little guy at that—five feet six and never more than 120 pounds. What really impressed Karpis about Devol was that he knew how to break into "boxes," the burglar's word for safes.[79]

The two young men chatted frequently for three years, when in the spring of 1929, they discussed the possibilities of breaking out of Hutchinson. Prior to December 19, 1903, there had never been a successful escape from the reformatory. On a dark and dreary night of December 19, 1903, an inmate by the name of Elmer Slider, who was a trustee at the director's residence, slipped off into the darkness and had never been heard from since. In 1903, the reformatory adopted the policy of photographing all incoming inmates. Pictures were taken in order to aid the parole and transfer officer and law enforcement agencies in apprehending PV parole violators who had absconded from supervision.[80]

Karpis' mind, however, was not idle whether he was in solitary confinement or the cell block, and he planned ways of escape before his release date. Slider had done it twenty-one years earlier and it could be done again. After plotting with Devol and another inmate, Charles Carroll, the four of them escaped from the prison through the reformatory garage with the aid of a couple of stolen saws appropriated from the prison workshop.[81]

Karpis and Devol split from the others, and after stealing guns and a big sedan, they made their way across Kansas and Colorado. In Pueblo they stole a Studebaker and drove to Oklahoma where they stayed awhile with Devol's parents in Tulsa, and then with his brother Clarence.

After hitting the road again, Devol was arrested in Chicago and returned to the reformatory. Karpis, who managed to get away, immediately rejoined his parents in Chicago. The parents, while appearing to be law-abiding citizens, refrained from notifying the Kansas State authorities of the location of their son Alvin. They justified their position by believing that Alvin was endeavoring to lead a law-abiding life, had found employment with various bakers in Chicago, and also secured employment with a concern which sold medical equipment.[82]

Despite his parents' hiding him out, his father tried to talk him into giving himself up so he could lead a normal life. Karpis took a job at Becker's Bakery, on the north side, as a baker's helper. His parents were delighted as they thought he was finally ready to settle down. The owner of the bakery, however, began losing money on the stock market, and was forced to let Karpis go.

But soon Karpis was joined by Larry Devol and the pair journeyed to Kansas City, Missouri. Devol had gotten transferred from the reformatory in Hutchinson to the Kansas State Penitentiary where a prisoner could have time knocked off his sentence by working in the coal mine. Devol worked the mine and had received an early release.

The two men headed to Kansas City following a whirlwind tour of robberies in Oklahoma, Nebraska, and Missouri. In Lexington, Missouri, Devol and an accomplice named "Dago" Howard, staged a robbery, and during their escape, Devol killed a police officer. Karpis later maintained he was not present during the robbery/murder.

In Kansas City, Karpis and Devol planned to rob a downtown poolroom, and on March 23, 1930, as they drove along McGee Boulevard with all their tools in the back, they were pulled over by two motorcycle officers. They were arrested and charged with auto larceny and safe blowing.

Karpis at this time had begun the use of aliases, and at the time of his arrest gave his name as Raymond Hadley. Karpis was not prosecuted on the charge of stealing the automobile, but on March 15, 1930, he was returned to the reformatory at Hutchinson, Kansas, for his earlier escape. Due to the record which he had made for himself at the reformatory, he was transferred to the Kansas State Penitentiary at Lansing, Kansas, on May 19, 1930.

"Ma"—The Life and Times of "Ma" Barker and Her Boys

Notes

[1] *Chicago Sunday Tribune*, April 22, 1934.
[2] *The* (St. Joseph) *Daily Gazette*, Wednesday, April 5, 1882—EXTRA.
[3] Ibid.
[4] *True Crime Most Wanted*, Alexandria, Virginia, Time-Life Books, p. 76.
[5] Dee Cordry, "The Outlaw and Lawmen Map of Oklahoma 1865-1935," Internet.
[6] FBI Files, RCS:TD I.C.#7-576, November 19, 1936, The Kidnapping of Edward George Bremer, St. Paul, Minnesota, History and Early Association of the Karpis-Barker Gang Prior to the Abduction of Mr. Bremer; Federal Bureau of Investigation Freedom of Information and Privacy Acts, Subject: Kate Barker "Ma," File Number 7-5768695, Memorandum Re: Kate Barker, August 19, 1955.
[7] "Ma Barker," Lawrence County Historical Society Bulletin, Number 120, July 1991.
[8] Federal Bureau of Investigation Freedom of Information and Privacy Acts, Subject: Kate Barker "Ma," File Number 7-5768695.
[9] "Supervisor" Rosen letter to St. Paul Special Agent K. R. MacIntire, December 29, 1955. Federal Bureau of Investigation Freedom of Information and Privacy Acts, Subject: Kate Barker "Ma," File Number 7-5768695.
[10] Myron J. Quimby, *The Devil's Emissaries*, South Brunswick & New York, A. S. Barnes and Company, 1969, p. 114.
[11] Nathan Boone Homestead State Historic Site, Missouri Department of Natural Resources Archives.
[12] Lew Louderback, *The Bad Ones Gangsters of the '30 and Their Molls*, New York, Fawcett Books, 1974, p. 14.
[13] Ibid.
[14] Miriam Allen deFord, *The Real Ma Barker*, New York, Ace Publishing Corporation, 1970, p. 16.
[15] Their marriage license is on file at the Lawrence County Courthouse, Mt. Vernon, Missouri, Book F, Page 341; Fountain & Journal, September 22, 1892 reported the issuance of the license.
[16] "Ma Barker," Lawrence County Historical Society Bulletin, Number 120, July 1991.
[17] Miriam Allen deFord, *The Real Ma Barker*, p. 17.
[18] Book G, page 349, Lawrence County Courthouse, Mt. Vernon, Missouri Archives.
[19] David Stewart Elliott, Last Raid of the Daltons, Coffeyville, *Coffeyville Journal*, 1892, pp. 13-56; Robert Barr Smith, Daltons! The Raid on Coffeyville, Kansas, Norman, University of Oklahoma Press, 1996, pp.116-134.
[20] Emmett Dalton, *Beyond the Law*, Coffeyville, Coffeyville Historical Society, Reprint of 1918 original, p. 153.
[21] Cherokee Nation Cultural Resource Center Archives, Tahlequah, Oklahoma.

[22]"Ma Barker," Lawrence County Historical Society Bulletin, Number 120, July 1991.
[23]Myron J. Quimby, *The Devil's Emissaries*, South Brunswick & New York, A. S. Barnes and Company, 1969, p. 114.
[24]Nancy B. Samuelson, "The Passing of Chris Madsen," *Oklahombres Journal*, Volume II, Number 3, Spring 1991; Nancy B. Samuelson, "Chris Madsen: Soldier, Oklahoma 89'er, and Deputy United States Marshal," *Oklahombres Journal*, Volume IV, Number 4, Summer 1993; Nancy B. Samuelson, "Bill Doolin was Killed, and Killed, and Killed," *Oklahombres Journal*, Volume VII, Number 3, Spring 1996.
[25]Floyd Miller, *Marshal of the Last Frontier*, Garden City, New York, Doubleday & Company, Inc., 1968, p. 166-172.
[26]Nancy Samuelson, *Shoot from the Lip, The Lives, Legends and Lies of the Three Guardsmen of Oklahoma and U.S. Marshal Nix*, Eastford, CT, Shooting Star Press, 1998, pp. 67-69.
[27]Glenn Shirley, Bud Ledbetter, *The Fourth Guardsman*, Austin, Texas, Eakin Press, 1997, pp. 61-67.
[28]Book 90, p. 124, Lawrence County Courthouse, Mt. Vernon, Missouri Archives; "Ma Barker," Lawrence County Historical Society Bulletin, Number 120, July 1991.
[29]Anthony Gish, *American Bandits*, Girard, Kansas, Haldeman-Julius Publications, 1934, pp. 68-69; Myron J. Quimby, The Devil's Emissaries, South Brunswick & New York, A. S. Barnes and Company, 1969, pp. 114-115.
[30]Alfred Bryce Gordon, King of the Ozarks, *Mount Magazine*, Magazine, Arkansas, Alfred Bryce Gordon, 1999; pp. 387-388.
[31]John Toland, *The Dillinger Days*, New York, Da Capo Press, 1995, pp. 44-45.
[32]Theodore C. Blegen, Minnesota, *A History of the State*, Minneapolis, University of Minnesota Press, 1963, pp. 461-462.
[33]Diana Nelson Jones, "Y2K a Breeze When Compared to Life in 1900 When Our City Had No 'H,'" *Pittsburgh Post-Gazette*, December 31, 1999.
[34]Paul M. Chapman, "A Dartmoor Mystery," Sherlock Holmes The Detective Magazine, Issue 43, 2001, pp. 6-7.
[35]Ibid.
[36]Lew Louderback, *The Bad Ones Gangsters of the '30 and Their Molls*, p. 16; John Toland, *The Dillinger Days*, pp. 44-45; Anthony Gish, American Bandits, Girard, Kansas, Haldeman-Julius Publications, 1934, pp. 68-69.
[37]Glenn Shirley, *Henry Starr Last of the Real Bad Men*, New York, David McKay Company, Inc., 1965, pp. 167-172.
[38]*Chandler News-Publicist*, April 2, 1915.
[39]Robert J. Conley, *The Saga of Henry Starr*, New York, Doubleday, 1989, p. 163.
[40]Dee Cordry, "The Outlaw and Lawmen Map of Oklahoma 1865-1935, Internet.

[41] Myron J. Quimby, *The Devil's Emissaries*, South Brunswick & New York, A. S. Barnes and Company, 1969, p. 116.
[42] Jay Robert Nash, *Bloodletters and Badmen Book 2*, New York, Warner Paperback Company, 1975, pp. 28-29.
[43] *Tulsa Tribune*, March 22, 1949; FBI Files Freedom of Information Act.
[44] Ibid.
[45] Autobiographical Interview with Ray Terrill as told to Meredith Williams, " I Tried Crime." This series appeared in the *Oklahoma News* for five consecutive weeks during November of 1936.
[46] *Tulsa Tribune*, March 22, 1949; FBI Files Freedom of Information Act.
[47] *St. Paul Pioneer Press*, December 25, 1887.
[48] Catherine H. Poholek, "Prohibition in the 1920s, Thirteen Years that Damaged America," Online, May 6, 1998; Mark Thorton, "Policy Analysis: Alcohol Prohibition Was a Failure." July 17, 1991 , p. 13. Online. Netscape. 23 April 1998.
[49] Ezra Bowen, ed., *This Fabulous Century*, 6 volumes. New York: Time Life Books, 1969, p. 175.
[50] Behr, Edward. *Prohibition: Thirteen Years That Changed America*, New York, Arcade Publishing, 1996. p. 192.
[51] Ray R. Cowdery, *Capone's Chicago*, Lakeville, MN., Northstar Maschek Books, 1987, p. 91.
[52] Behr, Edward. *Prohibition: Thirteen Years That Changed America*, p. 192.
[53] *Outlook Magazine*, June 8, 1928.
[54] Harry S. Truman, *Memoirs, Volume II, Years of Trial and Hope* (Garden City, New York, Doubleday & Company, 1956, p. 291.
[55] Federal Bureau of Investigation Archives.
[56] Harry S. Truman, *Memoirs, Volume II, Years of Trial and Hope*, p. 291.
[57] Federal Bureau of Investigation Freedom of Information and Privacy Acts, Subject: Kate Barker "Ma," File Number 7-5768695; "Ma Barker, Crooks Ran in Her Family," *Pageant Magazine*, December 1959.
[58] G. Russell Giradin and William J. Helmer, *Dillinger, The Untold Story*, Bloomington & Indianapolis, Indiana University Press, 1994, pp. 268.
[59] Federal Bureau of Investigation Freedom of Information and Privacy Acts, Subject: Herman Barker, (Death of), File Number 26-9961.
[60] Ibid.
[61] Tulsa World, December 30, 1926.
[62] Federal Bureau of Investigation Freedom of Information and Privacy Acts, Subject: Herman Barker, (Death of), File Number 26-9961.
[63] Laramie County, Wyoming Sheriff's Department.
[64] Federal Bureau of Investigation Freedom of Information and Privacy Acts, Subject: Herman Barker, (Death of), File Number 26-9961.

⁶⁵Autobiographical Interview with Ray Terrill as told to Meredith Williams, "I Tried Crime." This series appeared in the Oklahoma News for five consecutive weeks during November of 1936.

⁶⁶Federal Bureau of Investigation Freedom of Information and Privacy Acts, Subject: Herman Barker, (Death of), File Number 26-9961.

⁶⁷John Toland, *The Dillinger Days*, p. 46.

⁶⁸Miriam Allen deFord, *The Real Ma Barker*, p. 24.

⁶⁹Federal Bureau of Investigation Freedom of Information and Privacy Acts, Subject: Herman Barker, (Death of), File Number 26-9961.

⁷⁰"Ma Barker," *Lawrence County Historical Society Bulletin*, Number 120, July 1991.

⁷¹Autobiographical Interview with Ray Terrill as told to Meredith Williams, "I Tried Crime." This series appeared in the *Oklahoma News* for five consecutive weeks during November of 1936.

⁷²Alcatraz History—Prisoner: Alvin "Creepy" Karpis (#325-AZ); Tim Hrenchir, "Other 1930s Outlaws Had Topeka Ties," *Topeka Capital-Journal*, date unknown.

⁷³Alvin Karpis, Bill Trent, *Public Enemy Number One: The Alvin Karpis Story*, New York, Coward, McCann & Geoghegan, Inc., 1971, pp. 18-24,.pp. 27-29.

⁷⁴Ibid.

⁷⁵Jay Robert Nash, *Bloodletters and Badmen Book 3*, New York, Warner Paperback Library, 1975, p. 180.

⁷⁶Alvin Karpis, Bill Trent, *Public Enemy Number One: The Alvin Karpis Story*, p. 29.

⁷⁷Kansas Department of Corrections.

⁷⁸Alcatraz History—Prisoner: Alvin "Creepy" Karpis (#325-AZ); Tim Hrenchir, "Other 1930s Outlaws Had Topeka Ties," *Topeka Capital-Journal*, date unknown.

⁷⁹Alvin Karpis, Bill Trent, *Public Enemy Number One: The Alvin Karpis Story*, pp. 30-31.

⁸⁰Kansas Department of Corrections.

⁸¹Alvin Karpis, Bill Trent, *Public Enemy Number One: The Alvin Karpis Story*, pp. 35-43.

⁸²FBI Files, RCS:TD I.C.#7-576, November 19, 1936, The Kidnaping of Edward George Bremer, St. Paul, Minnesota, History and Early Association of the Karpis-Barker Gang Prior to the Abduction of Mr. Bremer.

Chapter Two

The Barker-Karpis Gang

"Probably the real reason Ma liked me, or at least one of the reasons, was that I was always showing her a good time. We went to movies and carnivals, and once, when we were staying in Reno, I took her on a side trip to San Francisco. We went by plane, and she got a real bang out of it. Actually, she liked simple pleasures more than expensive treats. Bingo, for instance—Ma was nuts about bingo, and I took her to many games. Bingo bored me, but I didn't mind showing Ma a good time."

—Alvin Karpis[1]

The decade of the 1920s had drawn to its close. A new hotel built in the Gateway district of Minneapolis did little to upgrade the rest of the area. The illicit booze trade still flourished in the city center. According to an October 1929 article in the *Minneapolis Journal*, federal agents moved in on soft drink bar operator George Johnson and charged him with possession of liquor and "maintaining a nuisance" at his establishment at 121 Marquette Avenue South. The agents expressed surprise in discovering that liquor was the only stock the "soft-drink" operator carried on his premises.[2]

As the decade of the 1930s opened, Minnesotans looked forward to even greater prosperity than they had enjoyed during the 1920s. In

(Courtesy Library of Congress)

September 1929, the signal event in the closing of the decade was the opening of the Foshay Tower in downtown Minneapolis. The event was marked by three days of enthusiastic celebration with the John Philip Sousa Band performing a specially commissioned march to celebrate the opening. But celebrations such as this were short-lived.[3]

That same year Minnesota and the nation were ripped apart by the opening onslaught of the Great Depression. On October 29, 1929, Black Tuesday, the stock market crashed. Minnesotans were reluctant to believe that a reversal in the New York financial district could affect the Middle West. Wall Street was just too far away. On October 29, 1929, in the face of this news, Minneapolis newspapers reported that leaders had found business still good in the Northwest and fundamentally sound. Both bankers and farmers remained optimistic.[4]

But then the roof caved in. An inflated Minnesota company went suddenly bankrupt, leaving unpaid twenty-million dollars of debts. The head of the organization was sent to prison in 1934. The Depression engulfed the

(Courtesy Library of Congress)

country, and by the spring of 1933, Wall Street had reduced the value of American stocks to below one-fifth of their October 1929 level.

Federal Bureau of Investigation: Barker-Karpis Files.

Many blamed the crash on speculation and the growing-rich that had recently entered the market. In an October 30 editorial, one newspaper stated, "Here and there in the United States, business has receded from its record-breaking volume. The slump in the stock market means a real danger unless it is soon checked. The newspaper played down any threat to the frightened business community. "American business has not been shaken from its sound foundation," the editorial continued. "But speculation that cannot margin its super-optimism has been badly hurt."[5]

Already in mid-November 1929, activity at the Wall Street Exchange slowed as the "disaster" month finally ended. The wreckage of the financial machine stunned Americans and thirty-billion dollars of paper values had vanished. The business leadership of Wall Street had all but collapsed. The country's credit system had begun to deteriorate, and unemployment began to rise.

The city of Minneapolis was affected early. On October 24, 1929, before Black Tuesday, a panic occurred at the Grain Exchange. But things were just getting started. The amount spent on Minneapolis Poor Relief in 1930 was $215,000. In a single year, it had risen by almost $50,000, and Minneapolis boasted the fewest unemployed and indigent men of any American city in 1930.[6]

A young Alvin Karpis. (Author's collection)

Unemployment continued to worsen. Right behind it followed a massive drought in the Midwest. The ferocious winds tossed the topsoil into boiling clouds of black dust and blotted out the sun. Farmers had plowed too much land, and there had been very little rain. The Red Cross reacted to assist the starving in many states and hundreds of the newly-poor roamed the streets of Minneapolis. In February 1931, homeless numbers exploded.[7]

Five hundred men and women led allegedly by Communists rioted in the city at 6:00 P.M., Wednesday, February 24, 1931. The riot came after an "International Unemployment Day" meeting at Bridge Square where powerful speeches were made by the insurrectionists. These speakers urged the city's poor to fight for their rights. The crowd then moved down

Hennepin Avenue and stormed into a grocery store and meat market, smashing plate-glass windows and taking what commodities they could carry. Chester E. Doxey, owner of the grocery, confronted the rioters with a revolver, but he was beaten to the floor and later taken to the hospital.[8]

After the store break-in, homeward-bound factory and office workers encountered the disorderly crowd. Suddenly more than 3,000 people were jammed together in the city's lower loop. One hundred policemen rushed to the scene with fire hoses and tried to disperse the angry crowd with water. Nine persons were arrested and escorted off to jail.

Many of the dissidents were young people as thousands of boys and girls had become transients. These young people usually took refuge in the cities—in the case of Minneapolis, the Gateway, but stayed only briefly before moving off to another retreat.[9]

By 1931 the industrial depression had thrown millions of Americans out of work, and the fall in crop prices had begun taking its toll on the Minnesota farmers. By the winter of 1931-1932, the full impact of the Depression had shaken the Twin Cities.[10]

Prohibition. (Courtesy Library of Congress)

"Ma"—The Life and Times of "Ma" Barker and Her Boys

In additional to the financial disaster, prohibition was still in effect, and the "soft drink" bars continued to operate, barmaids and all. The barmaids sat in sixteen shops in windows facing First Street, Marquette Avenue, Second Street, and Second Avenue South. Behind the windows, they shuffled "packs of grimy playing cards" and were joined in games by loggers, ditch diggers, camp cooks, and harvest hands fortunate enough to have jobs.[11]

On December 20, 1930, Frank "the Enforcer" Nitti, Capone's murder, finance and alcohol chief, pleaded guilty to income tax fraud in Federal Judge Charles E. Woodward's court and was sentenced to eighteen months in the Leavenworth Penitentiary and also fined $10,000. A stay of execution was granted until January 10th when Nitti would be taken to the federal penitentiary.[12]

"Scarface" Al Capone, on February 27, 1931, was found guilty of contempt of court by Federal Judge James H. Wilkerson and was sentenced to six months in the Cook County Jail. Judge Wilkerson overruled a motion for a new trial and an arrest of judgment. He ordered the district attorney to prepare a formal order and announced that it would be entered Monday.[13]

Frank Nitti. (Courtesy Library of Congress)

Capone's lawyers, however, were granted leave to appeal the case to the United States Court of Appeals. The judge granted them thirty days to file a bill of exceptions and allowed the $5,000 bond which Capone had posted for his appearance in the contempt case to stand for the appeal. Capone was told he would be at liberty until the case was settled by the higher courts.

"Ma"—The Life and Times of "Ma" Barker and Her Boys

Al Capone. (Courtesy Library of Congress)

Capone had been leaning forward, looking "glummer and glummer" as the judge's review of the testimony gave little indication of hope. When sentence was pronounced, he slumped back in his chair and his jaw dropped.

With his shooting hand all wrapped in bandages and useless, cop killer Francis "Two Gun" Crowley gave an interview from his bed in New York's Bellevue Hospital on May 9, 1931. Crowley broke down during the session and related, "Aw, I know I'm going to burn and I want to get it over with—right away. What's the use of fooling around with a trial?" Crowley had been indicted for the murder of Patrolman Frederick Hirsch.[14]

But not everyone associated with criminal activity was going into prison during these months. While in the Kansas State Penitentiary, the friendship between Alvin Karpis and Fred Barker was formed. Karpis was assigned to work in the coal mines at the Kansas State Penitentiary, and while engaged in this occupation, he arranged with other prisoners to buy their "pay coal," in order to hasten his release from the penitentiary. The prisoners were required to dig a certain quantity of coal each day, and for each ton mined over the required assignment, the prisoner was given good time. Through his own efforts and the support of those whose "pay coal" he purchased, Karpis was released from the penitentiary on May 31, 1931.

"Ma"—The Life and Times of "Ma" Barker and Her Boys

Following his release, Karpis proceeded to Tulsa, Oklahoma, to visit Freddie Barker's mother, Kate. Karpis had been told by Freddie that, upon his release, he should go visit Ma Barker in Tulsa, who would give Karpis an address for Barker, so the two could join forces. On the way, Karpis stopped and visited Carol Hamilton, who was Herman Barker's widow and Ma's daughter-in-law. Carol gave him directions to Ma's house out on Archer Avenue.[15]

The house with a shabby tarpaulin roof was situated in a field of weeds on the north side of the railroad tracks. As Karpis drew closer, he saw a "little, dumpy old woman" with stringy hair and a pair of bib overalls over a man's sweater standing on a box. Ma Barker was attempting to pound a nail into the frame of a window screen but she could barely reach it.

Karpis asked if she was Mrs. Barker, and she answered that she was. Ma appeared to be somewhat chubby, about five foot two inches tall, and about 140 pounds. She wore gold-rimmed glasses and sounded to Karpis like a real Ozark hillbilly.

"You only had to spend a few hours with Ma to see she wasn't the criminal type," penned Karpis years later. "She was just an old-fashioned home body from the Ozarks. I never understood why her sons turned out to be major league criminals. Ma wasn't, and she brought the Barker boys up. She was a simple woman. Her spare time was spent working jigsaw puzzles and listening to the radio—the way any mother would whose family had grown up. Ma was superstitious, gullible, simple, cantankerous and, well, generally law-abiding. She wasn't suited for the role in the Karpis-Barker Gang."[16]

Ma agreed to send a telegram to Freddie. Karpis hammered the nail in for her and followed her into the house. There

Ma Barker (Arizona Donnie Clark Barker) January 16, 1935. (Courtesy FBI Files)

was no bathroom inside, just an outhouse in back of the house. There was an old washtub on the porch, an oilcloth on the table, two lanterns—one on the table and the other on a rickety old dresser, no electricity, an old sink with no taps, and a bucket beneath the sink.

Ma went to town to send the telegram while Karpis returned to Carol Hamilton's. Alvin told her about the visit and Carol began talking about Ma's husband, whom she was anything but fond of. "He's a worthless bastard. A guy named Arthur Dunlop. Too lazy to work and too lazy to steal. They're just barely getting by. I buy them groceries now and then."

Ma came by with a telegram from Freddie saying he wanted Karpis to take the train to Joplin where he would be waiting to pick him up. Freddie kept his word. Karpis moved in with the Barkers shortly after that first visit, and was told by Freddie that Ma liked being with him more than with her own sons. Karpis did not get on her nerves the way Freddie did.

The following month, on June 10, 1931, Karpis was arrested by the police department at Tulsa as George Haller was on investigation for burglary.

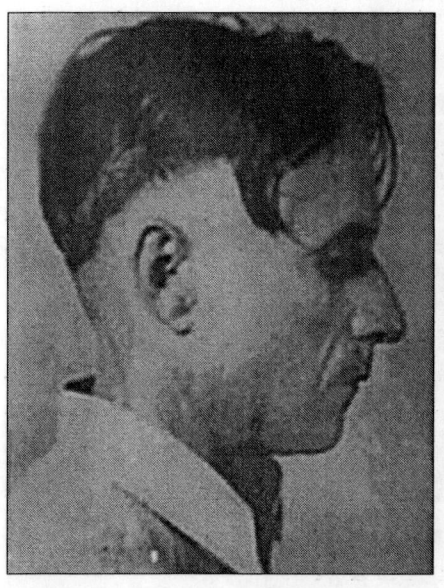 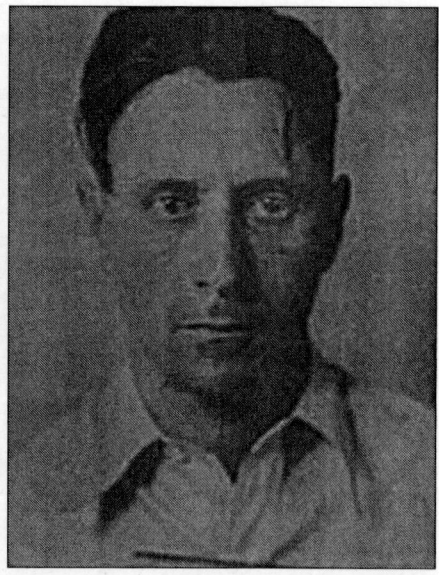

Fred Barker. (alias: F.G. Ward, Ted Murphy and J. Darrows). (Photographer: Bureau of Criminal Apprehension, Photograph Collection 1931, Location no. por 16550 r1, Negative no. 91503)

Fred Barker was also arrested on this charge, which grew out of the theft of some jewelry.

Capone, too, was having his share of problems. On June 13th, he was indicted on 5,000 separate offenses, 4,000 of which concerned the transportation of beer trucks with their loads of thirty-two barrels each. Capone and sixty-eight of his followers were indicted in a twenty-million-dollar-a-year beer operation.[17]

The evidence of the dry-law violation piled up against Capone and his men and constituted the greatest prohibition conspiracy on record, according to federal agents. The indictment revealed the rise of a gigantic industry with total receipts of $200,000,000. In addition to barrels of beer, truckers carried firearms in case they had to shoot it out with dry agents as they moved their product around.

On September 10, 1931, Alvin Karpis, after entering a plea of guilty, was sentenced to four years in the Oklahoma State Penitentiary on a charge of burglary, but, as restitution had been made, the court paroled him. Fred Barker also avoided serving a penitentiary sentence for this offense, and he and Karpis proceeded to Missouri.[18]

Fred Barker told Karpis he knew of a bank in Mountain View, Missouri, that would be easy to take. The Mountain View heist required four men, so ex-cons Bill Weaver and Jimmie Wilson were recruited. The plan called for Karpis and Weaver to break into the bank at three o'clock in the morning and wait for the employees to arrive. Weaver lay down on a table in the conference room where they were waiting and fell asleep.

Just before nine o'clock, the thieves heard two employees enter the bank, so they quickly tied handkerchiefs over their faces and drew their guns. A lady walked in, and upon noticing the masked men holding guns, panicked. Weaver grabbed her while Karpis warned her not to move. One of the employees opened the vault for them, and Weaver and Karpis scooped up all the money inside, shoved the employees into the vault, left it unlocked, and told the employees not to move for at least ten minutes.

Freddie had the car idling, and the bank robbers spun down the main road sprinkling two-inch roofing tacks on the road in their wake to slow up any police that gave chase. When they were far out of town, they counted the money and discovered they had taken close to $7,000.

Federal Judge James H. Wilkerson, meanwhile, sentenced Al Capone, "King of Gangdom," to eleven years imprisonment for evasion of the income tax laws on October 24, 1931. Capone also was fined $50,000 and ordered to pay the costs of his prosecution. Judge Wilkerson ordered the marshal to take Capone to the penitentiary at Leavenworth.[19]

Capone, standing before the bench, his hands behind his back, accepted the sentence stoically. His pendulous lips twitched a bit, and his fingers clenched tightly as the judge read the somewhat complicated sentence. The defendant was attired in a dark purple pinch-back suit and lavender tie. The index finger of his right hand was bandaged. His swarthy face was quite solemn as he stood there, listening to the ominous words of the judge: "It's all over!"

On December 18, 1931, Alvin Karpis and Fred Barker robbed C.C. McCallon's Clothing Store in West Plains, Missouri, of $2,000 worth of merchandise. Apparently they entered the store through a back window after removing two metal bars. The stolen clothing had been carefully selected as the two men were only interested in the latest fashions—the most expensive socks, ties, gloves, sweaters, and shirts. They fled in a 1931 blue De Soto sedan.[20]

Early the following morning, a blue DeSoto drove along East Main Street, pulling into the Davidson Motor Company. The three men in the car needed two tires repaired. One of the mechanics began fixing the flats. Sheriff C.R. Kelly had just finished his coffee and was walking into the post office across from the garage. While the flats were being fixed, the garage owner, Carac Davidson, noticed that the men in the car were wearing clothes that looked like the stolen merchandise from C.C. McCallon's store. Also, the tires on the blue DeSoto made tracks similar to those found behind the building where the break-in occurred. Quietly, Mr. Davidson slipped away to use the phone. He called Mr. McCallon, asking him to come to the garage and see if the men were wearing the clothing from his store.

As McCallon arrived at the garage, Sheriff Kelly was also coming out of the post office. Carefully, Davidson walked across the street to tell him what might be happening. Sheriff Kelly stepped over to his car, got his gun from the back seat, and slipped it under his coat. Then Sheriff Kelly crossed East Main Street, entering the garage to question the men with the blue DeSoto.

Just as the sheriff opened the car door, shots suddenly rang out.... Karpis and Barker knew they had been recognized. One of them ran outside, reloading his pistol as he fled. Turning down an alley at the side of the garage, he quickly made his escape. Tires screeched as the blue DeSoto roared out onto the street. The car hit the curb hard and bounced, causing the right, rear door to swing open accidentally. The DeSoto disappeared down East Main leaving Sheriff Kelly dead. Kelly had been shot twice in the chest and two more times in the left arm. His right hand was still inside his overcoat, reaching for his gun.

The citizens of West Plains began looking for the outlaws that had killed the Howell County sheriff. The only thing they found belonging to the man who escaped on foot was a red scarf. M.C. Stephens, a West Plains policeman, led a group of men in search of the sheriff's killers. Crowds of people gathered in front of the police station, waiting to hear whether or not the gang had been caught. State lawmen came to West Plains to help with the manhunt. It was soon discovered that the killers had headed south toward Thayer, Missouri.

The blue DeSoto was accidentally found by a group of hunters. The car had been abandoned. When the hunters found bullet holes in the back of the car, they knew something was wrong and reported it. After checking the license, the officers discovered that the car belonged to Karpis.

When the lawmen arrived in Thayer, Missouri, they found a farm that had been rented by a Mr. and Mrs. Arthur Dunlop of Oklahoma. The Ma Barker Gang was using the farm as a hideout, but when the police raided the place, the killers were already gone. The front gate was booby trapped to make a bell ring inside the house if the gate was opened, allowing the gang to know when the lawmen were coming. Half the clothes stolen from C.C. McCallon's store were found in the farmhouse. Some of the clothing had been burned in a wood stove to hide the evidence, but officers found a drawing of the First

National Bank of West Plains. The Ma Barker Gang had intended to rob the West Plains bank, but Sheriff Kelly had ruined their plans.

Things were even worse that same December 18th for Jack "Legs" Diamond. Cornered like a rat in his bedroom, Diamond was shot and killed in an Albany, New York, lodging house about 4:45 in the morning after celebrating his acquittal in a kidnapping case. Two men followed the slightly tipsy gangster from a speakeasy to his room where one of them held him down on the bed while the other pumped three bullets into his head.[21]

"Oh, hell, that's enough!" Mrs. Laura Woods, proprietor of the rooming house exclaimed following the third shot. She looked out her front window in time to see two men climb into a car and speed away.

Meanwhile, Kate Barker, Fred Barker, and Alvin Karpis had fled from the cottage in Thayer to the home of Herbert Farmer near Joplin, Missouri. Upon Farmer's advice and instructions, they proceeded to St. Paul, Minnesota. Herbert Farmer, who possessed an extensive criminal record, had been a close friend of the Barker family for many years, and he was particularly friendly with Fred Barker.[22]

According to Karpis, Ma Barker never took part in any of the actual robberies. She knew "her boys" were criminals, but she never wanted to know all the details. She almost never read newspapers or magazines, and the only radio stations she listened to were hillbilly oriented and did not carry news programming.

J. Edgar Hoover had dubbed St. Paul "the poison spot of America." The city was known by gangsters, corrupt police, and G-men as a safe city— a place where criminals on the lam could go to cool their heels. The O'Connor Layover System, named for turn-of-the-century Police Chief John J. "The Big Fellow" O'Connor, was devised in 1924 and allowed known criminals to take refuge in the city, provided they committed no crimes within the city limits, checked in with the police department's unofficial gatekeeper Dan "Dapper Dan" Hogan at his bar, the Green Lantern, and made a donation to the police department's "retirement fund."[23]

Danny Hogan, owner of the Green Lantern speakeasy in St. Paul and an underworld leader who kept gangsters in the city on their best behavior, was killed by a bomb when he started his Paige coupe in the garage behind his house at 1607 W. 7th St., on December 4, 1928. "Dapper Dan," called "the Irish Godfather," was known nationally as a corrupt man able to settle gangsters' feuds and launder money through his saloon.[24]

He served as Police Chief John O'Connor's agent in allowing them to live in St. Paul as long as they committed their crimes somewhere else. Hogan himself was charged in January 1927, along with former St. Paul Police Chief Frank Sommer, in connection with a $35,000 mail robbery in South St. Paul. Friends quickly put up his $100,000 bail, and the case against Hogan and Sommer was dismissed.

1607 West Seventh Street (near May Street and I-35E entrance). (Author's collection)

Police characters and businessmen trooped to the hospital to donate blood for Hogan as efforts to save him lasted through the day, but he died about 9 P.M. The next morning's *Minneapolis Tribune* reported that "There will be fewer turkey dinners in St. Paul this Christmas as a result of his death, according to the talk in the soft-drink bars."

Within a year, it was obvious to police and Federal agents that the illicit liquor trade, the syndicate, and mob violence, had moved into St. Paul with murders committed virtually in the shadow of the State Capitol. The St. Paul Dispatch proclaimed:

"Three men are under arrest in the investigation of the triple murder early Sunday of two men and a woman believed by police to have been brutally slain in the third outbreak of gang warfare in the Twin Cities within two weeks."[25]

"Ma"—The Life and Times of "Ma" Barker and Her Boys

The system initiated by John J. O'Connor and "Dapper Dan" Hogan protected citizens and also encouraged gangsters to come into the city to spend money. The major enterprise for gangsters during this time was bootlegging liquor, and the prohibition kingpin in the city known as the "Al Capone of St. Paul" was Leon Gleckman.

Gleckman maintained his headquarters for business dealings during these times in a suite at the Saint Paul Hotel. Built in 1910, it was the Twin Cities' finest with its beautiful lobby, complete with Waterford chandeliers, its bountiful English gardens, and its Victorian teas. In fact, much of the third floor of the hotel was rented by gangsters, politicians accepting payoffs, or FBI and federal agents engaging in surveillance efforts. Mike Malone, a U.S. Treasury Department official who had infiltrated the Capone syndicate in Chicago, rented a room to observe Gleckman's many guests, which included high-ranking politicians, underworld characters, and police accepting "registration fees" or payoffs.

It was also during these times that prohibition spurned many of St. Paul's wealthiest and most prominent figures to grace the hotel's corridors in pursuit of the finest liquor, available at the hotel by deliveries through bellhops and paid for by cash, reportedly as much as $25 per gallon of booze.

Caught with the goods. (Courtesy Library of Congress)

But few could afford such luxury. Some of the more desperate sufferers, who roamed the streets of Minneapolis with little to eat, turned to crime. On March 2, 1931, a robber had shot his way out of the Northwestern Building at 320 Hennepin, after trying to rob the City Loan Company. The fleeing man killed two detectives during the foray before he was shot to death on the streetcar tracks at

Hennepin and Fourth Street, his body riddled with bullets. The gunman was identified as Leroy Martin, age twenty-six, a substitute postal clerk. Hundreds of people witnessed the killings.[26]

One big haul for the Feds. (Courtesy Library of Congress)

The *Minneapolis Journal* also produced a story of a stag party held on the second floor of 232 Hennepin Avenue, which was raided by Minneapolis police. Unfortunately, some police members were among the crowd of 200 spectators watching eight unclothed women dancing on a stage. Spectators fled upon the arrival of the raiding officers but two police badges were discovered on the floor. Fifty-five men were arrested but only one of the women. The *Journal* saw some amusement in the flight of the undressed females who were much better in giving their pursuers the slip.[27]

These hard times made it tough for anybody to make a dollar in any line of work. The Depression even hit the criminals, and only those who were dedicated to "the profession" and knew how to select their partners were able to get by. Everybody was out of work and many of them wanted to be a crook. According to Alvin Karpis, the Department of Justice published some statistics in 1936 claiming that crooks outnumbered carpenters four to one, grocers six to one, and doctors twenty to one.[28]

In St. Paul, numerous high-profile criminals roamed freely about their favorite restaurants and nightclubs, such as Castle Royal, the Boulevards of Paris and Coliseum ballrooms, and the Hollyhocks Club casino, while the city's administration and civic leaders supported the activities because of assurances from gangsters that the citizens would be safe. When Howard Kahn, crusading editor of the *St. Paul Daily News*, spoke out against it, he was accused of "sensationalism."[29]

Ma Barker & Arthur Dunlop. (Courtesy FBI Files)

In 1933 and 1934, state and federal liquor laws were repealed. St. Paul was divided on the issue. Twenty-four clubs demanded that the legislature repeal the liquor laws, while opponents bombarded the state senate with thirty-one petitions. One of these stated:

"We, the members of the congregation of Dayton Avenue Presbyterian Church, assembled in worship of almighty God, heartily endorse the action of the members of the senate in refusing to repeal the enforcement act of our state; and we pray you will stand strong and firm against all efforts to flood our beloved land with intoxicating liquor so destructive of the physical, moral, and spiritual welfare of our people."[30]

But, of course, the clubs had their way. Among the popular clubs frequented by gangsters was Hollyhocks, a spacious three-story club on the Mississippi River Drive, north of West Seventh Street. Formal dress was required—black tie for men and evening dress for women—while wealthy customers often arrived in chauffeur-driven cars.

The Prohibition era began in 1920, following the ratification of the Eighteenth Amendment to the Constitution of the United States in 1919. The amendment banned the sale or manufacture of alcoholic beverages. Here, government agents dump alcohol confiscated from bootleggers. Prohibition ended in 1933 when the Eighteenth Amendment was repealed. (Author's collection)

The more notorious clubs thrived as well—the Green Dragon Restaurant on Snelling and University avenues, the Boulevards of Paris at Lexington and University, the Brown Derby on Seven Corners, the Plantation at White Bear Lake, and the Hollywood Club at the east end of the Mendota Bridge.

Alvin Karpis' favorite hangout was the Green Lantern Bar and Supper Club at 545 ½ Wabasha Street, which he described in his 1971 memoir:

"It was like a perpetual party. But the greatest blowout was on New Year's Eve, 1932.... There was probably never before as complete a gathering of criminals in one room in the United States as there was in the Green Lantern that night. There were escapees from every major U. S. penitentiary. I was dazzled."[31]

Among the who's-who of criminals were Tommy Holden, Francis Keating, Phil Courtney, Gus Winkler, Harvey Bailey, Big Homer Wilson, Tommy Gannon, Tom Philbin, Tommy Banks, Frank Nash, and Isadore "Kid Cann" Blumenfield.

The first post-prohibition beer in Minneapolis is served at Schiek's Restaurant (45-47 South 3rd). (Author's collection)

By the time prohibition ended in 1933, Kid Cann had diversified, making himself into a leading national power in high-stakes sports bookmaking. He had also invested heavily in Miami real estate; back home he was so entrenched in Minneapolis politics that even reformist Mayor Hubert H. Humphrey was advised by his close friend and campaign fundraiser Fred Gates to leave Cann's less visible operations alone."[32]

Another popular club was the Plantation at White Bear Lake, which had opened its doors with an invitation-only Grand Opening on July 2, 1930. Decorated like a plantation, the club catered to patrons such as Jack Peifer, Morris Roigner, Jimmy Keating, Tommy Holden, Frank Nash, and Capone gunman Fred Goetz. The manager, Ben Harris, was connected to the Barker-Karpis Gang and other criminals.[33]

The White Bear Lake press, however, was moved to print poetically: "Beautiful trees spread their branches, forming a canopy and creating a

"Ma"—The Life and Times of "Ma" Barker and Her Boys

Patrons crowd in for their first taste of beer in years. (Author's collection)

bower of foliage. The check room is a splendid replica of an old shed, in one corner of the Plantation."

The club closed at the end of the 1933 season due to financial problems and police pressure.

After prohibition was repealed and illicit profits dwindled, the gangs turned to bank robbery and kidnapping. The murder of Sheriff Kelly caused the flight of William Weaver, commonly known as Phoenix Donald, another criminal from the vicinity of Thayer, Missouri, to St. Paul. Weaver had been paroled from the Oklahoma State Penitentiary on June 20, 1931, where he had previously been sentenced to serve a term of life imprisonment on the charge of murder. Weaver felt that his move to St. Paul was necessary because the automobile which had been used by Fred Barker and Alvin Karpis at the time of the murder of Sheriff Kelly had been abandoned near the Weaver home.

William Weaver, in addition to his other aliases, was also known as "Lapland Willie" by his cronies, due to his having been reared in that part of Arkansas adjacent to Missouri known as "Lapland." He had launched his criminal career in July 1916, when he was arrested for vagrancy by the police department at Joplin, Missouri. He also was arrested on May 26, 1922, by special agents of the St. Louis-San Francisco Railway at Sapulpa, Oklahoma on a charge of auto theft, but was not prosecuted on this charge. Weaver was next involved with the law at Garden City, Kansas in July of that same year when he was arrested by the Sheriff's Office for attempting to assist in a jail delivery, but again was not prosecuted on this charge. Weaver, as Phoenix Donald, on April 7, 1925, was received at the Oklahoma State Penitentiary to serve a life term for murder, a crime he committed while attempting to escape after committing a bank robbery in the State of Oklahoma. In this attempted escape, he killed a member of the posse which was pursuing him and it was from this sentence he was paroled in 1931.

While serving time in the Oklahoma State Penitentiary, Weaver became acquainted with Ma Barker's son, Arthur, commonly known as "Doc," who had entered the penitentiary on February 10, 1922, for the murder of Thomas J. Sherrill, a night watchman in Tulsa, on August 26, 1921. Weaver also became acquainted with Volney Davis, who had been convicted with "Doc" Barker for the murder of that same night watchman during the burglary. A Tulsa County jury had sentenced both to life in prison.

Prior to the sentencing of Barker and Davis, Okmulgee investigators had received word from Tulsa of the arrest of the two men for the murder of the night watchman at St. John's Hospital. Officers of the Okmulgee Police Department were seeking two suspects for the murder of Captain Homer Spaulding.

Picking up their first post-Prohibition case of Gluek's. (Author's collection)

Early on the morning of Sunday, January 8, 1922, Captain Spaulding, Detective Mark Lairmore and Patrolman M.E. Spence received a hot tip that a robbery of the local jewelry store was planned. About 3:10 A.M., the lawmen spotted a big Buick touring sedan parked along the roadside. Two men were working on the engine of the vehicle while several others were sitting inside. Spaulding, who was driving, parked the police cruiser in front of the Buick with the headlights pointing directly towards the parked car.[34]

When the lawmen stepped from their cruiser and approached the Buick, Spaulding asked if they needed assistance. One of the men leaning over the engine stated they could use a flashlight. Officer Lairmore eased toward the back of the Buick to get a better look at the occupants. Noticing several shotguns and rifles lying on the back seat, he commented to his fellow officers to "be careful boys, they are armed."

Suddenly one of the men working on the engine pulled a gun and shot Spaulding in the thigh. Shots were fired back and forth with Lairmore getting struck in the leg, although he shot one of the gunmen in the arm. He and Spence also shot the man in the head, who had blasted Spaulding. The gunman died instantly.

Noticing a man inside the car trying to load a shotgun, Lairmore fired several rounds into the car wounding the suspect. At this point, two other suspects bolted from the car with the officers firing at the fleeing men. A blood trail was later found indicating that at least one of the assailants had been hit. Captain Spaulding later died from his wounds.

When officers searched the crime scene, they found various weapons, a bottle of nitroglycerin, and an assortment of burglary tools. The following day, Tulsa authorities officially identified the dead bandit as Jimmy Sexton, a small time hood, who had grown up with Fred and Doc Barker, Harry Campbell, and Volney Davis in Tulsa's Central Park neighborhood.

Although Ed Lansing was later convicted of first-degree murder and given the death penalty, he appealed the decision and his sentence was reduced to life in prison. Frank Hadley claimed self-defense but the jury wasn't convinced. He was sentenced to twenty-five years in prison. His lawyer promptly appealed and the Oklahoma Court of Appeals overturned the verdict and he was set free

Volney Davis, however, matched the description of one of the suspects who had fled the Spaulding murder scene. Detective Lairmore traveled to Tulsa the following day where he positively identified Davis. The suspect was left in custody of Tulsa authorities awaiting the outcome of the murder charges he was facing in connection with the night watchman's death. Okmulgee County Judge Bozarth ordered a hold to be put on the suspect in case he was somehow released or proven not guilty on the Tulsa murder charge.

After he was handed out his life sentence, Davis appealed the verdict for the killing of Sherrill and his case went before the Oklahoma Court of Criminal Appeals but to no avail. The court record reads:

"Davis v. State, 227 P. 848, 27 Okl.Cr. 319, Oklahoma Court of Criminal Appeals, (Syllabus.) 1. Homicide—Instruction for Verdict of Murder or Acquittal Held not Erroneous. Where the evidence shows that the homicide was committed while the accused or his confederates were attempting to commit a robbery and there is no evidence tending to show that the offense was manslaughter or excusable or justifiable homicide, it was not error for the court to instruct the jury they should either find a verdict for murder or acquit the defendant.

"2. Homicide—Evidence Sustaining Conviction for Murder. The evidence held sufficient to sustain the verdict. Appeal from District Court, Tulsa County; W.B. Williams, Judge. Volney Davis was convicted of murder, and he appeals. Affirmed. Luther James, for plaintiff in error. The Attorney General, for the State. BESSEY, J. Plaintiff in error, Volney Davis, defendant below, was on January 27, 1923, in the district court of Tulsa County, convicted of murder for the assassination of an aged night watchman in an attempted robbery of a safe in the watchman's charge. This is a companion case to the case of Doc Barker v. State, 27 Okla. Cr. 305, 227 P. 846, recently affirmed by this court. The state's evidence in the two cases, so far as it affects the important issues involved, was for the most part the same, or similar. Two important witnesses for the state may have been accomplices, but the trial court in apt language instructed the jury as to the necessity for corroboration of the evidence of accomplices. The record shows also that there were a number of facts and circumstances proven by other disinterested witnesses which sufficiently corroborated the accomplices, if indeed both were accomplices. The assignments of error are that the evidence is insufficient to sustain the verdict, and alleged erroneous instructions to the jury. The facts and circumstances which were outlined in general in the Barker Case need not be here reiterated. We find the evidence in the instant case sufficient to sustain the verdict rendered. The defendant excepted to the following instruction:

"'You are instructed that homicide is the killing of one human being by another, and is divided into five degrees or classes, namely: Murder, first degree manslaughter, second degree manslaughter, excusable homicide, and justifiable homicide. Homicide is murder: First, when perpetrated without authority of law and with the premeditated design to affect the death of the person killed or any other human being; second, when perpetrated without design to effect death by a person engaged in the commission of a felony. You are instructed that there has been introduced in this case no evidence showing or tending to show that the alleged killing is first-degree manslaughter, second-degree manslaughter, excusable or justifiable homicide, as such terms are used in the statute. The issue thus formed as determined by the court for you to decide is only whether or not the defendant is guilty of the crime of murder.'

"Under the evidence there was no showing of manslaughter in either degree, nor of excusable or justifiable homicide. The accused and his several confederates under the evidence were either guilty of murder or entitled to an acquittal. Lovejoy v. State, 18 Okla. Cr. 335, 194 P. 1087. This homicide was committed in the course of an attempt to rob a safe in the custody of Thomas J. Sharrill, and old night watchman, by the use of deadly and dangerous weapons, evincing extreme moral depravity on the part of the perpetrators, and an utter disregard for human life. Defendant complains that instruction No. 8B in relation to those features of the evidence was erroneous because the court told the jury that, if they found that the homicidal act was perpetrated by the accused while in the act of committing a felony or under circumstances imminently dangerous to others, evincing a depraved mind, regardless of human life, 'with or without a premeditated design to effect the death of Thomas J. Sharrill,' the accused was guilty of murder. This was a correct statement of the law on premeditation, as embodied in subdivisions 2 and

3 of section 1733, Comp. Stat. 1921, defining murder in practically the language used by the court. Ray v. State, 10 Okla. Cr. 403, 136 P. 980; Lovejoy v. State, supra. The other objections to instructions criticized are unimportant, and without merit. The judgment of the trial court is affirmed. MATSON, P.J., and DOYLE, J., concur."[35]

Davis succeeded in escaping from the Oklahoma State Prison on January 8, 1925. Thirteen days later, however, he was apprehended at Kansas City, Missouri, and returned to the penitentiary.[36]

When Kate Barker, A. W. Dunlop, commonly known as "Old Man" Dunlop, Fred Barker and Alvin Karpis sought refuge in St. Paul, Minnesota, they rented a house at 1031 South Robert Street in West St. Paul from Nick Hannegraf. The landlord's ten-year-old niece, Bernice Hannegraf, had been living next door with her mother and grandparents since her father passed away. The three Hannegraf-owned houses had been built in a row at 1025, 1031, and 1035 South Robert Street.[37]

Bernice Hannegraf Grossman recalled that Ma Barker was always very friendly. Unbeknownst initially to the Hannegrafs, the fugitives, who were then being sought by the various state law enforcement authorities, did not lead normal lives at the Robert Street address and this eventually aroused her suspicions. She and her mother observed that Ma's two "sons" constantly carried violin cases when leaving and returning to the house, which caused everyone to believe that they played in orchestras.

An older man, A. W. Dunlop, owned a little, short-haired, black-and-white dog which he walked every day on the cement sidewalk that bordered the rear of all three houses. While exercising the dog, this man always seemed to keep one hand in his pocket as if he were holding something of value.

But the Hannegrafs were not the only neighbors suspicious of the strange activities of their new neighbors. Ernie Langula, a young man employed at his father's hardware store, had waited on Arthur Dunlap and the Barker boys several times, and like everyone else, was fooled by the violin cases.

Anthony O'Tremba, who ran a filling station and auto repair across the street from the Barker house, noticed that one of the "boys" always kept a close eye on him while he serviced their car. Still, they were good customers.

Another neighbor, Harry Trost, delivered milk to Ma Barker and noted that someone always met him at the door with empty bottles and money. Unlike most of his customers, they never questioned the price nor did they ask for credit.

Rhea McBride, granddaughter of Henry Ehlers, the founder of the West St. Paul State Bank, remembered: "We lived two doors away from them on South Robert Street and noticed the boys coming in late at night with their violin cases. They claimed they were playing at lake resorts around the Twin Cities, but of course, they were robbing banks. They never bothered our bank, but the old man used to come in and get change."[38]

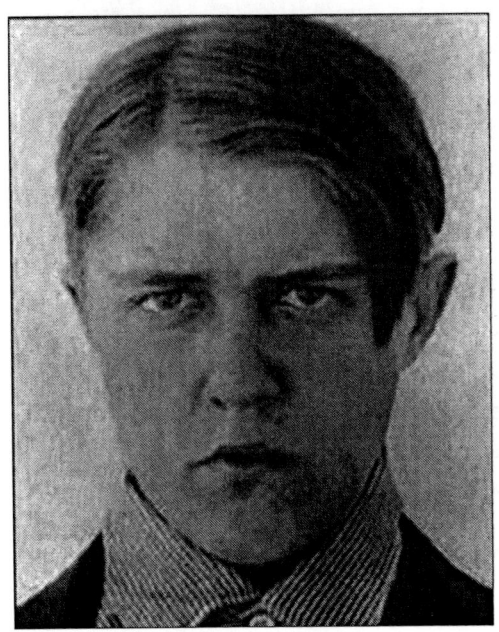

Alvin Karpis. (Author's collection)

In St. Paul, Fred Barker, Alvin Karpis, and Ma Barker became acquainted with Harry Sawyer, whose correct name was Harry Sandlovich, the "Kingpin and Fixer for the underworld in St. Paul." Sawyer was born in Russia, immigrated to this country and settled in Lincoln, Nebraska, later moving to St. Paul, where he went into partnership with the notorious underworld character, Dan Hogan. This contact for Karpis and Fred Barker was made for them through Herbert Farmer, who knew Sawyer could provide protection to wanted individuals.[39]

Karpis and the Barker boys felt that their fast moves were complicated by the fact that Ma's boyfriend traveled with them. She seemed to be attached to him and let him live with her. They concluded, however, that Dunlap was a user and was sponging off of Ma. Dunlop looked presentable enough—a slim, gray-haired man, about a head taller than Ma, who kept himself neat and clean. But according to Karpis, he was "a pain in the ass."[40]

Whenever Karpis took Ma to the movies, he always had to take Dunlop along, and when they were shopping for food or clothes, they had to remember to pick up something for him. Dunlop didn't work, did not take part in any holdups, did nothing around the house, and did a poor job of taking care of Ma.

It did not take long for Freddie and Karpis to discover that Dunlop was a drunk and an "ingrate." He never thanked anyone for anything, hated the moves from place to place, and did not like being told what to do by "young punks." His constant whining caused Freddie to despise him, and instead of calling him by name, referred to him simply as "the old bastard."

Dunlop was drunk much of the time and did not know how to handle liquor. Alcohol would make him mean and he would abuse Ma until Karpis or Freddie would shut him up or take him out of the room. Karpis' worst fight with "the old bastard" came after giving him a .38 in a "weak moment." Dunlop had the pistol sticking out of his pants pocket and had been heckling Ma and Karpis all evening. Karpis lured him into the kitchen by promising him another drink, and when they were out of Ma's hearing, Karpis demanded the gun. Dunlop told him "to go to hell." Karpis pulled his own gun and forcibly removed the other from Dunlop.

On April 24, 1932, nearly one thousand veterans marched through the lower loop of Minneapolis. Their march was joined by a rear guard of Communists with red banners, although they had not been asked to participate. The marchers demanded the return of beer and the payment of a special bonus to assist former service men.[41]

Some city residents lived on Prosperity Row, in a line of shacks on the banks of the Mississippi River. These crude dwellings were located a half-mile from the Broadway Bridge on the south side near an emptying sewer. The average shack in "the Row" cost thirty cents to build. Olaf Larson and "Bulldog" Hans Olson, former saloon workers, lived there with a number of others who subsisted on the fish they caught in the dirty river and on stale bread they were given from restaurants and bakeries.[42]

Nick Hannegraf owned and operated the Drovers Tavern and Restaurant in South St. Paul, and once the bar had closed, he sat down and began reading a detective magazine before going home. He became startled when he recognized a familiar face in one of the magazine photographs. There was no doubt about it—the man in the picture was one of Ma Barker's boys.[43]

Hannegraf closed the tavern, rushed to his mother's place, and related to the family what he had discovered. Early the following morning, Nick went to see Police Chief Paul Braun and reported the find. Braun, however, was less than enthusiastic and gave the impression that he did not wish to get involved with the apprehension of Ma Barker and her boys.

According to Alvin Karpis, the woman who owned the house in West St. Paul where they were living had a son, who ran a couple of speakeasies and liked to sample his own product. He and Dunlop would sit together and get drunk on the hooch and shoot the breeze. Both Freddie and Karpis were afraid of what information he might have been passing on.[44]

Right—Charles and Hannah Saunders. Sheriff Saunders, who was the sheriff at the time of the murder, dragged Arthur Dunlap's body out of the mud. Charles and Hannah rotated the sheriff position in Burnett County for many years. The other older couple is identified only as Anna and Orin. (Courtesy of Burnett County Historical Society)

The day after the skirmish in the kitchen, Karpis received an early morning call from Harry Sawyer. Photographs of Freddie and Karpis had appeared in *True Detective Stories* two weeks earlier, and according to Sawyer, an informant had visited the police with the pictures and other information regarding their presence in St. Paul. Sawyer's man on the police force was stalling the raid to allow him time to warn Ma's boys to get out of the house at once.

Karpis was certain the landlady's son had been the informant and he knew that Dunlop had spilled everything during one of his drinking bouts. Since Freddie was away, Karpis hustled Ma and Dunlop out of the house, and in two minutes flat, they were driving away.

Word soon reached St. Paul Chief of Police Thomas E. Dahill and Chief Inspector James Crumley. At about seven that morning, on April 25th, the police conducted a raid on Ma's house but found that the criminals had already fled.[45]

That same morning, Chief Braun and officers of the local police department, still had not checked out the Barker place. Their procrastination was costly as, approximately six hours earlier, Fred Barker, Alvin Karpis, Kate Barker and A. W. Dunlop packed their belongings and hurriedly departed from West St. Paul.

As Dahill's officers searched the house, they found that breakfast was still cooking on a lighted gas stove, the lights were still on, and all the clothing belonging to the Barkers was still in the house. The gang left with nothing but their guns and the little dog. Bernice Hannegraf became the recipient of Ma Barker's brown fur coat, which was restyled by Kastner's Furs at Bernard and Robert Streets.

Special Agent Madala of Chicago later filed a report which stated that A. W. Dunlop alias George Anderson, Ma's husband, had rented a cottage a mile and a half from Thayer, Missouri, on or about October 12, 1931. Fred Barker and Alvin Karpis moved in with Ma and A. W. on December 18th.

Madala's report verified that Karpis and Fred Barker had robbed the store in West Plains, Missouri, and the following day, they were about to be questioned by Sheriff Kelly, at which time Karpis fired on the sheriff, killing him. A. W. Dunlop's house was raided by police but it was found to be abandoned shortly before the officer's stormed the house.

Certain letters, however, were discovered indicating that Ma Barker had four years earlier resided at 401 Cincinnati Street in Tulsa, apparently owning this property. When things had gotten hot for the Barkers, Dunlop and Ma had fled northward from Tulsa, to the house they rented in West St. Paul, where they lived with Fred and Karpis.

"Ma"—The Life and Times of "Ma" Barker and Her Boys

When Karpis told Ma and her paramour about the snitch, Dunlop, too afraid to lie, admitted he had talked too much. He tried to excuse himself by explaining that he had been very drunk at the time. Karpis called him "a rotten son of a bitch" and checked him into a hotel under a false name.[46]

Ma Barker was in a state of shock and Karpis wanted to talk with her. Driving to a friend's house, they discussed Dunlop for a couple of hours and he told her she'd be better off without him. She would not criticize her husband but she agreed. Karpis suggested that she, Freddie, and him should move to Kansas City, give Dunlop some cash, and send him off to Chicago.

The following morning the body of A.W. Dunlop was found on the shores of Lake Fransted, near Webster, Wisconsin. It was stripped of clothing and an examination of the body disclosed that Dunlop had been shot three times at short range. A blood-stained woman's glove was discovered not far from the body. Federal agents determined that Dunlop was killed by Fred Barker and Alvin Karpis, inasmuch as they believed he had tipped them off to the police.[47] According to Karpis, however, Dunlop was killed by Jack Peifer, not by him and Freddie. They had often done jobs for Peifer and this was his way of returning the favor.

Kate Barker and her son, Freddie, with Alvin Karpis, found it necessary to temporarily leave St. Paul, Minnesota, and find another refuge due to the investigation by law enforcement agencies into the murder of Dunlop. The fugitives proceeded to Kansas City, Missouri, where under the disguise of being respectable citizens, they established a residence in an exclusive residential district known as the Country Club Plaza. Alvin Karpis posed as the son of Kate Barker and Ma frequently referred to her sons as being in the insurance business.

Meanwhile, on May 4th, Al Capone in leg irons and under heavy guard was taken to the penitentiary in Atlanta. Weeping and ranting at the "injustice" of his sentence, Capone, for seven years overlord of America's underworld, bade farewell to his family and started for Atlanta to begin serving his ten-year sentence.[48]

In Kansas City, Fred Barker and Alvin Karpis were thrown in their lot with criminals Francis Keating and Thomas Holden, escaped federal prisoners

Harvey Bailey. (Author's collection)

from the United States Penitentiary at Leavenworth, Kansas; Harvey Bailey, a nationally known bank robber; and Larry DeVol, Karpis' friend with whom he had been arrested in Kansas City. With this gang was Bernard Phillips, a policeman who had turned bank robber.[49]

The mob was residing in close proximity to each other in Kansas City and planned new depredations. On June 17, 1932, Fred Barker, Keating, Holden, Bailey, DeVol, Karpis, and Phillips made a raid on a Fort Scott, Kansas bank, but early in the robbery Fred became fidgety and threatened to kill everyone in the bank if they didn't shut up. Two tellers dropped to the floor, and when one of them reached for an alarm button, Karpis kicked his hand.

As they were cramming money into bags, a messenger from the local Light and Power Company walked in to make an $800 bank deposit. Relieving him of the cash, the robbers suddenly noticed that the street was filling up with people and some police officers and sheriff's men were headed straight to the bank.

The robbers took $47,000, grabbed three women customers, and headed for the door. When one of the girls fainted, they placed the other two on the running boards and made their escape. Fred Barker fired his "tommy-gun" out the rear window and the pursuing police officers backed off. The women were released a few miles out of town and the robbers returned to Kansas City and split the loot in the apartment occupied by Fred Barker, Ma Barker, and Alvin Karpis, located at 4804 Jefferson Street, Kansas City, Missouri.[50]

The "Tommy" Gun, or Thompson Sub-machine Gun the robbers carried, had been named after its inventor, Brigadier General John T. Thompson, who served as director of arsenals during the First World War. Because it was developed too late for the trenches of Europe, the submachine gun was placed on the open market Auto Ordnance Corporation of New York.[51]

Military agencies in the United States and overseas had little or no interest in the Thompson, nor did law enforcement agencies. Gangsters such as Alvin Karpis and the Barkers, however, loved it since it weighed only eight and a half pounds, had a range of five hundred yards, and fired a thousand .45 caliber pistol cartridges per minute. And just as impressive was the cost—only $175 by mail orders.

On the very day of the robbery of the bank at Fort Scott, another criminal who was to join the Karpis-Barker Gang was released from the Kansas State Penitentiary at Lansing. While in the penitentiary, Fred Barker and Alvin Karpis had become acquainted with Jess Doyle, who had been imprisoned March 19, 1927, to serve a five-to-ten-year sentence for second degree burglary and grand larceny. Doyle had served a previous five-year sentence in the Oklahoma State Penitentiary for the larceny of an automobile. Less than a year later, Doyle found himself in the state penitentiary at Lansing, Kansas.[52]

Prior to Fred Barker's release, he had made arrangements with Doyle to meet in Kansas City, Missouri, at the expiration of Doyle's term June 17, 1932. Jess Doyle immediately proceeded to Kansas City upon his release and met Barker in front of the Majestic Hotel. Fred Barker was well supplied with money at this time and from the spoils of the Fort Scott bank, Fred gave Doyle four or five hundred dollars for clothes and other expenses.

At Barker's apartment that night a celebration was held to celebrate the successful robbery of the bank and the release of Jess Doyle from the penitentiary. Those who attended this party were Francis Keating, Thomas Holden, Harvey Bailey, Larry DeVol, Alvin Karpis, and Bernard Phillips.

"Ma"—The Life and Times of "Ma" Barker and Her Boys

Kate Barker, with her son Fred and Karpis, lived at the Longfellow Apartments in Kansas City from May 12, 1932, until July 5, 1932, when they moved from the building as a safety measure, and began living at an apartment at 414 West 46th Terrance, in the same city under the aliases Mrs. A. F. Hunter and sons. Ma Barker was the housekeeper for Fred and Karpis and for a few days they enjoyed the homelike atmosphere which Ma Barker endeavored to create. Larry DeVol was also living in the same apartment building.

"In time, I became one off 'Ma's boys,'" wrote Alvin Karpis years later. "She and I grew very close in the years all of us—Freddie, Doc, Ma, and I, and various assorted friends and wives—lived together."[53]

Although he agreed with Karpis' statement about Ma and her boys, FBI Chief J. Edgar Hoover took a little dimmer view of the situation: "Everybody knew that . . . Ma, for all her killing ways, was still filled with maternal love for her 'murderous brood.'"[54]

This tranquility enjoyed by the gangster element, however, was disturbed on July 8, 1932, by Special Agents of the Federal Bureau of Investigation, who had been planning the apprehension of Francis Keating and Thomas Holden to return them to Leavenworth to complete the sentences which they were serving for mail robbery. Special agents had learned that Keating and Holden were golf enthusiasts, and a special agent, in checking the golf courses in Kansas City, located Keating, Holden and Harvey Bailey playing golf on the Old Mission Hill Golf Course.

Bailey, Holden, Keating, and Fred Barker were getting ready for a round of golf, waiting on their friend Bernard Phillips to appear. Bailey was anxious to tee off and decided they should begin without Phillips. Barker, who cared little for the game, declined and headed off in another direction while the group of three began their game. When they approached a ditch on the course, eight officers appeared heavily armed. They knew who Holden and Keating were and one of the officers suggested letting Bailey go because they weren't looking for him. That idea was nixed and when officers searched Harvey Bailey, they found a $500 liberty bond from the Fort Scott bank robbery, connecting him to the crime.

"Ma"—The Life and Times of "Ma" Barker and Her Boys

Holden and Keating were apprehended on that date and returned to the United States Penitentiary at Leavenworth, Kansas, where they had escaped on February 28, 1930, with the help of "Machine Gun" Kelly. Kelly had worked in the Bertillion Room in the prison and had access to prison files, passes and such. He made two fake passes and with the help of Frank Nash, civilian clothes were smuggled in. Holden and Keating simply walked out the front gate with the passes. Harvey Bailey was removed to Fort Scott by state authorities and identified as one of the participants in the robbery of the bank. He was later convicted and received a ten-to-fifty-year sentence to be served in the Kansas State Penitentiary.

Harvey seemed to accept his imprisonment, was positive he would live to be paroled, and settled into the life of a convict. But Wilbur "the Tri-State Terror" Underhill changed that for Bailey by enlisting his aid with smuggling guns. On June 1, 1933, Bailey, Underhill, Bob Brady, Jim Clark, Ed Davis, Frank Sawyer and five others escaped the Kansas prison. Bailey saved the life of the Warden, Kirk Prathers, whom they took hostage. Underhill hated the prison warden and wanted to kill him, Harvey refused to allow this to happen.

Bailey was shot in the kneecap during the escape and was bleeding badly. Prathers offered to take him to the hospital when he was released and seemed greatly concerned for Harvey. When the Warden was released unharmed as Harvey had promised, he gave Prathers five dollars for bus fare home.

When asked about Ma Barker's involvement with the gang and the possibility of her serving as the ringleader, Bailey replied: "The old woman couldn't plan breakfast. When we'd sit down to plan a bank job, she'd go into the other room and listen to *Amos and Andy*, or hillbilly music on the radio. She just went along with Freddie because she had no choice. Freddie loved his mother and wouldn't leave her to fend for herself."[55]

The fourth member of the foursome who had been playing golf with Holden, Keating, and Bailey on the Old Mission Golf Course that day was Bernard Phillips, who by chance was not with the other three men at the time of their apprehension. Phillips apparently carried the news to other members of the gang, for Kate Barker and her son Fred, with Alvin Karpis, hurriedly departed from their apartment about 5:30 P.M., on the same date that the arrests took place, leaving a fully cooked meal on the table. The condition of the apartment when later examined by special agents, clearly indicated that the fugitives had made a rapid departure.[56]

From Kansas City, Missouri, Fred Barker, Kate Barker, Alvin Karpis, Bernard Phillips, and Jess Doyle fled to St. Paul Minnesota and later, on July 9, 1932, they rented a cottage from Mr. and Mrs. John Lambert at Mahtomedi, a summer resort on White Bear Lake. Lambert, an eighty-year-old retired grocer, who once was a neighbor of Edward, Mollie, and a young F. Scott Fitzgerald on Laurel Avenue in St. Paul, was taking a trip to Scotland with his wife and renting out his cottage.

Ma Barker told the Lamberts that her name was Mrs. Hunter and that Freddie and Alvin were her sons, Freddie and Raymond. When Ma agreed to the Lambert rule of no drinking, partying, or carousing, the elderly couple rented them the house. For the most part, the "Hunters" were quiet and limited their revelry to nights at the nearby Silver Slipper roadhouse, the area's premier speakeasy.[57]

Driving into St. Paul several days a week, the mob relaxed there by frequenting the saloon operated by Harry Sawyer at 545 Wabasha Street, and also found entertainment at the Hollyhocks, the night club operated by John "Jack" Peifer.

While Fred Barker and Alvin Karpis were living at White Bear Lake, they were associated with a criminal attorney, J. Earl Smith of Tulsa, Oklahoma, and subsequent to the robbery of the Fort Scott bank and the apprehension of Harvey Bailey, Smith was retained to defend Bailey at his trial. Smith reportedly turned in two bonds in the denomination of one thousand dollars to Fenner & Beane Brokers in Tulsa. These bonds were part of the loot from the Fort Scott Bank robbery.[58]

Smith defended Harvey Bailey at his trial and the racketeer was found guilty. Smith later admitted to authorities that the bonds he had left with the brokers had come to him from a third party, who had gotten them from Fred Barker. After Bailey was convicted and sentenced, Smith received a mysterious telephone call, presumably from Karpis, on the morning of August 13, 1932, telling him that Fred Barker wished to see him in Tulsa. The next morning Smith's body was found bullet riddled at the Indian Hills Country Club, fourteen miles north of Tulsa, Oklahoma.[59]

Earl Christman, a confidence man who was a fugitive from the Indiana State Penitentiary, with his moll, Helen Ferguson, sought refuge in St. Paul and through Harry Sawyer, Earl Christman, and Helen Ferguson became acquainted with Alvin Karpis, Fred Barker, and other members of the gang who at that time were frequenting St. Paul. The members of the gang at this time included Frank Nash, also an escapee from the United States Penitentiary at Leavenworth, Kansas, and Nash, like Fred Barker, was an intimate friend of Herbert Farmer of Joplin, Missouri.

His nickname was "Jelly" Nash because apparently he had something of a large belly that wiggled like jelly. Frank was also known as the "Gentleman Bandit" because Frank was quite erudite, very smart. Nash was very polite, even as he robbed a bank he would be very courteous to the people that he was robbing.[60]

Born in the small town of Birdseye, Indiana on February 6, 1887, Frank "Jelly" Nash had a hard life from the start. His mother died when he was two and a cast of relatives took turns raising him. In 1902, his father, John, opened the Nash Hotel in Hobart, Oklahoma, and sent for his son to help operate his new business. After only two years, Nash left to join the Army. When he returned three years later, he worked as a hotel handyman and cook, but spent most of his time listening to tales from the travelers. With an affinity for fine things and a strong dislike of hard work, Nash ran out of income and began to pay for his worldly goods by robbing stores.[61]

In May of 1911, he was arrested for burglarizing a store. He was arrested six more times in six months, none of which resulted in a conviction. In 1913, Nash's accomplice, Nollie Wortman, was found dead near Hobart. Nash was charged with his death and found guilty of murder and was sentenced to life in prison at the Oklahoma State Penitentiary in McAlester. Nash talked his way into a parole so he could do his part in the war effort. He was then given a full pardon after the war.

Nash didn't learn his lesson in prison the first time around and in October 1919, he was arrested and convicted for robbing a bank and sentenced to twenty-five years. During his stay at the state penitentiary, he met Al Spencer, a member of the Henry Starr Gang. In 1922, Spencer escaped. Soon, Nash received sixty-days leave for "business reasons." His business, of course, was robbing banks. He didn't return. In the twenty months following, Spencer's gang robbed somewhere between twenty and forty banks. Nash was there for many of them.

After the Katy Limited train robbery, a massive manhunt for the Spencer Gang ensued. Within a month, every member except Nash was dead or in custody. Nash escaped to Mexico until U.S. Marshals lured him back to the States where he was promptly arrested. He arrived at the federal penitentiary in Leavenworth, Kansas to serve twenty-five years for assaulting a U.S. Mail custodian.

On October 19, 1930, Nash picked up his favorite book, *The Complete Works of William Shakespeare*, from the prison library and simply walked out of prison. He headed for the criminal haven of St. Paul, Minnesota. It was here that Nash became close with Verne Miller. In May 1933, Nash wed Frances Luce in Hot Springs, Arkansas.

On July 26, 1932, Karpis and Fred Barker with their augmented gang left their hideout at White Bear Lake, and staged a daring daylight robbery of the Cloud County Bank at Concordia, Kansas, appropriating about $240,000 in bonds and an indefinite amount of cash. With Karpis and Barker were Lawrence Devol, Jess Doyle, and Earl Christman.[62]

According to Karpis, Christman was along because he was badly in need of money. A specialist in con games and swindles, he had recently escaped from the penitentiary at Jackson, Michigan, while some lawmen were escorting him from Seattle to the coast, where he was to testify at a trial of three train robbers.

The initial step was to run the roads in the Concordia area before the robbery. This act was standard procedure by the boys, as they would familiarize themselves with every highway, dirt road, and gravel track so they could plan their escape route, plus possibly fool the police. While running the roads, the gangsters hid gasoline at strategic points because the police would often shoot at their gas tanks.

In mid-morning, the boys hit the bank with Jess Doyle waiting outside to drive the getaway car. Christman stood just inside the bank door, holding some dollar bills in his hand, as if he had just made a deposit. His role was to take charge of any customers that might enter the bank during the holdup.

DeVol, Fred, and Karpis looked the room over and noted there were seven or eight employees behind the counter, and the only customers were two old men sitting on a bench eating their lunches. The robbers pulled their guns and quietly ordered everyone into the small back room. The employees did as they were told but the two farmers just kept eating, even though the boys were waving their guns at them. Finally DeVol told them that they were robbing the bank and the two farmers dashed into the back room where the employees were.

The cashier, reminiscent of Joseph Lee Heywood, who had refused to open the vault of the First National Bank of Northfield, Minnesota, for the James-Younger Gang in 1876, would not unlock the vault even when he was threatened with death. When a female customer, in fear for her life, begged the cashier to cooperate, he merely told the robbers she did not belong to him and didn't care if they shot her. After forty-five minutes, the gangsters gave up, pushed the cashier into the back room, and left, leaving the money in the vault.

An eye witness, Marie Fredrickson had secured a position at the Cloud County Bank in the early 1920s and became secretary to the president, J. C. Peck. She later recalled that the robbery didn't go smoothly due to problems with the time release of the safe, and the gang had to spend nearly an hour in the bank instead of the planned ten minutes. Employees were beaten, and Marie had a gun held to her head by Freddy Barker. She was told she would be killed if the safe wasn't opened. She was later taken as a hostage when the gang left the bank, but luckily was released several miles out of town. Following a successful escape, the gang returned to their hideout at White Bear Lake.[63]

"MA"—THE LIFE AND TIMES OF "MA" BARKER AND HER BOYS

Notes

[1] Alvin Karpis with Bill Trent, *The Alvin Karpis Story*, New York, Coward, McCann & Geoghegan, Inc., 1971, p. 84.
[2] *Minneapolis Journal*, March 9, 1929.
[3] Joseph Stipanovich, *City of Lakes An Illustrated History of Minneapolis*, Minneapolis, Windsor Publications, Inc., 1982, p. 26.
[4] Theodore C. Blegen, *Minnesota A History of the State*, pp. 521-522.
[5] *Minneapolis Journal*, October 30, 1929.
[6] *Minneapolis Journal*, September 4, 1930.
[7] David L. Rosheim, *The Other Minneapolis or A History of the Minneapolis Skid Row*, Maquoketa, Andromeda Press, 1978, p. 114.
[8] *Minneapolis Journal*, February 25, 1931.
[9] Kenneth Alsop, *Hard Travelin'*, New York, New American Library, 1967, p. 187.
[10] Joseph Stipanovich, *City of Lakes An Illustrated History of Minneapolis*, pp. 26-28.
[11] *Minneapolis Journal*, April 10, 1931.
[12] *Chicago Daily News*, December 20, 1930.
[13] *Chicago Daily News*, February 27, 1931.
[14] *New York Daily News*, February 9, 1931.
[15] Alvin Karpis with Bill Trent, *The Alvin Karpis Story*, pp. 81-83.
[16] Ibid.
[17] *Chicago Daily Tribune*, June 13, 1931.
[18] Alvin Karpis with Bill Trent, *The Alvin Karpis Story*, pp. 81-83.
[19] *Boston Evening American*, October 24, 1931.
[20] Edwin J. (Ed) Riege, "The Barker-Karpis Rouges," *Minnesota Police Journal*, August 1991.
[21] *Brooklyn Daily Eagle*, December 18, 1931.
[22] Edwin J. (Ed) Riege, "The Barker-Karpis Rouges," *Minnesota Police Journal*, August 1991.
[23] Virginia Brainard Kunz, *St. Paul Saga of an American City*, Woodland Hills, California, Windsor Publications, Inc., 1977, p. 126.
[24] *Minneapolis Tribune*, December 5, 1928.
[25] *St. Paul Dispatch*, April 25, 1927.
[26] Ibid., March 3, 1931.
[27] Ibid., March 16, 1932.
[28] Alvin Karpis, Bill Trent, *Public Enemy Number One: The Alvin Karpis Story*, pp. 118-119.
[29] Virginia Brainard Kunz, *St. Paul Saga of an American City*, p. 128.
[30] Ibid., p. 126.
[31] Alvin Karpis, Bill Trent, *Public Enemy Number One: The Alvin Karpis Story*, Richmond Hill, Ontario, Canada, Pocket Books Canada, 1973.

32. Dara Moskowitz, "Minneapolis Confidential," *City Pages*, Volume 16, Number 775, October 11, 1995.
33. Cynthia E. Vadnais, *Looking Back at White Bear Lake, A Pictorial History of the White Bear Lake Area*, White Bear Lake, Sentinel Printing Company, Inc., 2004, p. 148.
34. Okmulgee, Oklahoma Police Department Archives.
35. Davis v. State, 227 P. 848, 27 Okl.Cr. 319, Oklahoma Court of Criminal Appeals.
36. Alvin Karpis, Bill Trent, *Public Enemy Number One: The Alvin Karpis Story*, Richmond Hill, Ontario, Canada, Pocket Books Canada, 1973.
37. Lois A. Glewwe, author and editor, *West St. Paul Centennial 1889-1989. The History of West St. Paul, Minnesota*, West St. Paul, West St. Paul Centennial Book Committee, the Mayor, and City Council, 1989, p. 146; Paul Maccabee St. Paul Gangster History, 1981-1995, Research Files, Minnesota Historical Society; Edwin J. (Ed) Riege, "The Barker-Karpis Rouge," *Minnesota Police Journal*, August 1991.
38. Ibid.
39. FBI Files, RCS:TD I.C.#7-576, November 19, 1936, The Kidnaping of Edward George Bremer, St. Paul, Minnesota, History and Early Association of the the Karpis-Barker Gang Prior to the Abduction of Mr. Bremer.
40. Alvin Karpis with Bill Trent, "The Hollihocks, the Green Lantern and Other Pleasure Places of St. Paul," Capitol, *The St. Paul Pioneer Press & Dispatch Sunday Magazine*, March 28, 1971, pp. 4-9; Alvin Karpis, Bill Trent, *Public Enemy Number One: The Alvin Karpis Story*, pp. 86-89.
41. *Minneapolis Journal*, April 24, 1932.
42. Ibid., August 3, 1932.
43. Lois A. Glewwe, author and editor, *West St. Paul Centennial 1889-1989. The History of West St. Paul, Minnesota*, West St. Paul, West St. Paul Centennial Book Committee, the Mayor, and City Council, 1989, p. 146; Paul Maccabee St. Paul Gangster History, 1981-1995, Research Files, Minnesota Historical Society.
44. Alvin Karpis with Bill Trent, "The Hollihocks, the Green Lantern and Other Pleasure Places of St. Paul," Capitol, *The St. Paul Pioneer Press & Dispatch Sunday Magazine*, March 28, 1971, pp. 4-9; Alvin Karpis, Bill Trent, *Public Enemy Number One: The Alvin Karpis Story*, pp. 86-89.
45. Lois A. Glewwe, author and editor, *West St. Paul Centennial 1889-1989. The History of West St. Paul, Minnesota*, West St. Paul, West St. Paul Centennial Book Committee, the Mayor, and City Council, 1989, p. 146; Paul Maccabee St. Paul Gangster History, 1981-1995, Research Files, Minnesota Historical Society.
46. Alvin Karpis with Bill Trent, "The Hollihocks, the Green Lantern and Other Pleasure Places of St. Paul," Capitol, *The St. Paul Pioneer Press & Dispatch*

Sunday Magazine, March 28, 1971, pp. 4-9; Alvin Karpis, Bill Trent, *Public Enemy Number One: The Alvin Karpis Story*, pp. 86-89.

[47] Federal Bureau of Investigation Freedom of Information and Privacy Acts, Subject: Kate Barker "Ma," File Number 7-5768695.

[48] *New York Evening Graphic*, May 4, 1932.

[49] Federal Bureau of Investigation Freedom of Information and Privacy Acts, Subject: Kate Barker "Ma," File Number 7-5768695.

[50] L. R. Kirchner, *Robbing Banks An American History 1831-1999*, Rockville Centre, New York, Sarpedon Publishing, p. 47.

[51] Tom Hollatz, Gangster Holidays *The Lore and Legends of the Bad Guys*, St. Cloud, North Star Press of St. Cloud, Inc., 1989, pp. 6-7.

[52] FBI Files, RCS:TD I.C.#7-576, November 19, 1936, The Kidnaping of Edward George Bremer, St. Paul, Minnesota, History and Early Association of the the Karpis-Barker Gang Prior to the Abduction of Mr. Bremer.

[53] Alvin Karpis, Bill Trent, *Public Enemy Number One: The Alvin Karpis Story*, p. 84.

[54] Curt Gentry, *J. Edgar Hoover, The Man and the Secrets*, New York, Penguin Books, 1992, p. 167.

[55] L. L. Edge, *Run the Cat Roads*, New York, Dembuer Books, 1981; L. R. Kirchner, *Robbing Banks An American History 1831-1999*, p. 47.

[56] FBI Files, RCS:TD I.C.#7-576, November 19, 1936, The Kidnaping of Edward George Bremer, St. Paul, Minnesota, History and Early Association of the Karpis-Barker Gang Prior to the Abduction of Mr. Bremer.

[57] Paul Maccabee, *John Dillinger Slept Here*, St. Paul, Minnesota Historical Society Press, 1996, pp. 112-113.

[58] Federal Bureau of Investigation Freedom of Information and Privacy Acts, Subject: Kate Barker "Ma," File Number 7-5768695.

[59] *Tulsa World*, August 20, 1932.

[60] Paul Maccabee, Crime Historian & author of *John Dillinger Slept Here*, Interview 3/18/03 on Verne Miller by Brian Bull.

[61] South Dakota Public Broadcasting.

[62] Alvin Karpis with Bill Trent, *The Alvin Karpis Story*, New York, Coward, McCann & Geoghegan, Inc., 1971, pp. 18-24.

[63] Carl Fredrickson Family Archives, Document #19.

Chapter Three

Robbery and Murder

"What the future may have in store, no man can foretell, yet it is safe to assume that if men of equal ability, earnestness and loyalty continue to be selected as members of the Federal Reserve Board and as directors and officers of the Federal Reserve Banks and their branches; and that if wisdom and statesmanship are manifested in the halls of Congress, the Federal Reserve System will continue to serve the people of the United States and their government with the same efficiency and adaptability to changing conditions as it has done in the past."

—Seymour S. Cook[1]

Seven gunmen armed with sub-machine guns and high caliber revolvers held up the Second National Bank of Beloit, Wisconsin, about ten o'clock in the morning, on August 18, 1932, and escaped with between $40,000 and $50,000 in cash. B. P. Eldred, Sr., president of the bank, and Henry Cox, 602 Wisconsin Avenue, a customer, were slugged and knocked to the floor by the bandits.[2] The robbery was later attributed to members of the Barker-Karpis Gang.

In executing the largest cash robbery in Wisconsin in recent years and the first ever in Beloit, the bandits rode boldly into town, pulled up in back of the bank, and parked their car. All seven, heavily armed, however, entered the bank through the front entrance and quickly pointed guns at employees and customers. The apparent leader commanded everyone in the bank to lie down while the robbers ran to the window cages.

One of the bandits, a tall, heavy man, leaped the wooden railing behind which President Eldred sat and grabbed him by the head roughly. Eldred was pushed ahead of the robber to the open space in the general office and ordered to open the vault. When Eldred answered he could not do so, the gunman slugged him just above the ears on both sides of his head with the butt of the gun. The blows knocked Eldred to the floor.

Several of the robbers who had been guarding the windows came back into the bank office. One man was posted as a guard at the door, while another stepped on Miss Emily Menhall, who was lying on the floor near the front of the bank office. "Get up and help us get the money," the gunman demanded.

Two of the bandits carried laundry bags, one of whom was attired in overalls and a cheap shirt. With the gun placed at her head, Miss Menhall was commanded to walk around the drawers at the tellers' windows, remove the currency, and stuff it into the bags. When she appeared to be reluctant, one of her captors waved his gun menacingly and ordered her to hurry.

Cashier Russell Mason was forced to open the bank vault when one of the gunmen threatened to kill President Eldred and other employees. "I didn't think that the money was anything in comparison with the loss of one or more lives," Mason said later. Mason, however, did everything in his power to save the money inside the drawers. Every time he opened a compartment, he told the gunman there was no more money inside. Intentionally opening some empty drawers, the gunman fell for the ruse and believed him.

Leslie Laird, a farmer living on the Orfordville Road, was a customer in the bank at the time of the holdup. He thought it was a joke until a gunman pushed a gun in his side. Another man, who was lying on the floor near the bank vault, moved, causing a robber with a submachine gun to remark, "I guess we had better spray him a bit." The man pleaded with the bandit not to shoot and the gunman backed off. One of the bandits was overheard saying that at least part of the gang was in town the night before the robbery to make a final check so no details had been overlooked.[3]

Miss Ruth Woll, an employee of the First Savings and Trust Company, located across the street from the Second National, heard the alarm and called the bank to find out what was wrong. B.P. Eldred, Jr., answered the telephone, but was forced by one of the gunman to tell her everything was fine. Because the alarm continued to ring, Miss Woll crossed the street and went over to the Second National where she was confronted by a gunman. The robber informed her they were robbing the bank and made her line up with the other women captives who were held at the west end of the bank lobby.[4]

Desk Sergeant Fred Stockwell was alone at the police station when the Second National Bank burglary alarm sounded. He immediately turned on the call lights for officers on the beat just as a man ran up the stairs to the police station shouting, "The Second National's being robbed."

Sergeant Stockwell grabbed a high-powered rifle from a cabinet, threw in a shell to make sure the weapon was in working order, and rushed down State Street with the rifle in his hands. The front of the bank presented a peaceful appearance as Stockwell ran towards it and there was no strange car parked nearby. With the cocked gun in his hands, he went inside the bank through the front entrance.

One of the robbers, who had hidden at the left of the entrance, pressed the muzzle of a .45 caliber automatic revolver against the left side of the officer's abdomen. Another gunman grabbed the back of Stockwell's belt and pressed a revolver muzzle against the right side of his back. Another robber wrenched the rifle from the officer's hands and ordered him to line up with the other captives along the west side of the wall. In doing so, Stockwell faced the wrong way and was ordered to turn around and keep his eyes straight ahead.

Meanwhile, the gunman brandishing a sawed-off shotgun ordered the seven women to walk down the basement stairs past the vaults, and out into the alley where a seven-passenger Studebaker sedan was parked. The seven women were Miss Emily Menhall, Mrs. Louise Anderson, Miss Louise Wolfram, Miss Lola Peebles, Miss Elizabeth Evans, and Miss Ruth Woll.

Sergeant Stockwell was also taken to the basement of the bank. "This is a cop," said one of the robbers to another member of the gang waiting in the basement. "He came in to murder us." The apparent leader of the gang, however, felt they might have some use for him and ordered the other bandit not to kill the officer.

When the women approached the doors in the rear of the building, one of the robbers asked the women how to get out through the door. Miss Peebles tried to draw the bolt on the door and succeeded in opening it when the short, well-dressed robber, who seemed to be the ringleader, slammed the door shut. He told them, "I know this place like a book" and led them out another door.

Two of the men accompanied them outside, making them hurry. Miss Wolfram, who became hysterical when the bandits first entered the bank, was supported by Miss Menhall. According to the women, they had waited for what seemed like several minutes at the door until the rest of the robbers came.

Outside, Sergeant Stockwell was ordered to lie down on the ground beside the car. When he lay down on his back by the car, a gunman pointed the muzzle of a submachine gun toward his head and commanded him to turn over on his stomach. Stockwell later said that the most trying part of his experience was turning over from a face downward position after the robbers left:

"When I was commanded to lie face downward, one of the robbers was standing over me with the muzzle of a submachine gun about a foot from my body. I did not know how many cars the robbers were using and I did not hear the guard who was over me leave. I heard one car leave, but I was not sure that my guard was not waiting for a second car. I was afraid that I might get a few machine guns bullets in my back if I moved."[5]

Police Chief J. Stanley Dietz heard of the robbery and rushed into the bank just as the robbers were leaving. Seeing what the situation was, he ran out the front entrance, fired several shots into the air to summon aid, and went back into the building. Ambulance driver Owen Rex arrived a short time later. Patrolman Charles Blazier ran through the McNeany store when he received the emergency call, but the bandits' car was out of sight when he got to the end of the Chicago and North Western Freight Depot.[6]

"Ma"—The Life and Times of "Ma" Barker and Her Boys

The seven robbers climbed into the sedan holding their machine guns and ammunition, and forced all the women to stand on the running boards of the car. A small boy walked past the rear of the bank just as the girls were being taken away. One of the robbers pointed a submachine gun at him. They drove down the alley, crossing the Northwestern switch tracks, and one of the bandits who had seemed kinder than his cohorts asked Miss Peebles if she had ever seen a submachine before. She replied that she had but never wanted to see another again. He replied, "Don't worry, you won't get hurt."

Turning unto Broad Street by the Salvation Army Building, the women were told to get off, although the robbers did not bring the car to a dead stop. The women watched the car drive away east on Broad Street. Miss Wolfram and two other ladies copied down the license number of the vehicle. Once the car had disappeared, they ran back to the bank building.

All the women reported that they were treated well and that several of the bandits told them they would not be hurt. They used no rough language until the ladies were taken into the basement. The women all agreed that the men were good looking and well dressed. A few of the girls agreed to look at mug shot pictures, even though they had been warned by the bandits not to do so.

The robbers left behind a package containing two large crowbars. The bars were wrapped in cardboard with orange paper of the type used in hardware stores. Apparently they carried the bars only in case of emergency as the package was unopened. Some of the guns they carried into the bank were wrapped with the same type of paper.

Hundreds of people gathered in front of the bank within a few minutes of the holdup and it was necessary for special police to clear the streets for the passing of automobiles.

Beloit Police were besieged with callers reporting sightings of the bandits' car speeding away in every direction possible from Beloit. Officers considered the possibility of the robbers using two cars in the holdup rather than one. Authorities did not believe that the gangsters would have taken a chance of parking their car behind the bank. The men would have had to walk around Broad and State Streets to the front of the building holding machine guns. They believed instead that the driver of the car dropped the men off in front, then drove behind the bank, and either parked or used a second car to take the men to the front of the building.

Two reports came in stating a car matching the description of the one used in the robbery had been sighted speeding towards the east on Highway 14. The car turned off and went towards Shopiere on a side road about five miles east of the city. Another report claimed the car went west on the Liberty Street road and turned to the left on Beckman's Millpond Road. This report stated that there were seven men in a large, dark sedan, which was being driven at a high rate of speed. The driver sounded the horn frequently in order to clear the way.

The only possible connection authorities could see between the two reports, aside from the two car theory, was that the bandits could have doubled back after starting towards the east to fool their pursuers. Sheriff J. S. Fessenden ordered his deputies out to cover the highways, and American Legion men were requested to arm themselves and scour the surrounding country in an attempt to find a trace of the bandits.

The license plates on the car were issued to James W. Albano, Route 1, Sturtevant, for a 1916 Buick touring car. The car had been stolen a month earlier in Sturtevant, according to Beloit Police.

About noon of that same day, three bandits held up the First National Bank of LeSueur, Minnesota and escaped with $5,000. The holdup occurred when most of the bank's staff was out to lunch. Only J. A. Bachman, assistant cashier, was in the bank. The gunmen, brandishing automatic pistols, threatened to kill Bachman if he interfered with their plans. With the Barker-Karpis Gang in Beloit, it is doubtful that any of its members had anything to do with this robbery although Tommy Carroll may have been involved.

Bank officials, following a complete checkup, announced on Friday, August 19th, that the bandits who robbed the Second National Bank of Beloit got away with $71,000 in cash and a $1,000 bond. The entire amount was covered by insurance. Fifteen minutes after the holdup, Chicago banks announced they would send any amount needed by airplane at a moment's notice should the Second National require financial assistance.[7]

"Ma"—The Life and Times of "Ma" Barker and Her Boys

The newspapers wasted little time in revealing that the inefficiency of the Beloit Police Department's equipment benefited the bandits greatly. The dilapidated, light, low speed police cars; the small caliber revolvers and antiquated police rifles were useless in combating criminals equipped with a high speed car, submachine guns, and other deadly weapons.

Urging creation of a central states detective bureau, former stalwart Republican Governor Walter J. Kohler accused the Philip F. La Follette administration of failing to take proper steps to curb bank robberies. He said there had been an increase in crime in the state the past two years, pointing out there were forty-one bank robberies in 1931 as compared to thirty-three in 1930. The Beloit robbery was already the fourteenth of 1932.

"The administration cannot escape responsibility for the crime situation in Wisconsin," Kohler said. "Because it was elected on a promise to drive the gangsters out of the state, and has made no attempt to fulfill that promise; second, because it has consistently opposed every proposition for a modern method of dealing with crime; third, because it is the first and paramount duty of the state to protect its citizens."[8]

La Follette, however, had proposed many more measures than lawmakers were willing to enact. Disturbed by the effects of the Depression, La Follette continually argued that government must reorganize and act decisively to relieve the distress. Regulation by itself was not working, he said, and although he always was opposed to outright government relief, he felt that state government needed to take an active role in solving the problems at hand. Like his father, Robert M. La Follette, Philp F. La Follette was anxious and willing to break new paths if the legislature would only follow.

But Wisconsin was in no way the only state having trouble with inferior equipment in coping with the Barker-Karpis Gang and other hoodlums. An investigation in Mankato, Minnesota, revealed that police equipment included two tear gas bombs and one pocket-sized device for short range gassing; two 12-gauge automatic sawed-off shotguns with approximately 100 yard range; one .32-.20 calibre rifle; one .22 gauge rifle; eleven .32-.20 calibre revolvers; one .38 calibre revolver belonging to Chief of Police Jacob Hilgers.[9]

"Ma"—The Life and Times of "Ma" Barker and Her Boys

The Mankato investigation revealed that if officers were forced to pursue bandits into the country, they would be at the mercy of bullets from the robbers' car, as neither the heavy squad car nor the two lighter traffic cars were equipped with bullet-proof glass. With the exception of a single rifle, none of the weapons were fit for long range service. Should officers want better equipment, they were required to purchase their own. Along with Minnesota and Wisconsin, no state in the Midwest could match equipment used by the gangsters.

And that included the Dakotas. On Thursday, September 1, 1932, a few minutes after nine o'clock in the morning, five members of the Barker-Karpis Gang held up the First National Bank in Flandreau, South Dakota and netted themselves $7,543.55 and bonds to the amount of $2,600, for a total of $10,143.55. The plans for the holdup were evidently well laid, and the men had apparently visited the bank before the robbery, as they knew much about its interior.[10]

The car in which they came and left was a dark-colored Hudson sedan bearing license number 29-1688. The car was parked for an hour in front of the B. J. Francis residence with a driver sitting at the wheel "smoking cigarettes." When the hour came for the time lock in the bank vault to open, two men approached the front of the bank, and two entered through the back door. At the same time, the car came forward from the west and parked just outside the rear door.

The first the bank employees knew they were being held up was when one of the men grabbed Ray Coonrod by the shoulder and ordered him into the back room. A Mr. Bigelow was covered by another man and also ordered to lie down on the floor in the back room. All employees were told to lie down except Cortes Whealy, who was questioned as to the location of the funds and keys to the private boxes. Whealy refused to give the men the information they wanted and was struck on the forehead with a gun, but he maintained silence.

Customers entering the bank on business were taken to the back room and most of them "complied with alacrity when they looked into the mouth of a .44." James Snyder, the local depot agent, was one of the first to walk into the bank. His pockets were bulging with railroad funds, but he was not searched. When ordered to lie down on the rear-room floor, he gladly complied. He was placed between two women lying on the floor—one of them crying and the other laughing.

John W. Baker, who farmed north of town, came in after Snyder. When one of the robbers told him the bank was being robbed, he replied, "G'wan, yer kiddin'" and pushed him over the radiator. Baker was immediately clubbed behind the ear with the side of a revolver, which laid open a gaping wound and convinced him the men were not kidding. Although quite giddy from the blow, Baker wobbled into the back room and did what he was told.[11]

Mr. Bigelow's eye glasses troubled him while lying on the floor, and he asked permission of his guard to take them off. The "polite" robber gave him permission to do so.[12]

The robbers scooped up what funds were in sight together with the bonds, and went out through the rear door taking Alma Weide with them as a hostage. While held on the running board, she cautioned the driver he was going too fast, but he said, "You are all right, girl," and grinned.

When the car reached the corner where the road ran south to Egan, the driver slowed up and Miss Weide was told to step off. She later told reporters that the wild ride was the "thrill of her life." A passing motorist picked her up and brought her back to town. The robbers continued south to the Bennett corner, turned east on Highway 34, and headed in the direction of the Twin Cities.[13]

The holdup occurred so unexpectedly and was over so soon that the people standing across the street were not even aware there was a robbery. Sheriff Gray was one of those standing across the street at the Davis corner, talking with Davis, and didn't know about the robbery until the bandits were well on their way out of town.

The robbery, including the license number of the car, was phoned in to Sioux Falls and Yankton and both broadcasting stations in these cities had the news out within ten minutes. Several people on the street outside the bank heard the first news of the holdup over the radio.

Miss Marion Whipps, a bank employee, grabbed a gun as soon as the car sped away, rushed across the street, and asked Dr. Cooper to jump in his car and pursue the bandits. Cooper armed himself and asked Fred Lehman to take the wheel before the trio sped off in pursuit as far as the Bennett corner, where the gang turned east. The Hudson, however, was too fast for the Lizzie, and Cooper and Miss Whipps, ready to shoot it out with the gang, were very disappointed.[14]

At the very same time the robbery in Flandreau was executed, robbers struck at Whitewood, South Dakota, robbing a bank and kidnapping a cashier. Flandreau was in southeast South Dakota near the Minnesota border while Whitewood was in the extreme western part of the state in the Black Hills. Three bandits participated in the Whitewood raid where they grabbed an undetermined amount of money and raced out of town with the cashier Guy E. Bailey as their hostage.[15]

A third bank was robbed that same day when burglars climbed over the transom in the First State Bank of Swatara, Minnesota. Upon breaking into the vault, they escaped with a mere $120 in silver after failing to gain entry to the safe. The thieves, believed to be amateurs, used a drill to gain access to the vault. Then they used a chisel and tried to blow open the safe but were unsuccessful.

Arthur "Doc" Barker, during this time, was confined in the Oklahoma State Penitentiary and negotiations were under way towards securing his release. The Karpis-Barker Gang was now becoming well organized, and through the efforts of Ma Barker, as well as Fred Barker and Alvin Karpis, private detective Jack Glynn of Leavenworth, Kansas procured Doc's release from the penitentiary on September 10, 1932.

Doc immediately went to visit his father at Neosho, Missouri, on the western edge of the Ozarks, as the condition of his parole was that he should leave the State of Oklahoma and never return. He may have tried to go straight. His Leavenworth prison psychiatrist reported: "He states that he was unable to make his way by being employed in lawful economic pursuits and was forced to resort to other means of livilihood [sic]. Unfortunately, these were unlawful means."[16]

After a three month visit with his father, Doc joined his mother and brother Fred in St. Paul, Minnesota. Ma Barker now had two sons to provide her with a life of luxury. Her oldest son, Herman, whose extensive criminal career had commenced March 5, 1915, when arrested by the Police Department of Joplin, Missouri, for a highway robbery and followed by several other arrests on various charges, had been cornered by police officers at Wichita, Kansas, on August 29, 1927, after he had killed a police officer.

Herman Barker and two accomplices were escaping from a holdup in Newton, Kansas. Two police officers stopped them near Wichita, and when one of the officers leaned down to look in the car window, Herman grabbed him around the neck and fired a Luger into his head. An officer on the opposite side of the car opened up on Herman and shot so many bullets into him that Herman turned the Luger on himself and committed suicide.

Lloyd Barker was also prevented from becoming a member of the gang due to his incarceration in the United States Penitentiary at Leavenworth, Kansas, where he had been received on January 16, 1932, to serve a twenty-five year sentence for robbing the United States Mail. Efforts on the part of Fred Barker and other members of the gang to secure the release of Lloyd Barker on parole were not successful.[17]

The gang struck again on September 23, 1932, when five men held up the State Bank and Trust Company in Redwood Falls, Minnesota, clad in new overalls. The bank, located in the center of the community of 2,600 people was relieved of $35,000 in cash, while its cashier and secretary were taken as hostages. Without firing a shot, the robbers snapped through the holdup like it was routine, and when two miles out of town, they released their captives unharmed after using them as human shields.[18]

Upon entering the front door of the bank, four of the gunmen herded five employees—A.F. Hassenstab, cashier, his secretary, Miss Mona Leavens, G.E. Engeman, and E.W. Whiting, assistant cashiers, and H.F. Peterson, teller—from behind four teller's cages and forced them to lie down on the floor faces down. A fifth robber waited in the car parked behind the bank.

While a robber held his pistol on them, the others quickly raked piles of silver, currency, and gold into sacks. None of the bandits bothered with the $1,000 in nickels, dimes, quarters, and half dollars left in the money changers in each cage. One of the robbers opened the back door and acted as a sentry during the brief operation of "lifting everything in sight."

Mrs. Cora D. Fox, proprietor of the Fox Millinery adjoining the bank, and Miss Matilda Buchholts, an employee, had perhaps the best look at the robbers. They first noticed strange men carrying sacks to a car parked behind the bank. Miss Buchholts remarked, "If we had a gun we could shoot them." At that very moment, the sentry at the back door stuck his head out and calmly stated, "Oh you wouldn't shoot us, would you?"[19]

They hurried out through a rear door a minute or so after entering, and in doing so, one of the bandit leaders tapped Cashier Hassenstab and Miss Leavens with his pistol and snapped, "Get up you two. We're going to take you with us and the rest of you stay put or we'll blow your brains out."[20]

Miss Leavens was forced to stand on one running board beside the driver and Hassenstab on the other, with his head perched above the top so he could not see into the car. The raiding car, bearing Iowa license plates, shot out of the alley, sped down Mill Street, and turned at three or four corners before leaving the city headed southward.

"The driver held on to me with his left hand and drove with the other," Miss Leavens later told the press. "He used profane language several times and told me to be sure and look the other way if I didn't want to get my head broken."

Hassenstab said a weapon he believed was a sawed-off shotgun was pressed against his stomach. Two miles out of town, the car stopped and the robbers released the hostages near the Robert Stewart farm before speeding down Highway 4 towards Sanborn and Windom. The loot was the second largest for bank robberies in Minnesota that year. In March, a Minneapolis bank had yielded $200,000.

After the car was out of sight, Miss Buchholts rushed to the telephone and called the telephone office while Mrs. Fox ran to the Redwood Grocery where she called Fred Swalm, who, in turn, called the sheriff.[21]

Sheriff L. J. Kise, "The Flying Sheriff," when notified of the holdup, immediately ordered aviator Jack Robinson to prepare to take off in the sheriff's cabin airplane in an endeavor to learn the route taken by the robbers.

Robinson hopped off with Fred Schwalm, a local resident, filled the plane with gas, and took off while Sheriff Kise and his son Douglas followed in an automobile.[22]

Miss Buchholts reported the bandits' car to be a Buick and Gazette employees who saw it leave the driveway verified this opinion. Later Fred Muckey and M. L. Pettis, who had brought the hostages back to town, also stated the car was a Buick. Other conflicting reports, however, insisted the car was a Hudson or a Studebaker. One witness said the first two numbers of the license were "76," while another was certain they were "38." Both of these agreed that the car bore an Iowa license as did Mrs. Fox.

The robbers, however, were not to be outdone. By spreading roofing nails in the path of Sheriff Kise, the bank bandits succeeded in eluding their pursuers on Highway 4, eight miles south of Redwood Falls. The tires of the sheriff's car had seven nails in them. Another car also attempted to get through but met a similar fate.

Tire repairman did a booming business that day as car after car came to town with three and four flat tires. Nails discovered in the vicinity of Morgan indicated the robbers had doubled back after giving the impression they were headed towards Sioux City, Iowa.

Meanwhile, the sheriff's airplane, piloted by Jack Robinson, shot ahead towards Sanborn and Tracy and landed on a ten-acre field in an effort to block the robbers, but he too, lost sight of them. Later in the day the plane scoured the woods along the Minnesota River but without success.[23]

The robbers were believed to have come from the Twin Cities the past evening. Charles F. Galles, a local merchant, and his son, Rex, were returning home from the Twin Cities and passed a car believed to have been occupied by the bandits. The Galles observed men dressed in overalls, as they sped past another car with Iowa license plates between Minneapolis and Chaska.[24]

Two men who had taken rooms the previous Thursday night were questioned and later released. Hotel employees said the men had registered under the names George and Romane Anderson without giving a home address. The men had left the hotel and did not pay their bill, although their luggage remained in the room.[25]

"Ma"—The Life and Times of "Ma" Barker and Her Boys

The lead was given some weight when a notebook listing buildings about the state with the notations "re-roofed" was found along with dates inside the grip. The men were later found on the street and established their identity with little difficulty. They were from Estherville, Iowa, and were roofers.

A filling station attendant at Delhi remembered filling a large sedan with eleven gallons of gas shortly before the robbery and lawmen believed the gunmen had entered Redwood Falls from that direction. The car seen in Delhi carried five passengers, most of them dressed in overalls.

Efforts to secure the release of Volney Davis from the Oklahoma State Penitentiary were successful and on November 3, 1932, less than two months after the release of his fellow murderer, Doc Barker, Davis was granted a leave of absence from the Oklahoma State Penitentiary, which permitted him to roam the country at will until July 1, 1934, when he was to again report to the Penitentiary officials. Davis, not surprisingly, failed to do so. It was suspected but never proven that Davis had been granted his release due to a payoff arranged by the Barker Gang to a state official.

The reunion between Volney Davis and Doc Barker took place at Leavenworth, Kansas, after which they immediately proceeded to St. Paul. Shortly thereafter, Davis took a vacation and with Kate "Ma" Barker made a trip to California where they visited her sister.

During November and December 1932, Fred Barker, Doc Barker, Alvin Karpis, and Jess Doyle were residing at the Twin Oaks Apartments in St. Paul. Larry DeVol also was also back in St. Paul and was residing in an apartment on Grand Avenue. The citizens of the Twin Cities and vicinity until this time had been unmolested so far as known from the depredations of the Karpis-Barker mob, but the gang planned new crimes.[26]

The Citizens National Bank in Wahpeton, North Dakota, figured to be a pretty routine job for Freddie and Doc Barker, Alvin Karpis, Larry Devol, and Jess Doyle. The bank had been robbed of $6,735 on May 30, 1930, by a gang led by Reinholt Engel and the Barker-Karpis boys expected their organized effort would be like "taking candy from a baby." Engel was serving a thirty-year sentence in the South Dakota State Penitentiary, but for a robbery in Ipswich, South Dakota, and not the Wahpeton raid.

"Ma"—The Life and Times of "Ma" Barker and Her Boys

The Barker-Karpis bandits swaggered into the bank shortly after 10 A.M. on September 30th and ordered ten people—employees and customers—to lie down on the floor. One of the bandits walked up to B. P. McCusker, who had led the battle against the bandits in the former holdup, and told him they were holding up the bank. McCusker was forced to take the bandits into the outer vault and give them access to the money therein.

Another man walked into Bank Vice President J. P. Reeder's office and began cursing at him while ordering him out of the room and forcing him to join the other captives. Reeder, who was a victim in the previous robbery, was too slow in executing the demand, and was prodded with a pistol and yanked by his collar.

With clocklike precision, the robbers rifled the cash in the cashier's cages, while they deployed to advantageous positions about the bank. It took but six or seven minutes to empty the cash drawer, but Cashier S. H. Murray, who was in a back room when the bandits entered the bank, pressed the button for the burglar alarm. One of the robbers slugged him to the floor with his pistol butt, inflicting severe head wounds.

Miss Doris Stack, a clerk in the office of the county superintendent of schools, entered the bank while the robbery was in progress. She was met by a short man who grabbed her and yelled, "Come in here lady and you won't get hurt." The man took her into Vice President J. P. Reeder's office and ordered her to sit down.[27]

Believing no harm would come to her, Miss Stack did not become frightened as she obeyed his command. The robbery was progressing with lightning rapidity and soon she heard a bandit yell, "Bring her back here!" She was ushered into the back room where she was ordered to join the rest of the victims on the floor.

Ruth Whipps, the bank's bookkeeper, also found herself taken by surprise. "I did not see the robbers as they entered the bank due to the fact my back was toward the main banking room," she stated. "The first that I knew was when someone came into my department and commanded me to get out of there. I was forced into the rear room with all the other employees and Miss Doris Stack, a customer. There the bandits ordered us to lie down on the floor. The cashier had sounded the burglar alarm and while it clanged away the bandits ran about the place, grabbing the money and hollering that they would shoot the first person to move."[28]

    A. M. Anderson and August Ehrens were inside the bank while the robbery was in progress, but they managed to walk out unnoticed. The two men wasted no time in spreading the alarm, and the telephone operator dispatched the news to the sheriff and chief of police at once. Both the sheriff's party and the police arrived at the bank as the robbers were leaving with a take of $6,827.

    As they were running out the back door, Doyle yelled that cops were covering both ends of the alley. The alarm had summoned officers and townspeople, and the robbers were fired upon as they started out the back door. One of the bandits returned the fire with a submachine gun.

    The robbers did an about face, rushed back into the bank, and grabbed Ruth Whipps and Doris Stack. With pistols in their backs, they were marched out as human shields to the waiting car that was being guarded by the man with the submachine gun.

    Upon seeing the girls on the running boards, the police held their fire. A.M. Anderson, meanwhile, had rushed to the Montgomery Ward store next door and warned Jack Nolan and Doug Creasey of the robbery and the men rushed to the roof of the store armed with machine guns. Ehrens told Walter Hoppert.

    As the robbers left the alley with their two hostages on the running boards, the guns of local merchants blazed from rooftops. Deputy Sheriff Millard Rickert raised his rifle and took the shot he had been waiting for, and the rear tire of the bandit's car exploded as the high-power bullet hit it.

    The rest of the police officers also fired at the rear tires. Buckshot rained on the back of the car like hailstones, and within seconds, both rear tires were running on the rims, and the fender wells were reduced to mangled hunks of tin. One of the bandits answered by breaking out the rear window of their sedan and his barking rifle left a heavy cloud of smoke between them and their pursuers.[29]

    While the girls on the running boards continued screaming, one of them tried to jump from the car, which was traveling fifty miles an hour.

Devol leaned out the window and grabbed her around the waist as they swung onto a side road, almost colliding with another police unit waiting to intercept them.

Seeing the girls, the police, led by Sheriff D.S. McIlwain of Richland County, North Dakota, and Chief of Police Henry Schweizer of Wahpeton, held their fire until they were about a hundred yards away; then one of them again opened fire with a high-powered rifle. The first shots hit the rear of the car but the next hit one of the girls, who was pulled into the vehicle by DeVol. The other woman had to ride on the running board for about twenty miles before she was pulled into the car as well.

"I was shot once before we left town and once afterward before we left the highway," recalled Miss Stock, the first of the two ladies pulled into the car. "I remember the men in the car talking about it, saying that I had 'got it in the face' but I was on the outside of the car and didn't hear much of the conversation. The men said that I had been shot in the arm and that they thought my leg was broken.

"The car pitched terribly because of the punctured tire, which someone had struck with a bullet. I saw a machine gun on the rear seat, but I was too dazed to see what they were doing with it. The men began throwing roofing nails out of the windows. We had hardly got out of the city, it seemed, before a radio in their car began operating. It brought a report of the robbery. The bandits smiled.

"They didn't talk about their plans, but they did talk about the cars coming. I don't remember stopping on the road—we must have slowed down though. Standing on the running board was terrible and I begged them to take me into the car. Then one of the men pulled my head in and said, 'Don't look at us, please.' They held me by the arms and then around the waist. I kept asking them to leave us at a farmhouse and they finally dragged me through the back window and I sat between two of the men. One man sat on one of the little extra seats in the car."[30]

With the police still in pursuit, the bandits crossed the river; the route of their car concealed by the trees, and fled south. The police expected them to make a brief stand where they would attempt to change tires. The sheriff's car came up, but at that point the robbers had outdistanced them, and from then on, no one came within four miles of them.

The wounded girl yelled hysterically for another couple miles until the car turned into a prearranged turnoff point in a farmer's field. They bounced through a pasture, rumbled over a dry creek bed, and pulled up in front of a little schoolhouse, where they jumped out to examine the wounded girl. One of the men lifted her gently from the car and laid her down as comfortably as he could in the shade. The sniper's bullet had broken her leg. Karpis retrieved a medicine bag from the car and administered a shot of morphine to the wound.

But the bandits had to deal with other problems which required their attention. When their car had crossed the river bed, the gasoline tank struck a sharp stone and punctured a hole in it through which gasoline was leaking. With a leaky gasoline tank, a flat tire, and a posse not far behind, the bandits were in desperate straits.

While Karpis had administered aid to the wounded women, some of the bandits attempted to stem the leak in their gasoline tank. Others took off what remained of the ruined tire and the men climbed back into the sedan. The girls were left at the schoolhouse as the gangsters drove away on the rims.

"When they started again, we were left behind," remembered Ruth Whipps, who had been shot in the hip by pursuing police. "We screamed for help. I tried to crawl to the road but could make no progress. My leg was bleeding and hurt terribly and I was weak from loss of blood."[31]

The women were found by the occupants of a pursuing car driven by Dr. J. H. Hoskins of Wahpeton. "As we passed the abandoned farmhouse riding with a flat tire, we heard the 'moans' and cries of the girls for help," Dr. Hoskins said later. "They apparently both were shot right outside the bank when the townspeople exchanged gunfire with the gunmen."

The bandits drove a few miles farther before the dropping gasoline gauge warned them of impending disaster. The radio in the car brought reports of the hunt to which the robbers must have grimly listened. They picked out the most isolated spot they could find without a telephone line in sight. The men drove up to the Ed Lindbergh farm, six miles southeast of Doran, Minnesota, where the family had gathered for their noon meal.

The boys remained at the Lindbergh farm for an hour and a half while they attempted to repair the leaking gasoline tank, drank some liquor which they had with them, ate a little lunch, and helped Martin Lindbergh wash all the metal and glass fixtures in the car. The bandits drained gasoline from a tractor and another automobile.

Before leaving, one of the bandits told Lindbergh that he could keep the big Hudson sedan and that it was not a "hot" car. Traces of paint around windows indicated a recent new paint job, and the lack of striping convinced the Lindberghs the job had been done in a hurry. The wheels and body were painted in different colors, and the dashboard had been patched with varnish.

Paying the Lindberghs an undisclosed amount of money, the robbers drove off in the family's Essex Coach, warning the family not to follow or they "would get plugged." There was no telephone at the Lindbergh farm but the family rushed to the town of Tintah as fast as they could. Dr. Doleman of Tintah called the Farmer-Globe office in Wahpeton and Sheriff McIlwain, Deputy Rickert, Newspaperman Donald Lum, Lee Agnew, and Walter McIlwain rushed to the Lindbergh farm, arriving there only a half hour after the bandits had left.

Lindbergh showed them the bandit car, which the robbers had left behind—a 1932 Hudson deluxe seven-passenger sedan. The car had been newly washed to erase fingerprints and the radio was still blaring out details of the chase, which spread over most of Wilkin and Grant counties in Minnesota.

Police found fresh blood stains in the car from the wounded women and the sedan's fresh paintwork induced one of the officers to do a little digging on the exterior with a knife, which disclosed the car's original color was blue-black. Traces of a second coat of green paint were found on the hood vents and the wheels, and the last coat of paint was found to be black.

A heavy steel trunk offered as good protection as could be devised for the machine gunners and was effective in preventing high-velocity bullets from entering the rear seat. Vacuum bottles of water, a small arsenal, some alcohol and drugs were found inside the car. Also, to the posse's delight, the bandits left behind several cigars.

An investigation by police revealed that the 1932 Hudson had been purchased from the Butler Hudson Motor Company on Michigan Avenue in Chicago by Frank Murphy, 6518 Sheridan Road—a fictitious address as well as a fictitious name. Police were quite certain all the members of the gang were from Chicago, and when they found the Lindberg car abandoned in Zumbrota, Minnesota, in a direct route to Chicago, they became convinced.[32]

A few days later, a holdup in Holland, Michigan, was attributed to the Barker-Karpis Gang because of its similarities to the Wahpeton job although this was pure speculation on the part of the authorities. Six bandits armed with sub-machine guns robbed the First State Bank of $12,000, shot the chief of police and a citizen, slugged a deputy sheriff with a pistol, and got away from a posse of a hundred men.

As usual, the fleeing robbers threw roofing nails onto the highway, causing several pursuing automobiles to abandon the chase because of flat tires. Near Drenthe, the robbers came upon a truck driven by farmer George Boerman, whom they forced from the vehicle. Turning the truck crossways on the highway to block the road, they stood off the approaching posse with gunfire. According to Boerman, one of the bandits had a bullet wound in his neck and was bleeding profusely.

Speeding away from the posse, the bandits were surrounded near Jamestown, along a highway which extended through swamplands. They opened fire again on the posse and once more sped away and vanished. One member of the police suffered a slight wound when his cheek was grazed by a bullet from a sub-machine gun.

While the gang was making preparations for their next holdup, they made arrangements for Ma Barker, who was living with them, to be out of state. Ma went to Chicago for a few days, and then on to Reno, where the boys planned on meeting her. With Christmas only a little over a week away, they planned to hit one more bank and then spend the winter in Nevada with Ma.[33]

"Ma"—The Life and Times of "Ma" Barker and Her Boys

According to Alvin Karpis, two days before the date set for the robbery, there was an urgent telephone call from Ma Barker. She had been experiencing heart palpitations and had "hit the panic button." One of the gang members had to go to her in a hurry, and because Karpis was the only one who knew his way around Chicago, he had to go. Despite Karpis' claim, he did take part in the robbery.

The immunity which had been enjoyed by the citizens in St. Paul and Minneapolis was soon to cease, for on December 16, 1932, Fred Barker, Doc Barker, Larry Devol, Alvin Karpis, William Weaver, Verne Miller, and Jess Doyle robbed the Third Northwestern Bank of Minneapolis and netted $112,000.

Alvin Karpis. (Photographer: Bureau of Criminal Apprehension, Photograph Collection California 1925, Location no. por 20416 r1, Negative no. 95659)

Alston Purvis, son of FBI Agent Melvin Purvis, when asked how his father regarded the dangerous Verne Miller in a 2003 interview, declared: "Verne Miller was one of the few he talked about. And he felt that Verne Miller was one of the few who rivaled Baby Face Nelson as a dedicated and vicious killer. He considered him absolutely cold and was. . . . well, if my father had a soft spot for these characters, he didn't have one for Verne Miller."[34]

Verne Miller was a complex character and even his early life is surrounded by mystery. He even obscured his birthday, listing 1892, 1895 and 1896 and his birthplace as South Dakota, Iowa, or Illinois. No one quite understands why this good guy went bad. What is known is that Miller was a victim of divorce and was left on his own at an early age. By the age of ten, he had dropped out of school. In 1914, he moved to Huron, South Dakota, and began working as a mechanic. He joined the Army in 1916 and served on the Mexican border until 1917 when he returned to Huron and married. A month later, he left for France with the military service.[35]

Color Sergeant Verne Miller returned a hero, claiming decorations for being a marksman and sniper and receiving a French Croix de Guerre award for bravery. After his return, he joined the Huron city police force where he worked until 1920, when he resigned. By then, his name was on the ballot as the Republican candidate for Beadle County Sheriff. He won by forty-one votes.

The community was pleased with his service and Miller was on his way to re-election, when his wife, Mildred, fell ill and was rushed to a Rochester, Minnesota, hospital. Taking a short leave, Miller went to visit his wife and never returned. Deputies discovered $6,000 missing from the county fund and a criminal was born. In the beginning, South Dakota's papers had lauded his credibility as a war hero and law enforcement official. Only thirteen years later, a nationwide search was under way and he was deemed "the most dangerous criminal in the country."

A three-month search ensued, ending when a St. Paul, Minnesota, hotel clerk turned him in. Miller pled guilty to embezzling $2,600 in county funds and served two years in the South Dakota penitentiary. While there, he landed a cushy position as the warden's chauffeur and passed his time driving the warden around Sioux Falls. Paroled in 1924, he worked as a farmhand until his parole terms were satisfied. He left in search of new pursuits but was indicted for bootlegging, a crime for which be posted bond. He then left South Dakota.

Shortly after leaving Sioux Falls, Miller met Vivian Gibson (Mathis), an attractive, young farm girl from Leola, South Dakota. Vivian was born Vivian Gibson but married a man named Stanley Mathis, who went to prison in 1922 in South Dakota for shooting a night watchman who supposedly insulted her. At times, Vi Mathis also used the name Mathias.[36]

"Verne Miller was apparently at carnival in St. Paul or Minneapolis, of the Twin Cities of Minnesota," related author Paul Maccabee in a 2003 interview with Brian Bull. "And Vivian Mathis was working at a carnival booth. Apparently a gentleman refused to leave the booth. We don't know why, it's been lost to history, but he was recalcitrant about leaving. And Verne Miller gallantly leaped to Vi Mathis' aid, knocked the gentleman, the reluctant gentleman, to the ground. And saved her doing some kind of Sir Lancelot, white knight thing . . . and Vi became his friend and eventually Vivian became his lover, and the great romance of Verne Miller's life. . . . and it is so fascinating that the moment of gallantry that Verne Miller had was also moment of violence but it. . . . it was in defense of his lady love."[37]

From 1926-1929, Miller and Gibson were leading bootleggers in the Twin Cities and were known for their top-notch casino operations in Montreal, Canada. In 1930, he jumped from bootlegging to bank robbing when he joined criminals such as Harvey Bailey, Tommy Holden, Jimmy Keating, Frank Nash, "Machine Gun" Kelly and others. Over the years, this gang would be responsible for numerous bank holdups from the Dakotas to Texas.

Miller was part of the crew and later drove the getaway car for the Barker-Karpis Gang when they held up the Third Northwestern Bank of Minneapolis. The bank, which was the East Minneapolis affiliate of that banking system was located in a triangular building on one of Minneapolis' busiest and widest intersections—East Hennepin and Central Avenues and Fifth Street Northeast.[38]

There were two doors for customers—one at East Hennepin and Fifth Street, and the other at Central Avenue and Fifth Street—and there was a streetcar stop right in front of the bank. Because the building was all glass, Alvin Karpis equated the situation to "working in a greenhouse."

Because they figured the robbery could be a tough one to pull off, the Barker-Karpis Gang was well equipped with four submachine guns, two rifles, several pistols, and plenty of extra clips. Larry Devol suggested they use a big car for the big job, so they stole a luxury Lincoln with a gorgeous interior and headed to the bank.

At approximately 2:40 P.M. on Friday, December 16, 1932, the large black Lincoln sedan pulled up to the Third Northwestern National Bank at 430 East Hennepin Avenue. It parked alongside the bank on the left side of Central Avenue. Four men, who were of average size and appeared to be well dressed, got out of the car and quickly burst through the front door of the bank.[39]

The bank tellers were preparing to check up the business of the day, before closing shortly at 3 P.M. The hour could not have been more propitious and obviously was planned by men who had taken every angle and detail into consideration. Because Friday and Saturday were "heavy" days at the bank, an armored car had just delivered $19,000 in currency, and pulled away a few minutes before the black Lincoln arrived.

Once inside the bank, the four bandits, armed with pistols and a machine gun, commanded everyone to put their hands up. After the four men rushed in the front door, another robber took charge of the lobby. Waving guns and yelling, none of the employees or patrons made a false move, although a few customers argued and several women screamed.[40]

Ray C. Teuscher, vice president and head cashier of the bank, was busy at his desk when he looked up and saw two of the men with pistols coming through the front door. At the same time, he heard a demand to "hold up your hands." He stood up and raised his hands, and as he did so, he saw two other men brandishing pistols on the other side of the room.

Two of the bandits walked up a short, narrow passage that separated the bank cages from a railing behind which were desks used by employees of the bank's insurance department. The runaway led to a door which gave access to the space behind the tellers' cages. The door was locked but one of the robbers forced it open with his shoulder and walked around behind the cages. This robber forced Mr. Teuscher to lie on the floor alongside his desk, where he was invisible from the street.

While the robbery was in progress, a streetcar pulled up in front of the bank and the terrified motorman dropped to the floor with his hands on his head. The passengers, however, remained in their seats trying to see what was transpiring inside the bank.

Inside, the robbers gave the order for everyone to lie down, while the machine gunner waved his weapon menacingly. There were ten employees and six customers in the bank at the time. The bandits worked very quietly and methodically, and with a seeming lack of excitement. They started through the tellers' cages, scooping all the cash in sight into large canvas bags they carried.

One of the bandits reached down for a teller, Paul L. Hesselroth—pulled him to his feet, and ordered him to open a grill door to the vault, which was locked. The heavy main door to the vault was open. Meanwhile, unbeknownst to the robbers, the teller very methodically managed to step on the burglar alarm that sent the note of danger into police headquarters.

"We want the combination to the vault," the bandit shouted. The teller, managing to stand squarely on the burglar alarm again as he talked, said he did not know the combination. Without another word, the bandit brought his gun down over the fellow's head, cutting a deep gash and knocking the teller unconscious. He was revived later and taken to a doctor's office for treatment.[41]

Another employee, who had a key to the grill, was forced at the point of a pistol to open the vault and let them inside. Freddie and Devol moved quickly into the vault, forcing the employee to open the seven individual safes. They scooped money out of drawers and shelves and dropped it into laundry bags they had carried into the bank.

It was believed that the bank robbers had known that this was the time of day when the police patrol day shift was going off duty and the evening shift was coming on. The closest patrol car should have been at the East Side station, a mile or more from the bank. But one east side patrol car was three minutes behind schedule and still en route to the station when the bank alarm was broadcast. In this car were Patrolmen Ira L. Evans and Leo R. Gorski. They had decided to answer the alarm before reporting off duty.

Upon finishing with the vaults, one of the robbers shouted, "Don't get up" to the employees lying on the floor, and keeping their pistols leveled at the prostrate workers, commenced their exit, gathering inside the Central Avenue doorway. The robbery had taken only a few minutes.

As one of the men started to open the door, Devol looked out the window and thought he saw police officers on both ends of the block. As Evans' and Gorski's patrol car drew up at the Central Avenue entrance of the bank, Patrolman Gorski stepped out of the car and his partner, Patrolman Evans, started to slide out from behind the steering wheel.[42]

Both were in plain sight of the bandits, who were not more than fifteen feet away. The officers, however, had not seen the robbers and knew only that there was some sort of trouble at the bank. Before Evans could alight, the windows of the bank seemed to burst out with gunfire and a hail of bullets crashed into their police car. Witnesses could see the glass flying and the windows in the police car smashing.[43]

Four men came running out of the bank door, making a break for the Lincoln. Larry Devol, however, put a drum on his machine gun and went out into the street just as the patrol car had pulled up. Jess Doyle rushed over and backed him up and the two gangsters began shooting.

At close range, they sprayed the police car with a withering rain of bullets. The policemen didn't have a chance to get out. One of their doors swung open, and the man with the gun poured his fire directly into the car when the two policemen slumped down. Patrolman Ira Evans was killed instantly as he sat unable to defend himself in his seat. He slumped over the wheel, riddled with at least ten machine-gun slugs in his body.

Patrolman Leo Gorski had opened the door right in the face of the fire and tumbled out of the radio car from the seat beside Evans, his body torn by at least three slugs that made a sieve of their police cruiser. The four gunmen ran for their waiting car while carrying the loot, $20,000 in currency and securities. Both patrolmen, Leo Gorski and Ira Evans, who happened on the scene, were killed by the hail of machine-gun fire, although Gorski did not die immediately.

Devol lost his balance on the slippery pavement, his feet went out from under him, and he landed on his back. His finger, though, had remained on the trigger, and as he lay he was firing out of control into the sky. The guys suddenly discovered that the right rear tire of the big Lincoln was flat and the radiator punctured. Devol must have fired into the Lincoln as he hit the ground.

The doors of the big car slammed, and the motor roared. Jess Doyle was behind the wheel of the Lincoln, but as the gang piled inside, Miller took over the driving. As the robbers started their escape, a huge crowd, having been attracted by gunfire, began to assemble in the street and on the sidewalk in front of the bank. Two gun squads, patrolling the East Side, arrived within a few minutes of the bandits' departure.

Nathan Meshbesher, who operated a business across the street from the bank, saw the bandits run from the building. He climbed into his own automobile and gave chase, but lost sight of the bandit car after a couple of blocks. Two other men, who were passing the bank just after the holdup, ran to aid the wounded policemen, and volunteered to take them to the hospital in the police car. These men were Robert L. Jones, 346 North Fairview Avenue, St. Paul, and C.E. Harvey, 1813 Elliott Avenue South, Minneapolis.

The car sped over Fifth Street, swung back onto East Hennepin Avenue and bounced out the pavement, gathering speed as it went. The tire rumbled and began to shred as the car bounced over the pavement. One of the bandits threw the shredded tire as they reached Larpenteur Avenue, the St. Paul continuation of East Hennepin Avenue, but it did not slacken their speed.

Despite the flat tire, the gang raced away along a route, which, because it had been used so often in getaways, was dubbed "Bank Robbers' Row." The road offered them a way of reaching St. Paul from Minneapolis without crossing the bridge where the police usually set up their roadblocks.[44]

Rumbling over the pavement on the rim, it finally made its way to St. Paul, where the fleeing bandit gang had a smaller green sedan waiting. Having anticipated the possibility of trouble, the boys had parked a Chevy just inside the St. Paul city limits in case of an emergency. Upon reaching the site, some of the boys jumped into the Chevy and followed the Lincoln to Como Park. The tire and rim of the wheel on the Lincoln were gone and Miller had been driving over icy streets at sixty miles an hour.

The boys were in the midst of changing the hot plates on the Chevy for another set when a car drove up with two men inside. The driver stopped and craned his neck to get a look at the plates. Freddie told the men to leave but the driver ignored the warning. Barker pulled out his gun and shot the man in the head. As blood streamed down the side of the car, the other man pulled himself behind the wheel and drove off.

The driver of the car, who was shot in the head, was a twenty-two-year-old St. Paul Christmas-wreath salesman named Oscar Erickson. He was taken to the hospital where he was found to have been wounded twice, one bullet piercing his skull. He died at 4 A.M. without regaining consciousness.

Some accounts state that Doc, thrilled by his new freedom and the novel, explosive power of the gang's machine guns, did the killings himself. Erickson, however, was murdered because the robbers believed he was endeavoring to secure the license number of the gang's getaway car.[45]

While the gang returned to Freddie's apartment, 22-year-old Arthur Zachman, 1253 Grand Avenue, the man who had driven away with his mortally wounded friend, went directly to police headquarters in a state of panic. The police, by this time, knew all about the bank robbery, and when the hysterical man came in saying there was a badly shot up guy in the car, they immediately descended on the car, concluding the wounded man was one of the robbers.

"It happened so quickly I didn't realize for some time what it was all about," Zachman told police. Zachman said that Erickson and he had been riding along the Como Park road near Monkey Island when they came upon a group of excited men standing around two cars, one a large green sedan and the other a smaller sedan. He said Erickson slowed down and looked at the men. The men returned the gaze with deadly aims, and Erickson slumped down in his seat with a bullet in his head. Zachman escaped the fire, and after the car continued rolling driverless, he was able to crawl over and drive his mortally wounded friend to police radio headquarters.[46]

Alvin Karpis later recalled: "Bank robbery, dangerous as it was, could get to be routine. You had to be pretty wild and a little crazy to take on a bank like the Third Northwestern National in Minneapolis. It was triangular building smack on one of the city's busiest streets, with a streetcar stop right in front of it, and practically the whole goddamn place was in glass. We sometimes did things like that deliberately, maybe to inject some extra excitement into our work."[47]

St. Paul police later recovered the expensive sedan from where it was abandoned in the park. It had been stolen from a White Bear Lake car lot two days before the bank robbery. The gang split up and Verne Miller moved to Kansas City to cool off.[48]

Meanwhile, the gravely wounded Patrolman Gorski was driven to General Hospital by a citizen in his private car. The officer had been shot in the back, the abdomen, and the leg. The hospital immediately called for donors of blood, and several transfusions were administered from fellow members of the police force, as physicians battled to save Gorski's life. His temperature was reported at 107, and he seemed to be sinking.

Patrolman Gorski continued in critical condition into the next day, with a slight improvement shown late in the afternoon following a blood transfusion. But with Gorski's high temperature, attendants at General Hospital said his condition was in no way favorable.

Mrs. Ira Evans, wife of the patrolman shot to death by the bank bandits, was at work, within three blocks of the scene of her husband's death. The ominous clatter of the bandit machine gun penetrated to her desk in the office at 101 Central Avenue. A few minutes later, Patrolman Evan's radio cruiser, literally sieved by machine-gun slugs, was driven past the office where Mrs. Evans was employed. She was unaware of the tragedy until some time later when she was notified by police. Accompanied by her sister, she went to the Hennepin County morgue to claim the body.

On Saturday, December 17th, the city controller's office revealed that Patrolmen Evans and Gorski had been working three and one-half days without pay when Evans was shot to death and Gorski seriously wounded by the bank robbers. Police department paychecks for the first half of December were short two and one-half days pay, and Friday was the first day of the last half of December, in which policemen would receive no pay because of a shortage in the police fund.

The day following the robbery, Minneapolis Police Captain Frank Forestal expressed the opinion the raiders were members of a Kansas City mob which also was responsible for the $200,000 looting of another branch of the Northwestern the past March.[49]

Forestal said the police were seeking Mike Allegretto, thirty-two; Sam Hunt, thirty-one; James Hines, twenty-six; Ralph Pierce, twenty-five;

and Clyde Bridges, twenty-eight, all from Kansas City, in addition to Bernard Phillips. Forestal pinned his hope on identification through Bertillion pictures. He announced one man had been partially identified from a Bertillion photograph.

Adding weight to his theory was the recovery of a large, expensive sedan, abandoned where the St. Paul motorist was killed in Como Park. The car, police said, was the same sedan used in the North American robbery on March 29th. Forestal said it had been stolen from a White Bear garage two days before the North American Bank was held up. Police established also that the sedan tallied by description with the car stolen from L. J. Shields of White Bear Lake.

Three days after the North American robbery, Bernard Phillips, who was identified through pictures by employees of the bank as one of the bandit gang, appeared at offices of the Automobile Association of Cicero, Illinois, with a woman he said was his wife. He filled out an application for membership. The motor number, chassis number, and other numbers were taken in accordance with routine of joining the association.

Phillips did not show up again and officials communicated with police. The numbers were those of the car stolen from Shields. Phillips, it was also learned, later tried to sell the car in Kansas City. Phillips was under an indictment by the Hennepin County Grand Jury for the North American robbery. Pictures of Phillips, 37, known as "Big Phil" and Clyde Bridges under indictment for alleged participation in the March holdup were being studied that very day by victims of Friday's robbery. St. Paul police released four persons picked up for questioning following the raid, announcing they had no connection with the holdup.

Three men and a woman were taken into custody that same day for questioning by St. Paul police. They were detained after a railroad ticket agent at Osceola, Wisconsin, reported the group had tried to purchase tickets for Montreal. They were told they had missed the train and all left by automobile in the direction of St. Paul, where they were picked up by the police.

A price was placed on the heads of the bank bandits, when the Hennepin County Commissioners voted to pay $500 for each member of the gang apprehended "dead or alive." All available detectives on both the Minneapolis and St. Paul police departments were working around the clock to check out every lead or tip that came in. Witnesses were shown "mug-shots" of known bandits, and local hoodlums were rounded up and brought in for questioning. All of this without success, until the big break finally came early Sunday morning, December 18th.[50]

Notes

[1] Federal Reserve Bank of Minneapolis Archives.
[2] *Beloit Daily News*, August 18, 1932.
[3] *Beloit Daily News*, August 19, 1932.
[4] *Beloit Daily News*, August 18, 1932.
[5] *Beloit Daily News*, August 19, 1932.
[6] *Beloit Daily News*, August 18, 1932.
[7] *Beloit Daily News*, August 19, 1932.
[8] Ibid.
[9] *Mankato Free Press*, December 20, 1932.
[10] Moody County Enterprise, September 8, 1932; *Mankato Free Press*, September 2, 1932.
[11] *Mankato Free Press*, September 1, 1932.
[12] Moody County Enterprise, September 8, 1932.
[13] *Mankato Free Press*, September 1, 1932.
[14] Moody County Enterprise, September 8, 1932; *Flandreau Herald*, September 7, 1932.
[15] *Mankato Free Press*, September 1, 1932.
[16] U.S. Penitentiary Leavenworth, Kansas, Admission Summary for #46928 (Arthur Barker), June 3, 1935 (BOP Archive); Lawrence County Historical Society Bulletin, July 1991.
[17] FBI Files, RCS:TD I.C.#7-576, November 19, 1936, The Kidnaping of Edward George Bremer, St. Paul, Minnesota, History and Early Association of the Karpis-Barker Gang Prior to the Abduction of Mr. Bremer.
[18] *Mankato Free Press*, September 23, 1932.
[19] *Redwood Gazette*, September 29, 1932.
[20] *Mankato Free Press*, September 23, 1932.
[21] *Redwood Gazette*, September 29, 1932.
[22] *Mankato Free Press*, September 23, 1932.
[23] *Redwood Gazette*, September 29, 1932.

[24] *Mankato Free Press*, September 23, 1932.
[25] *Redwood Gazette*, September 29, 1932.
[26] Alvin Karpis with Bill Trent, *The Alvin Karpis Story*, pp. 45-50.
[27] (Wahpeton) *Richland County Farmer-Globe*, October 4, 1932.
[28] Ibid.
[29] Alvin Karpis with Bill Trent, *The Alvin Karpis Story*, pp. 45-50.
[30] (Wahpeton) *Richland County Farmer-Globe*, October 4, 1932.
[31] Ibid.
[32] (Wahpeton) *Richland County Farmer-Globe*, October 7, 1932.
[33] Alvin Karpis with Bill Trent, *The Alvin Karpis Story*, pp. 45-50.
[34] Alston Purvis interview conducted by Brian Bull, April 29, 2003.
[35] South Dakota Public Broadcasting.
[36] Rick Mattix letter to author dated January 6, 2006.
[37] Paul Maccabee, Crime Historian & author of *John Dillinger Slept Here*, Interview 3/18/03 on Verne Miller by Brian Bull.
[38] *St. Paul Pioneer Press*, December 17, 1932.
[39] MPD Federation, Police Officers Federation of Minneapolis Archives.
[40] Alvin Karpis with Bill Trent, *The Alvin Karpis Story*, New York, Coward, McCann & Geoghegan, Inc., 1971, pp. 43-45.
[41] *St. Paul Pioneer Press*, December 17, 1932; MPD Federation, Police Officers Federation of Minneapolis Archives.
[42] *Minneapolis Journal*, December 17, 1932.
[43] *St. Paul Pioneer Press*, December 17, 1932; MPD Federation, Police Officers Federation of Minneapolis Archives.
[44] Alvin Karpis with Bill Trent, *The Alvin Karpis Story*, pp. 63-66.
[45] U.S. Penitentiary Leavenworth, Kansas, Admission Summary for #46928 (Arthur Barker), June 3, 1935 (BOP Archive); Lawrence County Historical Society Bulletin, July 1991.
[46] *St. Paul Pioneer Press*, December 17, 1932; *Minneapolis Journal*, December 18, 1932.
[47] Anne E. Cowie, "Two Horses and One Buffalo Robe, The Ramsey Count Attorney's Office and Its 150 Years: All the Frailties of Human Nature," Ramsey County History, Fall 2000, Volume 35, Number 3.
[48] MPD Federation, Police Officers Federation of Minneapolis Archives.
[49] *Minneapolis Journal*, December 17, 1932; *Mankato Free Press*, December 17, 1932.
[50] *Minneapolis Journal*, December 19, 1932; MPD Federation, Police Officers Federation of Minneapolis Archives.

Chapter Four

Larry Devol & Earl Christman

"[Larry DeVol was] probably the most cold blooded man that ever entered the [Stillwater] prison. I have not the slightest doubt but that he would take any stand between him and freedom."

—Stillwater Warden John J. Sullivan[1]

Five days after the robbery, Larry DeVol, drunk from a celebration of his success in the heist, began annoying tenants at 928 Grand Avenue, by running around in the halls. DeVol kicked at the door of the Haskett H. Burton, an Associated Press telegraph operator, and then staggered into Burton's apartment where a bridge game was in progress. After Burton and other persons in the group ejected DeVol, he started upstairs, breaking a window on his way up the stairs.

"We had just finished playing bridge," Burton later told the press. "Our wives were getting something to eat for us, and we were sitting around chatting and smoking. Somebody had been making a racket for about an hour, but we didn't pay much attention. Suddenly someone kicked the door. I opened it as far as the chain would let it go, and saw this fellow. He looked like just an ordinary drunk.

"'I'm looking for a friend,' he said drunkenly. 'There's no friend of yours here,' I said. 'Get going!' 'Oh, yeah,' he said and went down the hall. I had gone into the hallway, followed by one of our party. The man started down the hall and we went back to my apartment."[2]

About fifteen minutes after the initial altercation, DeVol staggered back from the rear hall and Burton again went out into the hall to see what was happening. Burton again ordered him to leave, but this time DeVol drew a pistol and threatened the tenant. Burton returned to his apartment, locked the door, and called the police. With Burton and his wife at the bridge party were Mr. and Mrs. Harry R. Olsen and Mr. and Mrs. James Bibeau, all of 1186 Grand Avenue, and Mr. and Mrs. Raymond Du Puy.

"In a minute we heard the crash of glass," said Burton. "Then there was another crash. We went out into the hall again and saw this fellow coming down the hall toward us with a gun—a big one. About that time, we went back to my apartment and did some telephoning. In a few minutes, a squad car arrived, and the policemen went upstairs."

Patrolmen George Hammergren and Harley Kast, members of a radio squad, responded to Burton's call. "Kast and I were cruising when we got the call there was a drunk causing a disturbance in a hallway at 928 Grand Avenue," stated Hammergren. "When we got there we couldn't find anyone on the first floor so we went up to the second. There was no one in the hall there. . . ."[3]

Burton lived on the first floor. The apartment occupied by the bandits was on the second. The Burtons had resided there since September and told police they had never seen the man before.

Upon inspecting the halls of the building, the two officers found a door on the second floor slightly ajar. They entered and found a man, Newbern, dressing. Newbern told them there were no guns in the place, that his partner was "slightly drunk," and assured the officers he would prevent any further disorder.

Hammergren insisted upon seeing the other man and entered a bedroom. "I'm going to look this fellow over anyway," he told his partner. The man, clad only in his underwear and a fur coat, stood with his back to the door. Believing he was kidding a drunk, the officer said to the man, "Why, you're nothing but a drugstore cowboy; little boys like you shouldn't be playing with guns."

As Hammergren spoke, DeVol spun around with a pistol in his hand and attempted to fire. Hammergren, however, seized the pistol with both hands and tried to wrest it away. Unable to do so, he called out to Officer Kast" "This man has pulled a gun and I've got a hold on him."

Kast rushed into the bedroom and aided his partner in disarming the gunman. But as soon as Kast had left the outer room, the first man fled without a hat or an overcoat. The patrolmen took DeVol out to the squad car. Hammergren stayed with the prisoner while Kast telephoned headquarters for more men to search the apartment.

But as soon as Kast left, DeVol attacked Hammergren again—attempting to choke him and biting his left hand in the battle. As they struggled, they rolled out of the car into the street where DeVol broke loose for a second. Hammergren, however, drew his pistol, but instead of firing, clubbed DeVol with it, knocking him down.

The police by this time decided they had more than an ordinary drunk to care for. While they waited for the "wagon" to come, they decided to search his apartment, where they found $1,700 in currency with Northwestern National Bank wrappers on it, and $10,000 in securities. The man was taken at once to St. Paul police headquarters, where he was identified as Lawrence Devol, twenty-seven years old. He also went by the names Barton and Barker and he was wanted at Kirksville, Missouri, for the murder of a policeman, and the wounding of another in November, 1930.

Minneapolis police were notified and a squad of detectives, along with Chief William J. Meehan, rushed to St. Paul and started questioning Devol. Almost at once he broke down and confessed that he had been a member of the bank bandit gang. "I shot the two coppers," Chief Meehan quoted Devol as saying. "But you can't get me to say another thing. It wasn't me that shot the fellow in Como Park. It was a younger member of the outfit. We tried to stop him, but he shot before we could. I won't tell you who he is. I might as well take the rap for that, too."

As Devol sobered up, he became "cagey," in the words of the police. He gave Charles Tierney, assistant inspector of detectives, a statement in which he confessed to having a part in the robbery as the "lookout" man. He mentioned several names but Inspector Tierney was quite certain many if not all were false. After leaving Como Park, according to DeVol, the gang went to the apartment at 928 Grand Avenue, to divide the loot, where he was arrested.[4]

An old bullet wound was found in DeVol's left palm, which he claimed to have received in a Whiting, Illinois, nightclub just before he had come to St. Paul. The police said that he admitted being involved in various crimes throughout the country and he was "hot" everywhere. He also admitted he always went armed, and that he frequented clubs on the outskirts of St. Paul and Minneapolis, but never ventured downtown, fearing arrest. He carried a .45 caliber revolver in his hip pocket at all times and also a .25 caliber gun with a special holster under an armpit beneath his undershirt.

Questioned concerning the whereabouts of other members of the gang, he first gave two fictitious addresses in Minneapolis. He was "questioned rather severely" then, and finally gave the address of an apartment at 209 East Sixteenth Street. Detectives went to the Sixteenth Street apartment, and were "planted" there only a short time before they arrested two more suspected members of the gang, Robert Newbern and Leonard Hankins, a.k.a. Owen Lewis and "Louisville Slim."

At about the same time, a squad of St. Paul police "planted" in the Grand Avenue apartments, captured a fourth suspect—Clarence DeVol, brother of Lawrence DeVol—when he appeared at the apartment where Detectives Clarence Miller and John Coskran were stationed. The officers found $750 in traveler's checks on the Midwest National Bank of Lincoln, Nebraska, in his pockets—a bank which did not exist. He left parked at the curb a green automobile similar to one to which the robbers were to have transferred in Como Park following the holdup and killings earlier in the week. He carried no gun but officers found a .32 caliber shell in the car. DeVol also used the alias of James Colton.[5]

All four of the men arrested were ex-convicts and each had a long police record. Five women were also arrested. The arrests were made shortly before 7 A.M. Sunday, at which time police believed the bandits had planned to leave St. Paul in a new automobile, found in the rear of the apartment house. Detectives found the back of the car was outfitted with a complete arsenal, including two rifles and four automatic pistols fixed to shoot like machine guns.

When photographs of the four men suspected of participating in recent robberies were shown to employees of the State Bank & Trust Company of Redwood Falls, they identified pictures of Lawrence Barker [DeVol] and Owen Lewis as two of the men who robbed the bank there. A partial identification was also made of Robert Newbern. Police continued looking for another robber believed to have escaped the traps laid in Minneapolis and St. Paul. This man was believed to be already on his way to Kansas City by automobile.

One angle that puzzled police was what happened to the remainder of the loot from the bank robbery. They were sure the $1,700 found in the Grand Avenue apartment house was part of the loot, because the money had just been issued and records of the bank disclosed it had never been used. A calculation found on a bit of note paper in the apartment, indicated the bandits had obtained $22,400 in the robbery. Detectives were inclined to believe the rest of the loot was hidden somewhere in the Twin Cities, and an intensive search was started for it, without success. The successful roundup of the bank suspects came just a few hours before Patrolman Leo Gorski died from his wounds at General Hospital.[6]

The Board of Hennepin County Commissioners, meanwhile, announced it was planning to vote a reward that same day for the capture of the bandits and murderers.

"We promised Saturday we would vote a reward for the capture of the bandits, and we will keep our promise, even though it looks like they have already been captured," one board member said. "The only question is whether the law will permit us to offer a $500 reward for the capture of each bandit, or whether they will have authority to vote only one reward of $500 for the capture of all of them."[7]

On the day Patrolman Evans was buried, a police lineup was conducted for thirty-five people who viewed the four prisoners. More than an hour before "Barker" [DeVol] was taken from St. Paul to Minneapolis, the corridors of the Minneapolis City Hall were jammed with people hoping for a look at him. At 5:30 P.M., a car drove up behind the Third Avenue entrance. From the car stepped Al Marxen, junior captain of detectives, and Frank Forestal, captain of detectives. Between them was DeVol, each of his wrists handcuffed to the wrist of one of the detectives. DeVol was taken to the detective captain's office.[8]

Under orders of police, the six captives, each bearing a card with a number on it, were paraded before fifteen witnesses to the bank robbery and a group of twenty police officers and city officials. Two other men, selected at random from the city jail, marched before the witnesses with the prisoners. As they walked back and forth, each was required to take off his hat and put it on again, and speak short sentences. While this was going on, detectives circulated through the crowd of witnesses.

As they recognized the suspects, the witnesses whispered the information to detectives. The witnesses selected the men by numbers on their backs. Four persons identified Lawrence DeVol as the man who riddled the police car with machine gun bullets as it stopped in front of the bank while the holdup was in progress. Three people identified Robert Newbern as the man who carried the loot from the bank. Both Leonard Hankins and Clarence Devol were identified by three witnesses as members of the bank robbery gang, and they were seen shooting as they left the bank.

Based primarily on the witnesses' identification of the four prisoners, the Hennepin County grand jury returned indictments charging each man with two counts of first degree murder, and one count of bank robbery. Only Lawrence DeVol gave police a signed confession that he was the leader of the bandit gang and that he helped plot the robbery of the Third Northwestern Bank.[9]

DeVol, however, refused to sign a statement confessing he actually participated in the raid and denied to Hennepin County Attorney Ed J. Goff that he had told St. Paul Police that he was the gunman who shot and killed the two patrolmen.[10]

That same day, Frank Nitti was shot by Chicago Police during a gunfight in a skyscraper and reports stated he was expected to die. As "tough guy" Nitti lay in Bridewell Hospital, felled by police bullets, intoning prayers that he might live, doctors said it was only a matter of hours before he likely would die.

Criminals as well as police called him "the Enforcer"—the heir apparent to the throne of the liquor, vice, and gambling syndicate vacated by the imprisoned Al Capone. Nitti won his sobriquet in police circles for his reputation for giving orders to "rub out" enemies of the Capone Gang. Police said more than a score of persons had been murdered via the bullet and torture method of Nitti's orders.

Nitti was among seven men at what police called a "gangster rendezvous" on the fifth floor of the La Salle-Wacker Building downtown Chicago when officers conducted a raid. Four policemen burst in on the group unannounced. Surprised and unresisting, the seven men lined up peaceably. Nitti was not recognized initially.[11]

Then, unconcernedly, Nitti sauntered from the line toward an anteroom. Police officer Harry Lang saw him slip a piece of crumbled paper into his mouth and start chewing rapidly. Lang lunged at him, yelling, "Here! What are you doing?" Nitti whipped out a pistol. It belched lead and a bullet tore through Lang's hand. Lang staggered, pulled out his own gun, and their pistols spat flame and lead.

In the next room, Nitti's companions stood still, making no effort to aid him. Two of the officers at the first shot ran to Lang's side; however, they were not needed. Three of Lang's bullet had found their mark in Nitti's abdomen and chest and another lodged in his spine.

"The Enforcer," however, survived the shooting. (Frank Nitti shot and killed himself eleven years later on Saturday, March 20, 1943, after he was indicted for extorting more than two million dollars.)[12]

Back in Minneapolis on December 20th, Sheriff Frank Cords took Herbert Dredge, assistant cashier of the First National Bank of Amboy, Minnesota, and John Starkweather, a farmer, to view suspects of the gang which robbed the Third Northwestern National Bank of Minneapolis. During the police "show-up," at 3 P.M., they were to ascertain whether these were the same men who robbed the bank in Amboy of $1,890. Sheriff Cords also planned to investigate a tip that one of the women being held by Minneapolis police was a former Amboy girl.[13]

Following the police "show-up," Sheriff Cords announced that Dredge and Starkweather identified two of the men as members of the gang which robbed the bank in Amboy on October 18th. Lawrence Barker, alias Lawrence Barton [Larry DeVol], was recognized by Dredge, while both DeVol and R. V. Newbern were named by Starkweather as participants in the robbery. Glee Jordan Stone, one of five women arrested as companions of the suspects, had attended school in Amboy, according to both men.[14]

However employees of the North American branch of the Third Northwestern Bank, which was held up March 29th, failed to identify any of the suspects in connection with that robbery. The North American branch bank employees looked over the suspects with robbery victims from Milaca, Minnesota, and Flandreau, South Dakota, who also failed to recognize any of the men.

A report that several witnesses to the Third Northwestern National Bank robbery had received warnings from gangsters began circulating as the county attorney prepared to present the case against four suspects in the raid to the grand jury. None of the witnesses would confirm the report but the story persisted and there were rumors that anonymous telephone calls had been received threatening death if any of the witnesses appeared against the four men held.

County Attorney Ed J. Goff said he would ask indictment of the four the next day on two counts of murder and one count of bank robbery. Goff had already called in six witnesses that day and said three small children who saw the machine gunner outside the bank, while the robbery was in progress, might be called as witnesses.

The children had earlier told police they were certain Lawrence DeVol was the man who stood outside the bank with a machine gun while the holdup was being executed. They said they asked the gunman where he got "such a nice gun" and were told to "beat it."

When Goff questioned James Colton, the suspect denied any knowledge of the bank robbery but gave a statement of his whereabouts on the day of the raid. The county attorney also interrogated Larry DeVol, Robert Newbern, and Owen Lewis.

While the county attorney was preparing to present the case to the grand jury, another phase of the robbery case was developing by way of a civil suit filed in district court. Paul Hesselroth, 726 Monroe Street N.E., who had been struck over the head with the butt of a gun, brought a personal injury suit against the four men. Hesselroth asked for damages of $5,000.[15]

Extra guards were placed on duty in the city jail on December 22nd, when police heard a rumor that Chicago gangsters had come to town on Wednesday night bent on releasing the four suspects. Police Chief William J. Meehan told the press that he had received several reports about the Chicago underworld characters and that the reports seemed genuine. The jail elevator, only entrance to the city jail, was ordered left on the fifth floor to prevent the possibility of a concerted raid on the jail in an effort to free the prisoners.

Police authorities revealed that "Barker" had a long criminal record and was wanted in several cities, including Kirksville (Missouri), Omaha, Milwaukee, and Wichita. In Kirksville he was wanted in connection with the slaying of Police Officer John Rose in November 1930, and the wounding of Policeman George Scrivins.[16]

According to Kirksville police, the two officers had seen the suspect in his car near a theatre after midnight, walked up to question him, and were mowed down by gunfire. He was also wanted at Hannibal, Missouri, for a theatre robbery and at Carrollton for the theft of guns used in the Kirksville shootings from a hardware store.

Omaha police said DeVol had been sought for questioning there the past year regarding the murder of Sam Villella during a hijacking raid and in connection with shotgun attacks directed at Omaha bootlegger Charles Hutter.

On December 23rd, Alex Uttendorfer, indicted at Red Wing for bank robbery, escaped from a machine gun ambush by authorities at Lake Johanna near St. Paul. The ambush was set by state crime bureau operates, Louis Dedon, a Milwaukee detective and two St. Paul city detectives in a lakeside cottage. Uttendorfer drove down a main highway toward the house, but before he turned in, one of the officers fired prematurely. Uttendorfer, in a small coupe, fled before the officers could get their autos from concealment and pursue him. Uttendorfer had earlier escaped a similar ambush in Wisconsin when a girl warned him of the plant.[17]

Meanwhile, employees of the bank in Redwood Falls visited the Minneapolis jail and identified the four suspects as members of the bandit gang which robbed that bank on September 23rd. Roland Zeigel, county attorney of Adair County, Missouri, and J.M. Campbell of Kirksville also viewed the prisoners and identified DeVol as the gunman who shot and killed one officer and wounded another in November 1930.[18]

With the Grand Jury investigation being held, news reached Meehan that all four suspects had been positively identified as members of the gang that had robbed the bank. Eight witnesses were on hand when the investigation opened, and one of them was Clyde Walstad, said to have been inside the bank at the time of the raid. Walstad identified the suspects as the four men he had seen rob the bank.

The next witness was Ed Rankin, New Brighton coal truck driver who had chased the bandits following the raid. Rankin identified DeVol and Robert Newbern. County Attorney Ed J. Goff asked for indictments against the four men, charging two counts of first degree murder for the slaying of the two police officers. Goff had been under the impression that jury was considering only the case against DeVol. An application for custody of Lewis, one of the prisoners, was filed in the police department by police officers from Paducah, Kentucky.

In a telephone conversation with Chief Meehan, the Paducah chief of police said Lewis, who had been identified as Leonard Hankins, was one of the five men that broke out of the Paducah jail in September and escaped. He was tried on a robbery charge in Paducah and sentenced to serve ten years in the Kentucky Prison. He was charged with the $26,000 robbery of the Peoples National Bank of Paducah, May 29, 1932, in which the Paducah police commissioner was shot and wounded.

Police also declared that Newbern was a fugitive from Mobridge, South Dakota, where he was charged with larceny in connection with the passing of travelers checks. Kansas City police, meanwhile, were asked to search for Medford Stone, sought as the fifth member of the bank robbers. Police received a report that Stone had fled to Kansas City.

Three of the men were named in indictments by the Hennepin County Grand Jury on December 27, 1932. The indictments automatically dismissed application for a writ of habeas corpus, which had been brought in Hennepin County in an attempt to free one of the suspects. County Attorney Goff said he would move for trial of the four January 3rd, and would try Lawrence DeVol first, if the four demanded separate trials.[19]

Five witnesses appeared before the grand jury that day before the indictments were voted. Their identities were closely guarded, due to the fact some of them had received death threats. The grand jury also voted two "John Doe" indictments charging murder and bank robbery, in the belief two other men, although still unnamed, participated in the raid.

Larry DeVol received more bad news on December 29th when he was identified through photographs as one of the participants in the $20,000 robbery of the Plaza Bank of Commerce in Kansas City on December 8th. From a group of photographs submitted by Captain T. J. Higgins of the detective department, bank officials selected one of DeVol as resembling the bandit whose mask slipped off during the holdup.[20]

John O'Keefe, cashier, and Dunlap Vanice, Jr., assistant cashier, selected the same photo. They were unable to identify any of the other three because of the masks they were wearing.

Charging that the Hennepin County Attorney's office had failed to reveal the names of at least seventeen witnesses who appeared before the grand jury in connection with the robbery of the Third Northwestern National Bank, counsel for Robert V. Newbern demanded his immediate release in district court the following day. The charges and the demand for release were contained in a motion and an affidavit filed in district court filed by Eugene Rerat, Newbern's lawyer.[21]

The motion asked that two murder and one bank robbery charge against Newbern be dismissed and Newbern be freed on the grounds that he had been deprived of his statutory rights because he had not been given names of witnesses who testified against him.

"Ma"—The Life and Times of "Ma" Barker and Her Boys

On January 10, 1933, Larry DeVol pleaded guilty to a charge of second degree murder and was sentenced to serve life imprisonment in the Minnesota State Penitentiary at Stillwater, Minnesota. The twenty-seven-year-old gunman admitted that he had obtained $2,500 of the loot from the bank robbery as his "split." As he left the witness stand smiling, Devol joked with deputy sheriffs about the "big hotel" he was going to. (In May of 1936, he became "stir crazy" in Stillwater Prison, lost his reason, and became so violent that it was necessary to transfer him to the state asylum at St. Peter under heavy guard.)

The other three defendants denied any knowledge of the bank robbery. Leonard Hankins was brought to trial next. Even though he denied any knowledge of the robbery, he was found guilty of first degree murder and also sentenced to life in Stillwater State Prison, at hard labor. Hankins told his jailers, "I'm a high class gambler. I wouldn't stoop to a thing like bank robbery."

After lengthy delays in starting their respective trials, Robert Newbern and Clarence Devol used the delays to their advantage. Some witnesses could not be located, and other witnesses' memories became clouded and their identification of the men tentative. As a result, both men were acquitted of the charges and released.

In the aftermath of the crime and the needless loss of two protectors of the city, civic leaders asked that the police department be provided with armored cars and machine guns to combat gangsters already supplied with such weapons. The chief of police concurred:

"This bank robbery is a good example of the things our squads may encounter at any time," he said. "It is a crime to send police, armed with only pistols or shotguns against a gang of bandits wielding machine guns that fire as many as 600 shots a minute. Bandits get the best equipment they can buy or steal. Why should not the police be equipped as well?"

The chief requested a sufficient increase in the police department funding, so that members would not have to continue to be forced to take payless vacations, as they were doing that year. At the time of the robbery, each police officer had to take a fifteen-day payless vacation, and it appeared that the police would have to work an additional fifteen days without pay in order to make up a shortage in the 1933 budget.

Minneapolis Mayor William A. Anderson issued the following statement concerning the police department situation and the deaths of the two patrolmen: "Patrolmen Ira Gorski and Leo Evans, who fell before the bullets of a gang of ultra modern bandits, displayed a type of courage that is practically unprecedented in the police history of any city. Compared with the new type of efficient machine gun pistols used by the bandits who robbed the Third Northwestern National Bank, the equipment of the Minneapolis police department is woefully obsolete. We not only have no machine guns, but no protection against machine gun fire. Why?

"The whole reason is a matter of finance. We have been forced to curtail expenditures to a point which puts us at the mercy of organized and well equipped criminals. This condition is not due to the high tax rate. It is not the average taxpayer who is the most articulate in opposing necessary costs of government and adequate wage and salary scales. It is not the inability of the average citizen to pay his taxes that has cut so heavily into departmental budgets. The articulate and organized minority of large taxpayers, however, is the group mainly responsible for our financial embarrassment. Surveys made at my request show that if the so-called big taxpayers all would pay their just share, if they would buckle down and shoulder their share of the burden and as willingly and with as much uncomplaining sacrifice as the small taxpayers have, we would not now be unable to meet police payrolls.

"Patrolmen Evans and Gorski not only did their duty. They went far beyond the normal requirements of their position. Because the police fund was exhausted, they were not even on the city payroll when they were killed, trying, without a chance of success, to defend the property of a large and successful institution. While their heroism will be remembered as long as Minneapolis exists, their sacrifice reflects little credit upon the city. Certainly a community as prosperous as this, even in times of depression, should be able to pay an adequate wage for the protection we demand and should have.

"They not only gave their lives freely, but gave them without the chance even of their just financial reward. The laborer is worthy of his hire.

And now we are threatened with further wage reductions, and the group fighting for those wage reductions is the same that supported and approved budgetary curtailment which held policemen on duty without pay. Minneapolis should provide some fitting memorial to Evans and Gorski. I hope it can be done, and if it is, it should set forth the full account of their deeds, including the fact that the city was too poor to pay them for their work.

"The best memorial, however, and the one which would go furthest to remove this stain from Minneapolis' name, would be a spirit of cooperation among our best and wealthiest citizens, a determination to provide not only adequate wages for their protectors, but modern equipment, machine guns and armored cars, with which to combat clever and ruthless thugs. If this result is accomplished, it will set an example for other cities to follow, and perhaps the lives of Evans and Gorski will not have been given in vain."[22]

Immediately after the arrest of Larry DeVol, the news was carried to the other members of the gang by Harry Hull and a rapid exit was made from the Twin Cities by Fred Barker, Doc Barker, Alvin Karpis, Jess Doyle, William Weaver and Harry Hull, their destination being Reno, Nevada. At Reno they joined Earl Christman and Helen Ferguson, along with Kate Barker and Volney Davis who had returned from their vacation in California and were in Reno when other members of the gang arrived there.[23]

They had arrived in Reno in two cars. Karpis stopped briefly in Chicago, caught a plane, and showed up in Reno a couple days later. Having never flied before, he arrived in Reno somewhat shaken and sleepless and went directly to Bill Graham's Rex Club on Virginia Street where the others awaited him in the casino's back room.[24]

They spent two months in Reno playing keno at the clubs, going to movies, socializing with people "in their line of business," and just sitting around the Rex Club killing time. "Baby Face" Nelson rushed to the club to welcome them and clue them in on all the hot spots in Reno, as well as places to avoid.

Karpis, one year older, and Nelson hit it off almost immediately. Karpis wrote later that "Nelson and I hadn't known each other as kids, but when we found out we had lived in the same neighborhood in Chicago, we developed a kind of bond. We both hung out around West Division and Sacramento and even knew the same kids. We saw each other a lot. . . ."²⁵

Right after New Year's, Karpis, suffering from a sore throat, took Nelson's advice and visited Tobe Williams' hospital in Vallejo where his tonsils were removed. Ma Barker, whom Karpis considered "a good sport" to "put up with our gypsy way of living," went with him to the Bay area.

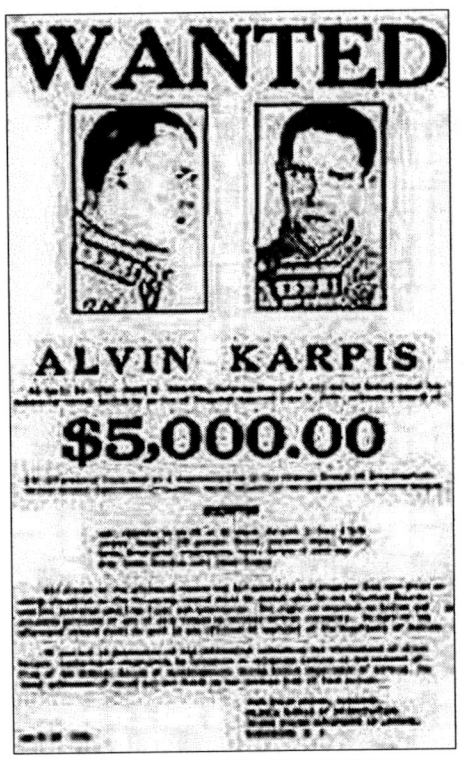

Wanted Poster of Alvin Karpis.

Following the operation, Ma and Karpis spent a couple days sightseeing in San Francisco and visiting some of Nelson's friends. During their stay, it was rumored that Ma became enamored of Tobe Williams and the two elders later spent a weekend together at Lake Tahoe.

Prior to the conviction of Volney Davis for murder in the State of Oklahoma, he had been associated with Edna Murray. Edna Murray was born in Marion, Kansas, on May 26, 1898, the daughter of H.D. and Luella Stanley. When Edna was still a small child, she moved with her father to Cardin, Oklahoma. Edna had one sister, Doris, later to become known as Doris O'Connor, and three brothers, Matt, Floyd and Harry. The family's income was derived from the rent of miners' shanties which were owned by Edna's father near Cardin, Oklahoma. Edna Murray, at the age of twenty-three, was working as a waitress and cashier at the Imperial Cafe in Sapulpa, Oklahoma, and it was here that she first became the sweetheart of Volney Davis.²⁶

After Davis was sentenced to life imprisonment, Edna Murray left her employment in Sapulpa, Oklahoma, and sought other means of livelihood in Kansas City, Missouri. Here she met and married Fred Sullivan, alias "Diamond Joe," a jewel thief. Edna had twice before been married. Her first husband's name was Patton and by this marriage she had one son, Preston. Her second husband was Walter Price. Edna after meeting Sullivan continued to live with him until the year 1924 when Sullivan was convicted of murder and subsequently electrocuted at Little Rock, Arkansas.

Jack Murray, a Kansas City, Missouri, bootlegger, was Edna Murray's next lover, and with Murray, Edna engaged in the illicit traffic of liquor, assisting Murray in transporting the same from New Orleans, Louisiana, to Kansas City, Missouri. These activities on the part of Edna Murray continued until the night of April 6, 1925, when she and Jack Murray were arrested and charged with the holdup of H.B. Southward at Kansas City, Missouri.

Both Edna and Jack Murray were convicted on October 1, 1925, and each sentenced to serve a twenty-five year sentence in the Missouri State Penitentiary. From the alleged activities of Edna Murray during this holdup, the press gave her the sobriquet of the "Flapper Bandit" or the "Kissing Bandit."

Edna Murray was confined in the Missouri State Penitentiary on December 3, 1925, and soon acquired another nickname—"Rabbits"—due to her agility in escaping from that institution on May 2, 1927. After this escape, Edna remained at large until she was arrested in Chicago, Illinois, and returned to the Missouri State Penitentiary on September 10, 1931.

Upon her return, Edna immediately began to plot another escape, and on November 4, 1931, she again succeeded in escaping; but on this occasion her freedom was short-lived and she was taken into custody the following day. Edna upon being returned to the penitentiary was placed in an individual cell, but she succeeded in conspiring with another inmate, Irene McCann, to escape a third time.

Edna Murray and Irene McCann succeeded in sawing the bars of their cells and escaped on December 13, 1932. Edna immediately proceeded to Kansas City. Volney Davis, who was then in Reno, Nevada, with other members of the gang, learned of her escape and proceeded to Kansas City where he met the woman who was to continue to live with him as his paramour and share in the loot of the notorious Karpis-Barker Gang. Edna and Volney joined the other members of the gang in Reno.

While in Reno, Nevada, dissension arose between Harry Hull and other members of the gang, when Hull purloined $250 and some clothes from Jess Doyle. Doyle anticipated that Hull would go to Kansas City, and he, with Doc Barker, took an airplane to locate and kill him. Their efforts in this regard, however, were unsuccessful.

Early in February 1933, the gang stayed in St. Paul, where they remained until March 4, 1933, when they were tipped off that the police planned to raid an apartment in which some members of the mob resided. The fugitives hastily took flight to the Chicago area.

During March, they found refuge in various apartments in Oak Park, Illinois, and found their entertainment at a roadhouse operated by Louis Cernocky in Fox River Grove, Illinois, which had long been a rendezvous for such notorious criminals as Francis Keating, Thomas Holden, and Frank Nash. They also found entertainment and refuge at the O.P. Inn, Maywood, Illinois, operated by Louis "Doc" Stacci, who had long been a known associate of criminals.

While in Chicago, they planned a robbery, and on April 4, 1933, the Fairbury National Bank, Fairbury, Nebraska, was relieved of $27,643.13 by Fred Barker, Volney Davis, Frank Nash, Doc Barker, Alvin Karpis, Earl Christman, Jess Doyle and Edward Green—commonly known as Eddie Green, an ex-convict who had joined members of the Karpis-Barker Gang in St. Paul.

Green was an accomplished bank robber and, due to the close friendship between Harry Sawyer and him, Green made numerous acquaintances with underworld figures, who were making St. Paul their haven. He became the close confidante of Volney Davis, Alvin Karpis, Fred Barker, and Doc Barker.

Picking a nice sunny April day, the gang drove into the town of Fairbury, Nebraska, armed with three machine guns, three rifles, half a dozen pistols, and several rounds of extra ammunition. It was city election day in

Fairbury, and before midnight, Frank L. Park would become the town's new mayor, the Fairbury Ministerial Association would be successful in its efforts to ban Sunday movies, and Mrs. Verneita London would announce to her East Ward School third graders: "Boys and girls, now don't get excited, but I understand the First National Bank has just been robbed!"[27]

The bank faced east, and to avoid the glare of the early morning sun, the blinds were pulled until about noon. This was a perfect situation for the robbers since no one on the sidewalk could see them doing their thing inside the bank.[28]

After pulling up outside the bank, the boys split up into pairs and descended upon the bank from different directions. Frank Nash is believed to have entered the bank first and did most of the talking. About the time Nash bounded up the stairs, Homer Yeakle, his daughter Gwen, and stepdaughter Wilma Vaughn reached the bank entrance. The ever-courteous Yeakle even held the door open for the robbers.[29]

As they entered the bank, a woman outside on the sidewalk started screaming hysterically, causing the teller inside, thinking the men were joking, to laugh. Karpis quickly let him know that it was not a joke by slapping him across the face with his gun. Cashier R.S. Wilfley was quickly accosted by the robbers and asked where the bank president was. Because President Luther Bonham had not come in yet, Wilfley was forced at gunpoint to open the vault.

Meanwhile, Assistant Cashier Frank Nelson, after waiting on a customer, looked up to see a revolver pointed in his face. He was ordered to back out and not touch any buttons. Nelson, with a gun pushed into his ribs, was shoved towards the safe along with Wilfley and Harold Livingston. Bank employee F.P. Conrad became so frightened he swallowed his chewing gum.

"While I was turning the combination," Nelson recalled, "the bandit stood back of me and said, 'I guess we will have to kill someone around here if there isn't more speed.'" Nelson added: "He jabbed me with his gun. Just then I had the door open and was getting the keys and he stepped up and put his hand into the money shelf. He took all of it."[30]

Karpis and Freddie Barker kept their guns on the tellers and customers while the others emptied money from the cages. Outside the bank, there was a great deal of commotion with at least a dozen people yelling, "Robbers!" Dr. C.E. Leach saw the start of the shooting from his office across the street from the bank building and ran to the telephone to call central to spread the alarm the bank was being robbed.[31]

B. A. Sedoris was standing on the bank corner and saw the whole robbery, but was compelled by a machine gun guard to stand very still. He said a passerby came by and said there was a holdup in the bank. Beginning to think the whole thing was a joke, Sedoris walked over and peered into a window on the east side of the bank. He was again confronted with the hard-boiled looking man with the machine gun and was told if he moved again, he was a dead man.

Sedoris stood in a direct line of fire and was very uncomfortable there. He had his hands in his pockets and did not dare to take them out. If he moved he would be shot, and if he didn't move, he might be shot anyway. But he kept his eyes open and his mind alert.

Mrs. F. R. Brill drove up about 9:30 P.M., saw the bandit's car parked on the wrong side of the street with the engine running, and parked her own car east of the bank. She saw the bandit guard standing on the east side of the bank but thought he was holding a musical instrument, perhaps a horn. Then she heard someone say, "Stop where you are."[32]

She turned around and asked the man, "Are you speaking to me?" He cursed and said he was, but she walked past him to the corner, turning west, intending to enter the bank. A neighbor, Ray Holtz, stopped her from going inside and told her the bank was being robbed.

Ruth Skidmore, one of fourteen employees forced to lie on the floor during the robbery, recalled being kicked by one of the gunmen, later identified as Frank Nash, when she raised her head and looked around: "I was too nosy for them. One led me toward the door, apparently intending to take me hostage, but then the shooting started. He let go of me and jumped through an east window."[33]

Frank Bell, a local resident, remembered the day the "Barker-Nash" Gang came to Fairbury: "A few election workers had gathered in the lobby of the Bonham Theatre hoping we could get a 'yes' vote for Sunday movies in Fairbury. We failed again. Archie Bowlen, one of our election workers, came into the lobby and told us that down E Street, one-half block south, a gang was robbing the bank and one of the men was pushing the bank's money through an east side open window, and another gangster was placing it in their seven-passenger sedan. Their sedan was parked on the west side of E Street, headed north and parallel with the traffic and against the curb. I ran to the street and then towards the entire operation. I stopped running at the bank in the alleyway north of the bank.

"Their lookout guard with his rifle was at the south end of their car. He stepped into E Street and ordered a car, which was just in front of the Globe, and when he didn't stop, the guard fired a shot through his windshield. The driver stopped his car and then ran into the lobby of the theatre."[34]

Meanwhile, word of the robbery had been phoned to the sheriff's office, and Deputy Sheriff W. S. Davidson and Glenn "Pete" Johnson of Des Moines, who were in the sheriff's office, rushed towards the bank. They were met by a woman who came running out of the bank screaming that a robbery was in progress. Gene Dickens, who was nearby, overheard her, and told Jay Brandenburg, clerk at the Twidale Shoe Store, to call the police.[35]

The editor of the *Fairbury Journal* came walking up the street from the west when Dickens accosted him and told him the bank was being robbed. Like so many others that day, the newspaperman thought it was all a joke until he saw the seriousness in Dickens' eyes. Dickens had not seen the bandits but had been told by Mrs. Lloyd Meyer as he had passed the bank.[36]

Mr. Dickens and the editor saw nothing. The sidewalk was deserted, except that Mrs. F. R. Brill came along around the bank corner and everyone began to realize that something was up. Then the crack of a gun, apparently fired inside the bank broke the stillness.

Just then, they saw Deputy Sheriff Davidson angling across the courthouse lawn from the north, moving at a dog trot with his gun ready to shoot. Suddenly he stopped dead in his tracks, aimed his rifle, and started shooting from across the street south of the bank. Several shots were returned by the bandits from inside the bank as glass flew outwards onto the sidewalk.

Davidson saw his predicament, took to his heals, crouched low, and raced south to the northeast corner of the courthouse lawn, where he crouched under a Ford Model T. Lying almost prone on the ground, he got off at least a couple shots at the bandits.

Karpis was concerned about Jess Doyle waiting out in the car, knowing that without a means of transportation, they would be sitting ducks. Karpis whispered to Nash, who was holding one of the machine guns, to move to the door where he could see all the way up the street to the courthouse. Karpis ran outside to check on Doyle.[37]

As Karpis made his way outside, he was temporarily shocked, since Doyle was not in the car as planned. Looking around, he saw Doyle crouched beside the bank wall, holding a .45 in each hand.

"The goddamned machine gun's jammed," Doyle shouted.

Karpis ran to the car and picked up the machine gun and tested its action. Doyle caught his attention and pointed up the street where several men carrying rifles were crouched down, moving towards them. The advancing citizens began firing and bullets ricocheted off the pavement and wall.

Karpis slipped a slug into the machine gun which had been jammed, and all of a sudden it went off and started spitting bullets down the street before he could control it. Many of the bullets shattered the glass fronts of a jewelry store and a drugstore, sending up a shower of glass, wood, and cardboard.

Injecting another fifty-shot drum into the gun Karpis flipped it to Doyle, who kept the men on the street at bay. Several police officers, however, began peppering the bank from cover in front of the courthouse. Nash was supposed to take care of them but his own machine gun jammed.

Earl Christman and Doc Barker had four hostages covered inside the door, when suddenly Christman headed for the car with two hostages in front of him, followed by Doc Barker and the other two. Both of Christman's hostages were men, and as the trio raced out, a man came out of the courthouse with a Luger in his hand. Hostage John Knobel, who was standing at one end of the car, dropped to the pavement when the shooting started, and escaped without injury. Fred Barker opened up with a rifle, and on the fourth or fifth shot, dropped the man with the Luger.

Karpis turned to find Christman blowing holes in the stomach of one of his hostages with a machine gun. When Karpis asked why he had killed the man, Christman answered, "These sons of bitches. The two of them separated so somebody could take a clear shot at me. I'm hit! Through the back!"

B.A. Sedoris, who was still standing in the street watched by Christman and another bandit looking out the east window, saw his chance when the gunman was hit and reeled back against the car. With the gunman in the window looking the other way, Sedoris rushed across the street to the Golden Rule corner.[38]

George Bliss, former manager of the Blue Valley baseball team, had been standing at this same Golden Rule corner. When the shooting started, he lay down and didn't even look up to see what was happening. Apparently, Sedoris brought him to his senses.

Frank Bell recalled: "A deputy sheriff [W. S. Davidson] and another man, reported to be an arms salesman [Glenn Johnson], ran from the courthouse to the middle of E Street, laid [sic] down and fired at the lookout [Christman]. The lookout returned the fire, hitting one of the men in the leg. The lookout was hit and as he flinched, he swung around wounding their male hostage also in the leg. (The hostage, Keith Sexton was later taken to Dr. Ainlay's office where he was treated. He miraculously survived five bullet wounds.)[39]

Sexton, the bank's bookkeeper, had been shot through the arm, shoulder, leg, and side; Glenn Johnson of Des Moines through the shoulder; and Deputy Sheriff Davidson in the knee. Sexton's condition was considered the most serious because of the shock caused by the four bullets.[40]

Karpis dragged the wounded Christman into the car while the others emerged from the bank with two women hostages as shields, who were forced to stand on the running boards.

"One thing I'll always remember is that they put me beside the man who was shot," recalled Mrs. Frances Wilson, a passerby, who had been pulled into the car as a hostage. "I can still see how white he was as he leaned against me."[41]

Herbert Aasendorf, came up the street on a motorcycle just after Deputy Sheriff Davidson was hit. Aasendorf grabbed the wounded deputy's gun and fired five shots into the rear of the bandit car as it started up the street. Dr. J.H. Bond leaned out of the window of his office in the bank building and scribbled the license number of the car—98-1355-1932, Iowa.[42]

The county board of commissioners was in session at the time of the robbery. Sheriff Emil Ackman had appeared before them to discuss the advisability of purchasing more equipment from the display of guns that had been brought to the sheriff's office by Mr. Johnson.

While they were discussing the matter, calls for the sheriff were heard and Ackman rushed to join the fight against the bandits. The commissioners and county officials watched the gunfight from a safe distance. Several bullets struck the corner of the courthouse building.

During the gunfight in the streets, plate-glass windows were well shot up. Several shots crashed through the windows of the Spear-Boswell Drug Store, diagonally across the street from the bank, tearing up a basket full of candy bars, and also smashed up the plate-glass mirror behind the soda fountain. F. L. Spear, one of the owners of the store, said that there were several clerks and customers in front of the store before the shooting started, but they were back behind the safety of the wall when the bullets began pouring through the windows.

A bullet pierced the window of the Howell-Diller Hardware Store, and also the front of E.L. Simpkins' jewelry store. Occupants of buildings along North E Street said that the bandits shouted, "Out of the way," as they started up the street and fired at random into the storefronts.

Windows north of Fifth Street were also smashed as the robbers kept up the barrage on their way out of town. Two bullets smashed the windows at Lambert's, one striking the wall and glancing off, and the other hitting a curtain rod. Customers and employees, as well as several bystanders, who had been outside when the car started up the street, found safety inside on the floor.

Another bullet penetrated the upper part of the glass front at the Fairbury Electric Shop. Mrs. Earl Morlan, an employee at McDonnell's Store, received a most unwelcome thrill when a bullet, which came through the glass and the back partition of a display window, struck a dust mop near where she was standing, toppling a mop and an aluminum kettle to the floor. Several other buildings were struck by bullets, and cars parked along the escape route had broken windshields.

The police at the courthouse ceased firing, and news of the holdup was quickly telephoned to the Associated and United Press Associations. Within an hour and a half after the shooting, Mrs. Johnson of Des Moines heard a radio news report of the shootings, and called to find how seriously her husband was injured.

After the rapid volley of shots had died away, local citizens with rifles and helmets flooded the streets making the scene look like a war zone. County Attorney A.J. Denney came running and assisted in caring for the wounded. Johnson, the traveling man, was lying prostrate in the street, just south of the bank entrance, his shirt front a mass of blood. Four men hurriedly carried him to the Potter-Hughes-Ainlay Clinic.

A checkup conducted by President Luther Bonham of the First National Bank revealed that instead of the robbers getting away with $27,000, the figure was closer to $150,000. After the cash had been gathered in by the bandits, they asked for the bonds. The bonds were pointed out and the gangsters stuffed them into a dirty flour sack.[43]

Bank officials found a black-leather briefcase left behind by the robbers on one of the marble customer tables in the center of the lobby. In the briefcase was a new pistol with several extra bullets, Kansas car licenses, and several copies of the Kansas City Star.

After the fugitives had driven about ten miles with no pursuit, they released their female hostages. They had been taken north on Highway 15 to one mile north of 14th Street, then a mile east on an off road before they were permitted to leave the car. The gunmen dropped roofing nails or, according to the ladies, "giant tacks" along the roads to slow their pursuers. The women caught a ride back with a passing motorist and arrived in Fairbury unhurt.

Driving on, out of sight of the women, the bandits stopped again to examine Christman's wound. A bullet had passed through his collarbone and left tiny splinters of bone where the bullet had entered his body. Karpis injected morphine into him and washed the blood with drugstore prescription whiskey.

On April 13th, the *Fairbury Journal* received a dispatch stating that three men—K. Stubblefield, Ray Fowler, and John Stanley were being held in Salina, Kansas, for investigation in connection with the Fairbury bank robbery. R. S. Wilfley and a number of Fairbury bank officials hurried to Salina and other points to aid in identifying the men if possible.[44]

Other developments in the Fairbury robbery case surfaced when Sheriff Tom Dunn telephoned from Beatrice reporting a clue involving a newly purchased car in southern Gage County. The owner was brought to Fairbury, but since no one in town could identify him, he was released.

Sheriff Emil Ackman reported an investigation made of a Kansas man who had strangely died as a result of frozen feet. Believing it was possible that he might have been the bandit shot by Deputy Davidson, the man's body was examined by Officer Joe Cook but no bullet was found.

Glenn Johnson, the Des Moines firearms salesman shot by bandits during the robbery, was released from the hospital in Fairbury a couple of weeks after the holdup. Johnson told the press that he was ready to resume his duties to urge law enforcement officials everywhere to be fully prepared with firearms for emergencies. With the bullet having been removed from his back, he told reporters he was going fishing.[45]

Deputy Sheriff W.S. Davidson was also permitted to leave the Fairbury Clinic and began recuperating at his home in the basement of the courthouse. When visited by reporters, he was seated at a table catching up on his book work in connection with police matters. His left ankle was still bandaged and swollen, and he wore slippers, as the swelling prevented him from wearing a shoe.

Earl Christman, meanwhile, had been rushed to the home of Vernon C. Miller at 6612 Edgevale Road in Kansas City by the bandits. The home of Miller was at that time considered a safe refuge for gangsters of the Middle West. It was later destined to be highly publicized as a rendezvous for Charles "Pretty Boy" Floyd and Adam Richetti, who gathered in Miller's home on the night of June 16, 1933 to formulate their plans for the unlawful delivery of Frank Nash, who was apprehended by special agents of the Federal Bureau of Investigation at Hot Springs, Arkansas, on June 16, 1933.

Notes

[1] Paul Maccabee, *John Dillinger Slept Here*, p. 124.
[2] *St. Paul Pioneer Press*, December 19, 1932.
[3] Ibid.
[4] *Minneapolis Journal*, December 20, 1932; *St. Paul Pioneer Press*, December 20, 1932.
[5] *Mankato Free Press*, December 19, 1932.
[6] *Minneapolis Journal*, December 19, 1932; MPD Federation, Police Officers Federation of Minneapolis Archives.
[7] *Minneapolis Journal*, December 19, 1932.
[8] *St. Paul Pioneer Press*, December 20, 1932.
[9] *Mankato Free Press*, December 22, 1932.
[10] *Mankato Free Press*, December 20, 1932.
[11] *St. Paul Pioneer Press*, December 20, 1932.
[12] *Chicago Daily Tribune*, March 20, 1943.
[13] *Mankato Free Press*, December 20, 1932.
[14] *Mankato Free Press*, December 21, 1932; *St. Paul Pioneer Press*, December 21, 1932.
[15] *St. Paul Pioneer Press*, December 22, 1932.
[16] *Mankato Free Press*, December 19, 1932.
[17] *Mankato Free Press*, December 23, 1932.
[18] *Mankato Free Press*, December 20, 1932.
[19] *Mankato Free Press*, December 27, 1932.
[20] *Mankato Free Press*, December 29, 1932.
[21] *Mankato Free Press*, December 30, 1932.
[22] MPD Federation, Police Officers Federation of Minneapolis Archives.
[23] FBI Files, RCS:TD I.C.#7-576, November 19, 1936, The Kidnaping of Edward George Bremer, St. Paul, Minnesota, History and Early Association of the Karpis-Barker Gang Prior to the Abduction of Mr. Bremer.
[24] Steven Nickel and William J. Helmer, *Baby Face Nelson Portrait of a Public Enemy*, Nashville, Cumberland House, 2002, pp. 78-79.
[25] Ibid.
[26] FBI Files, RCS:TD I.C.#7-576, November 19, 1936, The Kidnaping of Edward George Bremer, St. Paul, Minnesota, History and Early Association of the Karpis-Barker Gang Prior to the Abduction of Mr. Bremer.
[27] James Denney, "The Day the Barker Gang Hit Fairbury," *Sunday World-Herald*

Magazine of the Midlands, March 30, 1969.
[28] Alvin Karpis with Bill Trent, *The Alvin Karpis Story*, pp. 75-80.
[29] James Denney, "The Day the Barker Gang Hit Fairbury," *Sunday World-Herald Magazine of the Midlands*, March 30, 1969.
[30] Ibid.
[31] *Fairbury News*, April 4, 1933.
[32] *Fairbury Journal*, April 20, 1933.
[33] *Lincoln Journal*, August 29, 1979.
[34] *Fairbury Journal News*, April 23, 2004.
[35] *Fairbury News*, April 4, 1933.
[36] *Fairbury Journal*, April 6, 1933.
[37] Alvin Karpis with Bill Trent, *The Alvin Karpis Story*, pp. 75-80.
[38] *Fairbury Journal*, April 6, 1933.
[39] *Fairbury Journal News*, April 23, 2004.
[40] *Fairbury News*, April 4, 1933.
[41] *Lincoln Journal*, August 29, 1979.
[42] *Fairbury News*, April 4, 1933.
[43] *Fairbury Journal*, April 6, 1933.
[44] *Fairbury Journal*, April 13, 1933.
[45] *Fairbury Journal*, April 20, 1933.

Chapter Five

Hamm Kidnapping

"I want to talk to you and I want you to listen to what I'm going to say and don't butt in. We have Mr. Hamm. We want you to get $100,000 in twenty-ten and five-dollar bills. And goddamn you, see that they aren't marked. If you tell a soul about this or call in the police, it will be too damned bad for you and you will never see Hamm again."

—Alvin Karpis[1]

On the morning of June 17, 1933, a mass murder committed in front of Union Railway Station, Kansas City, Missouri, shocked the American public into a new consciousness of the serious crime problems in the nation. The killings, which took the lives of four peace officers and their prisoner, are known as "Union Station Massacre" or the "Kansas City Massacre."

The Union Station Massacre involved the attempt by Charles Arthur "Pretty Boy" Floyd, Vernon Miller, and Adam Richetti to free their friend, Frank Nash, a Federal prisoner. At the time, Nash was in the custody of several law enforcement officers who were returning him to the U.S. Penitentiary at Leavenworth, Kansas, from which he had escaped on October 19, 1930.[2]

Kansas City Massacre, June 17, 1933.

Nash's criminal record stretched back to 1913, when he was sentenced to life imprisonment at the state penitentiary, McAlester, Oklahoma, for murder. He was later pardoned. In 1920, he was given a twenty-five-year sentence at the same penitentiary for burglary with explosives, and again later pardoned. On March 3, 1924, Nash began a twenty-five-year sentence at the U.S. Penitentiary at Leavenworth for assaulting a mail custodian. He escaped on October 19, 1930. The Federal Bureau of Investigation launched an intensive search for Nash, which extended over the entire United States and parts of Canada. Evidence gathered by the FBI indicated that Nash had assisted in the escape of seven prisoners from the U.S. Penitentiary at Leavenworth on December 11, 1931.[3]

The investigation also disclosed Nash's close association with Francis L. Keating, Thomas Holden and several other well-known gunmen who had participated in a number of bank robberies throughout the

Kansas City Massacre, June 17, 1933.

Midwest. Keating and Holden were apprehended by FBI Agents on July 7, 1932, at Kansas City, Missouri. Information gained by the FBI as a result of the apprehension of these two indicated that Nash was receiving protection from his underworld contacts in Hot Springs, Arkansas.

Based on such information, two FBI Agents, Frank Smith and F. Joseph Lackey, and McAlester, Oklahoma, Police Chief Otto Reed located and apprehended Nash on June 16, 1933, in a store in Hot Springs, Arkansas. The law officers drove Nash to Fort Smith, Arkansas, where at 8:30 that night, they boarded a Missouri Pacific train bound for Kansas City, Missouri. It was due to arrive there at 7:15 A.M. on June 17. Before leaving, the lawmen made arrangements for R.E. Vetterli, Special Agent in Charge of the FBI's Kansas City office to meet them at the train station.[4]

While FBI agents were perfecting a plan, a number of outlaw friends of Nash had heard of his capture in Hot Springs. They learned the time of the scheduled arrival of Nash and his captors in Kansas City and made plans to free him. The scheme was conceived and engineered by Richard Tallman Galatas, Herbert Farmer, "Doc" Louis Stacci, and Frank B. Mulloy. Vernon Miller was designated to free Nash, and while at Mulloy's Horseshoe Tavern in Kansas City, he made a number of phone calls for assistance in the scheme. At about this time, two gunmen, "Pretty Boy" Floyd and Adam Richetti, arrived in Kansas City, and they agreed to aid in the mission.[5]

En route to Kansas City, Floyd and Richetti had been detained at Bolivar, Missouri, early on the morning of the 16th, when the car in which they were riding became disabled. While the two were waiting in a local garage for the necessary repairs to the car, Sheriff Jack Killingsworth entered the building. Richetti, who immediately recognized the sheriff, seized a machine gun and held the Sheriff and the garage attendants against the wall.

Floyd drew two .45 caliber automatic pistols and ordered all parties to remain motionless. Floyd and Richetti then transferred their arsenal into another automobile and ordered the sheriff to enter that vehicle. The two, along with their prisoner, drove to Deepwater, Missouri, abandoned the automobile and commandeered another.

After releasing the sheriff, they arrived in Kansas City about 10:00 P.M. on June 16th. There Floyd and Richetti abandoned the automobile and stole another car, to which they transferred their baggage and firearms. Finally, that same night, they met Verne Miller and went with him to his home. Miller told them of his plan to free Frank Nash. Early the next morning, Miller, Floyd

Kansas City Massacre, June 17, 1933.

and Richetti drove to the Union Railway Station in a Chevrolet sedan. They took up their positions to await the arrival of Nash and his captors.

Controversy still surrounds the Kansas City Massacre that left five men dead. Historians disagree on the identity of Verne Miller's accomplices. The FBI identified Charles "Pretty Boy" Floyd and Adam Richetti as the other gunmen. But other names put forth included Harvey Bailey, Maurice Denning, Solly Weissman, Wilbur Underhill, Bob Brady, and Jack Griffin. Even the motives of the Massacre are disputed. Many say Miller was trying to rescue a friend, convicted killer and robber Frank Nash. Others say the event, which resulted in Nash's death, was a gangland hit.

Alleged accomplice in the Kansas City Massacre Charles, "Pretty Boy" Floyd.

June 17, 1933, was a sad day for Kansas City's Union Station. It was an active, thriving landmark and centerpiece. However, at about 7:20 A.M., the station became an "arena of horror," according to Kansas City's newspaper, *The Star*. Events leading to the massacre began the day before, when escaped convict Nash was taken into custody at a horse race in Hot Springs, Arkansas, by Frank Smith and Joe Lackey, both agents of the Bureau of Investigation, which later became the FBI. They were assisted by Otto Reed, police chief in McAlister, Oklahoma. Devastated by his arrest, Frances Nash asked Miller for help.[6]

The agents escorted Nash to Kansas City by train, where he was to be transported in the car of agent Raymond Caffrey to Leavenworth

Penitentiary. With Caffrey were Bureau agent Reed Vetterli and two Kansas City detectives, W. J. Grooms, and Frank Hermanson.

While the lawmen waited, three men stood by, armed with machine guns, ready to free Nash. The train arrived on schedule at 7:15 A.M. and Nash was immediately taken to Caffrey's car. According to the official FBI version of events, as the party was getting into the car, two men—possibly three—rushed forward. One shouted, "Up, up!" There was no time for the lawmen to reach for their weapons. The next order came quickly, "Let 'em have it!" The group fired relentlessly with machine guns from all sides of Caffrey's car.

Verne Milller's friend, Frank Nash.

The result was truly a massacre. Hermanson and Grooms, exposed between the parked cars directly in the gunmen's line of fire, were killed nearly instantly. Caffrey fell with a bullet in his brain and died before he reached a hospital. Vetterli, wounded slightly, dropped down and crawled to the back of the car. He crouched and sprinted for the safety of the station.

In the agents' car, Reed was dead. Lackey took several bullets to the back and was paralyzed for life. Smith escaped unharmed after slumping to the floor and playing dead. Nash, slumped in the front seat, had his head blown apart and was the first to die in the massacre. After the gunfire stopped, a voice was heard, "They're dead. They're all dead. Let's go."

The death of Nash raised the possibility that the gangsters executed him because of his knowledge of underworld activities, rather than attempting to rescue him.

"I don't believe they planned to kill Nash," stated the wounded agent, Vetterli, in recounting the grisly details of the slaughter. "We went to the station to meet the officers who were bringing Nash back from Hot Springs. Raymond Caffrey and I drove to the station in his car. The two Kansas City detectives, Hermanson and Grooms, drove to the station in their car. We met the train and started over to Caffery's car, headed south on the station drive across from the east door of the station.

"There were eight of us, including Nash and seven officers. We were to enter Caffrey's car and the Kansas City detectives were to follow us to Leavenworth in their car. I was standing at the rear and west side of Caffrey's car. In the backseat were Lackey and Smith, the agents from Oklahoma, and Otis Reed, chief of police at McAlester, who came up with the prisoner.

"Caffrey was to drive. Nash had sat in the driver's seat temporarily until the car was loaded, and then he was to move over into the other front seat, which was folded up to allow the three men to enter the rear seat. Caffrey stood on the pavement beside Nash on the east side of the car waiting for Nash to slide over into the folding front seat. Hermanson and Grooms were standing on the west side of the car and toward the front.

"Suddenly I heard a man say, 'Put 'em up, up, up.' I looked and saw a man blazing away with a machine gun from near the southwest corner of the car. He seemed to be standing on something—perhaps the running board of a car. I don't know exactly but

Alleged accomplice in the Kansas City Massacre, Adam Richetti.

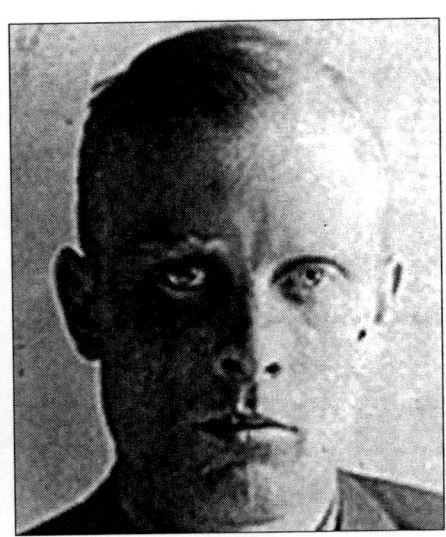

Verne Miller's FBI photo 1923.

he was very close to us. I crouched under the murderous fire. I believe there were other machine guns working, too. Hermanson and Grooms fell to the pavement in front of me, their bodies riddled. The windshield of Caffrey's car was splintering. The men inside of it were powerless before the red fire from the rattling guns.

"I fell to the pavement. I felt a stinging pain in my left arm. When the firing ceased—and it was all over in a flash—I leveled a pump gun at the escaping car...."[7]

Another popular theory was that one of the officers shot Nash as soon as the shooting started, but this version was highly unlikely and not taken too seriously.

Soon, Verne Miller, "Pretty Boy" Floyd and Adam Richetti were named as chief suspects in the violent massacre. Floyd, about twenty-nine years old at the time of the Kansas City Massacre, had been arrested on numerous occasions, the first by the St. Louis, Missouri, Police Department on September 16, 1925, for highway robbery. He pleaded guilty to that charge on December 8, 1925, was sentenced to the state penitentiary at Jefferson City, Missouri, and released on March 7, 1929. Two days later, on

Vi Mathis, her father John Gibson, and Verne Miller in 1932.

March 9, 1929, he was arrested by the Kansas City Police Department for investigation, and on May 6, 1929, for vagrancy and suspicion of highway robbery. In both instances, he was released.[8]

On May 20, 1930, Floyd was arrested by the Toledo, Ohio, Police Department on a bank robbery charge and on November 24, 1930, was sentenced to twelve to fifteen years in the Ohio State Penitentiary. Floyd escaped on his way to the penitentiary and was a fugitive when he became involved in the Kansas City Massacre.

Adam C. Richetti, about twenty-three years old at the time of the Kansas City Massacre, began his criminal career with an arrest in Hammond, Indiana, on August 7, 1928, for a holdup. Richetti was sentenced from one to ten years in the State Reformatory, Pendleton, Indiana, for that crime. He was paroled on October 2, 1930, and discharged from the parole on September 23, 1931. His next arrest occurred on March 9, 1932, at Sulphur, Oklahoma, for bank robbery; he subsequently served a sentence at the State Penitentiary, McAlester, Oklahoma, from April 5, 1932, to August 25, 1932, when he was released and placed on bond which he forfeited. Richetti subsequently was sought for jumping the $15,000 bond, and was wanted at Tishomingo, Oklahoma, for robbery.

The massacre triggered dramatic changes in the Bureau, then a relatively small agency called the Division of Investigation, composed of investigators without the authority to carry firearms or make arrests. A young J. Edgar Hoover did not miss the opportunity created by public outrage and the demand for more effective law enforcement.[9]

Miller's girlfriend Vi Mathis with her daughter Betty Mathis. 1928.

Less than a year later, President Franklin Roosevelt signed into law several statutes increasing the Bureau's jurisdiction. A month later, agents were given power of arrest and authority to carry firearms at all times. The agency, renamed the Federal Bureau of Investigation (FBI) on July 1, 1935, was given the mandate, power, and tools to fight gangster crime.

Herbert Farmer and Louis "Doc" Stacci of the Karpis-Barker Gang, were subsequently convicted in Federal Court at Kansas City for conspiracy to deliver Frank Nash from the officers and each was sentenced to serve two years in a Federal Penitentiary and pay a fine of $10,000.

At the time Earl Christman was being held in Verne Miller's home in Kansas City, Missouri, the associates of Christman frantically sought the aid of an underworld physician who was called upon to administer to his wounds. Christman, however, did not respond to this treatment and within a few days died. The Barkers and Karpis buried the body in a secret place. They had netted over $150,000, but paid the price.[10]

Christman's moll, Helen Ferguson, remained in touch with the gang after the death of Christman and later even lived with Ma Barker for a while on a Lake ShoreDrive apartment in Chicago. Most likely she was "pensioned" with Earl's share of the loot. (According to historian Rick Mattix, Helen also later bought one of the cars that the Dillinger gang left behind at Little Bohemia, which indicates the closeness of the two gangs.)

Verne Miller World War I.

The day following Christman's demise, Fred Barker expressed his desire for a woman companion. He had become enamored of a woman named Paula Harmon, whom he had previously met at the home of his friend, Herbert Farmer in Joplin, Missouri. Vivian Lattie, Verne Miller's girlfriend, telephoned Paula Harmon and asked her to visit Kansas City. Paula accepted this invitation and met Fred Barker at Vivian Lattie's home.

Paula Harmon was the widow of infamous bank robber, Charles Harmon, who was killed while participating in the robbery of a Wisconsin bank on November 19, 1931. She was a native of Demorest, Georgia, the daughter of Annie and Bird Drenon. When Paula was two or three years old, her family moved to Port Arthur, Texas, where Paula later attended grade

Verne Miller and his wife Mildred, 1917.

schools and attended an exclusive girl's finishing school in the South. She was first married to a man by the name of Dennis Hood at Port Arthur, Texas, in the year 1921. Hood was employed as a mate on a ship and Paula's marriage to him was dissolved in the year 1922. She married Charles Harmon, who had just been released from the penitentiary at Huntsville, Texas after serving a term for bank robbery. She soon met the associates of her husband, Frank Nash, Verne Miller, Herbert Farmer, and Fred Barker. During the married life of Paula and Charles Harmon, they quarreled frequently, and during one of these domestic disturbances, Paula separated from her husband and operated a house of ill repute in Chicago for a short period of time.[11]

On May 24, 1933, Paula Harmon and Fred Barker moved into a home at 204 Vernon Street, St. Paul, Minnesota, under the names of Mr. and Mrs. J. Stanley Smith. Fred agreed to rent the house through August at $45 a month and pretended to be a salesman for the Federated Metal Company of St. Louis. James and Gertrude MacLaren, who owned the home, described Mrs. Smith (Paula Harmon) as a "reddish-blonde with a Southern accent, a ring studded with eight diamonds, and a scarred nose that gave the appearance of once having been struck by a heavy instrument."[12] Other members of the gang established themselves in a cottage at Bald Eagle Lake in June.

During these early years of the 1930s, public indignation over the increase of crime in the country and the inability of the police to curb it was at an all time high. This indignation grew worse when the young son of Charles Lindbergh was kidnapped on March 1, 1932, from the family estate in Hopewell, New Jersey. The kidnappers demanded a $50,000 ransom, which the Lindberghs paid on April 2nd. The baby, however, was never returned, and on May 12th, the child's body was found in a shallow grave near their home. Because of Lindbergh's fame, the kidnapping and murder captured nationwide attention.[13] From that time on, every kidnapping case took prominence in the newspapers, with most Americans believing a wave of abductions was sweeping the country.[14]

Haskell Bonn, twenty-two, son of a St. Paul refrigerator manufacturer, was snatched in June 1932. He was returned alive within a week after his father paid $12,000 ransom. In February Federal agents put Gangster Verne Sankey into a South Dakota prison where he killed himself after confessing to kidnapping not only young Bohn but Charles Boettcher II, Denver broker.[15]

Tensions escalated when that same year two men, John M. Holmes and Thomas H. Thurmond, kidnapped young Brooke L. Hart in San Jose, California. After shooting him, they weighted his body, and threw it into San Francisco Bay. An angry mob formed outside the jail, went inside, and removed the two kidnappers, and hanged them from a nearby tree in front of 10,000 people, prompting the Governor of California to say publicly that the mob had done a "good job."[16]

George "Machine Gun" Kelly. (Courtesy FBI Archives)

On July 22, 1933, one of the most sensational kidnappings of the Roosevelt era occurred when George "Machine Gun" Kelly and his gang abducted Oklahoma City oilman, Charles F. Urschel, from a quiet bridge game and demanded a $200,000 ransom. Born to a wealthy family living in Memphis, Tennessee, George "Kelly" Barnes had flunked out of Mississippi

President Franklin Roosevelt signing new crime bill into law. Looking on from left: Attorney General Homer Cummings, J. Edgar Hoover, Director of the Bureau of Investigation, a senator and assistant attorney general Joseph Keenan 1934

State University, while pursuing a degree in agriculture, to pursue Geneva Ramsey, and then a life of crime.

    The couple married, had two children, but not wanting to rely on his family's money, he struggled to make ends meet. His father was also not inclined to help George because of what had happened at Mississippi State, and his displeasure as to Geneva. Money strained the relationship, and the couple soon separated. This was during prohibition, and George found work with a bootlegger. After a short time, he had several run-ins with the local

Memphis police, and he decided to leave town and head west, with a new girlfriend, Kathryn Thorne.

Rumor had it that Kathryn, an ambitious and domineering woman, had murdered a former husband. Nonetheless, she and George fell in love and married. She at once began scheming to build him up into a master criminal and introduced him to some of her own criminal friends who had robbed banks in Mississippi and Texas. Life was good to the Kellys in Fort Worth but Kathryn continued her plans to make it better. Her only mistake was in confiding in two undercover police detectives who had the Kelly's placed under surveillance.[17]

To protect his family and escape law enforcement officers, he changed his name to George R. Kelly. He continued to do small crimes and bootlegging. He was arrested in Tulsa, Oklahoma, smuggling liquor onto an Indian reservation in 1928 and sentenced to three years in the Leavenworth penitentiary, Kansas. Sent to prison on February 11, 1928, he was a model inmate and was released early.

It was Kathryn who came up with the idea to kidnap someone wealthy enough to have a $200,000 ransom paid for their release. She also chose Charles Bates, wanted in three states for bank robbery, to assist Kelly with pulling off the kidnapping of Urschel. The abduction of Charles F. Urschel and his friend Walter R. Jarrett, however, proved disastrous.

Kelly and Bates, one armed with a machine gun and the other with a pistol, opened the door to the screen porch, pointed guns at the two male bridge players, and inquired which of the two men was Mr. Urschel. Neither man would reveal his identity so both were taken away in the back seat of the kidnappers' Chevrolet sedan. Once Urschel was identified, Jarrett was put out of the car.

Urschel was blindfolded, but he was determined to foil his kidnappers by memorizing every possible link to his experience, such as carefully noting background sounds, counting footsteps and leaving fingerprints on every surface in reach. This in turn proved invaluable for the FBI in their investigation.

Mrs. Urschel, in accordance with the Attorney General's advice to the public, immediately telephoned J. Edgar Hoover, Director of the Federal

Bureau of Investigation, United States Department of Justice. Special agents were sent to Oklahoma City, where an extensive investigation commenced.[18]

At 1:00 A.M., Sunday, July 23, 1933, Jarrett made his way back to the Urschel residence. The victims had been driven to the outskirts of the city, where they had turned right on a dirt road parallel to the 23rd Street Highway and had proceeded northeast to a point about twelve miles from the city. After crossing a small bridge and arriving at an intersection, they had put Jarrett out of the car after they had identified him and had taken fifty dollars which he had in his wallet, warning him not to reveal the direction the kidnappers had chosen. He stated that after he was released the car proceeded south.

Kelly and Bates initially brought Urschel to Kathryn's stepfather's house in Paradise, Texas, and then to her stepbrother's place not far away.

Two day after the kidnapping, Urschel's wife, Bernice, told the press, "I am interested only in the safe return of Mr. Urschel and not what happens to the kidnappers after his return."[19]

That same day, E. E. Kirkpatrick, a friend of the Urschels was selected as one of two go-betweens and spokesmen for Mrs. Urschel. In addition to being their trusted friend, he was a newspaperman and a rancher. Kirkpatrick declared to reporters: "We will cooperate with the Federal and other officials, but we are ready to make a contact with the kidnappers themselves. If I could make a contact right now, I would do it in spite of everything."

A police guard was removed from the brick mansion of the Urschels during the day in order that any contact with the abductors might be facilitated, and Mrs. Urschel directed every move on her own. She slept soundly that night although her sixteen year old daughter, Betty Slick, paced the floor all night in her lighted room.

Several days elapsed before word was received from the kidnappers. On July 26th, J.G. Catlett, a wealthy oil man of Tulsa, Oklahoma, and another intimate friend of Mr. Urschel, received a package through Western Union. It contained a letter written to him by Mr. Urschel, requesting him to act as an intermediary for his release; a personal letter from Mr. Urschel to his wife; and a typewritten note directed to Mr. Catlett, demanding that he proceed to Oklahoma City immediately and not communicate by telephone or otherwise with the Urschel family from Tulsa. The package also contained a typewritten letter addressed to Mr. E.E. Kirkpatrick of Oklahoma City, which read in part:

"Immediately upon receipt of this letter you will proceed to obtain the sum of TWO HUNDRED THOUSAND DOLLARS ($200,000.00) in GENUINE USED FEDERAL RESERVE CURRENCY in the denomination of TWENTY DOLLARS ($20.00) Bills. It will be useless for you to attempt taking notes of SERIAL NUMBERS MAKING UP DUMMY PACKAGE, OR ANYTHING ELSE IN THE LINE OF ATTEMPTED DOUBLE CROSS. BEAR THIS IN MIND, CHARLES F. URSCHEL WILL REMAIN IN OUR CUSTODY UNTIL MONEY HAS BEEN INSPECTED AND EXCHANGED AND FURTHERMORE WILL BE AT THE SCENE OF CONTACT FOR PAY-OFF AND IF THERE SHOULD BE ANY ATTEMPT AT ANY DOUBLE XX IT WILL BE HE THAT SUFFERS THE CONSEQUENCE. RUN THIS AD FOR ONE WEEK IN DAILY OKLAHOMAN.

"'FOR SALE—160 Acres Land, good five room house, deep well. Also Cows, Tools, Tractor, Corn, and Hay. $3750.00 for quick sale. . TERMS. . Box # _____'

You will hear from us as soon as convenient after insertion of AD.'"

The ad was inserted. On July 28th, an envelope addressed to the "Daily Oklahoman," Box H-807, was received from Joplin, Missouri. A letter to Kirkpatrick read in part:

" . . . You will pack TWO HUNDRED THOUSAND DOLLARS ($200,000.00) in USED GENUINE FEDERAL RESERVE NOTES OF TWENTY DOLLAR DENOMINATION in a suitable LIGHT COLORED LEATHER BAG and have someone purchase transportation for you, including berth, aboard Train #28 (The Sooner) which departs at 10:10 P.M. via the M. K. & T. Lines for Kansas City, Mo. You will ride on the OBSERVATION PLATFORM where you may be observed by some-one at some Station along the Line between Okla. City and K. C. Mo. If indication are alright, somewhere along the Right-of-Way you will observe a Fire on the Right Side of

Track (Facing direction train is bound) that first Fire will be your Cue to be prepared to throw BAG to Track immediately after passing SECOND FIRE.

"REMEMBER THIS—IF ANY TRICKERY IS ATTEMPTED YOU WILL FIND THE REMAINS OF URSCHEL AND INSTEAD OF JOY THERE WILL BE DOUBLE GRIEF—FOR, SOME-ONE VERY NEAR AND DEAR TO THE URSCHEL FAMILY IS UNDER CONSTANT SURVEILLANCE AND WILL LIKE-WISE SUFFER FOR YOUR ERROR.

"If there is the slightest HITCH in these PLANS for any reason what-so-ever, not your fault, you will proceed on into Kansas City, Mo. and register at the Muehlebach Hotel under the name of E. E. Kincaid of Little Rock, Arkansas and await further instructions there.

"THE MAIN THING IS DO NOT DIVULGE THE CONTENTS OF THIS LETTER TO ANY LAW AUTHORITIES FOR WE HAVE NO INTENTION OF FURTHER COMMUNICATION. YOU ARE TO MAKE THIS TRIP SATURDAY JULY 29TH 1933."[20]

Although Kirkpatrick followed instructions, the kidnappers were delayed, and arrived too late in time to light the fire and meet the train. Kirkpatrick and John Catlett, felt they had been double-crossed. Kelly contacted Kirkpatrick again, and this time, set up a rendezvous in Kansas City.[21]

Again following orders, Kirkpatrick walked west from a designated hotel carrying the bag of ransom money. Kelly met him, took the money, and promised to release the victim within twelve hours. He did not attempt to conceal his identity and the passing of the money was carried out without a hitch.

When Bates and Kelly returned to the Armon Shannon farmhouse in Paradise, Texas, where Urschel was being held, they were greeted with more problems. Harvey Bailey and two friends who had escaped from prison were also hiding out at the farmhouse belonging to Kathryn's stepbrother. Although Bailey had not participated in the kidnapping, he was given a $1,000 share of the ransom money.

On August 1st, ten days after he had been abducted, Charles Urschel was driven to a point nineteen miles from Oklahoma City, given ten dollars for taxi fare, and released. Detectives Kathryn had trusted with information surrounded her stepbrother's farm and Harvey Bailey and the

Shannons were arrested. The Kellys, likely tipped off, left before the police raid.

An investigation conducted at Memphis disclosed that the Kellys were living at the residence of J. C. Tichenor. Special agents from Birmingham, Alabama, were immediately dispatched to Memphis, where, in the early morning hours of September 26, 1933, a raid was conducted and George E. "Machine Gun" Kelly was arrested in the Jackson, Mississippi, rooming house. Arrested with him were his wife Kathryn Kelly, twenty-nine, and two gang members, J. R. Tichnor, thirty, and S. E. Travis, twenty-six. Detective Sergeant W. J. Raney said Kelly met him at the door holding a pistol.

When Raney ordered Kelly to drop his gun, the gangster wanted in connection with the Kansas City Massacre, kidnapping of Urschel, and robbery charges, found himself without a weapon and cried, "Don't shoot, G-Men! Don't shoot, G-Men!" as he surrendered to FBI Agents. The term, which had applied to all federal investigators, became synonymous with FBI Agents. The trial of ten other defendants in the Urschel case resumed the same day.[22]

Investigation at Coleman, Texas, disclosed that the Kellys had been housed and protected by Cassey Earl Coleman and Will Casey, and that Coleman had assisted George Kelly in storing $73,250 of the Urschel ransom money on his ranch. This money was located by Bureau Agents in the early morning hours of September 27th, in a cotton patch on Coleman's ranch. They were both indicted at Dallas, Texas, on October 4, 1933, charged with harboring a fugitive and conspiracy, and on October 17, 1933, Coleman, after entering a plea of guilty, was sentenced to serve one year and one day, and Casey, after trial and conviction, was sentenced to serve two years in the United States Penitentiary at Leavenworth, Kansas.[23]

J.C. Tichemor and Langford Ramsey were indicted at Jackson, Tennessee, on charges of conspiracy and harboring and concealing a fugitive, for their part in concealing the Kellys at Memphis, Tennessee. On October 21, 1933, they were each sentenced to serve two years and six months imprisonment.[24]

Kidnapping, at the time, did not constitute a Federal offense but fell under the auspices of the state police. When it became apparent that the states could not be counted upon to capture criminals without Federal aid, Congress passed new legislation giving the Federal authorities jurisdiction over crimes which had formerly been under state control. President Franklin D. Roosevelt ordered the FBI to take charge of the investigations, including coordination of the efforts of local and state police with the Federal Government.

On June 17, 1932, Congress had passed the Lindbergh Law making kidnapping across state lines a federal felony. This act pitted the U.S. Government directly against the virulent "snatch" racket for the first time. Free from the corruption of local politics, superbly trained and equipped with tip-top morale, the Department of Justice's Division of Investigation buckled down to its new and difficult work with a will. By mid-October 1934, it had acted in thirty-one kidnapping cases, returning alive all but one kidnap victim. Of the seventy-four "snatchers" whom federal agents had helped to catch and convict, two had been sentenced to death, sixteen had been condemned to life imprisonment and the rest were given an aggregate of 1,186 years in jail. Two kidnappers committed suicide and two were lynched.[25]

J. Edgar Hoover wasted little time before going after John Dilllinger, who at that time had earned the title, Public Enemy Number 1, since Al Capone was sentenced to prison. Once Dillinger was shot down in Chicago, Hoover turned his attention to "Pretty Boy" Floyd, "Baby Face" Nelson, and Alvin Karpis.

One afternoon in April 1933, Jack Peifer asked Freddie Barker and Alvin Karpis over to Hollyhocks to discuss any interest they might have in executing a kidnapping. The risks, perhaps, would be higher than any job they had pulled but the rewards made up for the risks involved.

Peifer figured they'd ask for $100,000 in ransom money—he'd take a 10 percent cut for coordinating the affair, and "Shotgun" George Zeigler (Freddie Goetz) and Monty Bolton—both members of the Chicago Syndicate's execution squad who were involved in the St. Valentine's Day Massacre in 1929, Freddie Barker, Karpis and a few others would split the $90,000.[26]

In spite of the FBI's crackdown on kidnappers, the Barker-Karpis Gang was not intimidated. The gang decided to set up headquarters outside of St. Paul and Peifer rented them a cottage known as Idlewild at Bald Eagle Lake near Hugo, Minnesota. Peifer drove up to Idlwild in a La Salle coupe in May and paid the owner Alex Premo the $250 cash deposit. When Premo offered him a receipt, Peifer declined, preferring that there be no record of the transaction.[27]

The boys moved in and every day drove into St. Paul to watch William A. Hamm Jr.'s home and brewery. "We got to know so much about the guy that I was sick of him long before the kidnapping," penned Karpis.[28]

The brewery built in the 1850s and purchased in 1864 by Theodore Hamm was located in a deep ravine near Minnehaha and Payne Avenues, and expanded in 1901. With its clear spring water and cool caves for storage, Swede Hollow was a perfect place for brewing beer. Recognizing the valley's potential, Theodore Hamm started brewing at the north end of the Hollow in the 1860s. By 1894 the Hamm's brew house was an imposing five stories high, built of red brick and stone, with long rows of arched windows, ornate North Germanic gables, and a splendid baroque dome crowned by a cupola. At its opening, the expanded "Excelsior Brewery" drew a crowd of ten thousand curious people.

Crowning Dayton's Bluff was the Hamm mansion. For sixty-seven years the house would create an almost-medieval scene, standing like a baronial castle over Swede Hollow. Inside, the house offered twenty rooms, eight fireplaces, and all the other accoutrements of the good life in the 1880s.

"[Theodore] Hamm would throw very elegant parties," wrote historian Jim Sazevich. "The band would be imported from the city, a good German band. The lawn was all lit with Chinese lanterns, and he had tame deer that he kept in a barn below the bluff and peacocks. And these animals would roam among his dinner guests as they danced away the night. And I picture these children climbing up and peeking through the lilac bushes and seeing all of this, and, I think, being inspired by this grandeur, when their lives were being lived in abject poverty."[29]

The Hamm Brewery was incorporated in 1896, leaving Theodore with the title of president and William Sr., having the title of vice-president and secretary. The brewery continued to expand from 8,000 barrels in 1879 to 26,000 barrels in 1882 to 600,000 barrels in 1915. This growth, of course, was frozen from 1919-1933 during prohibition. Theodore died on July 31, 1903, leaving an estate valued at $1,114,388.20.[30]

William Hamm, Sr., having been indoctrinated to the brewery at a young age, was well prepared to take on the role as president of the brewery. He was the first Borealis Rex in the first St. Paul Winter Carnival in 1886 and was very much involved in the civic duties of the city. From 1889-1890, he was a city council member and council president in 1890. Then starting in 1890 and ending in 1902, he worked with the park board to develop the park system.[31]

When William Hamm, Sr., died on June 10, 1931, his estate totaled $4,225,247. William Jr. took over as president. During prohibition the plant was kept open while they produced an array of products including near beer, industrial alcohol syrups, and soft drinks. Soon after the death of his father, William Hamm Jr. started the greatest expansion effort in the tenure of the brewery. The capacity was doubled and the plant was modernized.[32]

668 North Greenbrier Street, St. Paul. (Author's collection)

Upon the proclamation of the end of prohibition on April, 7, 1933 the Brewery was ready to deliver. "As long-drawn whistle blasts signaled legalization of 3.2% beer at 12:01 today, long lines of trucks piled high with kegs and cases rumbled out of St. Paul's two brewery yards and one half hour later, those who wanted to were quaffing their first drink of their first beverage."

The repeal of prohibition had finally become a reality with the coming of Franklin Delano Roosevelt as President of the United States. One of the main things he promised during his presidential campaign was the repeal of the Eighteenth Amendment. After the elections of 1932-1933, some Republican senators gathered and drafted a new Amendment that would repeal the Eighteenth Amendment. This would become the Twenty-First Amendment. In this Amendment, the Senators proposed three things: (a) an end to national prohibition; (b) that the Federal Government retained the right to protect dry states against the import of liquor; (c) and that Congress should have concurrent power with the states to forbid the return of the saloon. After taking office on March 4, 1933, Franklin Delano Roosevelt requested a special session of the Congress on March 13th to revise the Volstead Act.[33]

On June 15, 1933, William A. Hamm, Jr., president of the Theodore Hamm Brewing Company, St. Paul, Minnesota, was kidnapped by Doc Barker, Fred Barker, Alvin Karpis, Charles J. Fitzgerald, Bryan Bolton, and Fred Goetz. Goetz, known to Capone's organization as "Shotgun George Ziegler," had brought along his bodyguard, William Byron Bolton, a tubercular graduate of Capone's organization who had been a carpenter, auto salesman, and golf teacher.

Hamm had left his imposing office adjacent to the brewery, and, as he always did at exactly 12:45 P.M. each workday, started the slow walk up the imposing hill to the family mansion at 671 Cable Avenue, in St. Paul. Hamm, thirty-nine, had inherited a fortune estimated to be at least $4.5 million in cash and probably double that in real estate and other commercial holdings. Separated from his wife, and a member of one of the city's oldest leading families, Hamm was said to be the most eligible bachelor in the Midwest.[34]

Two blocks from his house, at the corner of Greenbrier and Minnehaha, two men, probably Alvin Karpis and Freddie Barker, walked up to Hamm and stood in front of him. One man extended his hand and asked, "Mr. Hamm?" Hamm immediately thought it was someone he knew. When he reached to clasp hands, the second man grabbed him around the chest, locking in the brewer's arm and pushed him into the back seat of a large black coupe with a uniformed driver in the front seat. Hamm was shoved face down on to the floor of the back seat, a hood was slipped over his head, and the car sped away

The car stopped some twenty miles northwest of Chicago in front of the elegant home of Edmund Bartholmey (soon to be appointed local postmaster) on the main street of Bensenville. Bartholmey later claimed ignorance of the gang's plans. "George Ziegler" (Goetz) had persuaded him to let Barker, Karpis, Bolton, and their prisoner stay a few days. He told a prison psychiatrist: "I had nothing to do with [the kidnapping].... [A]s soon as I saw the man, I felt that there was something wrong, but I didn't know it was Hamm until the next day."[35]

Hamm was pulled gently out of the car "by the icy cold, but small hand of what I think was a woman," he later recalled. He was guided up a set of stairs into a small bedroom where he was allowed to take off the goggles. The room's window had been boarded up, and there was a chair, a bed, a small table with a lamp, and an un-shaded electric light.[36]

Alvin Karpis stayed with Hamm for the entire period he was their prisoner. Extra precautions had to be taken and the gang ordered Bartholmey to send his wife and daughter away for a visit. The postmaster slept on the downstairs sofa and the only time he was permitted upstairs was to use the bathroom. Despite the awkward arrangement, Hamm and Bartholmey never saw each other during the former's captivity in the house.

Over the next few days, only Fred Goetz talked to Hamm although Hamm never saw his face. He remembered that he was fed adequate though simple meals, and when he ate, he was forced to face downwards while Goetz discussed his views on prohibition and the new Roosevelt administration. Once, Goetz asked Hamm, "I see your advertisements about your booze, let me ask you something, is your stuff really special?" Hamm was silent a moment before replying, "Naw, it's all pretty much the same under the label." Goetz remarked, "Look, you seem all right to me, Mr. Hamm. But we had to snatch you. You see, I'm a man with champagne taste and beer income."

The day after Hamm was abducted, William Dunn, Hamm's business manager, received a telephone call from Alvin Karpis, who told him, that he had kidnapped his employer and would release him for $100,000 in small bills and then hung up. Freddie and Zeigler drove back to St. Paul from Bensenville to wait for a brewery truck which was to bring them the ransom money on a lonely stretch of highway.[37]

Only a few hours before the money drop was to take place, Peifer telephoned the two kidnappers and told them not to meet the truck. One of Peifer's police contacts had informed him that the police were laying a trap for them by placing a machine gunner under the truck's tarpaulin. Zeigler and Freddie stayed put.[38]

The machine gunner was former Police Chief Charles Tierney, then captain of detectives. Tierney was a small man, five foot three inches, and about one hundred twenty pounds. He had come up with the idea in which he would play the leading role with Dunn. He sent to headquarters for a machine gun with the idea that he would lie on the floor of the vehicle or in the trunk, and get the drop on the kidnappers.

Somehow there was a leak of information and Tierney's plan was shot down. During negotiations for a new drop at another location, Zeigler came up with an idea. The delivery man had to make the delivery in a Chevrolet coupe, and it had to be stripped of its side doors and the door on the trunk. If the police planned to send another man with a machine gun, he would be right out in plain sight.

After several notes and telephone conversations, Dunn began driving alone, north on Highway 61, towards White Bear Lake. His instructions were to drive twenty miles an hour. He was told he would get a signal of five blinking lights from a car that would follow him. He was then to drop the boxes of money out of the car.

After that he was to continue driving to Duluth and register at the leading hotel there to await the delivery of Hamm. Dunn noticed that a car was following him, then sped past him at a high speed. Dunn concluded that the car would wait on a side road until he passed, because the same thing had happened twice.

Finally he got the signal between Rush City and Pine City. The lights blinked five times and Dunn tossed out the boxes of money and drove on to Hinckley. He stopped there because it was a cold night, and with no doors, he was nearly frozen. After a rest, he drove on to Duluth and the hotel. He had dropped the money on June 17, 1933, in keeping with his part of the agreement. Hamm, however, was not delivered to the hotel as promised.[39]

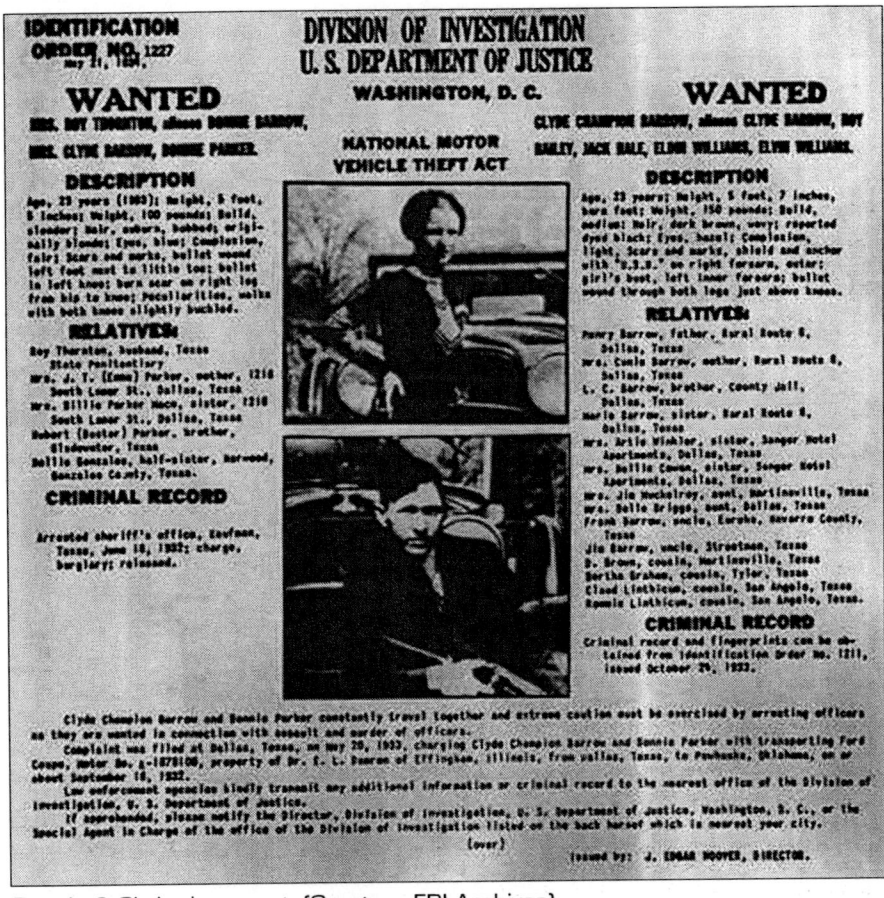

Bonnie & Clyde document. (Courtesy FBI Archives)

The day the ransom money arrived, June 18, 1933, Goetz told Hamm, "We have good news for you, Mr. Hamm, the ransom's been paid and you're going home."

He was given fresh clothes, a clean shave, blindfolded again, pushed on the floor of the car, and driven for ten hours before he was pulled out of the car and left in a vacant field in Wyoming, Minnesota, along Highway 61, about half way between St. Paul and the spot where the ransom money had been dropped. Hamm listened for the car to pull away, then removed the taped goggles from his eyes, and ran to a nearby farmhouse for help. Upon his release, Lu Heim (Shipstead), local telephone operator, took the call from him asking her to contact his family.[40]

The next day, newsmen, photographers and curiosity seekers blocked the main entrance to Hamm's estates. During a news conference, Hamm told reporters that he had been treated well and, "They said that if I ever want anything or if they could ever be of any service to me, just to let them know." A reporter asked the obvious question, "Did they leave a forwarding address?" "No," Hamm replied. "No, I'm afraid they neglected to do that." Despite Hamm's casual attitude towards the entire incident, the public was outraged by the kidnapping, made all the worse by the fact that Hamm's mother had died during his abduction.

On June 24th, three men inquired at an Excelsior, Minnesota, telegraph office about sending $1,000 to Chicago without having it clear through St. Paul. This incident gave police a new angle in the William Hamm kidnap hunt. Local detectives went to Excelsior, a short distance from Minneapolis, but were unable to find the men, according to Chief Thomas E. Dahill. Dahill said, however, that as a result of information gained at Excelsior, his men were investigating elsewhere.[41]

Mrs. Verne Sankey, whose husband had killed himself in prison after committing two kidnappings, asserted that she did not believe her late husband had been involved in any way in the Hamm abduction.[42] Police detectives were convinced, however, that the Touhy Gang, under the leadership of Chicago bootlegger Roger "The Terrible" Touhy, had committed the kidnapping, even though some gang members were already in jail in Milwaukee.

On July 20, 1933, Touhy, Edward McFadden, Gustav Schaefer, and William Sharkey were arrested near Elkhorn, Wisconsin, and charged with the kidnapping of William Hamm. They were transferred to St. Paul and confined in the Ramsey County Jail to await trial.[43]

FBI Agent Melvin Purvis declared he had an "iron-clad case" against Touhy. While being interrogated, Touhy later alleged that he refused to confess to a crime he did not commit and was beaten, starved, and denied sleep. Touhy may have been telling the truth having lost twenty-five pounds, seven teeth, and suffered three fractured vertebrae in his back.[44]

Their November 28, 1933, trial in the crowded, heavily guarded Old Federal Courts Building gained national attention as the first trial after passage of the Lindbergh Law. The suspects, however, were acquitted for lack of evidence but held for Illinois authorities on a charge of kidnapping Jake "the Barber" Factor. Rather than experience the ordeal of another trial William Sharkey hanged himself in his jail cell.[45]

Following the release of William Hamm on June 19, 1933, the gang fled once more to Chicago where Ma Barker was residing at 114 Home Avenue, Oak Park, Illinois. Ma had become a close friend of Helen Ferguson, the former girlfriend of Earl Christman. Volney Davis and Edna Murray had assumed the names of Mr. and Mrs. E. V. Davis and were living in an apartment at 219 North Second Avenue, Maywood, Illinois. The entire gang rented and established themselves in other apartments throughout Chicago.[46]

On July 24th, Clyde Barrow fought a machine gun battle with police in a wooded hideaway and by night was dodging through western Iowa with a network of men in airplanes, armored cars, automobiles, and motorcycles—all connected by wireless—in hot pursuit. Fleeing with him in a stolen car was a man identified as Jack Sherman and a woman, both of them believed to be badly wounded. They had hidden out in the woods for a week with a regular arsenal of two submachine guns, thirty-four automatic pistols, and five revolvers.[47]

During the gun battle, Clyde Barrow and his two companions escaped by wading through a stream and creeping through a cornfield. Marvin "Buck" Barrow, however, was wounded so badly he was not expected to live.

```
                Special Agent in Charge,
                Division of Investigation,
                U. S. Department of Justice,
                Located at:       Building          Tel. No.
        BIRMINGHAM, Alabama, 320 Federal            7-1755
        BOSTON, Massachusetts, 1002
                Post Office & Court House      Liberty 5600
        BUFFALO, N.Y., 612 Marine Trust Cleveland 2030
        BUTTE, Montana, 302 Federal                 2-4734
        CHARLOTTE, N. C., 234 Federal               3-4127
        CHICAGO, Ill., 1900 Bankers'       Randolph 6226
        CINCINNATI, Ohio, 426 U. S.
                Custom House & P. O.               Main 6720
        DALLAS, Texas, Post Office                  2-3866
        DENVER, Colo.,422 Midland Savings  Main 6241
        DETROIT, Mich., 907 Federal       Cadillac 2835
        EL PASO, Texas, 1331 1st Nat'l Bank Main 501
        INDIANAPOLIS, Ind., 506
                Fletcher Savings & Trust        Riley 5416
        JACKSONVILLE, Florida, 412 U. S.
                Court House & P. O.                 3-2780
        KANSAS CITY,Mo.,1616 Fed.Res.Bk.  Victor 3113
        LITTLE ROCK, Ark., 500 Rector Office   6734
        LOS ANGELES, Calif., 617 Fed.     Mutual 2201
        NASHVILLE, Tenn., 508 Medical Arts   6-6771
        NEW ORLEANS, La., 326 1/2 P. O.  Raymond 1965
        NEW YORK, N. Y., 370 Lexington
                Avenue, Room 1403        Caledonia 5-8691
        OKLAHOMA CITY, Okla., 224 Federal      2-8204
        OMAHA, Nebr.,629 1st Nat'l Bk.  Atlantic 8644
        PHILADELPHIA, Pennsylvania,
                414 Phila. Saving Fund         Walnut 2213
        PITTSBURGH, Pa., 620 New Federal   Grant 0800
        PORTLAND, Ore.,411 U.S.Ct.House  Atwater 6171
        SALT LAKE CITY, Utah, 503-A
                U. S. Court House & P. O.     Wasatch 3980
        SAN ANTONIO, Texas,
                1216 Smith-Young Tower         Fannin 8052
        SAN FRANCISCO, Calif., 405 P.O.  Hemlock 4400
        ST. LOUIS, Missouri,
                801 Title Guaranty            Central 1650
        ST. PAUL, Minn., 232 P. O.       Garfield 7509
        WASHINGTON,D.C., 5747 Justice   National 7117
```

Bonnie and Clyde document. (Courtesy FBI Archives)

"Ma"—The Life and Times of "Ma" Barker and Her Boys

On August 30, 1933, six bandits staged the robbery of a payroll being delivered to the Stockyards National Bank at South St. Paul, in which $50,000 was obtained. During the course of the robbery, two police officers were shot by machine guns fired by the robbers, one of the officers killed. At the time of the robbery, one of the officers was equipped with a Thompson submachine gun, which was taken by one of the bandits after the officer had been wounded.[48]

More than a year later, a hide-out of the Karpis-Barker gang was raided at Cleveland, Ohio, and police found a "getaway" chart, which investigation disclosed began at zero at the Stockyards National Bank, South St. Paul, a chart apparently used by the Karpis-Barker Gang in affecting their escape subsequent to the pay roll robbery.

The *South St. Paul Reporter* described the scene when gunshots rang out on Concord Street killing South St. Paul Police Officer Leo Pavlak and wounding fellow Officer John Yeamen:

"Blazing their way with death-dealing gunfire in the heart of South St. Paul's main district at an hour in mid-forenoon today when the street was jammed with traffic, six bandits in a big black sedan escaped with $30,000 in cash taken from the bank messengers in front of the post office building, leaving Officer Leo Pavlak of the South St. Paul Police force dead on the sidewalk where that had shot him down and Officer John Yeamen seriously wounded in his car in the driveway between the post office and the Great Western depot. The bandits who apparently had been awaiting the arrival of the money on the train from St. Paul began firing as the bank messengers, Joe Hamilton and Herb Cheyne, were intercepted and forced to deposit moneybags on the post office steps. They shot Officer Pavlak down after he had been surprised and forced to raise his hands. He sank as the withering fire of a sub-machine gun swept the front of the post office building. Officer Yeamen was also a target for the gunmen in their first fusillade and was shot while sitting in his car in the driveway between the post office and the depot. He was seriously wounded and later was taken to the West Side General Hospital in St. Paul.

"Hamilton and Cheyne set their bags of silver on the post office steps while Cheyne went into the post office to get the registered package of currency. As he came out he was ordered to place the package on the steps. The bandits slew Pavlak as Hamilton and Cheyne ducked under a truck. One of the bandits was shot in the back and crumpled up beside Pavlak's prostrate form, but he was grabbed and dragged into the car. Pavlak, with Hamilton, was standing guard over the money on the post office steps while Cheyne was getting the valuable package and they were to proceed together to the Stockyards National Bank . . .

"The truck under which the messengers hid was owned by Metzger & Nohl of Hancock, Minnesota. It was parked in front of the post office at the south end of the building. Mrs. Metzger was in the cab of the truck and a bullet passed through a slat of the body four inches from the cab. A spray of machine gun bullets was directed up and down Concord Street. Twenty-seven or more slugs struck the post office or shattered windows. Other places struck by bullets were Egan Chevrolet, Dakota County Beverage Co. and Minneapolis Shoe Company, both in the Rund Building.

"After the five or six bandits engaged in the holdup grabbed the packages of money they piled into the black car and drove toward St. Paul on Concord Street. Witnesses who took the license number observed that they did not travel at high speed . . .

"Alderman Joe Lenertz Sr., was within four feet of the bandits at the time the shooting commenced and if he had been armed he asserted that he could have accounted for all the gunmen. The crime was so well planned and executed that only a few minutes elapsed before the bandits were on their way. The bandit car which had been parked in front of the George Egan filling station on Concord Street at Leitch Street since seven o'clock was a veritable arsenal, and machine-gun fire was carried on from the time their lookout man gave the signal for the attack until the car was lost sight of down Concord Street."

The story continued, after describing the routine of the two messengers, which was no different than any other morning. "Then the bandit who stepped in front of Pavlak drew two pistols, covered Pavlak, made him raise his hand and, after disarming him, drilled him through the forehead. As Pavlak fell, this bandit shouted to Cheyne to set down the money on the steps, which he did. Hamilton said he grabbed Cheyne by the hand and ran, dragging him into the shelter of the big livestock truck parked at the curb.

"Two of the bandits who had been waiting in the Depot Café a few feet to the north, had entered and ordered glasses of beer. They set down cases, which looked like bags carried by salesmen . . . against a game machine at the left of the door. Val Papas, who served them their beer, said they drank part of it and that one, the shorter of the two, kept going over to the window. He grabbed his pal by the arm and said 'come on.' This was believed to have been a signal by the bandit in front of the post office who was seen to scrape his foot on the pavement. They grabbed their bags which seemed to fall open and exposed the machine gun and sawed-off shot gun as they ran out. They were seen to duck around the rear of Yeamen's car and their both opened fire and pulled Officer Yeamen out of the car.

"The utter abandon with which the gunmen operated was shown by the bandit who stood at the front of the automobile, and fired along the street. He wore a straw hat, and was well dressed in a gray suit."[49]

Witnesses saw one of the three bandits stagger during the shooting but an accomplice pushed him into the getaway car that drove north on Concord toward St. Paul. Several persons, who had been in the area at the time of the shooting, hid in a vault at an automobile dealer. It was later reported that the suspects were possibly seen in the area two hours prior to the shooting and had been in a beer parlor at 244 North Concord Street.[50]

The incident took place directly in front of the South St. Paul Reporter building and the Dakota Beverage Company where cashier Allen Burt escaped being hit by a bullet by a matter of inches, according to the report. "Shorty" Jensen's transfer company office, sustained broken windows as well.[51]

Dakota County Attorney Harold E. Stassen had his offices in the Farmers Union Building on Grand Avenue at the time of the robbery. His sister, Violet Stassen Crawford, was working in his office when she heard gunshots. She ran out to the street and hid behind a parked vehicle while she watched the gang escape "in a big black car."[52]

Officer Pavlak lay dead in the street and his partner John Yeamen had been hit as well. Violet recalled machine guns hanging out of the car windows, bullets flying in every direction. As the Barker Gang sped away, she rushed back to Stassen's office, reported what had happened, and collapsed from fright.

Rumors flew in the following hours as speculation arose concerning the identity of the gunmen. Chief McAlpine went to Minneapolis to seek assistance from that municipality's department in tracing the men whom he believed were still in the area. Walt Michels was named temporary police officer to fill in for the slain Pavlak and hospitalized Yeamen. Dakota County Attorney Harold Stassen, who arrived at the crime scene only moments after the shooting, assisted in the investigation by instructing passersbys to collect and turn in any shells found in the street or other evidence. Philip Roberge, whose sheet metal shop was located in South Park just north of Bryant Avenue, provided a lead that the bandits' car had remained on Concord Street and passed his shop at a high rate of speed. The license plates proved to have been stolen from a Duluth woman.

As officials continued their investigation, the community's grief turned to the families of the two police officers. Pavlak's wife and children, Eleanor, eleven, and Robert, nine, survived the thirty-five-year-old slain officer. An honor guard composed of twelve traffic officers from the St. Paul Police Force formed a double line facing each other from the curb to the church steps as their gesture of respect. Pallbearers were fellow officers Arthur and Ed Giguere, William Wagner, Fred Schulze, Louis Fuller, and Frank Farrell, who were all in full uniform. Officials from across the state attended the funeral to pay tribute to the officer slain in the performance of duty.

Reverend O'Callaghan of St. Augustine's spoke of Pavlak with affection, emphasizing the love all had felt for the man who was "ever ready to do a kindly deed." Mrs. Pauline Pavlak had only returned home from a hospital stay following major surgery a few days before her husband was killed and was unable to attend the funeral. The police escort and line of cars to the Calvary Cemetery was miles long, stretching from the Exchange Building to well past Swede Hollow on North Concord as the cortege left the city.

Fellow citizens of Pavlak and Yeamen contributed to a community fund established by the *Reporter* in the coming weeks. Officer Yeamen did recover from the 1933 attack but he was never truly well again, according to his son, John, or "Jack" as he was known. Several shotgun pellets remained in his body, one so near the jugular vein that surgeons had hesitated to operate, and another in his shoulder. He returned to the force late in 1933, suffered a relapse, and became disabled.

The bandits in the robbery stole the machine gun, which Officer Leo Pavlak was carrying on that fateful day in 1933. The confirmed identity of the gang was never positively achieved, but the gun was located by the FBI when they raided the New Orleans stronghold of Alvin Karpis.

On September 6, 1933, using a then state-of-the-art technology, now called "Latent Fingerprint Identification," the FBI Crime Lab raised incriminating fingerprints from surfaces that couldn't be dusted for prints. Alvin Karpis, Doc Barker, Charles Fitzgerald, and the other members of the gang had gotten away, but they'd left their fingerprints behind—all over the ransom notes.[53]

It's called the Silver Nitrate Method and its application in the Hamm Kidnapping was the first time it was used successfully to extract latent prints from forensic evidence. Scientists had just thought to take advantage of the fact that unseen fingerprints contain perspiration, chock full of sodium chloride (common table salt). By painting the evidence, in this case the ransom notes, with a silver nitrate solution, the salty perspiration reacted chemically to form silver chloride—which is white and visible to the naked eye. The FBI had finally found evidence that the Karpis Gang was behind the kidnapping.

Notes

[1] John Toland, *The Dillinger Days*, New York, Da Capo Press, 1995, p. 50.
[2] South Dakota Public Broadcasting.
[3] Federal Bureau of Investigation Files, Freedom of Information Act, Charles "Pretty Boy" Floyd Summary.
[4] South Dakota Public Broadcasting.
[5] Federal Bureau of Investigation Files, Freedom of Information Act, Charles "Pretty Boy" Floyd Summary.
[6] South Dakota Public Broadcasting.
[7] *Los Angeles Herald Express*, Night Edition, June 17, 1933.

[8] Federal Bureau of Investigation History Archives.
[9] *Los Angeles Herald Express*, Night Edition, June 17, 1933.
[10] U.S. Penitentiary Leavenworth, Kansas, Admission Summary for #46928 (Arthur Barker), June 3, 1935 (BOP Archive); Lawrence County Historical Society Bulletin, July 1991.
[11] FBI Files, RCS:TD I.C.#7-576, November 19, 1936, The Kidnaping of Edward George Bremer, St. Paul, Minnesota, History and Early Association of the Karpis-Barker Gang Prior to the Abduction of Mr. Bremer.
[12] Paul Maccabee, *John Dillinger Slept Here A Crooks' Tour of Crime and Corruption in St. Paul, 1920-1936*, St. Paul, Minnesota Historical Society Press, 1995, p. 155.
[13] *New York Daily Mirror*, May 13, 1932; Athan G. Theoharis, editor, *THE FBI A Comprehensive Guide from J. Edgar Hoover to The X-Files*, New York, Checkmark Books, 2000, p. 13.
[14] Louise I. Gerdes, editor, *The 1930s*, San Diego, Greenhaven Press, Inc., 2000, pp. 262-263.
[15] *Time Magazine*, February 20, 1933.
[16] *Los Angeles Herald Express*, November 27, 1933.
[17] Miriam Allen deFord, *The Real Ma Barker*, pp. 109-111.
[18] Federal Bureau of Investigation Archives.
[19] *Dallas Morning News*, July 25, 1933.
[20] Federal Bureau of Investigation Archives.
[21] *Dallas Morning News*, July 25, 1933.
[22] *Jackson Daily News*, September 26, 1933.
[23] Federal Bureau of Investigation Archives.
[24] George "Machine Gun" Kelly died of a heart attack at the Federal Penitentiary, Leavenworth, Kansas, on July 17, 1954. Kathryn Kelly was released from prison in Cincinnati in 1958.
[25] *Time Magazine*, October 29, 1934.
[26] Alvin Karpis with Bill Trent, *The Alvin Karpis Story*, pp. 127-132.
[27] Paul Maccabee, *John Dillinger Slept Here*, pp. 141-142.
[28] Alvin Karpis with Bill Trent, *The Alvin Karpis Story*, pp. 127-132.
[29] Larry Millett, Lost Twin Cities, St. Paul, Minnesota Historical Society Press.
[30] Moira F. Harris, *The Paws of Refreshment The Story of Hamm Beer Advertising*, St. Paul, Pogo Press, 1990, pp. 2-3.
[31] John T. Flanagan, *Theodore Hamm in Minnesota: His Family and Brewery*. Minneapolis, Pogo Press 1989, pp. 28, 65, 86.
[32] William Curtis, "Dateline April 7, 1933 PROHIBITION ENDS!" Brewery Age, March/April 1958.
[33] Dennis Sean Cashman, *America in the Twenties and Thirties- The Olympian Age of Franklin Delano Roosevelt*, New York, New York University Press; Thomas M. Coffey, The Long Thirst: Prohibition in America: 1920-1933, New York,

W.W. Norton & Company, Inc.

[34]John William Tuohy, "The St. Paul Incident," Part 1, *Gambling Magazine*, 1999.

[35]Parole Report by U.S. Attorney for 49369-L (Charles Fitzgerald), no date (1936?); Whelan, Parole report for Edmund C. Bartholmey, August 1, 1936 (cross-filed in Charles Fitzgerald file).

[36]John William Tuohy, "The St. Paul Incident," Part 1, *Gambling Magazine*, 1999.

[37]Alvin Karpis with Bill Trent, *The Alvin Karpis Story*, pp. 138-141.

[38]*St. Paul Sunday Pioneer Press*, August 6, 1972, Nate Bomberg, "Veteran Newsman Recalls Hamm, Bremer Kidnaps."

[39]Edwin J. (Ed) Riege, "The Barker-Karpis Rouge," *Minnesota Police Journal*, August 1991.

[40]Elsie Vogel, "In the Early 1900s, FL 'Law and Order' Unfolds," *Forest Lake Times*, May 21, 2003; Charles G. Zehnder, "Barker/Karpis Gang's $100,000 Stash," *Western Treasures Magazine*, June 1970.

[41]*Mankato Free Press*, June 24, 1933.

[42]*St. Paul Dispatch*, June 17, 1933.

[43]Edwin J. (Ed) Riege, "The Barker-Karpis Rouge," *Minnesota Police Journal*, August 1991; *Dallas Morning News*, July 25, 1933.

[44]Steven Nickel and William J. Helmer, *Baby Face Nelson Portrait of a Public Enemy*, p. 121.

[45]Virginia Brainard Kunz, *St. Paul Saga of an American City*, Woodland Hills, CA., Windsor Publications, Inc., p. 131.

[46]FBI Files, RCS:TD I.C.#7-576, November 19, 1936, The Kidnaping of Edward George Bremer, St. Paul, Minnesota, History and Early Association of the Karpis-Barker Gang Prior to the Abduction of Mr. Bremer.

[47]*Dallas Morning News*, July 25, 1933.

[48]*St. Paul Dispatch*, August 30, 1933; *St. Paul Pioneer Press*, August 31, 1933.

[49]*South St. Paul Reporter*, August 31, 1933.

[50]Lisa Lovering, "We Will Remember," .38 Special Press for police files.

[51]South St. Paul Centennial History, South St. Paul, South St. Paul Historical Society, 1987; *St. Paul Pioneer Press*, August 31, 1933.

[52]Lois A. Glewwe, author and editor, *West St. Paul Centennial 1889-1989. The History of West St. Paul, Minnesota*, West St. Paul, West St. Paul Centennial Book Committee, the Mayor, and City Council, 1989, p. 147; Paul Maccabee St. Paul Gangster History, 1981-1995, Research Files, Minnesota Historical Society.

[53]Federal Bureau of Investigation Headline Archives.

Chapter Six

Bremer Kidnapping

"You don't understand. I was offered a job as a hoodlum and I turned it down cold. A thief is anybody who gets out and works for his living like robbing a bank or breaking into a place and stealing stuff, or kidnapping somebody. He really gives some effort to it. A hoodlum is a pretty lousy sort of scum. He works for gangsters and bumps guys off after they have been put on the spot. Why, after I made my rep, some of the Chicago Syndicate wanted me to go to work for them as a hood—you know, handling a machine gun. They offered me two hundred and fifty dollars a week and all the protection I needed. I was on the lam at the time and not able to work at my regular line. But I wouldn't consider it. 'I'm a thief,' I said. 'I'm no lousy hoodlum.'"

—Alvin Karpis[1]

Buffalo, New York, had surpassed Minneapolis as the nation's milling center in 1930 due to the cheapness of water transport, and the Twin Cities' status as a commercial hub was effectively eclipsed. About all Minneapolis had to offer was a giant pool of unemployed miners, lumberjacks, railroad men, and millers; over 6,000 flour millers were laid off between 1919 and 1929. New industries did move in: linseed processing plants, silk mills, and clothing factories. But wages had lagged far behind the increase in the cost of living, and these were not happy factory workers.[2]

"Ma"—The Life and Times of "Ma" Barker and Her Boys

While the economy in the Twin Cities suffered, Ma's boys did not. Eight masked bandits held up two St. Paul Railway Express Company messengers at the door of their office on September 11, 1933, escaping with two large cash boxes police said contained between $60,000 and $100,000. The cash boxes were on a hand truck just inside the door of the express company office, near Union Station, ready to be delivered to Minneapolis.³

According to police, the eight robbers backed a big sedan under the depot concourse, not far from the express company office. Art J. Mangan, a guard, and B. Moles, a messenger, opened the door of the office to wheel out the truck carrying the cash containers. Five robbers quickly surrounded them.

The bandit leader, armed with a sawed-off shotgun, commanded the company employees to "stick 'em up and face the wall." Two bandits guarded the victims while the others hauled the truck to their waiting automobile and loaded the cash boxes into it. The stolen containers were thirty inches long, eighteen inches wide and eighteen inches high.

Two days later, the second of the two money chests stolen from Railway Express was found in the woods near Hayward, Wisconsin, 170 miles northeast of St. Paul. The first was located earlier in the day in St. Louis Park, Minneapolis suburb, along with the gang's automobile. Both chests had been stripped of their contents.

Two Wisconsin conservation wardens came upon four men in the woods near Hayward while the men were trying to conceal the 700 pound metal chest. The gangsters threatened to kill the wardens if they revealed their hiding place, but, the matter was reported and St. Paul authorities were notified. The box was located again and its top had been blown.

On September 13, 1933, four bandits, "believed to be the same men who hid a money chest stolen in St. Paul in Hayward [Wisconsin] yesterday," robbed the Union State Bank of Amery of $46,000 in cash and securities. The loot included $11,000 to $12,000 in cash and approximately $35,000 in securities, most of which were negotiable according to bank authorities.⁴

The robbers, believed to have been members of the Barker-Karpis Gang, broke into the bank the evening before the holdup by jimmying a rear door and hiding inside the bank. They overpowered two employees when they reported to work in the morning. The victims of the Amery holdup were O.M. Olson, assistant cashier, and B.H. Christensen, vice president.

When Olson entered the bank at 7:50 A.M., the four men stepped out from separate hiding places and covered him with a rifle, shotgun, and two pistols. One of the bandits demanded that Olson "put up his hands," and when he did so, another instructed him to put them back down. The leader, wearing a white mask, ordered him to give them the money from the vault.

As Olson was prodded toward the vault with a pistol jammed in his back, another kicked him and told him to hurry. As Olson was opening the safe in the vault, one of the robbers accused him of "stalling," and again reminded him he would blow his brains out if he didn't move faster. Again, the robber kicked Olson, admonishing him to "make it snappy."

The inner compartment of the safe was opened and the men forced Olson to hand over all the money, except for some pennies and other small change. With the robbery completed, Olson was taken to a back room and ordered to lie down on the floor.

While the robbery was taking place, one of the men had left the bank, apparently to get the car, which was parked up the street. As the bandits waited for their companion to return with the car, two of the men held pistols on Olson. The other stood by the door.

Lyle Luke, a twenty-year-old Amery grocery clerk, walked by the bank while the robbery was in progress and shouted to a waiting motorist, "Hey, fellow, your hub caps are missing." The driver got out, looked around, and courteously replied, "I guess you're right, kid. Thanks." Shortly afterwards, Luke learned that he had been conversing with one of the robbers.

After about twenty-five minutes elapsed, the bandit driver returned through the rear door. About the same time, B.H. Christensen, the bank's vice president, entered the bank, only to be greeted by a machine gun shoved into his ribs and a bandit ordering him to lie down on the floor next to Olson. The gunmen took extreme caution to avoid pursuit. They discovered two shotguns and two rifles belonging to their captives in a rear room and unloaded them. They also forced Olson to hand over the keys to his automobile that he had driven to the bank. Upon warning the two captives to remain quiet, the bandits departed through the back door.

The robbers, however, sped away in the same make of automobile that was used in hauling the money chest taken in the holdup of the St. Paul Railway Express robbery. Amery was only about eighty miles from the site in the Wisconsin woods where the men had dumped the chest.

Melvin Passolt, chief of the Minnesota Crime Bureau, told the press that there were strong indications that one gang had committed both jobs. "The fact that there were four men who took part in the Amery raid, coupled with the descriptions of the men tallying with those who hid the express company money chest, leads me to believe today's raid was committed by the same gang." The bankers telephoned police officers in surrounding communities in hopes of blocking the robbers' escape.

Ma and her mob retreated to Chicago, and in less than a month the newspapers reported the murder of a policeman during a Reserve Bank job. The murder occurred on September 22, 1933, as police officer Miles A. Cunningham endeavored to investigate an automobile accident near the intersection of Jackson Boulevard and Halsted Street. Officer Cunningham was unaware that a few moments before two bank messengers were held up by five men at Jackson Boulevard and Clark Street, seizing two sacks of registered mail, which proved to be of no value to the bandits.

As the messengers came out of the post office with the plainclothesmen, Freddie and Zeigler snatched the guns away from the cops and threw the mailbags into a Hudson. Doc whipped out into the middle of Jackson Boulevard in a Dodge, which left a thick cloud of greasy smoke over the street as the rest of the boys piled in. The two cars sped away over their planned escape route—one block west, another north, through an alley, a left turn on Adams, through the loop, across the river and Canal Street straight west on Adams.[5]

Everything seemed to be going smoothly until a car traveling in the opposite direction tried to squeeze through, causing a horrid crash with the Hudson. The accident took place in an area of skid row and police were on the scene at once. Doc began firing a .380 automatic from the side window while Bolton followed suit with a machine gun. One of Bolton's bullets caught Doc Barker in the hand causing him to let out a yell.

While the shooting continued, Freddie and Weaver stopped a Buick, kicked out its occupants, hauled in the mail bags, and the robbers swerved away down Ashland Avenue. Doc's keen eye noticed there was only a quarter tank of gas in the car. At Forty-eighth and Ashland, the boys threw a startled couple out of their four-door Ford sedan and again sped away; this time with a full tank of gas. Despite it all, they made it safely back to their hideout in Elmhurst.

Double jeopardy awaited them, however. In emptying the mailbags, they discovered that they had stolen checks but not a cent of cash. To make matters worse, they picked up a *Chicago Tribune* the following morning, only to be shocked by its headline, "Ten Thousand Police Hunt Cop Killers." Bolton, evidently, had hit one of the police officers when he opened up with the machine gun.[6]

It was time to skip town and head back to St. Paul. Picking up Ma, they drove back to Minnesota where they planned to get $5,000 from Sawyer and the same amount from Peifer. Word had preceded them about the botched Federal Reserve stickup and Peifer was quite angry with them.

That year William J. Harrison had become acquainted with members of the Karpis-Barker gang through Fred Goetz. Harrison originally was from St. Louis where he was born on September 27, 1900. He spent the major portion of his adolescent years in St. Louis. About 1926 he went to Calumet City, Illinois, where he operated numerous speakeasies during the prohibition era. He became acquainted with the Capone Syndicate of Chicago and fraternized with persons of such notoriety as "Killer" Burke, Gus Winkler and "Big" Homer Wilson. Harrison was a man of wide experience and as a result of his underworld activities was able to furnish members of the Karpis-Barker group some of their most valued contacts.

While various members of the Karpis-Barker Gang were on the rampage throughout the Middle West perpetrating bank robberies and kidnappings, Harry Campbell, a boyhood associate of the Barker brothers, committed a series of crimes in Oklahoma with Glen Leroy Wright and Charles

"Ma"—The Life and Times of "Ma" Barker and Her Boys

A story from a True Detective magazine on the Karpis-Barker Gang carried this photo of Wynona Burdette.

Cotner, who subsequently were incarcerated in the Oklahoma State Penitentiary. Harry Campbell was born on New Year's Day 1900 at McClintocville, Pennsylvania. His family later moved to Tulsa, Oklahoma, where he was released. Campbell joined the Barker boys, Volney Davis and Will Green. Green was later sentenced to serve a long term in the United States Penitentiary, Leavenworth, Kansas, and was one of the leaders of the gang which escaped in December 1931. Green later committed suicide rather than be apprehended.

In 1930 Campbell became acquainted with Wynona Burdette, a part Cherokee woman whose family was very poor. Wynona was one of more than a dozen children in the family. In the spring of 1933, Campbell frequented Casper, Wyoming, where it is alleged he engaged in safe-robbing, but he soon returned to Tulsa and remained in the company of Wynona Burdette. In September 1933, he received a communication from Fred Barker to join the gang at the Savoy Hotel, Hammond, Indiana, and was promised that there was big money to be had.

Campbell soon joined Fred Barker, Doc Barker, and William J. Harrison in Hammond, and at Campbell's request, Willie Harrison made arrangements for Wynona Burdette to join Campbell. The two Barkers, Harry Campbell and Wynona Burdette drove to St. Paul, where they joined other members of the gang who were temporarily located there. This group on or about October 6, 1933, motored to Reno, Nevada, where the gang had good contacts with the political bosses at that place.

Verne Miller's tombstone located in Huron's Riverside Cemetery. (Author's Collection)

On November 29, 1933, Verne Miller, the nation's most hunted outlaw at the time, was found murdered on the outskirts of Detroit—less than a month after he had shot his way out of a trap set by government agents. Although three mobsters had been slain during that single week through gang wars, authorities were certain Miller had been murdered by his friends because he had demanded they protect him from the government.[7]

His body—nude, strapped and bound, and wrapped in two blankets—was found in a roadside ditch on the north side of the city. Miller had been dumped from an automobile in typical gangland "ride" fashion. An examination showed that he had not been shot but instead, his skull had been crushed.

Alston Purvis, son of FBI Agent Melvin Purvis discussed Miller's demise with Brian Bull in a 2003 interview: "The theory that my father accepted was that he was found . . . I forget the town now, it was about 200 miles away they caught him in the bathtub and killed him there. And this disposal of the body—far away. It was that kind of murder was not unusual when they really wanted to wipe someone out. He was tied with clothesline, and his skull was bashed almost beyond recognition.

"They were sending a message at the same time they were killing him. That that kind of. . . . of . . . they were sending a message that that freelance operation that he was carrying out was not acceptable and was bringing heat down on them. He was not the only one put out that way, but certainly one of the better known ones."[8]

Detroit police had been hunting for Miller because of the September 22nd loop mail robbery in which Detroit Police Officer Miles Cunningham was shot to death and for an earlier mail robbery where $250,000 was obtained. But more importantly, police believed Miller was the man who fired the machine gun during the Kansas City Massacre.

After Miller's murder, a Detroit homicide detective and an FBI agent visited Harvey Bailey, Albert Bates, and Machine Gun Kelly at Leavenworth and asked the trio who might have killed Miller. Bailey and Bates refused to discuss it, other than Bailey saying he would have if he'd gotten the chance, but Kelly provided them with a long list of guys Miller had bumped off.[9]

Kelly included the 1930 "Fox Lake Massacre" at Manning's Resort on the Wisconsin border outside Chicago, in which three members of the Capone-allied Druggan-Lake mob were killed, which at the time had been attributed to the war between Capone and the North Side Moran–Aiello gang. According to Kelly, the killings were not a contract job or had nothing to do with the beer wars but were simply an act of vengeance because the three guys had killed Miller's friend Red McLaughlin (who did turn up in the Chicago River a few days after the Fox Lake killings).

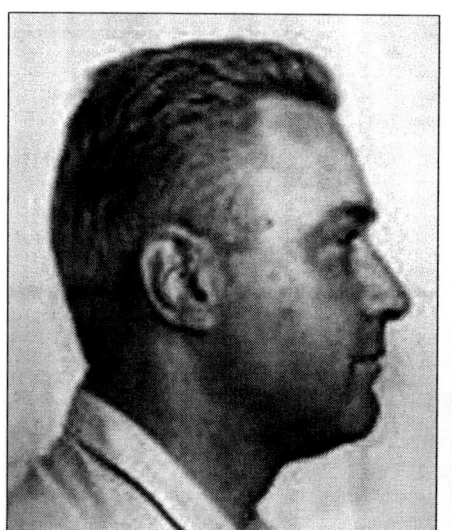 

1933 Memphis Police Department booking photo of Kelly.

As another example, Kelly mentioned that, also in 1930, Miller had killed Sam Stein, Frank Coleman, and Whitey Rusick at White Bear Lake because they had double crossed friends of his on a job in Kansas City. This trio had apparently been involved with Bailey, Kelly, Miller and others in the July 15, 1930, Willmar, Minnesota, bank robbery, in which the bandits made off with $70,000.

The FBI believed Miller was killed by the Eastern Syndicate, probably on orders of either Lepke Buchalter or Longy Zwillman. Miller had been connected to the New York mob for quite a while and his death certainly resembled a typical "Murder, Inc." job.

Many of Miller's former friends, including Alvin Karpis and Harvey Bailey, never really trusted Miller either, after they learned he had once been a lawman. Karpis told the Feds that he once asked Miller if he had been a sheriff in South Dakota. Miller denied the statement and conveyed that it was his cousin who had the same name who had been a sheriff. Later Karpis learned the truth and wanted nothing more to do with Miller. He had pretty much the same view of Bernard Phillips, a. k. a. Phil Courtney, who was a former Chicago policeman (and was probably murdered by Miller and Nash).

"Ma"—The Life and Times of "Ma" Barker and Her Boys

With a reward of $10,000 priced on his head, dead or alive, Miller had been the hottest criminal in the country. The same day, that the body was found, two Chicago women—Bobby Moore and Vivian Gibson—were being sentenced to a year and a day in the Alderson Federal Correctional Facility for having aided Miller in an earlier escape.

The Federal Prison at Alderson, West Virginia, had been dubbed the "College for Female Cons" by the press in the 1930s. Alderson played a major role in the commitments of the women who harbored the 1930s public enemies. Women from the Dillinger Gang, the Barker-Karpis and Nash/Holden Keating Gangs, and the assemblies of family members who helped Bonnie & Clyde, served time at Alderson between the years 1934 to almost 1940. They were all convicted of the Federal Harboring Law, Section 246, Title 18, U.S. Criminal Code, aiding and abetting in the escape of a fugitive. It was used to prosecute wives, girlfriends, mothers, and sisters of the notorious offenders of the 1930s Midwest and Southwest crime waves. Vivian Gibson was paroled late November/early December 1934.[10]

The *Minneapolis Journal* meanwhile reported that the city had undergone another hard year. The Minneapolis City Relief Fund was running in the red by September 1932. The relief demands were costing $7,000 per day and the mayor was deeply worried. Some federal aid the previous summer had created 8,000 jobs in the city, but the radicals continued to agitate on Bridge Square and politicians tried to no avail to inspire confidence in the minds of the voters.[11]

The Depression caused major changes in the political orientation of the citizens of Minneapolis and the entire state of Minnesota. For the first time in history, Minnesota gave its electoral votes to a Democratic nominee for the presidency in the 1932 election. Groups such as the Non-Partisan League, Farmer-Labor Association, and unrecognized unions found a voice in the Depression via Floyd B. Olson, a north Minneapolis native who became governor in January 1931.[12]

Although he was an avowed independent Farmer-Labor leader, Olson supported the candidacy of Franklin D. Roosevelt and became identified with the New Deal program. The *Journal* challenged Olson's campaign, however. Following Olson's sweeping victory, the *Journal* wrote, "While Governor Olson is a leader in the Farmer-Labor Party, he doubtless realizes that, as a party, it has no national future. He is too well grounded in logic and economics, moreover, to take stock in the more visionary of its projects. We believe he will carry on along safe and conservative lines for the most part, despite certain delusive and costly ideas of his party."[13]

Governor Floyd B. Olson enacted a state income tax to support state education and help limit the number of foreclosures of home mortgages. On a federal level, laws were passed that allowed the free organization of labor unions and the removal of restrictions upon them to enter into collective bargaining with their employers. This piece of legislation provided renewed life to unionization efforts in Minneapolis and the rest of the state.

During the national election of 1932, Herbert Hoover was up for re-election as president against Franklin D. Roosevelt who was seeking a first term. According to author David L. Rosheim, "The *Minneapolis Journal*, oblivious to the social conditions just outside their doorstep, endorsed Herbert Hoover for a second term, and Earle Brown for Minnesota governor."[14]

In its journalistic campaign to support Hoover, the *Journal* stated, "Why take a dangerous chance with a new and untried leadership, when a favorable trend in economic conditions is already under way, thanks to the measures the Hoover administration has taken and is taking."[15] In its "Where were the Jeremiahs?" editorial, the *Journal* attacked the Democratic Party for not having foreseen the Depression themselves, and pointed to Roosevelt's spending and taxing measures in New York State.[16]

Following Roosevelt's stunning electoral victory, 472 to 59, the *Journal* published an editorial straight from the philosophy of its owner, H. V. Jones: "We have had a bitter campaign full of partisan crimination and recrimination. This was perhaps inevitable in such tense times. But that is all over. The decision has been made with unprecedented partisanism. The nation should unitedly hold up the hands of its new president in his discharge of the momentous and critical task that has been entrusted to him."[17]

By 1934, however, Minnesota and the entire nation were devastated. Farm prices had plummeted and workers were out of work by the thousands.

"Ma"—The Life and Times of "Ma" Barker and Her Boys

Seventy percent of the iron range workers were jobless and farms were being lost through mortgage foreclosures. In Minneapolis and other cities, those fortunate to keep jobs, were suffering payroll cutbacks and were working extended hours for the same pay they had received earlier. In 1933, $9 million in relief costs were paid; one year later, the figure reached 33 million.[18]

On or about December 2, 1933, meanwhile, an automobile caravan left Reno. Among those who left Reno for St. Paul in December were Alvin Karpis and his moll, Dolores Delaney; sister-in-law to Pat Riley, a Dillinger mobster; Fred Barker and his girlfriend Paula Harmon; Volney Davis; Edna Murray; and Doc Barker. Harry Campbell and Wynona Burdette also accompanied Alvin Karpis and Fred Barker on their trek to St. Paul.

The members of the Karpis-Barker gang, with the exception of Alvin Karpis and Dolores Delaney, arrived in St. Paul in mid-December, 1933 and proceeded directly to the farm of Harry Sawyer, a bootlegger, ex-car thief and harborer of criminals. Harry Sawyer lived on a farm with his wife, Gladys, who also was an intimate associate of the gang.

Alvin Karpis and Dolores Delaney did not remain in St. Paul, but proceeded on to Chicago. Harry Campbell and Wynona Burdette, upon their arrival in St. Paul, took up residence at the Capital Hotel under the names of Mr. and Mrs. George Martin. Fred Barker and Paula Harmon rented an apartment at 628 Grand Avenue, under the names of Mr. and Mrs. Edwin Bergstrom. Volney Davis and Edna Murray, posing as Mr. and Mrs. V. E. Davis, moved into the Edgecumb Apartments, Osceola and Lexington. Doc Barker found shelter with William Weaver at his apartment at 777 Shelby Avenue. Weaver's girlfriend, Myrtle Eaton, native of Des Moines, Iowa, maintained an apartment at 565 Portland Avenue, which was frequented by the various members of the gang. Myrtle was a shoplifter and had been arrested by the Minneapolis Police Department on February 27, 1930, and fined $100. On December 9, 1930, as Sue Bond, alias Sue Hubble, she was arrested by St. Paul police for shoplifting, although these charges were later dismissed on motion of the County Attorney. On December 29, 1931, she was arrested by the police department at Des Moines, Iowa, as Mrs. Alice Martin on charges of investigation but again was not prosecuted.

"Ma"—The Life and Times of "Ma" Barker and Her Boys

In Chicago, Karpis, known to his friends as "Slim" or "Ray," and Dolores Delaney took up residency at the Orlando Hotel and later rented an apartment at 7133 Yates Avenue, under the names of Mr. and Mrs. William L. Lohman. Fred Goetz, with his girlfriend, Irene Dorsey, the daughter of a saloonkeeper, was living at 1954 Garfield Boulevard. Tubercular Bryan Bolton, alias Monte Carter, had been summoned from his health restoring activities in Arizona, and in December 1933, made his home with Goetz. Ma Barker was living quietly in an apartment on the exclusive South Shore Drive.

During the latter part of December 1933, Alvin Karpis and Fred Goetz joined the others in St. Paul where conferences were held to lay plans for a second kidnapping. These meetings were held in the apartments occupied by William Weaver and Myrtle Eaton, and were attended by Alvin Karpis, William Weaver, Fred Goetz, Doc Barker, Fred Barker, Volney Davis, Harry Campbell, and Harry Sawyer. One day Sawyer and Goetz visited a bowling alley and selected Edward George Bremer, scion of one of the wealthiest and most prominent families in St. Paul, as their victim.

Karpis had second thoughts about abducting Bremer but Sawyer told him all they had to do was hold Bremer for a couple of days and they'd get $200,000 out of it. Bremer was a big name, however—bigger even than Hamm—and his father had given $350,000 into Franklin Roosevelt's 1932 presidential campaign.[19]

Karpis had loaned his favorite Buick to Phil Courtney, and when he stopped at McCormick's Restaurant for coffee the next morning, a girl named Louise, whom he had promised to take riding, was visibly upset with him. When he inquired why she was mad, she handed him a newspaper showing a photograph of his Buick and a shocking headline which read, "Two Women Found Slain in Buick."

Indian Rose Walker, one of the slain was the widow of Bobby Walker, who had been killed in the Denver Mint robbery. The other woman was named Marjorie Schwartz. Both victims had been shot through the head; the car shoved into a snow bank where a group of farmers had to pull it out.

"Ma"—The Life and Times of "Ma" Barker and Her Boys

Karpis rushed over to the Green Lantern to tell the story to Harry Sawyer, but Sawyer had already heard about it. According to Sawyer, the two women found in the Buick had set a trap for a certain banker, but he had found out about it, and made arrangements to have the women killed. He had guaranteed $50 thousand dollars for the killings but hadn't paid a cent.

The banker had handled the Denver Mint bonds, and when he learned of the girls following him, he asked Sawyer to have them killed. Sawyer hated people that didn't pay up and the man with the Denver Mint bonds kept him sore for a long time. Bankers were a source of frustration and anger for Sawyer at the time, and when he learned of Edward Bremer in St. Paul, he immediately despised him. "I want him grabbed," he told Karpis.

The gang had originally planned to rob the Commercial State Bank, St. Paul, of which Edward George Bremer was president, but Sawyer in his dictatorial manner insisted that more money could be obtained if "Eddie Bremer was snatched." Definite plans were made for the kidnapping of Bremer, who was the son of Adolph Bremer, part owner of the Jacob Schmidt Brewing Company, and the nephew of Otto Bremer, Chairman of the American National Bank, St. Paul, and Manager of the Home Owners' Loan Corporation.

But on the night of January 13, 1934, the gang held a conference at Myrtle Eaton's apartment at the Kensington Apartments in St. Paul. Northwest Radio Operator Roy McCord, meanwhile, had been told by neighbors that peeping toms had been lurking the previous night at a friend's apartment and decided to investigate.[20]

McCord, who had the misfortune of looking like a policeman, was wearing his Northwest Airlines aviator's uniform, a military-appearing hat, and a dark jacket with brass buttons. About one o'clock in the morning, McCord and a friend spotted three suspicious men in a coupe riding down the alley behind and began tailing them. When he pulled up next to them and stopped, one of the occupants in the other car opened up on him with a machine gun. McCord was seriously injured.

Alvin Karpis later wrote: "We were sitting around an apartment in St. Paul where Bill Weaver lived with a shoplifter named Myrtle Eaton, when someone noticed a guy peeping through a window of an apartment across the alley." Karpis and Freddie dashed outside and jumped into their Chevy sedan with Freddie at the wheel. Karpis told Freddie to pull around a corner and stop suddenly, and when he did, Karpis leaped out with a machine gun. "I must have thrown twenty or thirty slugs into the cop car," wrote Karpis. "When we drove away that time, nobody was following us."[21]

After this occurrence, Harry Sawyer insisted that because of the heat the shooting had caused, the kidnapping of Mr. Bremer be postponed. The postponement, however, lasted only four days.

Everyday during the school year, Edward George Bremer drove his nine-year-old daughter "Hertzy" to the Summit School, a private educational facility located on Goodrich Avenue near Lexington. After taking Hertzy to school he would proceed up Goodrich, cross Lexington Avenue, and adhere to his duties at the bank. Each morning he brought his car to a stop at the traffic sign located at Lexington and Goodrich Avenues. This stop was made about a half a block from the apartment building occupied by Edna Murray and Volney Davis.

On January 17, 1934, Bremer, in keeping with his usual custom, drove his daughter to school and arrived at the stop sign at Lexington and Goodrich Avenues between the hours of 8:30 and 9:00 A.M. When he made the stop, a man approached the left front door of the Lincoln sedan Bremer drove, held a pistol to his side and told him "to move over." An accomplice opened the right front door of the car, struck Bremer over the head several times with a blunt instrument and pushed him to the floor of the car with his head under the instrument board. Taped goggles were placed over his eyes. Edward Bremer had been kidnapped by five men using two automobiles. Doc, Karpis, Harry Campbell, and William Weaver drove Bremer to their Bensenville, Illinois, hideout.

An eye-witness of the abduction told police of seeing a big sedan stop Bremer's car at Lexington and Goodrich Avenues, just one block beyond the school. James Quinehan, 582 Aurora Avenue, a driver for the Minnesota Milk Company, was found by an Associated Press reporter. Quinehan said he had seen the abduction between 8:20 and 8:30 A.M. Wednesday morning.[22]

"Ma"—The Life and Times of "Ma" Barker and Her Boys

Quinehan did not at first realize he had seen the kidnapping, but became convinced of it Friday morning after conversations with Miss Louise Bremer, 855 West Seventh Street, sister of the missing banker, and Mrs. Joseph N. Mounts, 1278 Lincoln Avenue, wife of the secretary of Police Chief Thomas E. Dahill, to whose homes he delivered milk. Quinehan also delivered milk to the home of Otto Bremer, 1344 Summit Avenue, uncle of the missing man and state manager of the Home Owners Loan Corporation

"I was driving east on Goodrich Avenue," related Quinehan, "until I reached Dunlap Street, where I stopped to let a bunch of kids cross the street to the school nearby. A block away, I saw two automobiles. The Bremer car had stopped before crossing Lexington Avenue, an arterial highway, when suddenly another big sedan pulled up squarely in front of it. It looked to me like an accident. It was between 8:20 and 8:30 A.M.

"I turned my head a moment to say, 'Hello' to some of the kids and when I looked back again I saw the kidnappers' automobile moving away with the Bremer car following. I must have stopped there about two minutes. I didn't see any of the men in the cars and I couldn't identify them."[23]

At about 10:40 A.M. on January 17, 1934, St. Paul Contractor Walter Magee, a close friend of the Bremer family, received a telephone call at his office, 118 West Central Avenue, in St. Paul from a man who gave his name as Charles McKee. The caller informed Mr. Magee that "they" had his friend Bremer and that Magee was to go outside his office where he would find a note. Magee complied with this instruction and immediately went to the side of the building in which his office was located, and there, under a side door, found a ransom note addressed to him as "Chas. McGee," which read as follows:

"You are hereby declared in on a very desperate undertaking. Don't try to cross us. Your future and E's are the important issue. Follow these instructions to the letter. Police have never helped in such a spot and won't this time either. You better take care of the payoff first and let them do the detecting later. Because the police usually butt in, your friend isn't none too comfortable now, so don't delay the payment. We demand $200,000. Payment must be made in five and ten dollar bills—no new money—no consecutive numbers—

large variety of issues. Place the money in two large suit box cartons big enough to hold the full amount and tie with heavy cord. No contact will be made until you notify us that you are ready to pay as we direct. You place an ad in the *Minneapolis Tribune* as soon as you have the money ready. Under the personal column (We are ready Alice.) You will then receive your final instructions. Be prepared to leave at a minute's notice to make the payoff. Don't attempt to stall or outsmart us. Don't try to bargain. Don't plead poverty we know how much they have in their banks. Don't try to communicate with us we'll do the directing. Threats aren't necessary—you just do your part—we guarantee to do ours."[24]

Also included was a note of verification from Bremer or someone posing as the kidnap victim, which read, "Mr. Chas. McGee. I have named you as payoff man. You are responsible for my safety. I am responsible for the full amount of the money. (Signed) E.G. Bremer. Deal only when signature is used. Chas. McGee. Personal."

The St. Paul Field Division for the Federal Bureau of Investigation, United States Department of Justice, and the St. Paul Police Department were immediately notified and an investigation commenced into the second major St. Paul kidnapping within six months.[25] The automobile which Bremer had been driving at the time he was kidnapped was found on the date the kidnapping occurred parked on Edgcumbe Road. The bloodstains on the steering wheel, the gear shift lever, the doorsill, the back of the front seat and on the floor of the car indicated to the investigators that a struggle had occurred. Relatives feared Bremer had been murdered.[26]

About six o'clock on the morning of January 20, 1934, Dr. H.T. Nippert received a telephone call and a voice told him to go to the vestibule of his home at 706 Lincoln Avenue, and see what he could find. Dr. Nippert immediately went downstairs and found that a bottle had been thrown through the plate glass front door. The doctor asserted that there was no message of any kind inside the bottle but he thought possibly it was a signal from the kidnappers, perhaps indicating the next contact might be made through him.[27]

Dr. Nippert's home was set back about thirty to forty feet from the sidewalk and the bottle made a clean hole through the plate-glass door one-fourth of an inch thick, continuing on to shatter against the inner door of the vestibule and cracking the glass. Nippert concluded the bottle must have been hurled with considerable force by someone standing only a few feet from the door.

Dr. Nippert was convinced the bottle was not thrown by a prankster, but by someone with a definite purpose. The physician had been a friend of the Bremer family for all of twenty years, and if the bottle incident was an indication he had been chosen as a contact person, he told police he would gladly assume responsibility.

"I would be perfectly willing to act as a contact man if I could be of any use to the Bremer family and help to end their long suspense," asserted the sixty-five-year-old physician.

Two days later, about 9:45 P.M., a large sedan stopped in front of Dr. Nippert's home, the car lights were flashed on twice, the porch light of the home came on for a second, and the car raced away. This time Dr. Nippert found an envelope addressed to him which apparently had been left under the door.

Two other envelopes were in the one addressed to Mr. Nippert. One of the enclosed envelopes was addressed to Walter Magee and the other to Mrs. Edward Bremer. Dr. Nippert promptly delivered the envelopes to Adolph Bremer. In the one addressed to Walter Magee was a note beginning "Chas. McGee" which read as follows:

"You must be proud of yourself by now. If Bremer don't get back his family, [he] has you to thank. You've made it almost impossible but were going to give one more chance—the last. First of all, all coppers must be pulled off. Second the dough must be ready. Third we must have a new signal. When you are ready to meet our terms, place a N.R.A. sticker in the center of each of your office windows. We'll know if the coppers are pulled or not. Remain at your office daily from noon until 8.00 P.M. Have the dough ready and where you can get it within thirty minutes. You will be instructed how to deliver it. The money must not be hot as it will be examined before Bremer is released. If Dahill is so hot to meet us you can send him out with the dough. Well try to be ready for any trickery if attempted. This is positively our LAST attempt. DONT duck it."

Included was a second note reading: "Mr. Chas. McGee. I have named you as payoff man. You are responsible for my safety. I am responsible for the full amount of the money. E.G. Bremer."

There was also a note in the handwriting of Edward Bremer addressed to Dr. H.T. Nippert, Lowry Building, St. Paul, Minnesota, which read as follows: "Dear Doctor: I am enclosing herewith two letters which please dilivir [sic} for me at once. Diliver [sic] them both to my father at the house—655 West 7th St. or at the office, wherever he may be—it is very important that they be dilivered [sic] right away as it means a lot to me. Be sure however not to say a word to anyone else that you have been given these letters to diliver [sic]. The reason I am writing to you is because I know you can be trusted not to say anything. Edward G. Bremer."

There were also two notes written in the handwriting of Mr. Bremer, one addressed to "Dear Walter" and the other to Mrs. Edward Bremer, in which Bremer addressed her as "Dearest Patz.": "Dear Walter: I'm sorry to have called on you but I felt you were the old standby. Assure Emily and Pat that I'm all right. I knew you would use your head & work on this all alone—no police. The people that have me have given the impression that you are not working alone. Walter, please do. I know you will for me. I've been told that the reason the first plan was not gone through with was because you were working with the police. Again I say please work all alone & I'm sure everything will come out all right. Be sure now—no strings allow[d] here. You & You alone. These people are going to give you a new plan. Work according to their directions—& again I say—alone—no police—just you. Edward E.G. Bremer."

The other read: "Dearest Patz. Please don't worry. I hope everything will come out all right. Tell Hertzy to be good little girl, her daddy is thinking of her all the time and to see you or her again is all that I want. I suppose you are worrying about the blood in the car. I have a cut on my head which bled a lot but it has been dressed & is all right now. Tell Pa too [sic] not to worry. I'm treated nice & the only thing I have to ask is to keep the police out of this so that I am returned to you all safely. Yours, Ed."

On January 21st, well authenticated sources stated that the abductors had conveyed a signal to the Bremer family for launching final negotiations, although definite contact had not been established. The same sources hinted that contact would be made with Walter Magee sometime that day through an unidentified third party. Disclosure of the pending contact, coming after a secret conference of postal authorities and city and county law enforcement officers, was preceded by an assertion by Chief of Police Dahill that he was confident that Bremer was unharmed.[28]

"He is okay," the chief told reporters. "There is no need to start worrying until Sunday or Monday."

Lending credence to the report of the impending contact with the kidnappers with the possibility of a ransom payment over the weekend, it was learned that old five, ten, and twenty dollar bills were transferred Friday at noon from the Ninth District Federal Reserve Bank in Minneapolis to the American National Bank in St. Paul, of which Otto Bremer, uncle of the missing man, was chairman of the board.

The bills, the numbers non-consecutive in accordance of instructions from the kidnappers, were in five black satchels and were transferred in the armored money truck of a national detective agency. Earlier Saturday, W. C. Robertson, Minneapolis postmaster, received an anonymous letter addressed to him in an unstamped envelope, stating that Bremer had been killed and signed "one of the gang." Police branded the letter a hoax.

Other developments included disclosures by a young man that he had seen a mysterious car following Mr. Bremer's automobile several days before the kidnapping. Investigation of reports that six or seven "big guns" of gangdom were registered in a Twin City hotel about ten days prior to the kidnapping and considerable police activities running down baseless rumors which flooded St. Paul.

Authorities searched the area around Anoka, Minnesota, on the strength of an anonymous letter received Saturday in Minneapolis and stating Mr. Bremer had been killed "by accident" and his body hidden near that city. The letter was believed to have been another hoax but authorities were searching regardless of this belief.[29]

The name of a man who allegedly witnessed the delivery of the initial message from the kidnappers was not divulged, but it was learned from authoritative sources that he had told his story to police. He was standing in front of a store on West Central Avenue about 10 A.M. Wednesday. It was reported that he told police when a large, black sedan, similar to that believed to have been used by the kidnappers, passed him going east on Central Avenue.

His attention was drawn to the automobile, he said, because it went through a stop signal at Rice Street and Central Avenue. As the car passed him, drawing closer to the curb, he observed that a blanket had been thrown over some object on the floor in the back seat. The car stopped in front of Mr. Magee's office at 118 West Central Avenue, and one man jumped out carrying a piece of white paper in his hand. He ran towards the back of Magee's office building while the car continued slowly down the street.

Nothing further was heard from the kidnappers until the morning of January 22, 1934, when Mr. William P. Behrens arrived at his office, the Behrens-Whitman Coal Company, 972 West 7th Street, St. Paul, Minnesota, where he was given a note. The message had been found that morning by Mr. C. A. Stahlmann, when he arrived at Mr. Behrens' office where he was employed as a bookkeeper. Mr. Stahlmann found upon opening the door to the office an envelope with a typewritten address to Walter Magee or Adolph Bremer. Behrens opened the note and found the following typewritten message:

"Chas. Magee: If you can wait O.K. with us. You people shot a lot of curves trying to get somebody killed then the copper's will be heroes but Eddie will be the marteer [sic]. The copper's think that['s] great but Eddie don't. We're done taking the draws and you can go _____ now. From now on you make the contact. Better not try it till you pull off every copper, newspaper, and radio station. From now on you get the silent treatment until you reach us someway yourself. Better not wait too long."

In an effort to operate unmolested, the kidnappers demanded that the law enforcement agencies cease investigation. Edward's father, Adolph, a personal friend of President Franklin D. Roosevelt and Minnesota Governor Floyd B. Olson, begged law enforcement agencies to cease their efforts to free his son. "Wait, don't make a move that will endanger Eddie's safety," he pleaded with officers. With an undetermined number of Federal Department of Justice Investigators in town, as well as the city police and the State Bureau of Criminal Apprehension, feared for his son's life, should authorities press the search for the kidnappers too diligently.[30] A heavy police guard was placed in the home of Adolph Bremer. At least six detectives, headed by a high ranking police official, were at the home.[31]

Joseph B. Keenan, assistant United States attorney general, announced in Washington that Federal agents sent to St. Paul on the kidnapping "will take no action to jeopardize the safe return of Mr. Bremer." St. Paul Police continued their "hands off" policy.[32]

A twenty-three-year-old taxicab driver caused a furor when he displayed a purported note from the kidnappers but later admitted it was a hoax he had perpetrated to gain notoriety.

Friends of Edward Bremer asserted they were not alarmed over bloodstains found in his automobile, saying the banker was quick-tempered and probably struggled with his captors, receiving a bloody nose or other minor wound in the fracas.

Since the initial news of the abduction, a score of detectives had been kept each night at the Public Safety Building and Chief Dahill and Inspector Charles Tierney, head of the kidnap squad, remained there all night. Werner Hanni, Northwest chief of the Department of Justice division of investigation, also remained in his office in the post office until a late hour, but he was complying with the request Adolph Bremer to maintain the "hands off" policy.

In ill health and considerably upset, though bearing up fairly well, friends said the elder Bremer maintained a vigil with his unmarried daughter, Miss Louise Bremer, in their home near the Schmidt Brewing property. He voiced his plea after hopes had evaporated that the abductors would communicate either with the family or friends that night.[33]

For a time there was expectation that a contact might be made, chiefly because of an advertisement inserted in a morning Minneapolis newspaper in accordance with the kidnappers' instructions. Authorities agreed to abide by Adolph Bremer's wishes so that he would have a free hand in negotiating the freedom of his son.

"I am sorry the impression has been spread that information has been given to the police," Adolph Bremer said at his home. "Whatever information has been passed out has been given against my will and has created a false impression. Chief of Police Thomas Dahill has been fine in offering every help he can give us and we all appreciate it, but we do not want the police or the State or Federal authorities to do anything about it now. We want to get Eddie back home safe."

The advertisement that appeared in the *Minneapolis Tribune* read: "We are ready. Alice." The advertisement was interpreted as notification that the family was ready to pay the ransom.

Upon learning of the Bremer kidnapping, Frank J. Balke, Department of Justice Agent, who had played a prominent part in the Charles F. Urschell kidnapping case in Oklahoma, left Dallas on an airplane for St. Paul. Urschell, the millionaire oil magnate, had paid a ransom equal to that demanded by the Bremer kidnappers. Simultaneously, M. F. Kinkead, Ramsey County attorney, canceled a trip to Florida, and returned from Cedar Rapids, Iowa.

Mr. Bremer's abduction was the fifth in St. Paul within the past two-and-a-half years. William Hamm, Jr., had paid the largest sum—$100,000—for his freedom. St. Paulites Leon Gleckman, a finance company head; Morris Rutman, a dress shop owner; and Haskell Bohn, son of a well-to-do refrigerator owner, had paid $28,400 for their freedom. In addition, Eugene Gluek, son of a wealthy Minneapolis brewer, had been kidnapped in 1930, but was freed after one day without the ransom being paid.

Considerable excitement was generated meanwhile when two automobiles loaded with heavily armed deputies led by Sheriff John P. Wall of Hennepin County, raced westward out of Minneapolis to investigate a tip that gangsters, possibly the Bremer kidnappers, were in a hangout at a cottage on Medicine Lake. Residents about the lake had reported that two airplanes had landed on the lake the past two days, and said that there was unusual activity at the summer cottage with two large cars coming and going at all hours of the night.[34]

The tip, however, turned out to be worthless. Upon his return to Minneapolis, Sheriff Wall proclaimed that the ownership of the planes and cars had been established and had nothing to do with any the gangster activities.

However on that very same day, January 23, 1934, Mr. John Miller, 1209 Hague Avenue, St. Paul, received a telephone call between six and seven o'clock in the evening. The caller instructed Miller to go to his home and there he would find a Hill Brothers Coffee can on his front porch. Reaching home, Miller found that his wife had already discovered the note. This note instructed them that $200,000 must be delivered that night and the note was addressed to Chas. McGee or Adolph Bremer. It insisted that the tag which was enclosed with the note be taken to the Jefferson Lines Bus Station. This tag was a baggage check. This note carried a warning that the recipients of this note should not stall and were to follow instructions. The note further related that the baggage check was for the baggage checking locker in the waiting room of the station and further indicated that a handbag would be found at the bus station in which additional instructions would be contained. Mr. Magee was instructed that this handbag should not be opened one minute before 8:20 P.M.[35]

Walter Magee followed the instructions and proceeded to the bus depot where he found a black zipper bag which contained a pillow and an additional note, instructing him to assume the name of John B. Brakesham and to board a bus leaving St. Paul, at 8:40 P.M. for Des Moines, Iowa. The pay-off, however, was not accomplished on this night and it was subsequently learned by the investigators that a ransom note purporting to have been signed in ink by Mr. E. G. Bremer had been left at the New Hotel Brunswick, Faribault, Minnesota, by a man who was dressed in overalls and appeared to be a farmer. This individual stated to Arthur Murray, who was at the hotel, that a bus from the Twin Cities would arrive at Faribault about 10:30 P.M. and that he wanted to leave a package with Mr. Murray to give to a passenger on the bus and claimed that the package contained medicine, the man's father having forgotten to take it with him. As no one called for the package, it was held for one month by Mr. Murray before it was opened. When opened, it was found to contain a note addressed to "Chas. Magee" or pay-off man (John B. Brakesham). The note stated that all previous instructions were canceled.

On January 24th, Harry Bachman, salesman for a St. Paul wholesale grocery concern, told Duluth police that he may have crossed paths with members of the kidnapping gang. Bachman said while he was traveling north on Highway 1, two automobiles, one preceding and one following him, refused to allow him to pass the front car for two miles north of Hinckley. When he finally succeeded in passing the front car, he saw what he believed to be a pile of blankets on the back seat. A roughly dressed man wearing glasses was driving.[36]

Several miles further on, Bachman stopped in Sandstone and the two cars continued north. Later on, he passed both cars, and as he did so, one of the drivers leaned out the window and shouted, "You _____, beat it!"

Bachman reported the incident to State Highway Patrolmen at Moose Lake, and later that same evening two officers visited St. Paul Police headquarters, and following a conference with Chief Dahill, dictated a statement to a police stenographer. Neither of the patrolmen would divulge the nature of their report, and Chief Dahill said it was "nothing important."

Police, however, did consider the information significant, since the $100,000 ransom for William Hamm, Jr., the past summer had been thrown out of a car on Highway 1 near this same spot where the two cars had been seen by Bachman.

During the negotiations for the safe return of Edward Bremer, John Dillinger, whose banditry and depredations had caused the state of Indiana to mobilize the National Guard, was captured and tucked away in the Lake County Jail in Crown Point, Indiana. Dillinger was to await trial on an indictment charging him with the murder of Policeman William Patrick O'Malley during a holdup of the First National Bank of East Chicago January 15th.[37]

Dillinger arrived at approximately 7:35 P.M., approximately twenty-six hours after four Indiana law enforcement officials carried him, screaming and fighting, aboard an American Airlines plane in Tucson, Arizona where he and three members of his gang had been arrested. Manacled and meek, Dillinger was quickly transported to Chicago where no less than one hundred twenty policemen waited for him as guards.

"Ma"—The Life and Times of "Ma" Barker and Her Boys

From September 1933 until July 1934 Dillinger and his gang had terrorized the Midwest, killing ten men, wounding seven others, robbing banks and police arsenals, and staging three jail breaks—killing a sheriff during one and wounding two guards in another.[38]

John Herbert Dillinger was born on June 22, 1903, in the Oak Hill section of Indianapolis, a middle-class residential neighborhood. His father, a hardworking grocer, raised him in an atmosphere of disciplinary extremes, harsh and repressive on some occasions, but generous and permissive on others. John's mother died when he was three, and when his father remarried six years later, John resented his stepmother.

During adolescence, the flaws in his personality became evident and he was frequently in trouble. Finally, he quit school and took a job in a machine shop in Indianapolis. Although intelligent and a good worker, he soon became bored and often stayed out all night. His father, worried that the temptations of the city were corrupting his teenaged son, sold his property in Indianapolis and moved his family to a farm near Mooresville, Indiana. However, John reacted no better to rural life than he had to that in the city and soon began to run wild again.

A break with his father and trouble with the law because of auto theft, led him to enlist in the Navy. There he soon got into trouble and deserted his ship when it docked in Boston. Returning to Mooresville, he married sixteen-year-old Beryl Hovius in 1924 and the couple went to live in Indianapolis. Dillinger had no luck finding work in the city so he joined the town pool shark, Ed Singleton, in his search for easy money.

John Dillinger. (Courtesy Library of Congress)

Their first attempt occurred when they attempted to holdup a Mooresville grocer, but both were quickly and easily apprehended. Singleton pleaded not guilty, stood trial, and was sentenced to two years. Dillinger, following his father's advice, confessed, was convicted of assault and battery with intent to rob and conspiracy to commit a felony, and received joint sentences of two to fourteen years and ten to twenty years in the Indiana State Prison. Stunned by the harsh sentence, Dillinger became a tortured, bitter man in prison.

His period of infamy began on May 10, 1933, when he was paroled from prison after serving 8 1/2 years of his sentence. Almost immediately, Dillinger robbed a bank in Bluffton, Ohio. By then he had begun dating a sister of a convict named Mary Longnaker, who had been living in a boarding house at Dayton, Ohio. The police were alerted to this and on September 22, 1933, Dillinger was arrested there while he visited her. He was lodged in the county jail in Lima, Ohio, to await trial.

In frisking Dillinger, the Lima police found a document which seemed to be a plan for a prison break, but the prisoner denied knowledge of any plan. Four days later, using the same plans, eight of Dillinger's friends escaped from the Indiana State Prison, using shotguns and rifles which had been smuggled into their cells. During their escape, they shot two guards. All of the escapees got away except for Joseph Jenkins, who after being thrown from the getaway car, managed to commandeer a vehicle driven by a youth who was able to escape after tricking Jenkins into checking the gas tank. Jenkins was later shot and killed by local posse members on alert in Beanblossom, Indiana.

On October 12th, three of the escaped prisoners and a parolee from the same prison showed up at the Lima jail where Dillinger was incarcerated. They told Sheriff Jesse Sarber that they had come to return Dillinger to the Indiana State Prison for violation of his parole. When the suspicious sheriff asked to see their credentials, one of the men pulled a gun, shot him, and beat him into unconsciousness. Then taking the keys to the jail, the bandits freed Dillinger, locked the sheriff's wife and a deputy in a cell, and leaving the sheriff to die on the floor, made their getaway.

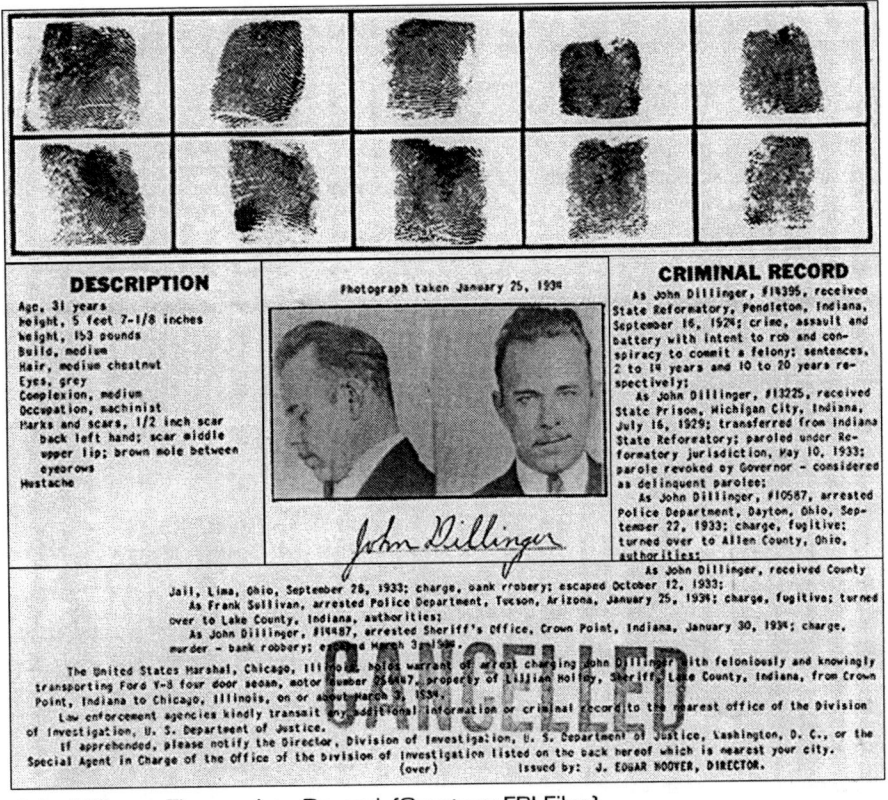

John Dillinger Fingerprints Record. (Courtesy FBI Files)

Although none of these men had violated a Federal law, the FBI's assistance was requested in identifying and locating the criminals. The four men were identified as Harry Pierpont, Russell Clark, Charles Makley, and Harry Copeland. Their fingerprint cards in the FBI Identification Division were flagged with red metal tags, indicating that they were wanted.

During the gang's stay in Chicago, several important events were to transpire. On November 15th, Dillinger, with his new girlfriend, Evelyn "Billie" Frechette, narrowly escaped a police ambush set up when an informant had notified the police that Dillinger would be seeing a dermatologist named Dr. Charles Eye. Dillinger eluded his pursuers after having his vehicle shot up in a high speed chase.

Dillinger and his gang, meanwhile, executed several bank robberies and even plundered the police arsenals at Auburn, Indiana, and Peru, Indiana, stealing several machine guns, rifles, and revolvers, a quantity of ammunition, and several bulletproof vests. On November 20th, the gang carried out a daring robbery in Racine, Wisconsin. With shots being fired, they escaped behind a shield of hostages. Then on December 14th, John Hamilton mortally wounded Sergeant William Shanley, when the detective tried to capture him in a garage where he had followed a lead on a gang vehicle being repaired there.

With the heat on and the development by the Chicago police of a special unit called "the Dillinger Squad," it was decided by the gang that they should lay low for awhile. Dillinger reportedly dyed his hair red and grew a mustache. John and Billie joined Makley, Clark, and Hamilton in Daytona Beach, Florida. On Christmas Eve, Dillinger and Billie had a violent argument which culminated with Dillinger beating her and throwing her out the following morning, providing her with a $1,000 and the keys to his car as a parting gesture.

Dillinger returned north two weeks later to go after Billie in her home state of Wisconsin. He and Hamilton decided to rob the First National Bank in East Chicago, Indiana, on January 15th. During the getaway Patrolman William O'Malley fired shots at Dillinger only to have them bounce off the bulletproof vest the outlaw was wearing. In the exchange of fire that followed Dillinger shot and killed the officer. Hamilton was wounded by police fire and was helped by Dillinger to the getaway car.

On January 23, 1934, Makley and Clark were forced out of hiding at the Hotel Congress in Tucson, Arizona, by a fire that broke out in the hotel that morning. One of the firemen, having recognized them from a crime magazine photo, notified the sheriff. Local police arrested them and also seized three Thompson submachine guns, two Winchester rifles mounted as machine guns, five bulletproof vests, and more than $25,000 in cash, part of it from the East Chicago robbery.

The same day, Dillinger and Billie Frechette arrived in town for the reunion of the gang. They did manage to meet on the 25th, but acting on a tip, the police first arrested Makley, and then Clark, at the house they had been staying in since the hotel fire. Later, following leads, the police were able to capture Pierpont. Dillinger, unaware of these events, arrived at the house where Makley and Clark had been grabbed, and was arrested by officers just as they were setting up their stakeout.

Dillinger became a national news item during his incarceration in the Pima County jail. Newspapermen and photographers poured in from around the country. While Dillinger and his gang gave interviews, there was much legal wrangling behind the scenes over which state would win extradition. He was eventually extradited to Indiana to stand trial for the O'Malley killing. The other three were sent to Ohio to be tried for killing Sheriff Sarber in the Lima breakout. Billie Frechette, arrested with Dillinger, was released.

On January 30th, the plane carrying Dillinger and his guards arrived at Chicago Municipal Airport. Waiting at the airport was a large contingent of police, in addition to the Dillinger Squad. With sirens wailing, the car carrying the outlaw was accompanied by a caravan of vehicles and motorcycle cops. Arriving at the sheriff's office in Crown Point, Indiana, he was greeted by numerous reporters with whom he cracked jokes. Photographers convinced Dillinger and Prosecutor Estill to pose, Dillinger cheerfully leaning his arm on his prosecutor's shoulder, with the sheriff looking congenially on.

The arraignment for the O'Malley killing took place on February 9, 1934. Louis Piquett, a Chicago attorney who specialized in representing underworld characters, acted as his lawyer. Following some legal maneuvering, Judge William J. Murray, set the trial for March 3rd. During the succeeding weeks there was little concern about a jailbreak, for along with the escape-proof reputation of the county jail and the fifty guards employed there, the sheriff had added armed citizens and National Guardsmen. Dillinger was sequestered at the county jail in Crown Point, Indiana, to await trial for the murder of the East Chicago police officer.

On February 5, 1934 Miss Lillian L. Dickman, secretary to Edward G. Bremer, received a note from a man who came to the back door of her home between 7:30 and 8:00 o'clock P.M. The man who delivered this note asked, "Are you Lillian Dickman" and when receiving a reply in the affirmative the man handed her a note and told her to take care of it. This note, which was in the handwriting of the kidnapped victim, was delivered to Adolph Bremer, urging that the ransom negotiations proceed in accordance with the instructions outlined by the kidnappers.[39]

The following day at about 4:30 P.M., Father Deere, a Catholic priest of Prior Lake, Minnesota, was approached by an unknown man at the door of his home who asked him if he was acquainted with a family by the name of Bremer. When the stranger learned that Father Deere knew the Bremer family, he thrust an envelope into his hand, containing a note addressed to Father Deere instructing him to deliver additional notes, which were in the envelope, to Adolph Bremer and Edward Bremer's wife. The note which was to be delivered to Adolph Bremer bore the salutation "Chas. McGee or Honest Adolph" and stated that "the coppers jimmied the last payoff." This note gave explicit instructions for the payment of the ransom money and warned that if the money was not paid on this particular night the ransom demand would be increased to $500,000.

Special agents of the Federal Bureau of Investigation worked quietly so as not to interfere with the payment of the ransom money if it were the family's desire to do so. Immediately after the first demand for ransom had been made, special agents caused the serial numbers of the ransom bills to be recorded, which act proved to be of inestimable value in subsequent investigations.

In compliance with the instructions contained in the ransom note addressed to "Chas. McGee or Honest Adolph," Walter Magee, on the evening of February 6, 1934, obtained a Ford sedan and with the $200,000 in ransom money consisting of five and ten dollar bills, drove in a circuitous route to 969 University Avenue, St. Paul. He arrived at approximately 8:00 P.M., where he found parked in front of that address a 1933 Chevrolet coupe bearing Shell Oil Company signs on each door. Mr. Magee transferred the ransom money from the Ford coupe and entered the Chevrolet car with the ransom money. In the left front door pocket of the Chevrolet coupe Mr. Magee found the keys to the car and an additional note which directed him further as to the delivery of the ransom. This not read as follows:

"Go to Farmington, Minnesota. The Rochester bus will arrive there at 9:15 P.M. and leave at 9:25 P.M. Follow one hundred yards in back of this bus, when it leaves Farmington until you come to four red lights on the left and proceed at fifteen miles per hour until you see five flashes of lights; then stop and deposit packages of money on the right hand side of the road. Leave the two notes; get in car and go straight ahead."

Mr. Magee, serving as intermediary, proceeded to Farmington and followed the bus to Cannon Falls and Zumbrota. Driving another four or five miles, he saw the four red lights on the left side of the road on the bank of a hill. When Magee came to this point he located a gravel road nearby leading to the left, down which he proceeded slowly. Upon traveling about one-half a mile, a car pulled up behind him and he saw the headlights of the car flash five times. Magee stopped the Chevrolet coupe, walked around to the rear of the car, opened the door of the right side and took out two suit boxes, placed them on the right hand side of the road and the ransom for the release of Edward George Bremer had been paid.

Bremer spent two weeks as the Barker's captive while Magee negotiated his release on behalf of the family. Doc, Fred, and Alvin took great pains to hide their identities and Bremer's whereabouts, even from him: they made Bremer wear a blindfold, feigned phony accents, and compelled his captors to follow their strict instructions for the payoff.

"It turned out to be a long grueling wait," penned Karpis. "Bremer wasn't exactly a model prisoner the way Hamm had been. The wound in his head didn't help his disposition, but even apart from it, he was just naturally a slightly miserable bastard."[40]

About 8:00 P.M. on February 7, 1934, Mr. Edward G. Bremer was released by his abductors at Rochester, Minnesota. When he arrived there with his kidnappers, he was instructed by them to get out of the car in the middle of the street and to stand with his back towards the direction in which the kidnapers' car was headed. He was also told to count slowly to fifteen, after which the bandage over his eyes could be removed.

After the automobile disappeared down the highway, Bremer, president of the Commercial State Bank, made his way as quickly as possible by train and bus. He appeared at 855 West Seventh Street, St. Paul, the home of his father, Adolph Bremer, president of Schmidt's Brewery, shortly after midnight. He bore marks of having been beaten about the head and face, and he had a full growth of beard.⁴¹

Once Bremer had returned safely to his home, special agents were free to vigorously pursue the investigation of the kidnapping. Although he had been injured during the kidnapping and had been blindfolded with taped goggles, Bremer had been able to hear various sounds en route to the hideout where he was held. The gang did not keep him blindfolded at all times at Bensenville and he was able to observe things which were later to be of assistance in identifying the place where he was held captive. Bremer was able to furnish the investigators with information that upon his arrival at the place where he was held he heard two dogs barking and these dogs appeared to be very close to the house and they barked on frequent occasions. He also heard a group of children playing in close proximity to the house and the noise of the children indicated that they were probably from four to eight years of age.⁴²

Edward G. Bremer and his father. (Author's collection)

"Ma"—The Life and Times of "Ma" Barker and Her Boys

Bremer told investigators that after the first few days of his confinement, the goggles which had been placed over his eyes at the time of his abduction were removed and he was permitted to sit in his room without any obstruction over his face. This privilege afforded him an opportunity to observe the furnishings of the bedroom in which he was held. He made a mental picture of the wallpaper and was able to describe it in such detail that similar wallpaper was traced by special agents and found to have been sold by a large mail order house. A specimen of this wallpaper was obtained and Bremer was able to positively identify it as being similar to that which was on the walls in the bedroom.

Despite a blindfold, Bremer was able to furnish information concerning the bathroom in which he was taken from time to time. He learned that the lever for flushing the toilet consisted of what appeared to be a metal screw. The enamel which had covered the screw had either been removed or broken. He observed a crack in the wall of the bedroom. Overhead Bremer heard a small child crying and estimated the age of the child to be about one year and he also heard another child approximately four years of age playing on the floor above him. He was convinced that there was a coal stove adjacent to the room in which he was held, as he heard sounds indicating that coal was being shoveled from a bin into a scuttle and that the coal was being kept in a position near the kitchen.

Bremer was also able to describe the sounds of traffic from the hide-out house. He could hear the brakes being applied to either buses or trucks, which gave him the impression that he was near a stop sign on a main highway. Sounds of trains could also be heard; probably interurban in character as they passed most frequently in the mornings and in the afternoons. In connection with the food which was served to him, he advised the special agents that he was of the opinion the food was cooked by a man, because it was always too well seasoned; that on one occasion he was served fish and on another fresh strawberry shortcake, which due to the season of the year was considered very unusual.

He was unable to state definitely the number of hours he was transported after being kidnapped at St. Paul, but after traveling several hours they arrived at the hide-out and his abductors dressed his wounded head, which wound had been inflicted upon him at the time of the abduction. He believed that he traveled through a city of medium size en route to the hideout, inasmuch as he heard streetcars. Bremer also was able to furnish the special agents with information concerning his return trip to Rochester, Minnesota. Bremer stated that upon leaving the hide-out sometime during the morning of February 7, 1934, he was placed in what appeared to be a one seated automobile by his abductors; that after riding a short distance he was transferred to another car and that this second car was a sedan. He was forced to enter the sedan and sit on the floor immediately behind the driver with his back against the front seat and his right side leaning against the left rear door. At this time his hand touched the butt of what appeared to be either a shotgun or a rifle on the floor. He also was able to ascertain that there was a tin can immediately on his left side on which he could comfortably rest his left elbow; that this can appeared to be an ordinary five gallon tin can which contained gasoline, as he could smell the strong odor of that fuel. He estimated that after approximately one-half of the distance had been covered between the hide-out house and Rochester, the car in which he was riding turned off from the paved road, and after ten or fifteen minutes, pulled to the side of a road. The two men who were in the front seat of the car and the one in the rear seat guarding him got out and took out of the car at least two tin cans containing gasoline. He heard his abductors pour gasoline into the tank of the car in which he was riding, after which the journey was resumed. He recalled that his abductors at the time the tank of the automobile was refueled turned off the paved highway, because he heard gravel striking the windows of the car.

Reporters were not allowed to talk with Bremer immediately after his return, because of the activities of the federal men and because of the fatigued condition of the kidnap victim. Bremer, however, upon revealing his experiences to friends, said that when his car was stopped at Goodrich and Lexington, one of the kidnappers climbed into the front seat with him holding a gun in his hand. Bremer quickly opened the door on his left and tried to escape.[43]

As he did this, another of the kidnappers met him on the side of the car and pushed him back into the seat, climbing in beside him. He was struck on the head by both men and did not remember being transferred from his car to the other vehicle. The next thing he knew, he had a bandage over his eyes and had no idea how many men were in the gang, but he expressed the belief that there must have been a dozen men, basing his opinion on the number of voices he heard in the place of his captivity.

The room in which he was kept was dark and the bandage had been removed from his eyes. During the entire time he was held, two men sat at his back and he was warned not to try to look around. "One look and we'll blow your damned brains out," Bremer related what he had been told.

The guards worked in relays. Two men would remain with him for a while and then would be relieved. A close friend of the Bremer family, who declined to allow his name to be used, stated: "He put up a hell of a battle. The blood in his car was not all his. He has a leg injury that he got when he stuck his foot out so they couldn't close the door. It seems they got the door closed and his leg may have a very bad bruise or worse. He was treated well enough while they had him, considering all the circumstances. Both he and his father were in bed this morning and under the care of a doctor and a nurse."[44]

After answering the agents' questions, Bremer was ordered to bed by a physician, Dr. Joseph Sprafka, who said that his patient was "very, very nervous," but that the wounds on his head, inflicted by two men, who had spirited him away, had healed. The family physician, Dr. H. T. Nippert, said he would be kept in bed for a day or two, adding that his chief suffering was from mental strain. Officers told the press that same night that they believed Bremer had been held either in Sioux City, Iowa, or in Kansas City, Missouri.[45]

Chief of Police Thomas E. Dahill was asked to make a public statement but he answered all queries with "I am not free to make any statement regarding the case tonight." When asked whether a report that Alvin Karpis and Freddie Barker, fugitives wanted for murders in West St. Paul and also West Plains, Missouri, were being sought in connection with the kidnapping, Chief Dahill said, "I can neither affirm nor deny that report."

After having slept in his father's home for several hours, Bremer, accompanied by his wife and daughter, went to his own residence at 92 North Mississippi River Boulevard, that evening. Discussing Bremer's condition that night, Dr. Nippert said: "He was still in a daze and very nervous when I visited him at 2 P.M. His drawn face and jumpy nerves showed the ordeal he had passed through. He was in a partially darkened room in his father's house because light hurt his eyes after being held so many days in a dark room. He told me that his kidnappers pummeled him considerably when they first took him, but that he never completely lost consciousness. He said that as soon as he realized what was up, he didn't offer any resistance."

The London Daily Mail called the Adolph Bremer home that afternoon by transoceanic telephone but failed to obtain an interview with the victim.

On February 8, 1934, special agents retraced the route taken by Walter Magee at the time he paid the ransom money, and at a point several miles south of Zumbrota, Minnesota, four flashlights were found equipped with red-film lens. These lights, which had been used as signal lights at the time Mr. Magee delivered the ransom money to the kidnapers, bore the trademark "Merit Product." The special agents then began the task of tracing these flashlights and it was learned that flashlights of this make were sold at the F. & B. Grand Silver Store, 67-7th Street, St. Paul. At this store a girl employee identified the photograph of Alvin Karpis as having purchased the flashlights from her prior to the kidnapping of Bremer.[46]

The car Walter Magee used to deliver the ransom money to the gang was a small coupe owned by E. J. Petronik of Owatonna. The coupe was reported to have had both side windows soaped and a rear window slightly opened. The windshield was not soaped.[47]

The following day the Federal Bureau of Investigation began the distribution of the printed list containing the serial numbers of all the currency which comprised the ransom. These lists were distributed to all banks in the United States and in some foreign countries, with the request that should any of the listed currency be detected in a bank the nearest division of the Federal Bureau of Investigation was to be immediately notified.[48]

With this information at hand, special agents continued their investigation, and on February 10, 1934, the Sheriff of Columbia County, Wisconsin turned over to the Federal Bureau of Investigation four large gasoline cans and a tin funnel which had been found by a farmer near Portage, Wisconsin. Due to the information furnished by Bremer concerning the refueling of the automobile used in the return trip from the hide-out house, these gasoline cans were immediately forwarded by special agents to the Technical Laboratory of the Federal Bureau of Investigation at Washington, D.C. The laboratory examination of the gasoline cans revealed a latent fingerprint, which fingerprint was identified as being identical with the right index fingerprint of Doc Barker.

Upon learning the identification of Arthur "Doc" Barker and Alvin Karpis, special agents were given definite leads. The special agents knew also that the gang which had extorted and robbed the citizens of the Twin Cities of more that $300,000 less than a year earlier was composed of desperate criminals. Barker and Karpis were in no way strangers to the special agents of the Federal Bureau of Investigation.

Thankful for the return of his son, Edward's father showed his appreciation by expressing his gratitude in a letter to the St. Paul Dispatch. His statement said: "I am so happy to tell you that my boy is back at last after his terrible experience. The hideous hours of suspense have been almost unbearable for all of us. I gratefully appreciate this personal interest of the president and the governor and the splendid cooperation given by the press and radio. The city, state, and federal law enforcing authorities have been most kind in their efforts and offers of assistance.

"Above all, I will never forget their humane willingness to stand by when my please convinced them that Edward's life was in serious jeopardy. No sacrifice has been to great for my brother Otto, Walter Magee, Clarence Newcome, and the others who at great risk have done their parts. It is my earnest prayer that other fathers and mothers will be spared the agony of a similar ordeal."[49]

St. Paul Mayor, William Mahoney, however, was noncommittal when interviewed by the press. "I don't want to say anything about it until I know more about it," he said. "I don't know anything about it at all."

"Ma"—The Life and Times of "Ma" Barker and Her Boys

Notes

[1] Lew Louderback, *The Bad Ones Gangsters of the '30 and Their Molls*, Greenwich, Connecticut, Fawcett Publications, 1968, p. 256.
[2] Dara Moskowitz, "Minneapolis Confidential," *City Pages*, Volume 16, Number 775, October 11, 1995.
[3] *Mankato Free Press*, September 11, 1933.
[4] *Mankato Free Press*, September 13, 1933.
[5] Alvin Karpis with Bill Trent, *The Alvin Karpis Story*, pp. 155-159.
[6] *Chicago Tribune*, September 21, 1933.
[7] *Chicago Herald and Examiner*, November 30, 1933.
[8] Alston Purvis, Son of FBI Agent Melvin Purvis, of the FBI Bureau in Chicago, Interview 4/29/03 by Brian Bull.
[9] Rick Mattix letter to author dated January 9, 2006.
[10] Ellen Poulsen, "Don't Call Us Molls: Women of the John Dillinger Gang," The Alderson Federal Correctional Facility Archives.
[11] *Minneapolis Journal*, July 24, 1932.
[12] Joseph Stipanovich, *City of Lakes An Illustrated History of Minneapolis*, pp. 26-28.
[13] *Minneapolis Journal*, November 10, 1932.
[14] David L. Rosheim, *The Other Minneapolis or A History of the Minneapolis Skid Row*, p. 121; *Minneapolis Journal*, November 3, 1932.
[15] *Minneapolis Journal*, October 31, 1932.
[16] Ibid., November 4, 1932.
[17] Ibid., November 9, 1932.
[18] Theodore C. Blegen, *Minnesota A History of the State*, pp. 524-526.
[19] Alvin Karpis with Bill Trent, *The Alvin Karpis Story*, pp. 161-163.
[20] Paul Maccabee, *John Dillinger Slept Here*, pp. 191-192.
[21] Alvin Karpis with Bill Trent, *The Alvin Karpis Story*, p. 165.
[22] *St. Paul Pioneer Press*, January 20, 1934.
[23] Ibid.
[24] FBI Files, RCS:TD I.C.#7-576, November 19, 1936, The Kidnaping of Edward George Bremer, St. Paul, Minnesota, History and Early Association of the Karpis-Barker Gang Prior to the Abduction of Mr. Bremer.
[25] *St. Paul Dispatch*, January 18, 1934.
[26] FBI Files, RCS:TD I.C.#7-576, November 19, 1936, The Kidnaping of Edward George Bremer, St. Paul, Minnesota, History and Early Association of the Karpis-Barker Gang Prior to the Abduction of Mr. Bremer.
[27] *St. Paul Pioneer Press*, January 23, 1934.
[28] *St. Paul Pioneer Press*, January 21, 1934.
[29] *St. Paul Pioneer Press*, January 22, 1934.
[30] *New York Times*, January 19, 1934.

[31] *St. Paul Pioneer Press*, January 23, 1934.
[32] *St. Paul Pioneer Press*, January 20, 1934.
[33] *New York Times*, January 19, 1934.
[34] *St. Paul Pioneer Press*, January 23, 1934.
[35] *New York Times*, January 19, 1934.
[36] *St. Paul Pioneer Press*, January 24, 1934.
[37] *Chicago Daily Tribune*, January 31, 1934.
[38] Federal Bureau of Investigation History Archives. United States Department of Justice.
[39] *New York Times*, January 19, 1934.
[40] Alvin Karpis with Bill Trent, *The Alvin Karpis Story*, p. 167.
[41] *St. Paul Dispatch*, February 8, 1934; *New York Times*, February 9, 1934..
[42] FBI Files, RCS:TD I.C.#7-576, November 19, 1936, The Kidnaping of Edward George Bremer, St. Paul, Minnesota, History and Early Association of the Karpis-Barker Gang Prior to the Abduction of Mr. Bremer.
[43] *St. Paul Dispatch*, February 8, 1934.
[44] Ibid.
[45] *New York Times*, February 9, 1934.
[46] FBI Files, RCS:TD I.C.#7-576, November 19, 1936, The Kidnaping of Edward George Bremer, St. Paul, Minnesota, History and Early Association of the Karpis-Barker Gang Prior to the Abduction of Mr. Bremer.
[47] *St. Paul Dispatch*, February 8, 1934.
[48] FBI Files, RCS:TD I.C.#7-576, November 19, 1936, The Kidnaping of Edward George Bremer, St. Paul, Minnesota, History and Early Association of the Karpis-Barker Gang Prior to the Abduction of Mr. Bremer.
[49] *St. Paul Dispatch*, February 8, 1934; New York Times, February 9, 1934.

Chapter Seven

Crackdown

"The men who fired the shots that night almost immediately agreed that no one would tell who killed Dillinger. I never have told, and I assume none of the others have. Most of us were young fellows. We had a feeling there was no great honor in taking part in the killing of a man."

—Melvin Purvis[1]

Dillinger lieutenant Eddie Green, posing as shoe salesman Theodore J. Randall had rented apartment 207 in the Charlou Apartments, 3300 South Fremont Avenue, in Minneapolis back in September 1933 to store the gang's armaments. Homer Van Meter, recently paroled from the Indiana State Prison, lived next door in the Josephine Apartments, 3310 South Fremont, apartment 201, with his twenty year old girlfriend, Marie Conforti during January and February 1934.[2]

The Federal Government, however, was cracking down on robbers, murderers, and kidnappers, and meting out severe punishment to offenders. On February 23, 1934, Roger "the Terrible" Touhy and two members of his gang—Albert Kator and Gus Schaefer—were sentenced to nintey-nine years in the penitentiary for the July 1 kidnapping of wealthy speculator, John Factor.[3]

"Ma"—The Life and Times of "Ma" Barker and Her Boys

Roger Touhy, the powerful bootlegging king of Chicago, and the merciless leader of the infamous Touhy Gang, became ill when the verdict of the jury was announced. Gagging and coughing, a handkerchief held to his face, the gangster who once defied the Capone syndicate, was assisted from the courtroom of Judge Michael Feinberg.

Solemnly the jurors watched him and his co-defendants exit the courtroom. Schaefer was white-faced. Kator, known as a cold-blooded gunman and killer, managed a last scornful grimace as he followed his companions.

During the spring of 1934, while the Federal Government began to win its war on crime, the City of St. Paul, too, commenced cleaning up its own act. An investigation within the St. Paul Police Department, through telephone wire-tapping, produced evidence which identified several members of the department who were in collusion with the underworld. Hearings were held for the persons charged, and by the end of 1936, disciplinary action had been taken on those on the take.[4]

Newspaper headlines, however, belonged to John Dillinger on March 3, 1934, when he escaped from the "supposedly escape-proof" county jail in Crown Point, Indiana, with the aid of a wooden pistol. He forced his captors to open the door to his cell, grabbed two machine guns, locked up the guards and several trustees, and fled.

A huge police force was immediately mobilized to recapture him under orders to shoot to kill. Ironically, Dillinger fled in an automobile owned by the county's woman sheriff, Mrs. Lillian Holley. He carried with him two hostages and headed for the Illinois border. Once across the state line, he released his hostages giving each four dollars in compensation for the ordeal. By doing so, however, he violated the National Motor Vehicle Theft Act, which made it a federal offense to transport a stolen motor vehicle across a state line.

A federal complaint was sworn charging Dillinger with the theft and interstate transportation of the sheriff's car, which was recovered in Chicago. After the grand jury returned an indictment, the FBI became actively involved in the nationwide search for Dillinger. Within three hours, three states had spread a net around the area, but Dillinger, armed with two machine guns and a pistol, made good his escape.[5]

Meanwhile, Harry Pierpont, Charles Makley, and Russell Clark were returned to Ohio and convicted of the murder of the Lima sheriff. Pierpont and Makley were sentenced to death and Clark to life imprisonment. But in an escape attempt, Makley was killed and Pierpont was wounded. A month later, Pierpont had recovered sufficiently to be executed.[6]

By March 4th, Dillinger, having rejoined Evelyn "Billie" Frechette, arrived in St. Paul to add the final members of his new gang. This was to include John Hamilton and old prison friend Homer Van Meter (paroled from the Indiana penitentiary nine days after Dillinger in May 1933). Van Meter brought in fellow criminals, Eddie Green and his partner Tommy Carroll. Also added was underworld character Lester Gillis, better known as Baby Face Nelson, with a reputation as a trigger-happy killer.

The following day, March 5th, a Mr. and Mrs. Irvin Olson (Dillinger and Frechette) moved into apartment 106 at the Santa Monica Apartments, 3252 Girard Avenue South, in Minneapolis. The Olsons seemed to be a strange couple in paying the fifty dollar advance on the apartment from a roll of dollar bills, and janitor Silas Lancaster later told the FBI that he found the shades in their apartment wired shut to prevent any light from escaping outside.[7]

According to Cathy Prachar, a neighbor, Dillinger had painted part of the curb in front of his house yellow so his underworld friends could recognize the house at night.[8]

And they came—Homer Van Meter, Eddie Green, John Hamilton, and Lester Gillis alias "Big George" a.k.a. "Baby Face" Nelson. On that very day they made plans to rob banks in South Dakota and Iowa.

On March 6th, the gangsters robbed the Security National Bank and Trust in Sioux Falls, South Dakota. As Dillinger and Van Meter collected $49,000 in cash and bonds from the vault, and with the alarm blaring, a large crowd of onlookers gathered in the street. Nelson, spying off-duty policeman Hale Keith peering through the window, fired through the glass, wounding the man.

"MA"—THE LIFE AND TIMES OF "MA" BARKER AND HER BOYS

The bold headlines in the *Daily Argus Leader*, South Dakota's leading newspaper, evening edition, told the story in a few succinct words: "Bandits get $46,000; Hostages Freed, Trail Car, Keith Alive. Six Men Armed With Machine Guns hold Police; Crowd at Bay as They Rob Security National; Robber Gang Last Sighted Near Luverne—Car is Abandoned."[9]

G. Oliver Nordby, loan officer in the bank, later stated in an interview that he was at his window that day and there was $1,500 in the drawer in cash. A little before ten that morning, men wearing long, dark overcoats and dress hats pulled over their faces, walked into the bank lobby carrying machine guns. When one of the men announced, "This is a holdup," a bank stenographer pushed a security button setting off a screeching burglar alarm. The bandits became angry and all pandemonium broke loose.

"We were ordered to open our cash drawer and then hold hands over heads," recalled Nordby. "There were about thirty employees and bank customers who were all ordered to line up with their faces to the wall and hands extended. Some of us remained at our stations so we were able to see the action . . . we had our hands up, of course! One man carried a hand gun rather than a machine gun. He gave orders by cursing, threatening and seemed eager to use his gun.

"Fred Anderson, a bank officer, was kicked twice and told to open the money cages. A robber scooped up the bills including those in my drawer. The bank president, China Clarke, was ordered to open the bank vault but he couldn't work the combination. A man, I believe was Dillinger, then commanded the head-teller, Bob Dargen, to open the vault. When it was opened, the man said, 'Drop that dough in the sack!' This took only a brief time. He took the vault money and then used a shield of people to carry it to the waiting car. It all happened so fast that we didn't have time to be scared."[10]

While the vault was being emptied, Lester Gillis, alias "Baby Face" Nelson, who was guarding people in the lobby, glanced out the north window and noticed Hale Keith, a motorcycle policeman, racing toward the bank. Nelson leaped on top of Trust Officer Adolph Lodmell's desk and fired at Keith through the closed window.

To make their getaway, the bandits took hostages—Mrs. Mildred Boswick, Mrs. Alice Blegen, Emma Knobach, and Mary Lucas—to ride the running boards of their Packard, acting as human shields. Once they arrived at the main highway, the bandits threw nails into the road in order to slow down any pursuing police. When the Packard overheated due to a police bullet hole in the radiator, the gang stole another car just as the police closed in. This led to a running gun battle, which nevertheless they were able to escape from, heading back to their Twin Cities hideout.

But their stay in the Santa Monica Apartments was cut short, according to Evelyn Frechette: "[John] Hamilton was taking off his coat one evening when he pulled his pistol from its shoulder holster. The weapon clattered to the floor and discharged. We packed our clothes and were on our way in less than ten minutes."[11]

At about the same time, a panic arose in Lima, Ohio, at the trial of Pierpont and Makley, as word got out that Dillinger might try to break them out. The writer of an article in the *Moody County Enterprise* was at a loss for words, declaring simply, Dillinger Seen in All Parts of South Dakota."[12]

On March 13, 1934, what was described as a well-armed and experienced gang robbed the First National Bank in Mason City, Iowa. Most accounts agree that the robbers had a dark blue Buick sedan, that there were seven of them, that they escaped with approximately $52,000, and that one of them was John Dillinger.[13]

First National Bank Robbery. (Courtesy of the Lee P. Loomis Archive of Mason City History)

"Ma"—The Life and Times of "Ma" Barker and Her Boys

A combination of witness identifications and gangster confessions later determined that the other participants were John "Red" Hamilton (the actual leader), "Baby Face" Nelson, Eugene "Eddie" Green, Tommy Carroll, Homer Van Meter, and either Joseph Burns or Red Forsythe. The fact that the seventh identification caused a problem is interesting because in one account, as reported by the *Des Moines Tribune* on March 14, 1934, there were six men and one woman.[14]

The gang parked their automobile on State Street, near the alley behind the bank. At least two of them remained by the car while Tommy Carroll stationed himself in the doorway of Mulcahy's Prescription Shop. "Baby Face" Nelson was across the street, on or near the sidewalk by the alley. One gangster was probably in the car. In some accounts it was Tommy Carroll, in others, it was Homer Van Meter. It may have been the woman reported in the *Tribune*.[15]

(Courtesy of FBI Archives)

The other gang members either went into the bank or stood guard outside. The most probable versions place Dillinger in front and perhaps one or two others in the bank. Tom Walters, the bank guard, said in one story that he saw five gangsters inside. The gangsters entered the bank shouting orders and shooting their guns into the ceilings and walls. Walters was in his elevated bulletproof observation booth, built into the wall near the front entrance. He followed procedure and fired a tear-gas cartridge, which hit one of the robbers in the back. The tear-gas gun jammed, however, and Walters was out of the fight.

One of the gang members sprayed the bulletproof glass with gunfire, shattering it but missing Walters. While one or two of the gang cleaned out the teller's cash drawers, another, probably John Hamilton, took bank cashier Harry Fisher to the vault. Tom Barclay, a bank employee, saw what was going on, retrieved a tear-gas bomb from another office and threw it on the floor.

Meanwhile, Hamilton and Fisher were at the vault. There the gang member made the mistake of allowing a steel gate to close between him and Fisher. Fisher proceeded to hand small denomination bills out through the bars to Hamilton. Margaret Johnson (Giesen) was a switchboard operator in the bank; her office situated on a balcony above the vault. When the robbery started, she crawled across the floor and shouted out of a south window the news of the robbery—to "Baby Face" Nelson, who brandished his machine gun and said, "You're telling me, lady?"

Earlier in the day, a newsreel cameraman shooting footage of the bank had attracted onlookers. Now, however, a bigger crowd gathered as the word spread that the bank was being robbed. People on the street, as well as customers in the nearby Nichols and Green Shoe Store, were used by the gangsters to shield them from the police. Officer James Buchanan realized a robbery was going on, armed himself with a shotgun, and took cover behind the GAR monument in Central Park.

The gangsters in front of the bank shot at him but missed. Buchanan was unable to return fire with the shotgun he was carrying because of the human shield around the robbers. Police Chief Patton watched helplessly from the C.L. Pine Co. across the street in the "Weir" (Frank Lloyd Wright) Building.

Mayor Laird owned a shoe store in the IOOF building a few feet away from the gunmen on State Street. At first, he thought he heard a car backfiring; then he realized it was gunfire. As he later observed, if the police had interfered, there certainly would have been many people injured or killed. As it was, only one person was wounded deliberately by the gangsters.

R. L. James was walking up to the corner of State and Federal, intending to go into the bank, when he heard the gunfire. Realizing what was happening he turned around and headed back down State. He ducked beneath the windows, hoping he would not be noticed. Baby Face Nelson, according to the newspaper, ordered him to stop. James did not hear the order and Nelson fired a burst from his machine gun. The bullets hit James in the leg and he fell to the sidewalk.

A few moments later Dorothy "Ransom" Crumb and her mother turned out of the alley behind the bank on to State Street. They pulled their car up behind the parked gangster's vehicle and stopped. Baby Face Nelson ordered them out of their car and onto the gangsters' car. Dorothy argued with the gunman and eventually he let them stay in their own car and they watched as numerous hostages climbed aboard the getaway car.

Francis DeSart, a teller at the bank, was one of the hostages. His wife, Ruth, was working at the Style Shop at 1 South Federal that day. She saw her husband being led out of the bank and forced to stand on the rear bumper of the car as it moved slowly north on Federal Avenue. The coat that Francis DeSart wore received a bullet hole in the tail of it caused by a gangster's gun shooting out of the rear window of the car toward trailing police.

As soon as the car, loaded with gangsters and hostages, turned up Federal Avenue, a policeman, pulling R.L. James behind him, jumped into the back of Dorothy Crumb's car and told her to hit the horn, stop for nothing, and drive as fast as she could for the nearest hospital.

Deputy Sheriff John P. Wallace was behind the Civil War monument in the park and apparently fired a few shots at the getaway car as it drove up Federal. One of the robbers reportedly told a hostage that if the shooting didn't stop someone would be hurt. Chief of Police Patton, Detective Leo Risacher, and record superintendent Ray Oulman followed the bandits with their hostages as far as a road house called "The Farm," 2053 4th SW, west of town.

The hostages were let off the car individually and in groups during the next hour. The holdup car was found that night in a quarry near the community of Hanford, four miles south of Mason City. Although many accounts point to Dillinger as one of the robbers, the holdup was also charged to the Barker-Karpis Gang. Back in Minneapolis, both Dillinger and Hamilton were treated for their wounds. John's plans to use his share of the $240,000 to leave the country had to be abandoned.

The March 13th robbery of the First National Bank in Mason City, Iowa, netted only $52,000 of an anticipated $240,000. Both Dillinger and Hamilton received shoulder wounds and a bystander was wounded when fired on by Nelson. The gang once again escaped behind a shield of hostages, all of whom were released after about forty-five minutes.

Fleeing to Chicago the gang allegedly stopped at the Weir tourist stand and gas station on the west side of Tama near the Mesquakie Indian settlement. As reported by Charles Weir, his father met Dillinger and his pals at the gas pump. Mr. Weir recalled the bandits as being "real polite" and filled their tank. He also gave them a spare tire—quite a gift as a new one in 1934 cost roughly one week's wages for a working man. Weir kept Dillinger's visit secret because he did not want the gangsters to return to his station.

Mrs. Frank Cargin, at the Evening Star Camp Filling Stations on Mt. Vernon Road, east of Cedar Rapids, claimed to have recognized Dillinger and one of his henchmen back in April 1934. She recalled that the visitors conducted inquiries regarding a cabin for the night and were told the cabins were not open for business and ready to rent yet. However, for the next few nights a single cabin was broken into and it appeared to have been used for the night's lodging. Mrs. Cargin was so frightened, she didn't notify the police.[16]

After one of Dillinger's men, Tommy Carroll, was shot and killed by Waterloo police in early June, the Evening Star became known as a "hideout." Carroll and his wife had stayed at the camp the previous night.

"Ma"—The Life and Times of "Ma" Barker and Her Boys

On March 30, 1934, a federal agent talked to the manager of the Lincoln Court Apartments, 93 South Lexington Avenue, in St. Paul, who reported two suspicious tenants, Mr. and Mrs. Hellman, who acted nervous and refused to admit the apartment caretaker. The FBI began a surveillance of the Hellman's apartment. The next day, an agent and a police officer knocked on the door of the apartment. Evelyn Frechette opened the door, but quickly slammed it shut. The agent called for reinforcements to surround the building.

While waiting, the agents saw a man enter a hall near the Hellman's apartment. When questioned, the man, Homer Van Meter, drew a gun. Shots were exchanged, during which Van Meter fled the building and forced a truck driver at gunpoint to drive him to Eddie Green's apartment.

Suddenly the door of the Hellman apartment opened and the muzzle of Dillinger's machine gun began spraying the hallway with lead. Under cover of the machine gun fire, Dillinger and Evelyn Frechette fled through a back door. They, too, drove to Green's apartment, where Dillinger was treated for a bullet wound received in the escape.

At the Lincoln Court Apartments, the FBI found a Thompson submachine gun with the stock removed, two automatic rifles, one .38 caliber Colt automatic with twenty shot magazine clips, and two bulletproof vests. Across town, other agents located one of Eddie Green's hideouts where he and Bessie Skinner had been living as "Mr. and Mrs. Stephens." On April 3rd, when Green was located, he attempted to draw his gun, but was shot by the agents. He died in a hospital eight days later.

On that same April 3rd, Arthur "Doc" Barker and Alvin Karpis were named by the Department of Justice in Washington as the kidnappers of Edward Bremer. The Justice Department immediately launched a widespread search for the pair.[17]

In April, also, the FBI raided John Dillinger's "safe house" in the Charlou Apartments on Fremont Avenue in Minneapolis and found a small arsenal. A bullet-proof vest, a loaded 50-round machine gun, a Thompson submachine gun, a .45 automatic pistol, and a high-powered rifle were seized.[18]

Dillinger and Evelyn Frechette, meanwhile, fled to Mooresville, Indiana, where they stayed with his father and half-brother until his wound healed. Then Frechette went to Chicago to visit a friend and was arrested by the FBI. She was taken to St. Paul for trial on a charge of conspiracy to harbor a fugitive. She was convicted, fined $1,000, and sentenced to two years in prison. Bessie Skinner, Eddie Green's girlfriend, got fifteen months on the same charge.

Meanwhile, Dillinger and Van Meter robbed a police station at Warsaw, Indiana, of guns and bulletproof vests. Dillinger stayed for a while in Upper Michigan, departing just ahead of a posse of FBI Agents dispatched there by airplane.

Dillinger eluded the police for another month, shooting his way out of the ambush in St. Paul and dodging the FBI. He arrived in Chicago in late June and proceeded to rob a South Bend, Indiana, bank and kill a police officer and four civilians. John and Billie next moved on to the Dillinger farm in Mooresville, staying there while he recovered from his leg wound.

Authorities soon learned that they had returned to Chicago and were quickly able to track down and arrest Billie Frechette as she entered a bar. On seeing the arrest of his girlfriend, Dillinger quickly drove away. She was taken to St. Paul to stand trial on harboring charges. She was sentenced in May 1934, receiving two years in jail at Milan, Michigan.

On April 13th, Dillinger and Van Meter robbed the Warsaw, Indiana, police station, making off with guns and three bulletproof vests. This heist set off an intense manhunt and prompted hundreds of reports of sightings. In mid-April Dillinger and Hamilton stayed at Hamilton's sister's home in Sault Ste. Marie, Michigan.

On April 20th, having received a tip, the FBI arrived in town only to discover that the two outlaws had already moved on. In just over a year, Dillinger has robbed six banks, killed two police officers, two FBI agents, escaped from jail twice, and had escaped from police and FBI traps six times.[19]

On March 20, 1934, Fred Goetz was murdered by members of the underworld at Cicero, Illinois, outside the closed Minerva Restaurant, 4813 West Cermak, by killers in a passing automobile. Having just crossed 22nd Street, he walked alone to his car and was inserting the key on the driver's side when ~~he~~ someone called to him from behind. The buckshot also hit the windows of 4811 West Cermak, then a saloon belonging to Fenton M. Mangan. The slugs narrowly miss hitting Mangan and several patrons drinking there at the time. The killer's car disappeared eastward into Chicago.

Goetz's killers eliminated him from further participation in the criminal activities of the Karpis-Barker gang by several shotgun blasts to the face, which prevented recognition. He was identified by fingerprints. Found with a $1,000 bill in his pocket, Goetz's body was taken to Frances Willard Hospital. On his body besides the $1,000, they found several cards with variations of his name for different clubs. In his leather belt they discovered six slender steal blades concealed within. This led police to believe that Goetz was ready for any escape should he be jailed. Police searched his luxurious apartment and came up with landscaping plans for a farm he had in Wisconsin and a cultured taste in books.

Goetz also had various bank accounts and dabbled heavily in distillery stocks. His car, an expensive coupe, was found abandoned at 79th street and Cottage Grove Avenue. The registration in the car listed the owner as J. George Zeigler, 40 Chicago Avenue, Oak Park. Investigators found a filling station at this address, where Goetz had been receiving his mail. His car had been purchased from Joseph Bergl, a well known Cicero automobile dealer with connections to gangsters, and who was apt at modifying gangster's vehicles in making them fast and bulletproof.

After the death of Fred Goetz, investigation revealed that he had participated in the abduction of Bremer. Efforts were made by special agents to locate Irene Dorsey, with whom Goetz had been living. Interviews with the parents of Irene Dorsey, and Fred Goetz produced no information concerning her whereabouts other than that Irene Dorsey was somewhere in the West. Continued investigation revealed that Irene had sent her parents the following telegram:

"No contracts, no signing partner to settle read and think. Use your wits, neither cloud is under control and all need Indian orders wait for them. Answer yes at once." (Signed) "Irene Dorsey, Larna Hotel, San Francisco, California."[20]

Irene Dorsey was not found at the Larna Hotel but in the mental ward of a hospital. Her association with the criminal Fred Goetz had been too much and her mind faltered under the strain. Subsequent investigation by the Federal Bureau of Investigation revealed that Fred Goetz, with Fred Barker and Volney Davis, had carried on ransom negotiations in St. Paul and had collected the $200,000 from the intermediary. It was further learned that Volney Davis had been the individual who had openly approached Lillian Dickman and Father Deere in the negotiations for the payment of the ransom money.

Most Minnesotans showed concern over the recent kidnappings, but by 1934, Minnesota and the entire nation were devastated. Farm prices had plummeted and workers were out of work by the thousands. Seventy percent of the iron range workers were jobless and farms were being lost through mortgage foreclosures. In Minneapolis and other cities, those fortunate to keep jobs, were suffering payroll cutbacks and were working extended hours for the same pay they had received earlier. In 1933, nine million dollars in relief costs were paid; one year later, the figure reached 33 million.[21]

Toward the close of 1933, the trucking industry workers were putting in between fifty-three and ninety hours a week and they were paid only twelve to eighteen dollars weekly for their service. Teamsters' Local 574 came to the conclusion that it had taken enough abuse. Minneapolis had long enjoyed the reputation of being a "pro-company" town but now talks of striking were quite unprecedented.

Transportation was a strategic key to Minneapolis' commercial life, and the union officials knew a strike would cause economic paralysis. Neither the Teamsters, nor the Citizens' Alliance, the employers' organization, were ready to back down.[22] Local 574 organized nearly all the Teamsters in the city of Minneapolis. The organizing effort was led by Karl Skoglund, the Dunne brothers—Miles, Grant, and Victor—and William "Bill" Brown. The leadership of the group was avowedly Socialist, ideologically the adherents of Leon Trotsky's interpretation of Marxism, but throughout the strike they adhered only to the unionization effort and not ultimate political gains.[23]

The Citizens' Alliance represented more than 800 city businesses and retained a permanent staff as well as a network of paid informers. The organization boasted a long and successful record of combating unions, and it geared up immediately for a showdown with the Minneapolis truck drivers.

The union leaders made preparations and called a mass meeting in April. Governor Olson attended and urged the workers to "organize and fight for their demands." That Monday evening more than 2,000 drivers attended the meeting at the Eagles' Hall, Fourth Avenue So. and Eighth street. To be sure, this was more than the big hall accommodated, but drivers came and went as their different times for reporting for work and quitting work occurred. It is conservatively estimated that at least 2,000 were present at various times.[24]

A strike committee of seventy-five was selected. It met Wednesday evening at Labor Headquarters. It voted to recommend to the big meeting Monday evening that a strike be declared unless in the meantime a settlement has been reached.

Floyd B. Olson had been elected governor on a platform that declared: "Capitalism has failed and immediate steps must be taken to abolish it." Olson had been brought up in poverty on the streets of Minneapolis, not unlike Kid Cann, and would always side with the poor. He was the first governor in the history of the United States to call in the National Guard to protect labor rather than crush it.[25]

Having gained the support of the governor, the workers were assured the state would not intervene and break a strike. With preparations complete, the union leaders attempted to enter into collective bargaining with the employers. The employers, however, refused to negotiate.

In May 1934, truckers, in a very good position to strike, demanded a wage increase and a closed shop town. William "Bill" Brown, president of local 574 of the American Federation of Labor, announced the strike and claimed the closed shop issue needed attention before any discussion of rights could be worked out. Brown stated, via the *Journal*, that "Wage agreements are not much protection to a union man unless first there is a definite assurance that the union man will be protected in his job."[26]

Within days, the union literally closed the city of Minneapolis. All transportation, except for necessary foodstuffs, was non-existent and even gas stations were picketed on the theory that truckers, wanting to ignore the strike, could obtain gas from their cars, which were free to move about the city.[27]

The strikers gained considerable support from the citizenry of Minneapolis, and within three days the union received $15,000 in contributions. Governor Olson even contributed a $500 donation. The strike proceeded under relatively peaceful conditions for several days.[28]

The *Minneapolis Journal* was slow to react to the strike threat. It did, however, give good coverage to the pre-strike discussions, and during the first few days of the strike, *Journal* reporters were on the scene during incidents that they decidedly reported pro-labor.

One of these verbal incidents was that of picket leader Alfred Johnson who told the *Journal*: "There can't be any drinking on this job. We have to be orderly. And we aren't going to allow any agitators or troublemakers to do anything around here. We're good Americans and we don't want any of this Communist stuff."[29]

On Saturday morning, May 19th, 500 strikers attempted to halt two C. Thomas Stores' trucks from making a downtown Minneapolis delivery. Twelve squad cars of club-wielding police and special deputies charged the pickets. According to the *Journal*'s report, twenty people, sixteen of whom were strikers, were taken to the hospitals. That same evening three cars carrying men and women from strike headquarters were forced into entering Tribune Alley, next to the Journal and Tribune buildings on Fourth Street, and were severely beaten with clubs and saps and kicked mercilessly into unconsciousness. Strikers suddenly got the message. That weekend they padded caps and gathered war clubs.[30]

Labor leaders indicated that the strikers were unarmed but the *Journal* report disagreed: "Nearly 500 strikers swooped down on the trucks moving produce with rocks and clubs. Twelve police cars were rushed to the scene. The fight was on. Strikers were clubbed and fought back with clubs. Ambulances screamed to the scene."[31]

"Ma"—The Life and Times of "Ma" Barker and Her Boys

The *Journal* pointed out in its editorial that the strike methods used by Local 574 were dividing the people of Minneapolis. According to its report, "It matters not what are the right and wrongs of this labor controversy. There are powerful and lawful methods by which to settle them. Usurpation of authority, intimidation and violence are emphatically not in that category.

"If it be a fact that the striking truck drivers have labored under injustices that their employers refuse to correct, it does not follow that these strikers have the right to starve and abuse a whole city to bring about the redress they seek. The battle for civic freedom, for human rights, is on. There can be only one upshot. The reign of law and order must be, will be, restored."[32]

The employers, however, assembled an army of men, handed out billy clubs, and issued a complete set of instructions from its headquarters at 1328 Hennepin Avenue. Many of the "army" members did not consider themselves strikebreakers. Instead, they felt they were doing their duty in keeping the streets open. The men were officially made special deputies, and each wore a badge, but to the strikers, they were still strikebreakers.[33]

The strikers, too, had become well armed. Six hundred of them moved into the market area while special deputies were on hand to greet them. When the deputies saw the large disciplined force, however, they retreated hastily, leaving the police to fend for themselves. Quickly, the police officers formed a square, drew their guns, and held the strikers at bay. One striker, not to be outdone, drove his car into the square and dispersed the police force. Each officer was thus exposed to the savage beatings of the strikers and the striker victory came to be called the "Battle of Deputies Run."[34]

According to one *Journal* reporter, it was "the first time since the crash that the strikers were nearly all armed . . . . They were equipped with hundreds of 18-inch lengths of gas pipes and with clubs and sticks." Thirty-seven people were injured in the melee, all but seven, members of the police.[35]

On March 6, 1934, J. Edgar Hoover ordered Melvin Purvis to develop a network of informants "in the event of an emergency arising," and to "put forth every effort" to capture Dillinger. After his escape from jail at Crown Point, Indiana three days earlier, Dillinger had committed a federal crime by driving a stolen vehicle across state lines. Hoover had previously avoided the pursuit of Dillinger because he wasn't sure it could be done legally. Now that he was forced by political pressure to go ahead with it, he covered himself by upbraiding Purvis for not having taken action in the past.

On April 1st, Clyde Barrow and Bonnie Parker killed two State Highway Patrol officers near Grapevine, Texas. The officers, E.B. Wheeler and H.D. Murphy, both of Fort Worth, were gunned down as they approached a car parked on a side street. Clyde and the cigar-smoking Bonnie had been parked since mid-morning awaiting the arrival of Raymond Hamilton, who had escaped from a prison farm with the aid of Barrow and Parker's machine gun fire.[36]

Bonnie Parker. (Photo Courtesy of Rick Mattix)

On April 23, 1934, the elusive John Dillinger and eight members of his gang escaped from a Federal trap following three gun battles in which two officers were killed and four others wounded. Hundreds of Federal agents from a half dozen cities hastily swore in posse men as deputies from the Lac de Flambeau Indian Reservation in northern Wisconsin.

The FBI had received a tip that the Dillinger gang was staying there and would be leaving that night. Because of the distance involved, Melvin Purvis and several other agents in Chicago flew to Wisconsin. From

Clyde Barrow and his Ford V8. (Photo Courtesy of Rick Mattix)

Rhinelander, an FBI task force had set out by car for the Little Bohemia Lodge on Spider Lake in northern Wisconsin. Two of the rented cars broke down along the way, and, in the uncommonly cold April weather, some of the agents had to make the trip standing on the running boards of the other cars. Two miles from the resort, the car lights were turned off and the posse proceeded through the darkness.

When the special agents arrived at the lodge, the owner's dogs started barking. Purvis, who had no map of the place, told the men to surround the building. In the darkness, two agents got entangled in a barbed wire fence; two others fell into a ditch. As the agents spread out to surround the lodge, machine gun fire rattled down on them from the roof. Swiftly, the agents took cover.

The special agents returned the gunfire, which was coming from the second floor. They also fired tear gas shells, but the wind blew the tear gas back in their direction, making the agents sick. One of them hurried to a telephone to give directions to additional agents who had arrived in Rhinelander to back up the operation.

While the agent was telephoning, the operator broke in to tell him there was trouble at another cottage about two miles away. Special Agent W. Carter Baum, another FBI man, and a constable went there and found a parked car which the constable recognized as belonging to a local resident. They pulled up and identified themselves.

Inside the other car, "Baby Face" Nelson was holding three local residents at gunpoint. He turned, leveled a revolver at the lawmen's car, and ordered them to step out. But without waiting for them to comply, Nelson opened fire. Baum was killed, and the constable and the other agent were severely wounded. Nelson jumped into the Ford they had been using and fled.

As the Federal agents fought it out with Dillinger at the lodge, they noticed a car carrying three men pulling away from the lodge. Believing that the car's occupants were members of the Dillinger Gang attempting to escape, they fired at them. Passengers John Hoffman and John Morris were wounded; Eugene Boiseneau was killed. They turned out to be local Civilian Conservation Corps workers who had innocently come to the lodge to have a few beers and got caught in the middle of the battle.

Although the police greatly outnumbered the fugitives, withering fire from the doors and windows of the resort forced them to retreat into the woods. Although three women members of the gang were arrested, Dillinger and eight of his men escaped.[37] Purvis admitted the operation was a failure. He offered his resignation to Hoover, who refused to accept it.

Emil Wanatka, owner of the Little Bohemia Resort, told the press: "John Dillinger had been here at Little Bohemia only about four hours when I recognized him. I had seen his picture in the newspapers many times. After supper, Dillinger and four of his gang invited me to play cards with them. We sat there playing two-bit limit poker when I suddenly recognized his features. I was frightened. I knew I should not do anything that would cause Dillinger and his pals to hurt me so I kept my mouth shut. I played along and lost sixteen or eighteen dollars. Dillinger won. It was a gentlemanly game and Dillinger enjoys cards. He is a good player. The women played rummy.

"Last Friday afternoon, a man and a woman came here and asked for accommodations. I showed them the rooms and they said more people were coming. About two hours later another car came."[38]

With an army of federal, state, county, and city police patrolling every road between St. Paul, Stillwater, Hastings, and Prescott, Dillinger, Tommy Carroll, and John Hamilton were engaged in a gun battle with a Dakota County Sheriff's deputy near St. Paul Park. As the gangsters fired machine guns at the police car, other units from both St. Paul and Minneapolis joined in the fray.[39]

After racing through the town of Afton, Dillinger abandoned the vehicle near Hastings. The car, blood-soaked and bullet riddled, was found on Highway 53, only five miles from the St. Paul city limits. Police found that one of their bullets had entered the rear of the car at a point where it could not have missed hitting one of the fleeing suspects, and the blood-soaked seats were another indication that one of the robbers had been wounded.

"We were stationed at the bridge at Hastings," Officer Fred McArdle told the press. "We saw the Ford coupe coming from the spiral bridge and we jumped into Joe Heinen's car. There were Joe, Norman Dieter, and Larry Dunn (all Dakota County deputies) and myself. Just as we were going to cut this coupe off at the bridge, a cattle truck pulled in front of us, the coupe got on the bridge, and we couldn't pass the truck until after we got across the bridge. Then the coupe was way up ahead and going fast.

"We took out after them, and we were almost up to St. Paul Park before we could begin shooting. They began shooting back. I guess there were about fifteen or twenty shots fired from each car. One of the bullets hit our car in the wood framework above the windshield, and just above Joe Heinen's head.

"At St. Paul Park, they turned off east, and took to the hill roads over toward Cottage Grove. We kept after them and did some more shooting, but they got away from us on those roads. We went as fast as we could on those roads but they outdistanced us. So we finally lost them. . . ."[40]

During Dillinger's escape, John Hamilton was seriously wounded. Refuge was sought and obtained by Dillinger, Homer Van Meter, and the wounded Hamilton from members of the Karpis-Barker Gang. Because Hamilton was dying, Dillinger took him to Dr. Joseph Moran in his office in the Irving Park Hotel. The underworld physician had been working almost exclusively for the Barker-Karpis Gang the past year.[41]

Moran, an alcoholic, was a qualified physician who had lost his license for performing illegal abortions. Rumor had it that he had accidentally killed two of his patients by poisoning them. His function with the

Barker-Karpis Gang, however, was treating bullet wounds as well as trying his hand at plastic surgery.

He was anything but a specialist in the field of plastic surgery although he did his best to alter physical characteristics of wanted men, including Alvin Karpis, to whom he gave ear lobes which the gangster had not possessed before. He also performed the very painful process of shaving fingerprints although he was not skilled enough to realize that fingerprints grew back and could not be permanently destroyed. Nonetheless, Dillinger pinned his hopes of saving Hamilton's life on him.[42]

Dr. Moran, however, was both outraged and terrified finding the most wanted man in America on his doorstep and refused to treat Hamilton. When Dillinger demanded medical assistance, Dr. Moran put him in touch with some of his physician friends also affiliated with Barker.[43]

Hamilton was eventually taken to the apartment of Volney Davis at 415 Post Street in Aurora, some forty-five miles southwest of Chicago. Since the Bremer kidnapping, the Barker-Karpis Gang had been lying low. Freddie Barker and Alvin Karpis were hiding out in Ohio while Davis and others took refuge in Chicago.

Dillinger, Van Meter, and the dying Hamilton comprised a risk that the Barker-Karpis element could ill afford. The following day, federal agents arrested former politician and sometimes member of the Barker Gang, John J. "Boss" McLaughlin, and commenced a rigid interrogation procedure. This interrogation placed them all in dire straits.

Shortly after the arrest of McLaughlin, Doc Barker, Harry Campbell, and William Weaver joined Davis at his apartment. As dangerous as it was, they allowed Dillinger and his friends to stay. While Hamilton was pumped full of pain-killers, the others stood guard in case McLaughlin squealed and a raid was carried out.

Through mutual contacts, who were members of the Capone Syndicate, Dillinger was put in touch with Elmer Farmer at Bensenville, Illinois, and through him, arrangements were made to take Hamilton to the home of Volney Davis at Aurora. Hamilton, however, died at Davis' home and was buried by Davis, Doc Barker, John Dillinger, Homer Van Meter,

William Weaver, and Harry Campbell in a gravel pit near Oswego, Illinois. The body of Hamilton was later recovered on August 28, 1935, by special Agents of the Federal Bureau of Investigation.[44]

Shortly after the gun battle at Little Bohemia, the Chicago Field Division of the Federal Bureau of Investigation received information that an individual appeared at the Uptown State Bank, 1050 Wilson Avenue, Chicago, and presented $900 in five dollar bills and $100 in ten and twenty dollar bills and requested that $100 in bills be given in exchange. The teller at the bank was suspicious of this exchange and compared the serial numbers appearing on the five and ten dollar bills with the ransom list. It was found to be ransom money. Special Agents of the Federal Bureau of Investigation acting promptly on this lead and having obtained a description of the individual who passed the money redoubled their efforts to locate him.

On April 26th, an individual requested a hundred dollar bill for ten $10 bills, which were determined by the officials of the bank to be ransom money. Again the Chicago Field Division of the Federal Bureau of Investigation was immediately notified and investigation disclosed that the individual who had exchanged the money had made the remark that he was a "bookie."

William Edward Vidler was arrested by special agents at a bookmaker's establishment at 226 South Wells Street, in Chicago with $2,665 identified as part of the Bremer ransom money. Vidler admitted that he was the man who had been exchanging the money in Chicago but denied that he knew it was ransom money. Federal agents also learned that Vidler's associates in the exchange of the money were John J. McLaughlin, commonly known as "Boss" McLaughlin, John J. McLaughlin, Jr., and Philip Delaney.[45]

On April 28, 1934, Boss McLaughlin had been taken into custody by special agents. He was indignant that he should be arrested. Telegrams were dispatched to the President of the United States and to the attorney general by McLaughlin's wife, protesting the arrest. The attempt failed and McLaughlin remained in custody. The ex-Illinois state legislator was unable to gain his freedom by endeavoring to use political influence.

John McLaughlin, Jr., and Philip Delaney were also arrested and charged with being money-changers. When questioned concerning his part in the transaction, John J. McLaughlin stated that he first negotiated with one Frankie Wright in the lobby of a prominent hotel in Chicago; that he was later introduced by Wright to individuals known only to him as "Izzy" and "Slim"; and that he agreed to exchange the money on a 5 percent cut basis and understood from information furnished him by the two men that the first $100,000 to be exchanged was the Hamm ransom money paid by William A. Hamm of St. Paul to effect his release from a gang of kidnappers and that $200,000, paid by Edward G. Bremer, would be forthcoming at a later date to be exchanged.

Special Agents of the Federal Bureau of Investigation also learned that McLaughlin had visited "Izzy" and "Slim" at a hotel on Irving Park Boulevard in Chicago. Investigation disclosed that the hotel in question was the Irving Hotel on Irving Park Boulevard and that the room for the office in which John McLaughlin had visited was rented by Dr. Joseph Moran.

Additional rooms had been rented at the hotel by Dr. Moran on April 23, 25, 26, and 27, 1934. This investigation disclosed that an individual known as Roy Gray, of 626 Waveland Avenue, Chicago, was a frequent visitor to Dr. Moran.

Special agents of the Federal Bureau of Investigation obtained a photograph of Roy Gray, and after examining it, discovered that it was identical with the photograph of Russell Gibson, for whom the Federal Bureau of Investigation had previously prepared an Identification Order, showing Gibson to be wanted for violation of the National Motor Vehicle Theft Act and also for robbing the American First National Bank messenger at Oklahoma City, Oklahoma, on May 24, 1929. Special Agents of the Federal Bureau of Investigation through their investigative efforts identified "Izzy" as Oliver A. Berg, who was wanted by the Illinois State Penitentiary at Joliet, Illinois.

Special agents on the night of August 22, 1934, arrested Oliver A. Berg at the home of his sister, 5248 North Winthrop Avenue, Chicago. Nearby in a desk of the room in which Berg was taken into custody were found fully loaded revolvers which Berg had no opportunity to use. Berg did not surrender peacefully and although he was advised of the identity of the special agents, he screamed that he was "being taken for a ride." Berg boasted that he was one of the few surviving members of the so-called "Bugs" Moran mob, which had terrorized Chicago in the early prohibition days. Most members of that gang had been annihilated on February 14, 1929, in the St. Valentine's Day Massacre, in which Fred Goetz is alleged to have been one of the machine gunners.

Berg's record indicated he had been received at the Southern Illinois State Penitentiary on December 15, 1926, to serve a sentence of ten years to life imprisonment after conviction on a charge of robbery with a gun. He appealed his case and while it was receiving consideration of the Appellate Court, he was released from the Illinois State penitentiary on bond on November 7, 1931. The Appellate Court, however, sustained the sentence of the Lower Court and Berg did not return to the penitentiary until after his apprehension by Special Agents of the Federal Bureau of Investigation.

Notes

[1] Federal Bureau of Investigation Files, Freedom of Information Act, Melvin H. Purvis, File Number 67-7489.

[2] Paul Maccabee, *John Dillinger Slept Here, A Crooks' Tour of Crime and Corruption in St. Paul, 1920-1936*, St. Paul, Minnesota Historical Society Press, 1995, pp. 213-214.

[3] *Chicago Daily Tribune*, February 23, 1934.

[4] Edwin J. (Ed) Riege, "The Barker-Karpis Rouges," *Minnesota Police Journal*, August 1991.

[5] *New York World Telegram*, March 3, 1934; "Public Enemy #1 - John Dillinger," EyeWitness to History, www.eyewitnesstohistory.com (2000).

[6] Federal Bureau of Investigation, United States Department of Justice, History Archives.

[7] Paul Maccabee, *John Dillinger Slept Here*, p. 208.

[8] Cathy Prachar interview with author March 16, 1983, Plymouth, Minnesota.

[9] (Sioux Falls) *Daily Argus Leader*, March 6, 1934.

[10] Ardyce Samp, *The Dillinger Robbery of the Security National Bank & Trust Company of Sioux Falls*, Sioux Falls, Rushmore House Publishing, 1992, pp. 4-7.

[11] Paul Maccabee, *John Dillinger Slept Here*, p. 213.

[12] *Moody County Enterprise*, March 15, 1934.

[13] Lee P. Loomis Archive of Mason City History, First National Bank Robbery, Mason

City Public Library.

[14] *Des Moines Tribune*, March 14, 1934.

[15] Lee P. Loomis Archive of Mason City History, First National Bank Robbery, Mason City Public Library.

[16] *Cedar Rapids Gazette*, June 9, 1934.

[17] *Casper (Wyoming) Tribune-Herald*, April 3, 1934; FBI Files, #32-16384, Alvin Karpis and Fred Barker.

[18] Paul Maccabee, *John Dillinger Slept Here*, p. 213.

[19] *St. Paul Sunday Pioneer Press*, April 1, 1934.

[20] FBI Files, RCS:TD I.C.#7-576, November 19, 1936, The Kidnaping of Edward George Bremer, St. Paul, Minnesota, History and Early Association of the Karpis-Barker Gang Prior to the Abduction of Mr. Bremer.

[21] Theodore C. Blegen, *Minnesota A History of the State*, pp. 524-526.

[22] Charles Rumford Walker, *American City*, New York, Farrar and Rinehart, Inc., 1937, pp. 85-88.

[23] Joseph Stipanovich, *City of Lakes An Illustrated History of Minneapolis*, p. 179.

[24] *Minneapolis Labor Review*, May 11, 1934, Volume 27, No. 403. Official organ of Minneapolis Central Labor Union and Hennepin County, the Minneapolis Building Trades Council, the United Card and Label Council, and the Minnesota Pipe Trades Association .

[25] Dara Moskowitz, :"Minneapolis Confidential," City Pages, Volume 16, Number 775, October 11, 1995.

[26] *Minneapolis Journal*, May 17, 1934.

[27] Ibid., May 16, 1934.

[28] Joseph Stipanovich, *City of Lakes An Illustrated History of Minneapolis*, p. 180.

[29] Ibid.

[30] Ibid., May 19, 1934.

[31] Ibid.

[32] Ibid.

[33] George H. Mayer, *The Political Career of Floyd B. Olson*, Minneapolis, University of Minnesota Press, 1951, pp. 196-198.

[34] Ibid.; Joseph Stipanovich, *City of Lakes An Illustrated History of Minneapolis*, p. 180.

[35] George H. Mayer, *The Political Career of Floyd B. Olson*, p. 196; Minneapolis Journal, May 21, 1934.

[36] *Dallas Morning News*, April 2, 1934.

[37] *St. Paul Daily News*, April 23, 1934.

[38] *St. Paul Pioneer Press*, April 24, 1934.

[39] *St. Paul Daily News*, April 23, 1934.

[40] *St. Paul Pioneer Press*, April 24, 1934.

[41] Steve Nickel & William J. Helmer, *Baby Face Nelson, Portrait of a Public Enemy*, p. 255.

[42] Miriam Allen deFord, *The Real Ma Barker*, p. 35.
[43] Steve Nickel & William J. Helmer, *Baby Face Nelson, Portrait of a Public Enemy*, p. 255.
[44] *St. Paul Pioneer Press*, April 24, 1934.
[45] *St. Paul Pioneer Press*, April 28, 1934.

Chapter Eight

Assassinations

"Doc and I shot the son of a bitch. Anybody who talks to whores is too dangerous to live. We dug a hole in Michigan and dropped him in and covered the hole with lime. I don't think anybody's ever going to come across Doc Moran again."

—Freddie Barker[1]

An investigation into the background of Dr. Joseph P. Moran revealed that he had an extensive practice in medicine, most of his patients being members of the underworld. Dr. Moran himself had served a sentence at the State Penitentiary, Joliet, Illinois, for the crime of abortion. He was received at the penitentiary on November 17, 1926, for LaSalle County, Illinois, under sentence of one to ten years. He was paroled April 7, 1930 and having violated the terms of his parole was returned to the penitentiary on January 23, 1931. He was again paroled on December 15, 1931.[2]

While in the penitentiary, Dr. Moran engaged in medical work and is said to have operated upon approximately 4,500 people, including prisoners and officials during the period of his incarceration. Also during his incarceration, Dr. Moran met various labor leaders who visited that institution and through these contacts he became the physician for the Chicago Chauffeurs, Teamsters, and Helpers' Union, with headquarters in Maywood,

"Ma"—The Life and Times of "Ma" Barker and Her Boys

Fred Goetz. (Courtesy FBI Files)

Illinois, subsequent to the time he was released from the penitentiary.

As physician for this union, Dr. Moran became very closely associated with the Touhy mob and the Capone Syndicate. During August of 1933, the union was reorganized and at the time Dr. Moran was dropped as its physician. He opened an office on Irving Park Boulevard, where many of his friends from the underworld continued to call upon him.

Fred Goetz and Irene Dorsey, subsequent to the release of Mr. Bremer, moved from their apartment at 1934 West Garfield Boulevard, to another located at 7827 South Shore Drive, in Chicago. After the collection of the ransom money from the Bremer family, it was taken to the apartment of Fred Goetz by Volney Davis, Goetz and Bryan Bolton, but later in order to better conceal the loot, Goetz took the ransom money and buried it in the garage of Simon Cinotto, Irene Dorsey's uncle, at Wilmington, Illinois.

At the time Mr. Bremer was being held for ransom, the women members of the mob concealed themselves in apartments in Chicago. Edna Murray, Wynona Burdette, and Paula Harmon secured an apartment together at 6212 University Avenue. The arrangements for this apartment were made by William J. Harrison.

Ma Barker at this time was residing in an apartment at 7269 South Shore Drive, in Chicago, which she occupied until September, 1934. Here she waited patiently for her sons to successfully consummate their latest crime. Harrison also did other favors for the gang and on January 27, 1934, Harrison, with Wynona Burdette and Edna Murray, traveled from Chicago, Illinois, to Toledo, Ohio, and registered at the Algeo Hotel.

The purpose of this trip was to secure license plates for the automobile of Fred Barker. Harrison during the time he was operating speak-easies at Calumet City, Illinois, had as a partner, Bert Angus, who at the time of the visit in February 1934 of Harrison to Toledo, was operating a roadhouse known as the Casino Club, Point Place, Ohio, a suburb of Toledo, in partnership with his ex-convict brother, Ted Angus. Immediately upon Harrison's arrival in Toledo, he contacted his old friend Bert Angus and through a bartender arranged for the purchase of a set of license plates.

That same afternoon, Edna Murray, Wynona Burdette, and Harrison were sleeping in their rooms at the Algeo Hotel. Captain George Timiney, in charge of the so-called "hoodlum" squad of the Toledo Police Department, played a practical joke on Harrison by sending two officers to arrest him. Harrison pleaded that he was a good friend of Bert Angus, but the officers refused to heed his pleadings, but finally agreed to take him to the Casino Club to ascertain whether Angus would vouch for him. As a part of the hoax, Bert Angus and Captain Timiney refused to recognize Harrison.

Kate "Ma" Barker. (Author's collection)

In the meantime, the women in the hotel were frantic. They feared that possibly the Karpis-Barker gang had already been identified as the kidnapers of Mr. Bremer. Immediately after securing the license plates, Harrison, with Wynona Burdette and Edna Murray, returned to Chicago.

Just prior to the release of Mr. Bremer, dissent arose

among Edna Murray, Wynona Burdette, and Paula Harmon. Paula rented another apartment, located at 6708 Constance Avenue, Chicago, where Fred Barker presumably resided with her after the collection of the ransom money. The landlord later complained that this apartment was vacated without notice the latter part of February 1934 and left in a disorderly condition. Due to the reliable contact that Harrison had established in Toledo, Fred Barker and Paula Harmon, after vacating the apartment on Constance Avenue, proceeded to the vicinity of Toledo as Mr. and Mrs. A. J. Bredford, and rented an apartment at 4905 Summit Street in Point Place.

In late February, 1934, Volney Davis, posing as a gambler and ex-prize fighter, with Edna Murray, moved to Aurora, Illinois, where they had an apartment at 415 Fox Street. Volney and Edna believed that they would be in less fear of apprehension if they did not live in too close proximity to other members of the gang.

Their wishes in this matter were soon shattered, as William Weaver and Myrtle Eaton also moved to Aurora, and rented a room at 50 South 4th Street, and later moved into an apartment at 411 Claim Street. "Doc" Barker also made his home with Weaver and Myrtle Eaton at the latter address. Weaver represented himself to the citizens of Aurora as being William Thornton, a man engaged in the slot-machine business. "Doc" Barker was known as Mr. Morley.

After the assassination of Fred Goetz, the gang deemed it advisable to move the ransom money from its burial place at Wilmington, Illinois. On March 23rd, Kate Barker and Irene Dorsey contacted Volney Davis at his apartment in Aurora, and on that night Davis, with Kate Barker and Irene Dorsey, removed the ransom money from Wilmington, and transferred it to the apartment of Fred Barker in Chicago. Fred had just returned from Toledo. Thereafter the ransom negotiations with "Boss" McLaughlin began on or about April 18, 1934, and the money was taken to the apartment of William Weaver at Aurora. The money was then routed through Dr. Moran to the money-changers in Chicago.

During the months of March and April 1934, Moran's rooms at the Irving Hotel were used as a rendezvous by Doc Barker, Oliver A. Berg, Boss

McLaughlin, Russell Gibson, and other members of the Karpis-Barker gang. Dr. Moran's rooms contained at various times many thousands of dollars of the ransom money. After the money had been exchanged, it was returned to Dr. Moran's rooms, where percentages were paid for the exchanges.

Additional quantities of ransom money were given to McLaughlin for further exchange. Moran received his cut for the assistance which he rendered. Oliver A. Berg, Russell Gibson, and James Wilson, the nephew of Dr. Moran, were assisting the mobsters by making trips with them to Aurora to secure money for purposes of exchange in Chicago, and Wilson was running other errands which were required. James Wilson became involved with this notorious mob because he had hoped that his uncle, Dr. Moran, would secure sufficient remuneration from the exchange of the ransom money to permit his uncle defraying his expenses for a medical course in college.

Special agents of the Federal Bureau of Investigation ascertained that on or about the 10th of March, 1934, Dr. Moran operated on the fingers and faces of Alvin Karpis and Fred Barker in his rooms at the Irving Hotel, in an unsuccessful effort to alter their fingerprints and facial characteristics to prevent identification.

The operations cost Barker $500 and Karpis $750. The extra $250 charged Karpis was for patching up his face and included a shot of morphine which put him under through the whole procedure. The fingerprint operation was very painful. Dr. Moran began by looping plastic bands tightly around Karpis' fingers at the first joints. After freezing the fingertips with an injection of cocaine, he began scraping with a scalpel. According to Karpis, "he really took the meat off," and in finishing each finger, he removed the plastic band and bandaged the scraped tip with cotton.[3]

After these operations, Alvin Karpis and Fred Barker convalesced in a room provided for them by Oliver Berg at the home of his sister on Winthrop Avenue in Chicago. Fred Barker was suffering from operations the night Fred Goetz was killed. This prevented him from taking an active part in the removal of the ransom money from Wilmington, Illinois. Fred Barker was referred to as a "raving maniac," because of pain caused by the unsuccessful operations performed by the ex-convict doctor.

"Ma"—The Life and Times of "Ma" Barker and Her Boys

On the day that "Boss" McLaughlin was arrested with his cronies in Chicago, a dramatic incident occurred at Aurora. The gang did not know whether McLaughlin would talk. They anticipated that if he did, the gang's hideout at Aurora would become known and decided to be prepared. Doc Barker, Harry Campbell, Volney Davis, and William Weaver, together with their guests John Dillinger and Homer Van Meter, guarded the windows and the doors of Volney Davis' apartment all through the night, each armed with a machine gun, anticipating a raid by special agents.

The following morning, Russell Gibson brought them the details of what he had learned concerning the arrest of the money-changers. With the announcement in the press on April 28, 1934, of the arrest of John J. McLaughlin and the others, Dr. Joseph P. Moran abandoned his rooms at the Irving Hotel and together with Oliver A. Berg, Russell Gibson, and James Wilson, fled to Toledo.

Prior to the occurrences at Aurora, and immediately after the release of Mr. Bremer, Harry Campbell, and Wynona Burdette, under aliases of Mr. and Mrs. George Nelson, rented an apartment at the Jarvis Apartments in Toledo, and later, on March 25th, as Mr. and Mrs. George Winfield rented a house at 2831 131st Street, Point Place, Ohio. Harry Campbell returned to Chicago and Aurora on various occasions during the ransom exchange negotiations.

On April 18th, Alvin Karpis and Dolores Delaney rented rooms at the Jarvis Apartments in Toledo as Mr. and Mrs. Edward L. Baudry, where they resided until May 18th.

Edna Murray, after fleeing from Aurora subsequent to the apprehension of "Boss" McLaughlin, traveled to Kansas City, Missouri, and later joined Volney Davis in Toledo, where on May 9th they rented an apartment at the Burdella Apartments under the names of Mr. and Mrs. H. J. Morley.

The investigation by special agents revealed that although the gang had fled from Chicago and Aurora, they were making every effort to avoid detection and identification. Arrangements were made at Toledo for Volney Davis, Harry Campbell, and Doc Barker to undergo facial and finger operations similar to those which had been performed on Karpis and Barker at Chicago.

On the night Dr. Moran was to perform these operations, with the assistance of James Wilson, at the home of Harry Campbell in Point Place, Campbell alarmed the other members of the gang by saying that he believed the house was under surveillance by police officers. The operations were postponed while Fred Barker made inquiries, through Ted Angus, whether that situation really existed. Upon receiving information that there was nothing at which they should be alarmed, Dr. Moran performed the operations.

Harry Campbell, as was revealed later, lacked the courage in going through with the operations; so he postponed it by advising his associates that there was danger of a police raid. Volney Davis, Harry Campbell, and Doc Barker were nursed during their convalescent period by James Wilson, Wynona Burdette, and Edna Murray. They suffered severe pain in their fingers and had to be hand-fed by those attending them.

The favorite hang-out for the mob after their flight from Chicago was the Casino Club. Here the gang spent their money freely and enjoyed the fruits of their crime. Charles J. Fitzgerald, better know as "Old Fitz" or the "Old Man," was with other members of the gang in Toledo and enjoyed the recreation and entertainment at the Casino Club with them. Fitzgerald was popular among the members of the club and others who visited that place, as he would frequently buy a beer and a whiskey for the house.

In Minneapolis, lawlessness continued to increase. Newspapers announced there would be a movement of trucks the next day. But another clash was unavoidable when a thousand special deputies and a small number of police squared off with 2,500 strikers in the market place. *The Minneapolis Journal* estimated that 3,000 persons joined the crowd in case any of the trucks decided to move. A union official estimated the crowd at 60,000. Radio broadcasters were on the spot with live coverage when an unidentified person hurled a crate of tomatoes through a store window. Baseball bats, saps, and rocks smashed skulls, and as deputies and police fled, several badges were found and displayed by the strikers. Several members of the Citizens' Alliance were killed, one deputy died, and another was mortally wounded.[4]

"Ma"—The Life and Times of "Ma" Barker and Her Boys

C. Arthur Lyman was an innocent bystander who happened to be in the wrong place at the wrong time. Lyman was struck by a rock thrown by one of the strikers and killed. On the ground, their confederates turned over trucks.[5]

The *Journal's* editorial page mourned the passing of C. Arthur Lyman, the vice-president of the American Ball Company. The piece condemned the lawlessness and overbearing actions of the strikers that had resulted in the death of an important businessman. The *Journal* contended that Communists were in control of the strike and blamed not the "honest American strikers, but the red revolutionaries who managed the bloody riot of Tuesday . . . .who killed Arthur Lyman."[6]

The following Sunday an agreement was reached between the Teamsters and the employers. The agreement, however, was subject only to voluntary compliance on the part of the employers. It soon became clear the employers were not about to honor the agreement. On July 16th, the Local 574 leaders called for a new strike to compel the employers to honor the May agreement. On July 20 a truck carrying fifty heavily armed policeman ambushed a group of strikers, killing two of them and wounding sixty-seven others. Governor Olson declared martial law on July 26th.[7]

The *Journal* published its account of the July 20th incident inaccurately blaming the strikers rather than the police: "The strikers rushed forward. They swarmed over the truck and onto police squad cars, laying about them strenuously with fists and clubs. Literally fighting for their lives, the police fired once into the air in an effort to frighten off the strikers. It did no good. On they came. Finally one policeman aimed his gun at the crowd and fired. A striker toppled over. Then another policeman fired. Another striker fell. The mob started to move back under the more rigorous tactics of the police. For a moment it seemed that more gunfire would be averted, but the rioters congealed in another group again and when ordered to disperse, defied the police."[8]

The *Journal's* fabrication of the wrong "bad guys" irked many of its subscribers. Governor Olson appointed a committee to investigate the shooting and found that police officers were at no time endangered, pickets were unarmed, pickets did not attack the officers, the truck movement was a "plant," and the police department became an agency to break the strike. "The decoy itself was dastardly; the deliberate attempt by the *Journal* to tell the public an incorrect version was reprehensible."[9]

At the end of July, Minnesota guardsmen pulled an early morning raid and peacefully arrested the leaders of Local 574, with the exception of two who had slipped away. John Belor, who had been shot by the police during "Bloody Friday," died that same day. The *Journal*'s headline read "Troops Jail Four Strike Leaders, Seize headquarters, Arrest 25 in Truck Riots; Striker Wounded in Shooting Affray Dies." No mention was made that Belor had been shot by a policeman and it gave the impression he had been a victim of rioters.[10]

Bonnie Parker. (Photo Courtesy of Rick Mattix)

Two days later, Governor Olson sent Lieutenant Kenneth Haycraft and a detachment of troops to raid the headquarters of the Citizens' Alliance. They found "a sheaf of dictaphone records and confidential letters." The evidence proved a close relationship had been maintained by the Citizens' Alliance and the Employers' Advisory Committee. Haycraft later found that the Alliance had been "tipped off" and four files had been removed the previous day.

The strike ended in August. Martial law was lifted by Governor Olson, troops were dispersed, and Minneapolis went back to Depression-era normalcy. The *Journal* attributed the death of the strike to secret elections. President Roosevelt, however, after meeting with Governor Olson, had issued an order "to the Reconstruction Finance Corporation to withdraw its loans to banks that were financing employer resistance. The pressure proved decisive because Twin City banks had served as the principal coercive agency of the Citizens' Alliance. Deprived of life-and-death financial power over debt-ridden employers, the Alliance could not keep the strike from collapsing."[11]

On May 18th, President Roosevelt signed seven anti-crime bills designed to put teeth in the federal search for John Dillinger and other public enemies. At the same time, he issued a somewhat militant statement that the Department of Justice was going after every criminal "big and little."[12]

Only five days later, a posse of six officers ambushed and killed Clyde Barrow and Bonnie Parker near Arcadia, Louisiana. Neither Barrow nor Parker fired a shot but Clyde was reaching down for his gun when the police unleashed their deadly fusillade. The car careened to one side of the road as

Bonnie and Clyde death car. (Photo Courtesy of Rick Mattix)

Barrow fell backward and Parker slumped forward. Fearing a trap, the officers stepped from their ambuscade and poured more lead into the wrecked automobile. But Bonnie and Clyde were already dead.[13]

"Today we got them," proclaimed Dallas Deputy Bob Alcorn, who had been on the trail of the fugitives for ten long months. "They won't kill anyone else now."

In June 1934, William Weaver and Myrtle Eaton, as Mr. and Mrs. J. A. Orhee, rented a cottage at Grand Forest Beach, Ohio. Likewise Edna Murray and Volney Davis took a cottage on Lake Erie near the cottage of William Weaver and Myrtle Eaton, in an effort to avoid the company of other members of the gang, but this was unsuccessful, as various members congregated at these cottages. Discord was aroused among various members, and as a result, William Weaver and Volney Davis, who were characterized as the malcontents of the gang, were given their share of the ransom money, which to the best information obtainable, was approximately between $18,000 and $20,000 each.

After securing his share of the ransom money, Volney Davis made a trip to Buffalo, New York, where he exchanged a portion of his share of the ransom money for unmarked currency. Davis secured a Ford truck, left Grand Forest Beach, Ohio, and proceeded to Glasgow, Montana, where he was later joined by Edna Murray. Davis intended severing his connections with the Karpis-Barker Gang forever and contemplated going into business at Glasgow with Corey Bates, with whom he had become acquainted while in Aurora.

At Glasgow, Davis and Bates leased a plot of land near the Fort Peck Dam and built a night club which was also to be used as a gambling establishment. Volney Davis and Edna Murray enjoyed the free life of the West for only a short time, however, as they received information that special agents were conducting an investigation in the vicinity of Glasgow, concerning them, and they immediately fled to Kansas City.

William Weaver, after securing his share of the ransom money in August, left the other members of the gang and proceeded with Myrtle Eaton to Allandale, Florida, where they took up residence on a small chicken farm.

Alvin Karpis also reasoned that if so many of the gang continued to remain together, it would ultimately cause their apprehension, so he, with Dolores Delaney, moved to Cleveland, where in early May of 1934, they rented an apartment, the location of which has never been determined. They were soon joined by Fred Barker and Paula Harmon, who on May 20th, rented an apartment at 10515 Parkhurst Avenue, where they resided under the names of Mr. and Mrs. J. Earl Matterson.

On June 8th, Karpis and his moll, as Mr. and Mrs. H. G. Milgreth, rented a house at 18109 Flamingo Avenue, where they stayed until July 6th, before renting a house at 5973 West 140th Street. On August 16, 1934, as Mr. and Mrs. J. Earl Matterson, Fred Barker and his woman began living at 4419 West 171st Street, Cleveland.

Harry Sawyer, following the kidnapping and release of Mr. Bremer, continued to reside with his wife, Gladys, in St. Paul until April, 1934, when they fled to Las Vegas, Nevada, to avoid prosecution in connection with the abduction of Mr. Bremer. Harry Sawyer had not received his share of the ransom money, and in June, 1934 he communicated with Alvin Karpis by letter at General Delivery, Cleveland, Ohio, and made arrangements to meet Karpis in Cleveland, and thereafter did join other members of the gang in that city.

As for Dr. Joseph P. Moran, special agents ascertained that he was last seen, according to the best information available, at the Casino Club in Toledo during the latter part of July 1934. Dr. Moran had been at the club with Doc Barker, Russell Gibson, and other members of the gang and become quite intoxicated. His associates tried to quiet him and it is alleged that Dr. Moran made the remark, "I have you guys in the palm of my hand."

This statement apparently was the signing of his death warrant as Karpis suggested he should be punished and Ma Barker approved of the plan. She was still distressed with the failed operation the doctor had performed on Freddie, and members of the gang felt he had been talking too much. He left the club with two of the gang and did not return.[14]

Shortly afterwards, Moran was shot to death, his legs buried in a barrel of cement, and he and the barrel tossed into the Chicago River. Rumors circulated that Fred Barker had taken him for a boat ride on Lake Erie. The present whereabouts of Dr. Moran is best determined by a remark Fred Barker made to a member of the mob—"Doc will do no more operatin'. The fishes probably have eat him up by now."[15]

Needing a break from Cleveland, Freddie and Karpis drove to Chicago to visit Ma Barker. In taking her to a movie theatre, a special announcement flashed on the screen reading, "These Men are Public Enemies," followed by photographs of John Dillinger, "Baby Face" Nelson, Doc, Freddie, and Karpis. Then came the line, "Remember, one of these men may be sitting beside you." The lights came on in the theatre and everyone looked around giggling.[16]

In Washington, meanwhile, FBI Director J. Edgar Hoover assigned Special Agent Samuel A. Cowley to head the FBI's investigative efforts against John Dillinger. Cowley set up headquarters in Chicago, where he and Melvin Purvis, Special Agent in Charge of the Chicago office, planned their strategy. A squad of agents under Cowley worked with East Chicago policemen in tracking down all tips and rumors.[17]

"By July of 1934, our agents were receiving reports that Dillinger was in the Chicago area," recalled Melvin Purvis later. "At that time, I was special agent in charge of the Chicago office of the Department of Justice's Division of Investigation, which was the forerunner of the FBI."[18]

Late in the afternoon of Saturday, July 21, 1934, the madam of a brothel in Gary, Indiana, contacted Sergeant Martin Zarkovich of the East Chicago, Indiana Police Department with an important tip. This woman called herself Anna Sage; however, her real name was Ana Cumpanas, and she had entered the United States from her native Rumania in 1914. Because of the nature of her profession, she was considered an undesirable alien by the Immigration and Naturalization Service, and deportation proceedings had been started. Anna was willing to sell the FBI some information about Dillinger for a cash reward, plus the FBI's help in preventing her deportation.[19]

During a meeting with Anna, Cowley, and Purvis were cautious. They promised her the reward if her information led to Dillinger's capture, but said all they could do was call her cooperation to the attention of the

Department of Labor, which at that time handled deportation matters. Satisfied, Anna told the agents that a girlfriend of hers, Polly Hamilton, had visited her establishment with Dillinger. Anna had recognized Dillinger from a newspaper photograph.

Anna told the agents that she, Polly Hamilton, and Dillinger probably would be going to the movies the following evening at either the Biograph or the Marbro Theaters in Chicago. She said that she would notify them when the theater was chosen. She also said that she would wear a red dress so that they could identify her. Purvis, however, later stated she was wearing an orange skirt that night and he couldn't recall the colors of her other clothes.[20]

On Sunday, Cowley ordered all agents of the Chicago office to stand by for urgent duty. Anna Sage called that evening to confirm the plans, but she still did not know which theater they would attend. Therefore, agents and policemen were sent to both theaters. At 8:30 P.M., Anna Sage, John Dillinger, and Polly Hamilton strolled into the Biograph Theater. Purvis phoned Cowley, who shifted the other men from the Marbro to the Biograph.

Cowley also phoned J. Edgar Hoover for instructions. Hoover cautioned them to wait outside rather than risk a shooting match inside the crowded theater. Each man was instructed not to unnecessarily endanger his own life and was told that if Dillinger offered any resistance, it would be each man for himself.

"Around 8:30 P.M., I saw a man approach the marquee with two women, one of them 'the woman in red,'" later wrote Purvis. "The man was coatless, he sported a small mustache, he wore gold-rimmed dark glasses, a straw hat, a white shirt. Having committed countless photos of Dillinger to memory, I took a long, hard look. Yes, the man was Dillinger. The deadly killer calmly purchased three tickets (admission price, 30 cents each) and entered the movie house with Mrs. Sage and Polly Hamilton."[21]

When Dillinger walked into the theater that night, he had unknowingly been set up by Anna Sage, who had taken him there at the request of the FBI. Sixteen police officers and FBI agents waited over two hours outside the theater for Dillinger to exit. They even walked the aisles of the theater several times to make sure that he was still there.[22]

"We had originally planned to take Dillinger by surprise inside the theatre," wrote Purvis. "The idea was to take a seat behind him, pin his arms and capture him without raising a fuss. But the closest seat I could get was three rows away. The movie was packed. We decided to take him on the way out.

"So all of us waited, and waited. It was the longest two hours and four minutes in my life. My knees kept hitting together the whole time and I had a double hitch in my stomach."[23]

About 10:30 that evening, July 22, 1934, a dapper-looking John Dillinger, wearing a straw hat and a pin-striped suit, stepped out of the Biograph Theater on North Lincoln Avenue in downtown Chicago where he and his two lady friends had watched a film called *Manhattan Melodrama* starring Clark Gable. Accompanying him from the theater were Anna Sage, the notorious "Lady in Red," and Polly Hamilton. He had been hiding out in Polly's North Halstead Street apartment for months while pursued diligently by Melvin Purvis, the head of the Chicago branch of the FBI.[24]

A nervous Melvin Purvis, Special Agent in Charge of the Bureau's office in Chicago, stood near the Biograph box office. He'd seen Dillinger walk into the crowded theater about two hours earlier with two women, including one in an orange skirt (often called a "red dress") who had tipped off authorities that the wanted criminal would be there. Now, Purvis was waiting for Dillinger to re-emerge.

Suddenly, Purvis saw him and later recalled: "I waited under the marquee, for I had the responsibility of making the identification. When I was absolutely certain that the man was John Dillinger, I lighted a cigar. There I was nonchalantly puffing on a stogie as the gunman and his party strolled right in front of me and headed south on Lincoln Avenue.

"The cigar was the signal of identification. When I struck the match it signified that I took full responsibility that the man under observation was Dillinger and that we should take him. As Dillinger moved away, I gave a second signal. It was a wide sweep of the arm. Anyone who saw it would know that it meant: 'Let's close in.'"[25]

The pre-arranged signal with the cigar alerted the Bureau agents and local police officers taking part in the operation, but in the thick crowd less than half a dozen of the men saw it. But on this night, the bureau was prepared. The arrangement of agents, the setting of the signal, and the careful preparation were evidence that the bureau was learning how to catch the most violent criminals. The plan was not perfect, but it was sound, with agents covering all theater exits and directions Dillinger might take.

Agent Charles B. Winstead later wrote in his memorandum that he "located Special Agent in Charge Purvis, and Special Agent C. O. Hurt, and was informed by them that Dillinger had gone to the theatre from the south, and likely would return in that direction. [Winstead] stepped in a doorway where Special Agent Hurt was standing and it was agreed that when Mr. Purvis gave the signal that Dillinger was leaving the theatre, if he had gone south, Hurt was to take the right side, and this agent the left side, and endeavor to apprehend Dillinger before he reached an alley about forty or fifty feet from where we were standing. Mr. Purvis gave the signal a few minutes before 11 o'clock. Agent Hurt turned to this agent and stated, 'That is Dillinger with the straw hat, and the glasses.'"[26]

As Dillinger started down the street, agents fell in behind him and closed in. Recalled Purvis: "We had previously arranged that the other agents would run if I ran, walk if I walked, etc. In that way we would all get to Dillinger at the same time. No one wanted to win that race and get to Dillinger first, and alone.

"So I moved in from behind. Other agents sauntered out of a doorway. Another came up on Dillinger's right. The others moved in closer. Suddenly an agent barked: "Stick 'em up, Johnny. We have you surrounded."[27]

Dillinger had sensed something was wrong, and when Purvis stepped out, he quickly realized what was happening and acted by instinct, as he stepped down from the curb, passing the alley entrance. As Agent Charles Winstead would later describe, the gangster "whirled around and reached for his right front pocket [where he had a .380 Colt automatic pistol]. He started running sideways toward the alley."[28]

But it was too late; five shots were fired from the guns of three FBI agents. Three of the shots hit Dillinger and Public Enemy Number One crumbled to the pavement, his left eye shredded by one of the shots fired by the other agents who lay in wait. He had been struck by bullets fired from the front and from his rear. Two bullets slightly grazed his face next to the left eye. A third, the fatal shot, entered the base of his neck, traveled upward until it hit the second vertebra, then exited below and to the outside of his right eye. A fourth bullet, fired from the front, entered his left clavicle and exited his left side.

Two innocent bystanders, both women, were hit by bullets during the shooting although neither was injured seriously. "They shot John Dillinger and they shot me too," stated one of the victims, Mrs. Etta Natelski, to the press. "I'm not very badly hurt but I'm pretty mad."

Melvin Purvis later described the morbid scene in the alley:

"Probably I will never forget, although I would like to, the morbidness displayed by the people who gathered around the shooting. Craning necks of curious persons, women dipping handkerchiefs in Dillinger's blood."

Purvis found a spot of Dillinger's blood on his own pants cuff and a few days later was offered $50 for the trousers. At 10:50 P.M. on July 22, 1934, John Dillinger was pronounced dead in a little room in the Alexian Brothers Hospital. The successful conclusion to the Dillinger manhunt was the beginning of the end of the gangster era and a cornerstone in the evolution of the Bureau. With new powers, new skills, and within a year, a new name—the Federal Bureau of Investigation—it was well on its way to becoming a premier law enforcement agency respected around the globe.

The agents who had fired at Dillinger were Charles B. Winstead, Clarence O. Hurt, and Herman E. Hollis. Each man was commended by J. Edgar Hoover for fearlessness and courageous action. None of them ever said who actually killed Dillinger. The events of that sultry July night in Chicago proved to the public that law enforcement officers could, and would, triumph over criminals. Eventually, twenty-seven people were convicted in federal courts on charges of harboring, and aiding and abetting John Dillinger and his cronies during their reign of terror.

"Who killed Dillinger?" Melvin Purvis wrote many years later in response to questions directed to him by the media. "Officially, no one knows. The men who were there—and I was one of them—made a pact never to reveal who fired the shot that actually killed him. Now, a quarter of a century later, the pact is still binding.

"I have been credited with capturing him. I have been credited with killing him. All I have ever said was that I was with the group that captured Dillinger. That's what I stand on. After all, does it really matter that much who killed him?"[29]

"I have been advised by Mr. Purvis and Mr. Cowley that it was you who shot and killed John Dillinger. I wanted to write and to express to you not only my official, but my personal congratulations and commendation for your fearlessness and courageous action in this matter. We are all indeed proud of you. It is particularly gratifying that Dillinger was shot and killed by one of our own men. I am informed that the manner in which you handled yourself on this occasion was indicative of the usual calm, deliberate and at the same time fearless manner which has reflected itself in your work since you entered the department.

"I wanted you to know that I did personally, as well as officially, appreciate the effort and application which you have given to this case since its inception, and in particular your courageous act of last evening, in shooting and killing the notorious desperado."[30]

The FBI received some criticism over the manner of how they killed John Dillinger. It has been speculated they had no intentions of taking him alive. Having been promised the halting of her deportation for turning in Dillinger, Anna Sage was nonetheless, later deported back to Rumania.

Homer Van Meter, notorious desperado and Dillinger henchman, was shot and killed by St. Paul police only a month after Dillinger near University Avenue and Marion Street. Surprised as he stood on the street corner, Van Meter fired two shots at officers, before dashing a half block into a blind alley. He fell dead in the alley from a withering blast from police machine guns and shotguns.

Five slugs pierced his chest, one reaching his heart. Both of his hands were ripped by bullets, his chin was crushed by another, and other shells were lodged in his head. Van Meter, like Dillinger and three other gang members, was betrayed by his girlfriend who had informed police of his whereabouts.[31]

"Ma"—The Life and Times of "Ma" Barker and Her Boys

On or about August 21, 1934, Harry Campbell and Wynona Burdette left their cottage at Grand Forest Beach, Ohio, and also moved into Cleveland, where as Mr. and Mrs. George Walcott, they rented an apartment at 7009 Franklin Boulevard. Doc Barker also resided at this address with them. Harrison also associated with those members of the gang living in Cleveland.

Alvin Karpis, Fred Barker, Harry Campbell, Harry Sawyer, Doc Barker, and William Harrison enjoyed their rest at Cleveland, frequenting the Harvard Club, a notorious gambling establishment in Newberg Heights, Ohio, a suburb of Cleveland, which was operated by James "Shimmy" Patton and a business partner.

The gang in September of 1934 still possessed approximately $100,000 of the original ransom money, and to avoid detection, efforts were being made by them to exchange it for money which could not be detected by the serial numbers. William Harrison and Harry Sawyer were designated as the emissaries of the mob to proceed to Miami, Florida, and make arrangements for this exchange, and on September 1st, Sawyer and Harrison took rooms at a hotel in Miami.

Four days later, the tranquility enjoyed by those who remained in Cleveland, was shattered when Wynona Burdette, Gladys Sawyer, and Paula Harmon visited the bar in the Cleveland Hotel where they indulged heavily in intoxicating liquors. They became boisterous and as a result they were arrested by the Cleveland police department on charges of being drunk and disorderly. They were taken from the hotel screaming, fearing that their identities would become known. Special agents learned of the arrest of the women and identified them as being associates of the Karpis-Barker gang.

Again it was time for the remaining members of the gang in Cleveland to move. Dolores Delaney was instructed by Karpis to immediately proceed to Toledo and register at the Algeo Hotel. There, Delaney received further instructions from Karpis to proceed to Chicago. Fred Barker and Alvin Karpis followed and Karpis met Dolores Delaney in Chicago. Fred Barker, meanwhile, met his mother and the next place of refuge was Miami, Florida.

Special agents, after the identification of the women were made, conducted an investigation at the various residences which had been occupied by the gangsters, but found that they had fled. Paula Harmon, Wynona Burdette, and Gladys Sawyer, after being questioned concerning the wanderings of the gang, were released. Gladys Sawyer returned to her home in St. Paul, but later rejoined her husband and proceeded to Mississippi.

After the release of Wynona Burdette, she proceeded to the home of her sister in Tulsa, Oklahoma, and later to the home of another sister near Hominy, Oklahoma. Wynona had vowed that she was through with gangsters and their activities. She expressed a desire that she could again secure a position in her native state and remain there as a law-abiding citizen. Paula Harmon, upon being discharged from custody, returned to her home at Port Arthur, Texas, later to be committed to a state hospital for mental disorders. She thereafter at no time associated with other members of the mob.

According to Agent McIntire, Paula Harmon had told agents that Kate Barker, while condoning the criminal activities of her sons, did not approve of their fraternizing with women. Upon instructions from the Barker boys, Paula delivered money to George Barker at Neosho, Missouri, during the summer of 1934. Jess Doyle later related that Arthur Barker retained some regard for his father because after Doc Barker's release from the Oklahoma State Penitentiary on September 10, 1932, he visited his father at Neosho before proceeding to St. Paul to join his mother and other members of the gang.[32]

William Harrison and Harry Sawyer had, in the meantime, started negotiations with Cassius McDonald to make further exchanges of the ransom money. Cassius McDonald, a man of fifty years of age, had for twenty-five years been engaged in gambling activities in Chicago, Detroit, and Havana, Cuba. He maintained a residence at Trombley Road and Lake St. Clair, Detroit, Michigan, where he entertained many prominent politicians. For ten years, McDonald had spent a considerable portion of his time in Cuba, as a result of which he gained control of the gambling activities in Havana.[33]

On September 5th, McDonald traveled by air to Havana where he contacted a brokerage firm, stating to the officials of that firm that he had a quantity of small denomination of American bills with which he desired to purchase Cuban gold. McDonald introduced himself to the brokerage firm as

Mr. O'Brien. McDonald exchanged $18,000 of the ransom money and received $14,000 in Cuban gold in exchange.

The following day McDonald went to the National City Bank in Havana, where arrangements were made for the sale of the Cuban gold through that bank and he received fourteen one thousand dollar bills in exchange. Later, on September 10th, McDonald under the name O'Brien again contacted the brokerage firm and made arrangements to exchange $72,000 in ransom money for larger bills. The representatives of the brokerage firm were Rene Bolivar and Juan Ruis, and on the occasion of his second visit to the firm, McDonald invited Bolivar and Ruis to his room at the National Hotel, at which place they observed William J. Harrison. McDonald, while in the hotel room, produced a newspaper-wrapped package which contained $72,000 in small bills. Bolivar thereafter went to the Chase National Bank in Havana with McDonald and the money was exchanged for one thousand dollar bills. The Chase National Bank charged a discount of one-fourth of 1 percent on the transaction.

On October 22nd, Charles "Pretty Boy" Floyd was shot and killed by policemen under Chief Hugh J. McDermott and federal agents at the Conkle farm, seven miles north of East Liverpool, Ohio. Officers had spotted Floyd attempting to hide behind a corn crib. Although he was armed with two automatic revolvers, Floyd did not fire his weapons, but instead tried to run over a hill. Police fired fifty shots while giving chase. Floyd died within a few minutes of being hit. His last words were, "I'm Floyd." His body was identified "without a doubt" by McDermott and Melvin H. Purvis, chief of the Federal agents on duty.[34]

Next to fall was the ruthless Lester Gillis, better known by his alias George "Baby Face" Nelson, who ended up killing three FBI agents, more than anyone in history. Despite his boyish looks, his violent temper had eventually caused even Dillinger to refuse to rob banks with him. The FBI's search for Nelson intensified in July 1934, after Dillinger was killed by Bureau agents.

On November 27th, two Bureau agents on a stake-out in Lake Geneva, Wisconsin, encountered Nelson. Nelson fled but was later spotted nearby by another agent, who wrote down his license plate number. With

Nelson in the vehicle were his wife, Helen Gillis, and John Paul Chase, Nelson's long-time partner.[35]

Samuel P. Cowley, an FBI Agent and Inspector, who was in Chicago to spearhead the search for Nelson, learned that "Baby Face" may have been heading towards Chicago. Cowley immediately dispatched Agents Bill Ryan and Tom McDade out to search for Nelson's car on the highway. Cowley then sent Agent Herman "Ed" Hollis out in a second car.

Agents Ryan and McDade spotted Nelson heading south on the highway; they made a u-turn and pursued him. Nelson saw them and quickly made two u-turns of his own, so that he was suddenly following the agents. A gun battle ensued, and although outgunned, one of Agent Ryan's bullets pierced the radiator of Nelson's car. Nelson's car sputtered and the agents raced ahead and pulled over.

Moments later, Agents Cowley and Hollis passed the still fleeing Nelson on the highway. Hollis made a u-turn and gave chase. His car disabled, Nelson pulled off the road near a park in Barrington, Illinois. Nelson and Chase jumped out of the car and took up positions with their weapons. Hollis skidded to a stop about 150 feet past the outlaw's car.

Chase and Nelson immediately opened fire on the Federal men. Both agents jumped out of their car and returned fire. Hollis was killed and Cowley mortally wounded. Nelson, despite being hurt badly, with seventeen gunshot wounds, climbed into the FBI car with his partners and sped off. Inspector Cowley died shortly afterwards, and about 8:00 P.M., Nelson succumbed near Wilmette, sixteen miles north of downtown Chicago.

Early in the morning of November 28th, police, acting on a tip, found Nelson's body lying in a ditch near a cemetery on a Niles Center prairie. He had been killed by ten sub-machine gun and shotgun slugs fired into his body by Inspector Cowley and Special Agent Hollis of the Department of Justice. Both Chase and Helen Gillis were caught within the month and sent to jail, closing the chapter on the Nelson gang. With Nelson dead, Alvin Karpis became Public Enemy Number One.[36]

Alvin Karpis and Dolores Delaney on September 20th registered at the El Commodoro Hotel in Miami as Mr. and Mrs. J. Wagner of Detroit,

Bay of the Hotel Park View. (Author's collection)

Michigan, but the following day they checked out of the hotel and took refuge in Havana. In Havana, they visited the Park View Hotel and presented to the Manager, Nathaniel Keller, a card signed by Joe Adams, the Manager of the El Commodoro Hotel, which bore the message "this man is all right."

Originally built in 1928, the Park View was located in a historical surrounding where old and new Havana met, which included the former Presidential Palace, and the well-known Prado Promenade. The Park View Hotel was one of the first hotels built with American capital and was one of the most luxurious hotels in Havana in the early part of the 20th century.

Karpis believed that in Cuba he would find relaxation from the pressing search being conducted by Special Agents of the Federal Bureau of Investigation. Through the efforts of Nathaniel Keller, Karpis rented a cottage at Veradero Beach in Cuba and he and Dolores once more settled down.

"Ma"—The Life and Times of "Ma" Barker and Her Boys

During the first half of the 20th century, Playa Veradero was the Caribbean playground for America's rich and famous. After the Duponts bought half the Veradero Peninsula for four cents a square meter, other tycoons soon followed and purchased winter retreats. During prohibition, many thirsty Americans in addition to members of the Barker-Karpis Gang, visited the clubs of Veradero. In nearby Veradero City, Al Capone owned a stone beachfront home where he often went to relax.[37]

Other members of the Karpis-Barker Gang, who during September 1934 registered at the El Commodoro Hotel, were Harry Campbell, Fred and Kate Barker. Ma Barker appeared at the hotel on September 30, 1934, and registered as Mrs. G. K. Ryan of South Bend, Indiana. Harry Campbell, as G.L. Summers, and Fred Barker, as T.C. Blackburn, of St. Charles, Illinois, registered at the hotel on September 29th and remained there until November 7th, as did Ma Barker.[38]

During the residence of Fred Barker at the El Commodoro Hotel, he expressed a desire to Manager Joe Adams that he would like to have a cottage where he and his mother could reside and enjoy a quiet life. Joe Adams had a friend who owned a cottage which he considered ideal for them. Adams, through this friend, secured the rental of a cottage for Fred Barker and his mother which was located on Lake Weir at Oklawaha, Florida. After this cottage was rented by Fred Barker, he and his mother left the El Commodoro Hotel on November 7th and took up their residency on Lake Weir.

Harry Campbell became lonesome for Wynona Burdette, and a few days before Thanksgiving 1934, he drove to Oklahoma to the home of Wynona's sister at Hominy and rejoined Wynona. Wynona cast aside the resolution she had previously made and returned with Campbell to the State of Florida, where they began living with Fred Barker and his mother on Lake Weir. Karpis, in the meantime, with Dolores Delaney, had continued to reside in Havana, but in the early part of December 1934, he again decided it was best to move. His photograph had appeared in the Havana newspapers and he feared someone might recognize him. The couple returned to Miami. Again Joe Adams came to the assistance of a member of the gang and assisted Dolores Delaney and Karpis in renting a house at 1121 95th Street, N.E., Miami, where the couple resided as Mr. and Mrs. S. A. Groom.

While these activities were taking place in Miami, Florida, and Havana, Cuba, James Wilson had not seen his uncle, Dr. Moran, for several weeks, so he left Toledo, and proceeded to Chicago, and then to Denver, where on September 4th, he surrendered to the Denver Field Division of the Federal Bureau of Investigation.

Notes

[1] Alvin Karpis, Bill Trent, *Public Enemy Number One: The Alvin Karpis Story*, p. 54.
[2] FBI Files, RCS:TD I.C.#7-576, November 19, 1936, The Kidnaping of Edward George Bremer, St. Paul, Minnesota, History and Early Association of the Karpis-Barker Gang Prior to the Abduction of Mr. Bremer.
[3] Alvin Karpis with Bill Trent, *The Alvin Karpis Story*, pp. 51-52.
[4] Ibid., May 22, 1934; Charles Rumford Walker, *American City*, pp. 117-122; Joseph Stipanovich, *City of Lakes An Illustrated History of Minneapolis*, p. 180; George H. Mayer, *The Political Career of Floyd B. Olson*, pp. 198-199.
[5] Mrs. Sally Koether telephone interview with author February 7, 1999; Mrs. Frances Siftar interview with author February 22, 1999.
[6] *Minneapolis Journal*, May 24, 1934.
[7] Joseph Stipanovich, *City of Minneapolis An Illustrated History of Minneapolis*, p. 180.
[8] *Minneapolis Journal*, July 21, 1934.
[9] Ted Curtis Smythe, "A History of the Minneapolis Journal, 1878-1939," unpublished thesis, p. 368.
[10] Ibid., p. 375.
[11] George H. Mayer, *The Political Career of Floyd B. Olson*, p. 221.
[12] *Chicago Herald and Examiner*, May 19, 1934.
[13] *Dallas Morning News*, May 24, 1934.
[14] Miriam Allen deFord, *The Real Ma Barker*, pp. 35-36.
[15] Jay Robert Nash and Ron Offen, *Dillinger Dead or Alive?* Chicago, Henry Rignery Company, 1970, p. 52.
[16] Alvin Karpis with Bill Trent, *The Alvin Karpis Story*, p. 176.
[17] Federal Bureau of Investigation, United States Department of Justice, History Archives.
[18] Federal Bureau of Investigation Files, Freedom of Information Act, Melvin H. Purvis, File Number: 67-7489.
[19] Federal Bureau of Investigation, United States Department of Justice, History

[20]Federal Bureau of Investigation Files, Freedom of Information Act, Melvin H. Purvis, File Number: 67-7489.
[21]Ibid.
[22]*Los Angeles Herald Express*, July 23, 1934.
[23]Federal Bureau of Investigation Files, Freedom of Information Act, Melvin H. Purvis, File Number: 67-7489.
[24]*The Evening Gazette* (Xenia, Ohio), July 23, 1934; Federal Bureau of Investigation Headline Archives.
[25]Federal Bureau of Investigation Files, Freedom of Information Act, Melvin H. Purvis, File Number: 67-7489.
[26]Special Agent C. B. Winstead Memorandum for File, July 25, 1934. Federal Bureau of Investigation Freedom of Information and Privacy Acts, Subject: John Dillinger, File Number 62-29777-1.
[27]Federal Bureau of Investigation Files, Freedom of Information Act, Melvin H. Purvis, File Number: 67-7489.
[28]Special Agent C. B. Winstead Memorandum for File, July 25, 1934. Federal Bureau of Investigation Freedom of Information and Privacy Acts, Subject: John Dillinger, File Number 62-29777-1.
[29]Federal Bureau of Investigation Files, Freedom of Information Act, Melvin H. Purvis, File Number: 67-7489.
[30]Memoirs and letters of former Agent, Charles Winstead, Red River Historical Museum, Sherman, Texas.
[31]*St. Paul Pioneer Press*, August 24, 1934.
[32]Federal Bureau of Investigation Freedom of Information and Privacy Acts, Subject: Kate Barker "Ma," File Number 7-5768695.
[33]*Los Angeles Herald Express*, July 23, 1934.
[34]*East Liverpool* [Ohio] *Review*, October 22, 1934.
[35]Federal Bureau of Investigation Archives.
[36]*Chicago Herald and Examiner*, November 29, 1934.
[37]Rick Millikin, "Cuba's International Playa Veradero," Travel Lady Magazine, internet.
[38]*Chicago Herald and Examiner*, November 29, 1934.

Chapter Nine

The Death of Ma Barker

"*The most ridiculous story in the annals of crime is that Ma Barker was the mastermind behind the Karpis-Barker Gang. I must have read in a couple hundred newspapers and magazines that it was she who trained her sons and the rest of us in the finer points of thieving, kidnapping, bank robbing and murder. The articles I've read are always going on about the 'crime school' she ran in Tulsa, Oklahoma. Ma Barker never ran a crime school in Tulsa or any other place. As a matter of fact, the legend of Ma Barker, whose full name was Arizona Clark Barker, only grew up years after her death and only then in order to justify the manner in which she met her death at the hands of the FBI.*"

—Alvin Karpis[1]

In the aftermath of the Dillinger ambush, Anna Sage was given a handsome reward for her part in setting up the gangster. Although the government had apparently promised her some sort of assistance regarding her immigration status (she was an illegal resident from Romania) she was quickly deported back to her homeland. J. Edgar Hoover was given, and graciously received accolades from an appreciative president and attorney general.

Over the next few months the remaining members of Dillinger's gang were hunted down, captured, or killed by Hoover's "Flying Squad." Other

"Ma"—The Life and Times of "Ma" Barker and Her Boys

public enemies who were exterminated by the squad during the same period, included the notorious Charles "Pretty Boy" Floyd and "Baby Face" Nelson.

Hoover and his staff then turned their attention to eradicating the members of the Barker-Karpis Gang. According to the Federal Bureau of Investigation, "this vicious band of hoodlums who had originally been based out of the north side of Tulsa, Oklahoma, was suspected of a dozen bank jobs along with nearly as many murders."

"Jelly" Bryce, who later made the cover of Life magazine, due to his fast draw skills and the fact he had shot nearly two dozen bad men in the line of duty during his career, along with Clarence Hurt, Charles Winstead, and several other members of the "Flying Squad" were ready to focus their attention on Ma and her boys.

Ma did not live with Freddie and Karpis constantly, and at times when the heat was on, they would leave her at a safe location with plenty of cash. Ma, of course, missed them while they were away on a job, and when they returned, she welcomed them with spreads of fried chicken, mashed potatoes, and Ozark biscuits.

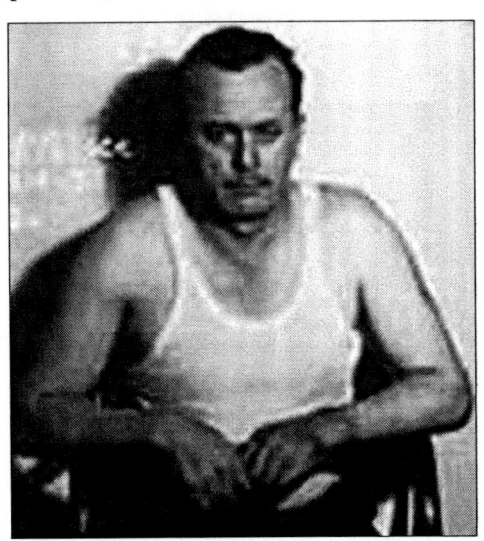

Arthur Barker. (Photograph Collection ca. 1939, Location no. por 14093 p1, Negative no. 85100)

Karpis later said Ma was an odd character at times. For one thing, she looked a little peculiar, and when they saw her propped up in one of their cars, Karpis and Freddie had all they could do to keep from laughing. She was very short and her head barely rose above the dashboard. Because she needed boosting up to see out, the boys purchased her an air cushion, and according to Karpis, it made her look like "a slightly nutty old queen."

What Ma did with her hair did not make her glamorous, and

when she felt like dolling up, she'd turn her hair into a mass of curls, which gave her the appearance of a little girl. But somehow, Ma's sixty-year-old face spoiled the effect.

Doc Barker, prior to going to Toledo in April 1934, had been termed by his associates as a woman hater, except for his frequent visits to houses of prostitution. At Toledo, Doc became infatuated with Mildred Kuhlman, who was a friend of Madeline Angus, the wife of Ted Angus, who had provided the gang protection. Mildred was also friendly with Thelma and Rene Holst, sisters of Madeline Angus.

After the gang had left the vicinity of Toledo and Cleveland, Doc persuaded Mildred Kuhlman with promises of many luxuries to return with him to Chicago. Through the investigative efforts of special agents it was established that Mildred Kuhlman on December 11, 1934 registered at the Morrison Hotel in Chicago. An immediate surveillance was instituted of this woman and it disclosed that Mildred Kuhlman resided at 432 Serf Street, Chicago, Illinois, and that she was friendly and almost in constant company with a woman known as Patricia Lonquest.

The investigation further disclosed that Doc Barker was residing with the Kuhlman woman at the Serf Street address and that Doc and Mildred were associating with William Harrison and Russell Gibson in Chicago. It was also ascertained that in keeping with the usual practice, Harrison had rented an apartment at 3920 Pine Grove Avenue, as J.B. Bolton, and special agents immediately determined that Russell Gibson and Doc Barker frequented the place.

The apprehension of these fugitives was delayed, as the information which had been obtained throughout the course of the investigation of the Bremer kidnapping had indicated that members of the gang usually resided in the same general vicinity, and it was not until investigation definitely disclosed that Alvin Karpis and other members of the gang were not associating with Doc Barker in Chicago that action was taken to apprehend those fugitives.

On the night of January 8, 1935, the apartment at 3920 Pine Grove Avenue, was surrounded. At about 10:45 P.M., as Federal men entered the front lobby of the apartment building, they met Clara Gibson, who was just leaving with her chow dog. She returned to her apartment, however, after being told to warn the others that the "agents were coming." A few minutes later, the front doorbell was rung and the first tear gas bomb was tossed, followed almost immediately by others.

One of these tear gas bombs, however, went through the window of Jay H. Twitchell, who lived in an adjacent apartment. Twitchell climbed out of a window with upraised hands, shouting that he surrendered. He was questioned, but later released after proving his identity.

The special agents continued flooding the suspects' apartment with tear gas and one of the agents gave the command to the occupants at 3920 Pine Grove Avenue, to surrender. Clara Gibson, wife of Russell Gibson, came staggering out of the apartment gasping and crying. Ruth Heidt, the ex-wife of William J. Harrison, and Bryan Bolton also complied with this command. Bolton was at first mistakenly identified as Willie Harrison, former golf professional and member of the Barker-Karpis Gang, but later, Harold Nathan, assistant to J. Edgar Hoover, announced the suspect was not Harrison.[2]

At the time, Nathan denied reports that the man [Bolton] was Karpis or one of the Barkers. He admitted, however, that the agents had been seeking Harrison as a member of the Barker-Karpis mob.

Ignoring the plea of his wife who frantically begged him to surrender, Russell Gibson, thirty-two, chose to fight it out against sixteen special agents. He equipped himself with a bulletproof vest, a .32 Caliber Colt automatic pistol and a Browning automatic rifle and endeavored to force an escape through the rear door of the apartment. Gibson cautiously opened the door, but upon observing a special agent guarding the entrance, Gibson raised the automatic rifle and attempted to fire, but his gun jammed. The special agent returned the fire and Gibson fell at the bottom of the stairway mortally wounded, not far from the spot where John Dillinger was killed the previous year.

Two shots fired by the special agent hit their mark; one of them finding a fatal spot, despite the fact that Gibson, also known as "Slim" Gray, was wearing a bullet proof vest. The bullet penetrated the vest. Before he died, Gibson was questioned by Agent Thomas Myers, but admitted nothing except the identity of himself and his wife, and to name his male companion as a man named Willie. He refused to answer any other questions. Gibson died a few hours later in a hospital in Chicago, with a curse on his lips for all law enforcement officials.

A few days later, ironically on his birthday, Gibson was buried in a cemetery at Chicago. There was no large gangster funeral, but only a few of his nearest relatives attended. There were no friends as pallbearers, but the employees of the cemetery due to the cold wind which was blowing, carried the casket which contained the remains of Russell Gibson from the hearse to the burial place.

Upon entering the apartment at 3920 Pine Grove Avenue, special agents found a small arsenal. Among the guns found were a .32 Colt automatic pistol #481720; a .38 police positive revolver #273652; two Browning 30.06 automatic rifles; a Auto burglar 20 gauge Ithaca Gun Company shotgun #361601; a .351 rifle fitted with front machine gun grip and Cutts compensator; together with a hundred rounds of ammunition hidden in a suitcase.

. Other special agents on that same January 8th evening, covered the address at 432 Serf Street, and at about 6:30 P.M., Doc Barker and Mildred Kuhlman left the premises and were taken into custody by special agents. Doc Barker had no opportunity to resist. An immediate search of the apartment which had been occupied by Barker and Mildred Kuhlman revealed a large black leather case which contained a Thompson submachine gun from which the serial number had been removed. The Technical Laboratory of the Federal Bureau of Investigation subsequently restored this number and it was found that it was the machine gun which had been stolen by members of the Karpis-Barker gang at the time they staged the pay roll robbery in South St. Paul on August 30, 1933, and killed a policeman.

Doc Barker was flown secretly from Chicago to St. Paul which federal agents called the scene of his biggest crime. His capture was not made public for nearly a week as Department of Justice operatives focused their attention upon Ma and Fred Barker. Lodged in the county jail when bail of $100,000 was not furnished, Doc was placed under a special guard with an entire cell block—six cells—all to himself. Responsible for keeping him in custody was Sheriff

"Ma"—The Life and Times of "Ma" Barker and Her Boys

Thomas J. Gibbons, former heavyweight boxer, who several years earlier stayed fifteen rounds with Jack Dempsey in Shelby, Montana.[3]

A map was found in the effects of Doc Barker on which appeared a penciled circle around the town of Ocala, Florida, encompassing the territory in which Lake Weir was located. Luckily for the feds, Doc had been dutiful enough to mark the map, indicating the exact site of the hideout of his mother and brother. Other information had been obtained by special agents that in the vicinity of where the other members of the gang were hiding out, the residents talked of an alligator known as "Old Joe."

Another clue was that of the "tattooed heart" which Doc's brother, Fred, carried on his arm. He had been hunting with a Bellevue man who had previously remarked on the resemblance of "Mr. Blackburn" to a man in a photograph he had seen posted in a post office. Barker killed a deer and rolled up his sleeves to skin the animal. His companion, whose name was not revealed, glimpsed the tattoo mark and notified federal agents, who reacted quickly in springing their trap.[4]

In possession of this valuable information, the FBI sent one of the smaller agents to Ocala. He was in his late 20s but appeared to be still of school age. This agent went into all the villages around the lakes where tourists were fishing and finally he came to the little town of Oklawaha on the Oklawaha River near where it empties into Lake Weir.[5]

A visit to the one barber shop revealed that a party of several fishermen had rented a large house on the lake and one of the barbers told of receiving a $50 bill for a tip. The agent felt he was nearing his journey's end. He pretended to be selling magazines "to pay his way through college" and he went house to house, although he now knew where the gang was located. He did not report his "find" as he had not identified them.

When he came to the house of the Barkers, he stepped inside and at once discovered high powered rifles behind nearly every door on the ground floor. He naturally paid no attention to the firearms but talked fishing with them, insisting he wanted to fish in Florida "more than anything in the world." He was invited to join them the next morning for an early try at the big-mouth bass.

"Ma"—The Life and Times of "Ma" Barker and Her Boys

The little FBI man was up early and claimed he hooked and landed "three whoppers." Following the fishing trip, he went to Ocala and wired in code to his headquarters.

Special agents had launched an extensive investigation in the vicinity of Ocala and Oklawaha, Florida, which disclosed that Fred Barker and his mother were residing in a cottage located on Lake Weir, this being the cottage which had been secured for them through the efforts of a Miami friend, Joe Adams. It was further learned that a few days prior to the location of this cottage, Harry Campbell, and Wynona Burdette had been visitors there.

Campbell and Burdette were not the only members of the gang staying with Fred and Ma Barker. Alvin Karpis stayed there a few days and put in some wonderful hours fishing. Karpis later described Freddie's place on Lake Weir: "It was a gorgeous layout. The cottage sat fifty yards from the lake, and it came with a boathouse and a launch. A stone fence, about waist-high, surrounded the property, and the grounds were crowded with grapefruit, orange, and lemon trees. It was a small paradise, and Ma had the luxury of a maid and a gardener."[6]

Wynona Burdett. There is a St. Louis Studio mark on the back of this photo. It is believed this was taken possibly at the time Wynona was running with Harry Campbell and the Karpis-Barker gang (1930-1935). (Courtesy Federal Bureau of Investigation Files)

Located in Marion County near the Oklawaha River, the Barker hideout, near the towns of Ocala and Gainesville, and about a hundred miles southwest of Jacksonville, was surrounded by rolling green hills, horse farms, and small cities lined with one hundred–year–old trees and crystal clear rivers. Although Lake Weir is a beautiful lake, bordered by orange groves and some of the oldest trees in the state, Karpis and Campbell were probably more impressed with its reputation as being excellent for fishing.

According to Harry Campbell, Fred Barker wanted him and Wynona Burdette, Alvin Karpis, and Dolores Delaney to live with them permanently at Oklawaha, but he and Karpis turned them down. Karpis became quite concerned however, when Campbell told him he had seen two men whom he believed were "casing" the house. When they warned Freddie and Ma that there could be something to this activity, they refused to believe that the cottage was under observation.[7]

During Karpis' stay, Harry Campbell, who frequently drove drunk, was speeding down a highway when he collided with a Model-T Ford, which had just run a red light. A man and his wife in the other automobile were killed and their baby somehow miraculously survived the crash.

Campbell was put in jail by the local sheriff, and when he sobered up, he realized that if his fingerprints were taken and sent to Washington, it would be curtains for himself and the Barker-Karpis Gang. The sly Campbell managed to talk his way out of jail by agreeing to purchase a car from the sheriff's friend, who was the local Ford dealer, and also donate $250 towards the baby who had survived the accident.

When Karpis decided he had to get back to Dolores in Miami, Ma Barker was very sad to see him leave. She made him promise to call when Dolores' baby was born and she'd come down to Miami and help with the baby. Karpis was shocked because Ma had never liked their women and hadn't been real friendly to Dolores in the past. She seemed a changed woman at Lake Weir and Karpis had never seen her so mellow. As he drove away from the lake, he was looking forward to Ma coming down for a visit.

Harry and Wynona went with Karpis to his place at Little River. After checking on Dolores, Campbell and Karpis left the girls and drove farther south on a fishing trip. They fished in the Gulf Stream, Biscayne Bay, and off Everglades City where trolling for mackerel turned out to be spectacular.

While the boys relaxed, the FBI was on the move. Willie Woodbury, a black cook who made meals for the Barkers and lived with his wife just west of the Barkers, told the FBI agents that the cottage had been a rendezvous for members of the underworld during the Barkers' stay. The Woodburys had heard strange whisperings outside the house several nights but it never occurred to them to investigate.[8]

Both Willie and his wife had worked for the "Blackburns" for about two months and the two of them agreed that Mrs. Blackburn was a strange woman. They also knew better than to stick their noses into the Blackburn's business, and especially the one room in the house they were ordered never to enter.

Whenever Willie or his wife wanted to leave the house for an errand, they had to obtain permission from Ma. Each time Willie had driven Freddie into town, he was given the third degree upon returning. Ma wanted to know whether her son had been drinking or playing around with women.

Other residents of the small town said that Fred Barker was lavish in his use of money in town, paying for small, inexpensive items with bills of large denominations and not waiting for change. Neighbors claimed that the Barkers had a radio in the house that stayed on twenty-four hours a day, plus two automobiles both equipped with radios.[9]

The lake truly was inhabited by the alligator named Old Joe. (Karpis and Freddie Barker had tried to rub out Old Joe by shooting a machine gun at him while trailing a live pig as bait behind their motor boat.) The FBI determined that Lake Weir was definitely the home of Old Joe, Ma and Fred Barker as well.[10]

The FBI agents finished going over their plans and caught a plane for Florida. After landing, they joined several of their colleagues near the white house on Lake Weir. "We'll surround the place and hope we can get them to surrender," explained the senior agent to his men. "If not, we'll blast them into the open and we're going to have plenty of guns with us."[11]

All roads leading to the two-story white cottage were blocked by 7 A.M. It was impossible for anyone unauthorized to get into the area, or to leave it. Federal agents toting machine guns were everywhere, ready to assault the house where a sixty-three-year-old woman with graying hair and a short dumpy figure awaited them with her favorite son.

"I was on investigation for the State of Florida in the 1930s and was, at day break one morning, driving south of Ocala, headed for Lake Weir when traffic was detoured around several men wearing long overcoats," recalled veteran newspaperman Vernon Lamme. "Recognizing immediately these men were strangers, I parked and approached them, showed them my badge and credentials and learned they were FBI agents and that they had the Barker gang holed up in a two-story frame house on Lake Weir. They said that Ma Barker and her son Fred and Paul [sic] Karpis were inside. The Barkers with Karpis on their latest caper had kidnapped a well known Minneapolis man and held him for a $200,000 ransom which had been paid, and the victim was released. The FBI wanted them."[12]

Some people whom Ma Barker met, especially bank managers and their assistants, had called her "a nice motherly-looking woman." But to FBI Director J. Edgar Hoover, she was "an animal mother of the she-wolf type."

At about 5:30 o'clock on the morning of January 16, 1935, Department of Justice Agents surrounded the Barker cottage, and Special Agent E.J. Connelley of Cincinnati (who functioned as an "assistant director" and whom the other agents often received their orders from), actually went up to the house, and knocked on the door demanding the occupants to surrender. One of the agents shouted, "We are Department of Justice men. Come on out!" After a period of approximately fifteen minutes, no answer was received.[13]

Finally Connelley was answered by Ma Barker. He told her that the FBI was there to arrest Fred Barker. Ma went to tell Fred this while Connelley waited; then a voice was heard to say "all right go ahead." The special agents interpreted this remark as meaning that Kate and Fred Barker were going to surrender. However, Fred Barker fired a full clip of .45 rounds at agents from his submachine gun and Connelley took refuge behind an oak tree, lucky to have escaped unharmed. Angry lawmen responded in kind, firing tear gas canisters, phosphorous grenades, and 300 rounds of hot ammo into the cottage.[14]

The Woodburys were sleeping when they were awakened by the clatter of machine gun fire. When a couple shots fired from the Barker cottage hit the bedpost right beside them, Willie and his wife hit the floor face down and remained there for five long hours. The FBI had been eyeing the servants' quarters since they arrived but they had made no attempt to enter it. Their curiosities finally got the best of them and a couple officers began pounding on the door demanding that those inside open up. Willie yelled back that if they wanted in, they'd have to do it themselves. The agents kicked in the door, saw the terrified couple on the floor and left.

Mrs. A.F. Westberry, whose home was opposite the house occupied by the Barkers, and her daughter fled from their home in a hail of bullets. "I was suddenly awakened by guns firing," she told the press. "I got out of bed, and as I stood up some bullets came through the closed door between my bedroom and the dining room and hit the head of my bed. I opened the door a crack and more bullets came through the window and hit the face of the door above my head.

"I looked out the window and saw the yard was full of men. From Mr. Bradford's house across the road there was a lot of shooting. I could see streaks of fire from the guns. I could see the blazes from the men's guns on the outside. There was a lot of rapid-fire-like machine guns. My daughter was in bed. I broke open the back window of our room and told her we had to get out. About that time some more bullets came smacking through the dining room window and hit the wall.

"My daughter and I climbed through the window and got down on the ground. We were going to run to my neighbor's house, about fifty yards back of our house. The house from which the bullets were coming was only about a hundred feet in front of my house.

"As we lay down on the ground for a moment we heard the firing coming louder. We got up and started to run to Mrs. Rex's house. As we ran some men yelled at us to stop. We did not stop.

"They began shooting at us. I learned later it was the federal men. We kept on running and they kept yelling and shooting. They must have shot at us two dozen times. They didn't know who we were. It was still a little dark. Finally we got to Mrs. Rex's house.

"There appeared to be fifteen or twenty federal agents. The shooting kept on all morning. Just before noon it stopped. We saw all of the federal men go into the house. Some of them came out in a few minutes. It was all over.

"My daughter and I went back to our house and inspected the damage. There were three holes in my bed just above where my head had been.

There were two holes in the door facing. In the window were two holes looking as if ten or twelve bullets had come through at the same time."[15]

The battle raged on. There would be a relentless barrage for about fifteen minutes followed by a lull in the action. One of the agents would eventually shift positions out in the yard and the fusillade would begin anew.

Freddie Barker and his mother Kate "Ma" Barker battled until death and residents of the little village described the six hour shootout as being "like a war." Fred Barker was thirty-two and his mother fifty-five. When the shooting stopped from the house about eleven o'clock that morning, the agents crept closer to the house and lobbed a few tear gas shells into an upstairs window. Previously, the shells had fallen short of their mark; some actually choking those who had hurled them.[16]

After forty-five minutes of no returning fire, the fifteen agents realized that an entry had to be made. None of them, however, wanted to be the first; each afraid of Ma Barker's wrath and Freddie's marksmanship. Special Agent Connelley sent for Willie Woodbury, who had been working there, and ordered him into the house.

Willie was terrified as he slowly ascended the front steps. Behind him, FBI agents encouraged him to keep moving from the safety of the oak trees which sheltered them from harm. Reaching the top of the stairs, Willie jumped to the door and tried it, but it was locked. A jubilant Willie Woodbury raced back and reported the locked door. He was told to go back, cut the screen, and kick the door down.

Again, he edged his way to the porch, removed his pocket knife from his pants, slit the screen, reached in, unlatched the door, and then kicked in the main door. The door suddenly opened, and although he expected to be hit by a barrage of bullets, there was only silence. Placing his handkerchief over his face, he went inside, choking from the tear gas fumes. A minute later, he appeared in the upstairs window yelling "They are all dead." The Barkers had perished in the crescendo of fire.[17]

One agent slowly stepped out from behind the oak trees and entered the house. His main fear was that Freddie Barker was holding a gun to Willie's head, forcing him to give the all clear. Nonetheless, he entered the

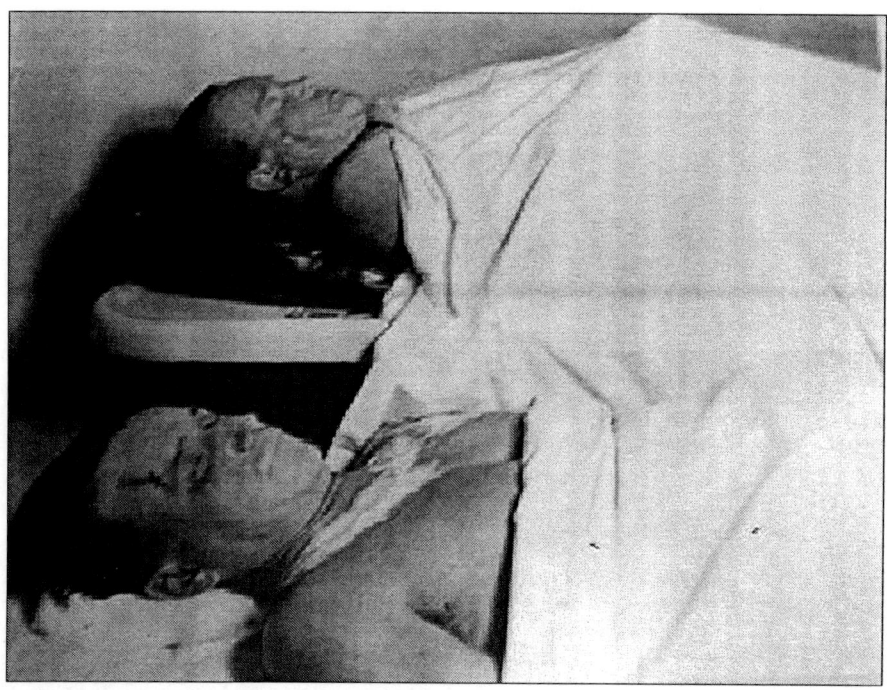

Ma and Fred Barker. (Courtesy FBI Files)

house and in a few minutes appeared at the same upstairs window and verified the deaths. Suddenly the house was swarming with agents searching and probing for other gang members who could be hiding somewhere inside.

When the house was entered by the agents, they found the bodies of Fred Barker and his mother. A .45 caliber automatic pistol was found near the body of Fred Barker and a machine gun lay at Ma Barker's left hand. A portion of the drum of ammunition had been exhausted. One shot had killed Ma Barker. Her son's body was sprawled on the floor with eleven machine gun bullets in one shoulder and three in the head. The dozen or more government agents escaped injury. A rumor prevalent was that the mother, seeing her son fall, and recognizing that capture was inevitable, took her own life.[18]

Initially, a report surfaced that two men and a woman had been killed in the house by federal agents. Word began to spread that Alvin

Karpis, co-leader of the gang, had also been slain, but after agents converged on the cottage, it was definitely established that only Fred Barker and his mother had been killed.[19]

A systematic search of the house after the battle had ceased disclosed $14,000 in $1,000 bills and investigation revealed that these $1,000 bills were a part of those which had been obtained by Cassius McDonald in Havana, Cuba, in exchange for Bremer ransom money. There was also found other currency of smaller denominations totaling approximately $293.[20]

With the lesson of the Lindbergh ransom money found in Bruno Hauptmann's Bronx garage as a precedent, floor boards were torn up and the garage and the yard searched with flashlights long after nightfall. A small arsenal was discovered in the house which consisted of two Thompson submachine guns, one Browning .12 gauge automatic shotgun, one Remington .12 gauge pump shotgun, two .45 caliber automatic pistols, a ._3 caliber Winchester rifle, and a .380 caliber Colt automatic pistol, together with machine gun drums, automatic pistol clips and a quantity of ammunition. Investigators also found a letter signed by "B. L. Barnes," which was a letter to Fred Barker from his brother "Doc." This letter read as follows:

"Hello everyone how is that old sunshine down there fine I hope. Boy it is not so hot up here, for we are having some winter. I Bet you and Buff are not catching no fish now for I think I caught then all when I was down there. I took care of that Business for you Boys it was done Just as good as if you had did it your self. I am Just like the standard oil always at your service ha ha. tell, Bo, you Know the Boy with the rosy cheek that Moxxy is up here looking for him and if it is alright to send him down. I have not seen chuck yet I have Been Busy on that other he was pretty hard to locate. But will see him right away, and see if he wants come down there. Tell mother that deer was mighty fine and I said hello and her and the squaw had better not let you Bums Beat them in catching fish haha well I will close for this tine as ever your Big Bud B. L. Barnes"

Definite evidence linking the kidnapping of William Hamm and Edward G. Bremer was announced in Washington by the Department of Justice later that same day following the killing of the Barkers. While maintaining close

Reward poster for Alvin Karpis and Fred Barker. (Photograph Collection ca. 1936 Location no. por 20416 p2 Negative no. 64393)

secrecy on the nature of the evidence pinning both the St. Paul kidnappings on the Barker-Karpis Gang, the information was known to have been obtained through clues opened up by disposal of the ransom money.[21]

With Ma Barker and her son Freddie both dead, justice operatives pressed on to round up the rest of the mob, which they had looked upon as "the most dangerous and most vicious gang at large." Seven or eight persons were believed to have been members of the gang that raked together more than a half million dollars in the two St. Paul kidnappings and bank robberies in a single year.

Leaders were identified as Alvin Karpis and Arthur "Doc" Barker, Fred's brother, and their mother Ma Barker was regarded as the brains of the troupe. The rest, according to the *St. Paul Pioneer Press*, were hangers-on. Fingerprints on a set of signal lights and a gasoline can led to the identification of Barker and Karpis as Bremer's abductors.

Having already disposed of most of the Dillinger and "Pretty Boy" Floyd gangs, agents had been hunting the Barkers for some time on clues they had come to Florida. The Barker-Karpis Gang had been described as the last of the free-running mobs at large in the United States.

On January 17th, the *St. Paul Pioneer Press*, printed the following editorial: "By a furious six-hour fusillade, in which its agents fired 1,500 shots, the Federal government has reaffirmed its policy of ruthless extermination for criminal gangsters. Two Barkers—mother and son—paid the extreme penalty for the complicity of the Karpis-Barker Gang in the Bremer kidnapping a year ago in St. Paul. The spectacle of a sixty-nine-year-old woman loosing a murderous stream of machine gun bullets should silence any mawkish sentimentality.

"Through this affair the accounting with gangsterism as an institution is almost complete. There are still at large a few gangsters of the Dillinger-Barrows-Babyface type but they are leading furtive, hunted lives as individuals who rarely if ever venture further gang operations and whose realization of their own offenses is such that they do not dare to come in and give themselves up. Ruthlessness as a cure for ruthlessness has proved effective not only in setting a period to depredations but also in discouraging recruits and the fair weather lenders of aid, comfort and concealment.

"The discredited, fugitive gangster has become indeed an outcast and a pariah whose chance for succor has faded with the magic of his brief success. There is hope that a dark chapter in the annals of this country is far toward its close and that the orderly processes of the law will soon be efficient to uphold the peace and dignity of government."[22]

Despite orders given on January 16th in Washington to "get" Doc Barker, reports from Chicago persisted that Arthur "Doc" Barker had been in Federal custody there for over a week, but Division of Investigation officers denied this.[23] D. M. Ladd, agent in charge of the Chicago office of the Federal Division of Investigation told reporters, "I have no comment to make."[24]

Many persons recalled that this was the same remark which covered up for days the fact that federal agents secretly held Mrs. Lester Gillis, the widow of the slain George "Baby Face" Nelson. The Chicago Evening American said that Doc Barker had been taken into custody about the same time federal agents raided a north side apartment and killed Russell Gibson and captured Byron Bolton and two women. The men were described by the agents as members of the Barker-Karpis Gang.

Arthur "Doc" Barker. (Courtesy Library of Congress)

Doc Barker, the newspaper stated, had been taken with a woman at a north side apartment, and it was assumed that his reported apprehension had given leads to enable the federal agents in Florida to locate the hideout of his mother and brother. This report was soon confirmed.

Alvin Karpis was being sought in Chicago that Thursday, according to the Associated Press. Strict secrecy surrounded the activity of federal agents as they swarmed into Chicago's north side in search of an apartment where Karpis was believed to be hiding.[25]

"Ma"—The Life and Times of "Ma" Barker and Her Boys

Doc Barker, indicted May 4, 1934, on conspiracy charges for the kidnapping of Edward Bremer, was being returned to St. Paul to stand trial during the April term of Federal Court, George F. Sullivan, United States District Attorney told the press. He would be tried under the Lindbergh Kidnap Law.

Arrested with Barker, stated the report, were three women and one man, all linked with the gang. One of the women, still unnamed by agents, surrendered with Barker. The others were Byron Bolton, alleged by police to have been the "finger man" in the St. Valentines Day Massacre of George "Bugs" Moran's gangsters in a Chicago garage, February 14, 1929; Ruth Hite; and Clara Gibson. The latter three had been arrested in a different part of Chicago from where Barker and his girlfriend were captured.

Both roundups were directed by Harold Nathan, assistant director of the Division of Investigation. Bolton, Ruth Hite, and Mrs. Gibson gave themselves up after federal agents had slain their companion, Russell Gibson. It was believed the prisoners furnished information which led agents to Oklawaha.

Arthur Barker and Alvin Karpis were named as the chiefs of the Bremer kidnapping. With eight others, including Gibson, they were named in the May 4th indictment in St. Paul. The others were John J. McLaughlin, William Vidler, and Philip Delaney, all of Chicago and free on bail pending trial; and four named as John Doe, Richard Doe, "Izzy" and "Slim." John J. McLaughlin, Jr. was indicted but was absolved of connection with the abduction. The "Slim" referred to, it was learned, was Russell Gibson.

"We intend to try Barker together with Vidler, Delaney, and McLaughlin," proclaimed District Attorney Sullivan.[26]

Vidler had been arrested by Chicago police the past spring and was found with $3,000 Bremer ransom money in his possession. Shortly afterward, the elder McLaughlin, his seventeen-year-old son, and Philip Delaney were arrested on charges of handling some of the $200,000 Bremer ransom money. Brought to St. Paul, the younger McLaughlin was exonerated, but the others were arraigned and subsequently released on bail to appear at the next session of Federal court in St. Paul.

Doc Barker's investigation was stepped up, even though the killings of Ma and Fred Barker continued to capture the headlines. Department of

Justice agents and city police worked to determine whether Doc should be tried for the Bremer kidnapping alone or for the Hamm abduction as well. Barker also would be facing witnesses in the shooting of Roy McCord of St. Paul, and Chief of Police Michael J. Culligan announced that he and South St. Paul Chief Ed McAlpine planned to have witnesses in the Swift & Company payroll messenger view the suspect as well.[27]

Harold Nathan of the Department of Justice announced that with the acquittal of the Touhy Gang for the Hamm kidnapping, he planned to have William Hamm view Doc Barker, and authorities planned to link the suspect with the murder of paint salesman Theodore Kidder of St. Louis Park, Minnesota.

The last Congress had enacted laws that attempts to rob and robbery of national banks and member banks of the Federal Reserve System would constitute a federal offense. These laws, of course, turned over jurisdiction to the Justice Department. As one method of preparation, steps had been taken to learn the identities and study methods of some of the country's known stickup men.

"The long road to eternal peace and security has no shortcuts," proclaimed J. Edgar Hoover. "Civilization's recourse is remorseless pursuit, complete punishment, and, if necessary and adequately provoked, elimination of the criminal individual."[28]

With the notorious reign of the Barkers at an end, a conference was held between J. Edgar Hoover and St. Paul Mayor Mark Gehan, in which the bureau chief told the mayor that St. Paul was rid of its professional underworld gangs in the opinion of the United States Department of Justice. Mayor Gehan was advised that Hoover had no suspicion that anyone high in the underworld was being harbored in St. Paul. Justice agents had come to the conclusion that the "big shots" of crime had left St. Paul to take refuge in Chicago and Florida.

During the conference which lasted over an hour, Mayor Gehan and the city's corporation counsel John L. Connolly were offered the utmost cooperation of the department in the solution of local crime problems. Division experts conferred with the two officials on the situation uncovered a year earlier when Attorney General Homer Stille Cummings said that some members of the police force did not have the full confidence of the department. The mayor did not disclose any definite advice gained in this connection.

Upon emerging from his conference with Hoover, Mayor Gehan expressed deep satisfaction at having learned that St. Paul had recovered its standing for law enforcement. Less than a year earlier, St. Paul had been branded "one of the poison spots of crime" by members of the Senate Crime Committee and singled out by Cummings, appointed Attorney General of the United States by President Franklin Delano Roosevelt on March 4, 1933, as one of the spots in America in need of cleaning up.[29]

M. F. Kinkead, county attorney, conferred with the St. Paul office of the Bureau of Investigation, Department of Justice, and offered congratulations on the breakup of the mob. "This is the finest piece of police work in recent years," he stated, "and special commendation is due the government for its persistence in this case. It should not be forgotten that this is another in a series of knockout blows against crime, in which the government is taking a leading role."[30]

Kincaid also said that although Barker and Karpis had been wanted since 1932 for the murder of Arthur W. Dunlap of West St. Paul, no prosecution could be carried out in St. Paul because the crime occurred in Webster, Wisconsin, and therefore was outside the jurisdiction of Ramsey County.

Meanwhile, E. J. Connelley, a stocky, thirty-eight-year-old federal agent, known throughout the service for his tenacity, was credited with being in charge of the operation that ended in the deaths of Fred and Ma Barker. Connelley, who headed the Cincinnati office of the Division of Investigation, had fifteen years of service and possessed detailed knowledge of the Barker Gang's personnel and their activities.[31]

Connelley had helped in laying a trap for Doc Barker and Alvin Karpis in Cleveland, Ohio the past September, and although the mission failed, he and his men contined their work on the case. Hailing from Columbus, Ohio, the agent was second in command of forty men rushed to the Louisville area in October, when social leader Mrs. Alice Speed Stoll was abducted and held for a $50,000 ransom. According to the department, the shootout with Ma and Fred Barker earlier in the day had done a great deal to crack the last of the roving gangs terrorizing America.

The bodies of Ma and Fred Barker were removed to a mortuary in Ocala, while the FBI continued its systematic search of the house, which lasted for over a week. Willie cooked for the agents every day they were there. When the agents departed, morbid curiosity seekers moved in, and when the crowds got out of control, the owners commenced charging admission.[32]

The day was an exciting one for the residents of Oklawaha, which had only a handful of scattered houses and stores. The town was situated about twenty miles southeast of Ocala, the county seat, and a hundred miles southwest of Jacksonville. The Barkers had been there about two months, renting the summer house under the name of T. E. Blackburn from Carson Bradford, president of the Biscayne Kennel Club of Miami. Neighbors knew little about the "Blackburns" except that they had a great deal of company, especially at night. A few days before the shootings, a couple known as "Mr. and Mrs. Summer" left for the north, where it was understood by neighbors they lived, after an extended stay.[33]

Many of the neighbors, warned by the agents of impending danger, deserted their houses before the battle commenced. About two hundred cars still remained parked around the lake and streets, and most of the neighbors saw the firing from safe vantage points. Many lay flat on the ground. Rifles and machine guns would crack for about fifteen minutes; then there would be a lull, followed by a renewal of firing from both sides. Most of the shooting from the besieged house came from upstairs, witnesses reported. The white house was pock-marked by bullets. The agents claimed they had fired 1,500 rounds of ammunition.

News of the battle traveled rapidly and several hundred outsiders flocked to the village. Newspaper men and camera men from the surrounding cities rushed to the scene. The village had only one telephone and a line was soon formed by those anxious to report the story.

"I am glad to see them meet justice," Mrs. Lulu Kelly told reporters from her home in West Plains, Missouri. Word that Fred Barker and his mother had been killed by federal agents in Florida was comforting news to

Howell County residents whose popular sheriff, C. R. Kelly, was mowed down by Barker guns in December 1931.[34]

Since the morning that her husband was slain as he was about to question Barker and a companion about a store robbery two days earlier, Mrs. Kelly had not relaxed her search. She told the press that "last night" her watchfulness had been rewarded.

"Not that I have murder in my heart, but I wanted to see them meet justice," she kept repeating. "I had hopes all the way through that we would find them, but naturally I thought the chances were better after the federal agents took it up. I appreciate all they have done and I feel mighty warm towards them. The officers all have been wonderful to cooperate with me."[35]

When her husband was killed, Mrs. Kelly was appointed to serve as sheriff until a successor was elected. When she left office, she kept up her search. Mrs. Kelly made several trips to view suspects. Her longest trip was to southern Mississippi where police were holding a man they believed to have been Alvin Karpis. As soon as she saw the suspect, she told police that he was not the man, and he was released.

Mrs. Kelly had also visited the Missouri State Penitentiary and the jail, hoping she might learn something about her husband's death. She corresponded with the heads of other penal institutions and she mailed circulars containing the outlaws' photographs and fingerprints to virtually every county seat in the nation.

Karpis and Campbell had returned to the girls at Little River, completely oblivious as to what was transpiring at Lake Weir. Harry and Wynona had planned to leave and go back to Lake Weir that day, but Harry told Wynona he really needed one more crack at those mackerel.

Karpis took him back to where the fish were biting and the two men made a day of it. Darkness had begun to fall when they came off the lake; their boat loaded with fish. They drove back to Little River and turned down Eighty-Fourth Street. About a block from the house, they saw Wynona and Dolores sitting in the front seat of a parked car. As Karpis pulled over to the curb, a hysterical Dolores ran over to the car and told them the FBI had just killed Ma and Fred.[36]

Home of Fred and Ma Barker in Florida where shoot out took place. (Author's collection)

J. Edgar Hoover was all smiles over the deaths of Ma and Fred Barker and the capture of Doc. "The backbone of the gang is broken," he told the press. "We intend to knock off everyone who ever worked with this gang. It may run to twenty-five or thirty people. We have always felt that the Barker-Karpis mob was the brainiest and most dangerous in the country. As long as it was at large, we felt that a kidnapping or a big bank robbery might take place at any time. It moved from the Pacific across the continent, through the Middle West and the South. We never heard of any of its activities around here, or New York."[37]

Hoover also had a few unkind remarks to say about Ma: "She was a jealous old battle axe. She dictated who her four sons' lady friends were to be. We even heard that when they wanted to go out on a party, they would go to another town, from the one she was. There is a legend that she taught her boys never to be taken alive; however, Arthur Barker is the second member of the family to be in federal custody."[38]

"Ma"—The Life and Times of "Ma" Barker and Her Boys

He also announced to the press: "It was the brainiest and most desperate of all—this Barker-Karpis Gang. We have been closing in on this gang and now the backbone is shattered. Only last week in Chicago, we killed Russell Gibson, a member of the gang, and arrested several men and women associates."[39]

"Ma Barker was the brains of the gang, a domineering woman of about sixty years, so clever that she never had been arrested. She was a domineering old battle-axe. She was so jealous of her sons that she would not even let them run around with women that she did not select. Ma's husband is still living an honest life in a small Missouri town."

Concerning the six hour gun battle near Oklawaha, Florida, in which Ma and Fred Barker were slain, Hoover said that when agents called for them to surrender, Ma Barker opened the door and shouted, "Let 'em have it!" She slammed the door and the shooting began. Bullets came from all windows of the house, indicating that Ma and her son ran up and down stairs with machine guns in their hands. When the agents finally burst in, they found Fred's body with fourteen bullets in it. Nearby was the body of Ma. Hoover said. "Both hands grasped a machine gun, which still was hot."

According to Hoover, "the house was a regular arsenal. We found ten guns, most of them machine guns and high powered rifles with a range of three miles. We also found twenty-five boxes of ammunition. There was a legend that Ma had advised her boys never to be taken alive. Ma traveled constantly with Freddie and Art. She was the brains of the whole organization. As long as the gang was loose, there was always the danger of kidnappings and bank robberies. The gang had ramifications from the Pacific coast to Chicago, and from there south into Florida and Texas."[40]

George Barker told the press in Joplin, Missouri, that he didn't care when or how his son Fred and former wife Kate were buried. "I don't care to have them brought back here, Barker, sixty-seven, said. "I wouldn't care to attend the funeral. I'd like to be left out of all this. They chose their path some years ago, and I followed mine. I haven't seen any of them in years."[41]

Alvin Karpis was devastated by Ma's death at the hands of the FBI. "Ma was always somebody in our lives," he wrote years later. "Love didn't

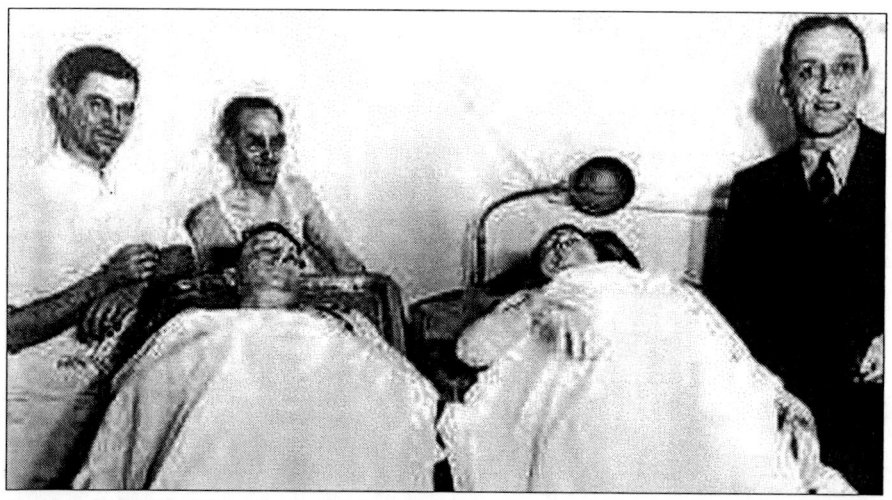
Bodies of Ma and Fred Barker after the shoot out in Florida. (Author's collection)

enter into it really. She was somebody we looked after and took with us when we moved from city to city, hideout to hideout.

"It's no insult to Ma's memory that she didn't have the brains or know-how to direct us on a robbery. It wouldn't have occurred to her to get involved in our business, and we always made a point of only discussing our scores when Ma wasn't around. We'd leave her at home when we were arranging a job, or when we'd send her to a movie. Ma saw a lot of movies."[42]

Ma and Fred Barker were going to be given a pauper's funeral, but Sheriff S. C. M. Thomas, of Ocala, received a telegram on January 17th from Sheriff Rogers of Jasper County, Missouri, forbidding the burial. George Barker, then in Carthage, Missouri, wanted to claim the bodies of his wife and son, as well as their property. George had read about the deaths in the newspaper and wanted to bring the bodies back to Oklahoma for burial next to his son, Herman, but he just didn't have enough money.[43]

The money discovered in the house at Oklawaha had been confiscated as evidence by the FBI, even though the serial numbers did not match those from the Bremer kidnapping. The cash was probably from a bank robbery but this could not be proven. Still, George Barker was denied receipt of any of the money.

"Ma"—The Life and Times of "Ma" Barker and Her Boys

The bodies of Kate and Fred Barker lay on slabs in an Ocala mortuary unburied from January 16, 1935, until October 1, 1935, while George tried to come up with enough money to return them to Oklahoma. Florida officials, anxious to get on with the burials, were stopped cold by George, who continued to refuse any burial in that state.

George Barker, the man Ma and her boys had turned their backs on, finally came up with the cash to permit him to take the bodies back to Oklahoma for burial. He showed up in Ocala in an ambulance and the mummified bodies of his wife and son were loaded into the vehicle. George drove back to Tulsa across country with the bodies, which would finally be given a proper burial.

From Tulsa, George had the bodies taken to Webb City. Hundreds of people viewed the coffins, but the caskets were not opened. The *Joplin News Herald* reported on Monday, September 30, 1935: "Hundreds of people visited the Haines-Woodard Funeral Home yesterday to view the coffins of Kate (Ma) Barker and Fred Barker, slain at Oklawaha, Florida, eight months ago in a gun battle with federal officers. The bodies were brought here last week for funeral services and burial. The caskets were not opened. Officials of the undertaking firm and Frank Dixon, one of George Barker's advisors, said that Barker, husband a father of the bandits, would not view the bodies. Brief funeral services will be conducted at the graves Tuesday afternoon in a cemetery northeast of Miami. The funeral procession, including two hearses, is expected to leave Webb City at 1 P.M., Tuesday for the cemetery."[44]

The funeral cortege left Webb City on October 1, 1935, for brief services at the cemetery near Welch, Oklahoma, where Herman had been buried in 1927. The *Joplin News Herald* ran only a brief notice on the day of the funeral: "Brief funeral services for Kate "Ma" Barker and her son, Fred Barker, who were slain eight months ago by federal officers at Oklawaha, Florida, were conducted at the graves this afternoon in a cemetery northeast of Miami."[45]

Ma and Freddie left an estate of $12,757.05. Following a long legal battle, George finally received $1,600 of his former wife and son's estate, and all household effects and wearing apparel. Attorneys received the balance.[46]

"Ma"—The Life and Times of "Ma" Barker and Her Boys

Ma, Herman, Freddie, were dead, with Doc soon to follow, and Lloyd, finally paroled from Leavenworth in 1947, died two years later.[47]

George buried Kate and their son Fred in an open field at Williams Timberhill Cemetery in Welch, Oklahoma, a countryside graveyard, overrun by undergrowth and weeds. The services were attended by a small number of relatives and curious onlookers. It was estimated that approximately twenty-five people attended the services which included six undertakers. The funeral sermon was preached to the living, with no mention being made of the deceased. The minister invoked the blessings of God upon the surviving members of the family and honored the request for such blessings with the statement, "If it by Thy will." The bodies were buried next to the grave of Herman Barker, Ma's oldest son.

Grave of Herman Barker in Welch, Oklahoma. (Author's collection)

A marker was later added for Arthur "Doc" Barker in Williams Cemetery but he is actually buried in Olivet Memorial Park Cemetery in Colma, California. Lloyd "Red" Barker, the last of Ma's sons to die, is buried in Elmwood Cemetery, Brighton, Colorado.

J. Edgar Hoover, FBI director, described Ma as having the "most resourceful criminal brain that America has produced in the past generation. She was the most dangerous lawbreaker in my experience. More so than John Dillinger or 'Baby Face' Nelson or any of the rest of our so called number one public enemies. In her sixty years she raised a spawn of hell. Of her four sons, one was a mail robber, another a holdup man, and the remaining pair highwaymen, kidnappers and wanton murders."[48]

Alvin Karpis saw Ma in a different light: "If you believe the legends, Ma was the most famous and the most feared woman in the United States at one time, a thief and a killer. Ma was none of these things. She wasn't a leader of criminals or even a criminal herself. The proof is that in her entire life she was never once mugged or printed by the police. There is not one official police photograph of her in existence or a set of fingerprints taken

End of the Barker-Karpis Gang. (Author's collection)

while she was alive. If she had been such a menace to society, the police would surely have had her mug shot and prints on file. I challenge the FBI to prove otherwise. . . .

"The idea that Ma was the brains behind our five years of holdups and crimes is strongly entrenched in North America. In books, kids' comics, detective fiction, and movies and, for that matter, in every other entertainment outlet Ma has been described as a genius of crime for so long that nobody will ever believe that she was to us, in the Karpis-Barker Gang, a simple woman and the mother of Freddie and Doc."[49]

The actual degree of Ma Barker's own criminality is of some doubt. Though her children were undoubtedly criminals and their Barker-Karpis Gang committed a spree of robberies, kidnappings and other crimes between 1931 and 1935, it appears that the popular image of her as the gang's leader and its criminal mastermind is a myth. Though she must have known of the gang's activities and it seems clear that she did help them before and after they committed their crimes, there is no evidence that she was ever an active participant in any of the crimes themselves or that she was involved at any level in planning them.

The cemetery where Ma was laid to rest was very near the clapboard filling station operated by George Barker. New super highways skirted the dirt road leading to the station and occasionally, but not often, a rare tourist would pull up for gas, oil, or water. George Barker would pull himself out of his chair in the Oklahoma sun and fill the tank while studying the lonesome road.[50]

Once a tourist filling up his tank happened to notice the clump of headstones peeking out of the tall weeds and asked George if what he saw was a graveyard. George Barker looked at him and calmly related, "That's Ma and the boys."

Notes

[1] Alvin Karpis with Bill Trent, *The Alvin Karpis Story*, pp. 80, 90-91.
[2] *Springfield Leader and Press*, January 9, 1935.

[3] *Springfield Daily News*, January 19, 1935.
[4] *Springfield Daily News*, January 17, 1935.
[5] Vernon Lamme, Florida Lore Not Found in History Books, 1973, privately printed.
[6] Alvin Karpis with Bill Trent, *The Alvin Karpis Story*, pp. 183-187.
[7] United States Bureau of Investigation, Report of Special Agent D. P. Sullivan, Chicago, Illinois, February 17, 1936; Paul Maccabee St. Paul Gangster History, 1981-1995, Research Files, Minnesota Historical Society.
[8] Myron J. Quimby, *The Devil's Emissaries*, p. 143.
[9] (Jacksonville) *Florida Times-Union*, January 17, 1935.
[10] *New York Times*, January 17, 1935.
[11] Jim Hounschell, "Ma Barker and Her Viper Brood," Lawmen and Outlaws, 116 Years in Joplin's History, published in cooperation with The Fraternal Order of Police Lodge #27, Walsworth Publishing Company, Inc., 1989.
[12] Vernon Lamme, Florida Lore Not Found in History Books, 1973, privately printed.
[13] *Springfield Leader and Press*, January 16, 1935; *Atlanta Georgian*, January 16, 1935; *Atlanta Georgian*, January 17, 1935.
[14] Patterson Smith, "Thomas McDade and the Annals of Murder," AB Bookman's Weekly, April 22, 1996; *Dallas Morning News*, January 17, 1935 [15] Ibid.
[16] Myron J. Quimby, *The Devil's Emissaries*, pp. 143-145; *Dallas Morning News*, January 17, 1935.
[17] (Jacksonville) *Florida Times-Union*, January 17, 1935; *New York Times*, January 17, 1935.
[18] *Tulsa World*, January 17, 1935; Charles G. Zehnder, "Barker/Karpis Gang's $100,000 Stash," *Western Treasures Magazine*, June 1970; *Dallas Morning News*, January 17, 1935.
[19] Springfield Daily News, January 17, 1935.
[20] FBI Files, RCS:TD I.C.#7-576, November 19, 1936, The Kidnaping of Edward George Bremer, St. Paul, Minnesota, History and Early Association of the Karpis-Barker Gang Prior to the Abduction of Mr. Bremer.
[21] *St. Paul Pioneer Press*, January 17, 1935.
[22] Ibid.
[23] *Springfield Daily News*, January 17, 1935.
[24] *St. Paul Pioneer Press*, January 17, 1935.
[25] *St. Paul Pioneer Press*, January 18, 1935.
[26] Ibid.
[27] *St. Paul Pioneer Press*, January 19, 1935.
[28] Ibid.
[29] Attorney General of the United States, 1789-1985, Washington D.C., U.S. Department of Justice, 1985.
[30] *St. Paul Pioneer Press*, January 18, 1935.
[31] *Florida Times-Union* (Jacksonville), January 17, 1935; *St. Paul Pioneer Press*, January

17, 1935.
[32] Myron J. Quimby, *The Devil's Emissaries*, p. 146.
[33] (Jacksonville) *Florida Times-Union*, January 17, 1935; New York Times, January 17, 1935; Springfield Leader and Press, January 16, 1935.
[34] *Springfield Daily News*, January 17, 1935.
[35] Ibid.
[36] Alvin Karpis with Bill Trent, *The Alvin Karpis Story*, pp. 185-187.
[37] Myron J. Quimby, *The Devil's Emissaries*, pp. 146-147.
[38] *Springfield Daily News*, January 18, 1935.
[39] *Springfield Leader and Press*, January 17, 1935.
[40] Ibid; *Springfield Daily News*, January 18, 1935.
[41] Ibid.
[42] Alvin Karpis with Bill Trent, *The Alvin Karpis Story*, p. 81.
[43] Myron J. Quimby, *The Devil's Emissaries*, p. 147.
[44] *Joplin News Herald*, September 30, 1935.
[45] *Joplin News Herald*, October 1, 1935.
[46] "Ma Barker," Lawrence County Historical Society Bulletin, Number 120, July 1991.
[47] J. Robert Nash, *Bloodletters and Badmen Volume 2*, pp. 34-35.
[48] Tulsa Tribune, March 22, 1949; FBI Files Freedom of Information Act.
[49] Alvin Karpis with Bill Trent, *The Alvin Karpis Story*, pp. 80-81.
[50] J. Robert Nash, *Bloodletters and Badmen Volume 2*, pp. 34-35.

Chapter Ten

Life Imprisonment

"Ma Barker and her sons, and Alvin Karpis and his cronies, constituted the toughest gang of hoodlums the FBI ever has been called upon to eliminate . . . Looking over the record of these criminals, I was repeatedly impressed by the cruelty of their depredations . . . murder of a policeman . . . murder of two policemen. . . . machine gun murder of an innocent citizen who got in the way during a bank robbery . . . kidnapping and extortion . . . train robbery . . . mail robbery . . . the protection of high police officials bought with tainted money . . . paroles bought."

—J. Edgar Hoover[1]

ederal agents, who had not only killed Ma and Fred Barker in the Florida gun battle, but eliminated John Dillinger, Pretty Boy Floyd, and "Baby Face" Nelson from the crime scene, settled down to their longest respite from chasing criminals in a year. One agent spoke for all of them when he told reporters that the shootout with Ma Barker "was the worst battle of them all. It was much worse than Little Bohemia. The house was a worse riddle."[2]

While they awaited developments in the chase for Alvin Karpis, the agents lolled about the spacious lawn fronting Lake Weir. They chatted amongst themselves and to the hundreds of curiosity seekers, who also had

Alvin Karpis. (Photograph Collection 1936, Location no. por 20416 p1)

assembled there. The conversations with the public were somewhat of a rarity as ordinarily the agents were a tight lipped, silent bunch.

"They're the best hand-picked squad in the country," E.J. Connelley told the crowd. He said that the sharpshooter of the squad, a former Texas Ranger known to outsiders as "Doc," had ended Fred Barker's life with three bullets to the head from his rifle. That same "Doc," Connelley added, was at his side when he had knocked on the door of the Barker cottage and had covered his retreat when the bullets started flying.

Meanwhile, the gray-haired mother of Alvin Karpis, America's new Public Enemy Number One, renewed her appeal for him to surrender and avoid possible death at the hands of Federal agents on January 19, 1935. Mrs. John Karpavicz talked with reporters at her home in Chicago's northwest side and reaffirmed that she was afraid her son would share the fate of Ma and Fred Barker.[3]

"I don't want my boy to look like that woman and her son," Mrs. Karpavicz said, referring to published photographs of the slain pair. The manner in which she said, "That woman"—expressing scorn and anger—indicated her bitterness against Mrs. Barker. "I want him to live, and to live he must surrender before the government men hunt him down."

Mrs. Karpawicz said she expected her son to answer her appeal: "Alvin has done wrong and he should pay—but I don't want him shot down like the others were. I want him to surrender—that is the only way he can save his life." She added he had not been home in three years.

"Ma"—The Life and Times of "Ma" Barker and Her Boys

"He probably doesn't care anything for his life now," she related. "But I suffer all the time for him. If he still loves me he will come back and give up."[4]

With the Oklawaha shootout all over the radio, Alvin Karpis and Dolores Delaney decided they could no longer stay in their house on 85th Street in Miami. Karpis was crushed by the deaths of his friends. Freddie Barker had been his best friend and Ma was like his very own mother.[5]

Dolores had received a call from the underworld earlier that day warning them to get out of their house before midnight. Although she did not know who made the call, she knew it came from Cleveland and was a tip-off that the feds were closing in. With the guys away fishing, she and Wynona wondered whether the Barkers had received a similar call.

Dolores had become skeptical of the safety of not only the Lake Weir hideout, but her own place in Miami as well. She decided to go to Atlantic City where she might be safe for a while. Wynona Burdette told her that she would come along and help take care of Dolores, since she was an expectant mother. Karpis told her they should all go first to Joe Adams' place in Miami to pick up some much needed cash and some advice.

It was time for Karpis and Campbell to renew their flight. Plans for the departure were made hurriedly and the gang's new errand boy, an orchestra leader by the name of Henry "Duke" Randall, was dispatched to the El Commodoro Hotel, where $1,200 was secured for Karpis from Joe Adams, who had been holding the same for Campbell Karpis and. Campbell, traveling apart from the women, stole a new Buick Special in Jacksonville, Florida and drove north.

Dolores Delaney. (Author's collection)

"Ma"—The Life and Times of "Ma" Barker and Her Boys

The night of January 16, 1935, found Dolores Delaney and Wynona Burdette on board a train bound for Atlantic City, New Jersey. They carried with them as credentials a note signed by Duke Randall addressed to William A. Morley, part owner of the Danmor Hotel in Atlantic City. The message requested Morley to take care of his friend Mrs. Graham and to see that she obtained a good doctor and good care. The women arrived at Atlantic City about 2:00 o'clock on the afternoon of January 18th and registered at the Danmor as Mrs. A.B. Graham and sister of Macon, Georgia.

At about 1:00 o'clock in the morning the following day, Karpis and Campbell appeared at the Danmor driving a Buick sedan bearing Florida license D-5-306. Karpis registered at the hotel as R.S. Carson and Campbell used the name of G.C. Cameron. Special agents had learned of the license number of the car in the possession of Karpis and a description of the vehicle and the desperate character of its occupants were broadcast.

The telegraphed tip that led to the unsuccessful attempt to arrest Karpis, who was wanted for the Edward Bremer kidnapping in St. Paul a year earlier, came from Florida police. It informed Atlantic City officers to watch for a car bearing a Florida license, and to be cautious as the car's passengers were "two bad men." The Atlantic City police investigation led them to the Coast Garage at the foot of South Kentucky Avenue near the boardwalk, and it was there the car was found. Inside the vehicle were a rifle and some ammunition. The Florida information had warned that the men were heavily armed and well supplied with ammunition.[6]

From the minute that Karpis and Campbell had arrived in Atlantic City, they both had the feeling they were being followed. Because Dolores was in her eighth month of pregnancy, Karpis, with surprising bravado, took her to see police surgeon, Dr. Carl Surran and made arrangements with him for the delivery of the baby when the time came.

"We've got plenty of dough, and we want the best for the little girl," Karpis said, according to Dr. Surran.[7]

In addition to the checkup by Dr. Surran, Karpis ran some other errands as well, shortly after arriving in Atlantic City. The whole time he was certain that he was being tailed. A man and woman, both in their forties, became prime suspects, as they seemed to be behind him everywhere he went. Although they undoubtedly made him nervous, he kept his temper and did nothing to throw additional suspicion on himself or on the other members of his little group.

That night he talked over the situation with Campbell, who was also convinced someone had been on his tail all day. They agreed to stay the night at the Danmor, then head for New York City. Karpis told the girls to get to bed before midnight and be all packed and ready for an early morning checkout.

Early on the morning of January 20, 1935, Patrolman Elias Saab located the stolen Florida automobile, a Buick coach, in the Coast Garage on Kentucky Avenue, a half bock from Atlantic City's boardwalk. After reporting his finding to the Atlantic City Detective Bureau, Saab, with two fellow officers of the Atlantic City Police Department proceeded to the Danmor Hotel to investigate.

The officers carefully made their way to the registration desk and learned that the two men had registered at the hotel the following Friday. The room they occupied was adjoined to the one taken by the two women, who had arrived in Atlantic City a day earlier.

The officers approached the third floor of the hotel with drawn guns and were soon joined by Detectives Edward Mulhern and Arch Witham. A third detective, George Brennan, waited downstairs to block the escape route.[8]

As they moved slowly down the hallway, they saw a crack of light under the doorway of Room 23, in which they had been told the owners of the car were staying. Detective Mulhern, with a revolver in his hand, put his shoulder to the door and broke it in. Detective Witham, with his revolver drawn, stood behind him. Karpis was sitting in a rocking chair directly opposite the door with a Thompson submachine gun in his lap, covering the entrance. Campbell sat on the edge of the bed in his underwear, also holding a submachine gun.

"Stick 'em up. We're officers," Mulhern demanded. The response was immediate. "Stick 'em up yourself, coppers. We're coming," Karpis retorted, firing at the detective. His first burst, fired as he lifted the submachine gun from his lap, missed the two detectives. Mulhern fired once, but was forced to back out of the door with Witham behind him, as Karpis and Campbell swung their weapons on them.

The surprised detectives retreated down the hall while firing the whole time. They concealed themselves around a bend in the corridor, where they could continue the fight from a safe position. Witham and Mulhern fired at the doorway from the hall whenever one of the fugitives approached it. Karpis, disregarding the bullets, stepped out into the hallway and fired another burst at the detectives. One bullet struck Detective Witham on the side of the face, penetrating his cheek and leaving a deep gash.

Meanwhile, the door of the next room opened and Dolores Delaney and Wynona Burdette rushed out into the hallway. A machine gun bullet struck Delaney in the leg. Both women charged back into their room and closed the door. Karpis dashed inside the room and bandaged her leg with a strip of bed sheet.

Out of ammunition, Mulhern ran to his wounded comrade, who had also fired his last cartridge. Although Detective Brennan had run upstairs upon hearing the firing, Karpis and Campbell backed toward a rear stairway, Harry Campbell toting the machine gun, Karpis his forty-five. The fleeing robbers could see the detectives from the second floor landing and slipped unseen down to the first floor, making their way through a back hallway that led to Westminster Alley.

Three uniformed officers were waiting for them—Patrolmen Saab and James Campbell, and Sergeant Joseph Florentino. The policemen fired at the fugitives until their revolvers were empty with Campbell and Karpis returning the fire. One bullet fired by one of the gangsters, struck a wall near Patrolman Campbell's head, so close that flying bits of cement knocked his cap to the sidewalk. Campbell later, while discussing the shootout, maintained that he and Karpis could have killed the police officers with their machine guns if they had desired to do so.[9]

According to the officers, more than 200 shots were exchanged. With no ammunition, the officers were driven away from the garage door by

Karpis and his gun. While he guarded the door, Harry Campbell rushed into the garage, only to find that their car was no longer there. The police had taken care of that.[10]

Harry Campbell came out driving a pea-green Pontiac sedan, the property of Mrs. Harold Brand, wife of an Atlantic City auctioneer. Karpis jumped in, and after several unsuccessful attempts to locate their girlfriends with numerous police cars pushing them hard, they drove off along Kentucky Avenue and out of the neighborhood.

Twice their unfamiliarity with Atlantic City thoroughfares almost resulted in the police having them cornered. The chase through the streets was anything but a test of speed or endurance. Upon a couple occasions, the fugitives drove their automobile down blind alleys, which ended at the boardwalk, but they were able to spin their car around, and with the underwear-clad Campbell standing up in the back of the vehicle pulling the trigger of a machine gun, they shot their way through the pursuing police forces; all of which added to the sensationalism of the escape.[11]

"I didn't know Atlantic City's downtown streets . . . [one] turn took me to a dead end at the Boardwalk," recalled Karpis years later. "The cops knew we'd trapped ourselves. They waited for us to turn around. 'We'll run right through,' I told Harry. 'Get the gun ready.' I wheeled the car in a 360-degree turn and raced it straight at the waiting cops. But partway down the street, I saw an alleyway I hadn't noticed before. We skidded and threw burning rubber all over, but we made the turn."[12]

Almost from the very first echo of gunfire, the city's traffic lights had been reset to blink on and off red, which was the manner in which a general police alarm was given in Atlantic City. This action spread a warning to the farthermost sections of the city, leading the police to believe it would be next to impossible for Karpis and Campbell to leave town.[13]

In spite of the blinking red lights, the two criminals easily outdistanced their pursuers and encountered little trouble penetrating police lines and getting out of the city. While the weather hindered police attempts to capture their prey, it gave cover to the disappearing act of the desperadoes, who vanished in the snow and rain before the police could get close enough to find them. Many patrol cars blocked streets in a certain area, believing the gangsters were headed toward Longford on the outskirts of Atlantic City.

The *Chicago Herald Examiner* described the shootout in somewhat sensationalistic fashion: "Alvin Karpis, America's public enemy number one, blazed his way with spitting machine gun fire early today from a police trap laid for him in a small hotel. With Harry Campbell, another hunted Midwestern gangster, he shouted defiance to the police command to surrender, fired on the police, stole a motor car, tried to rescue two women companions from police and then, with guns roaring, sped away. One policeman narrowly escaped death when a bullet pierced his cap."[14]

The *St. Paul Pioneer Press* also described the escape in colorful terms: "The nation's latest ace of bad men, the twenty-five-year-old Alvin Karpis, shot his way out of an Atlantic City police trap early today. With him, triggering a machine gun was another of the Middle West's hunted criminals, Harry Campbell. Behind them they left their women, one of them wounded and an expectant mother.

"Trapped before dawn in a hotel room to which they came to only Saturday, the two desperadoes—wanted for crimes from robbery to kidnap to murder—answered with gunfire the police demand to surrender. Fighting their way from their fourth floor quarters to an alley, blazing so close to policemen that one officer's hat was shot from his head, they stole an automobile and then, pursued by twenty policemen and with every traffic light in the city flashing on and off in a general police alarm, they drove toward Camden, distancing pursuit."[15]

Although wounded in the right leg, Delaney, with the aid of Wynona Burdette, succeeded in escaping from the hotel and crouched in the alley, awaiting the arrival of Karpis and Campbell to rescue them. Karpis and Campbell rode twice around the block, firing as they careened through the streets. They were attempting to reach the two women, and if possible, get them into the car with them.

However, during the period of time the girls were waiting for the fugitives, they deliberated upon the safety of their men and it was decided that to continue the flight with Karpis and Campbell at this time, due to the condition of Dolores Delaney, would only hinder their flight. Karpis and Campbell, finally realizing the hopelessness of the situation, drove away and were quickly lost to pursuers. The women remained in the alley until taken into custody by officers.

Doris Lockerman (Rogers), Melvin Purvis's FBI Secretary, later stated in an interview by Joshua Welsh: "At the time there was a joke—a rather bitter joke but interesting. . . . that the FBI rarely got their men but they always got the women. . . . They could always find a mate somewhere. . . . and it was of course, a ragged joke."[16]

Dolores Delaney, also known as Louise Graham, was taken to Atlantic City Hospital where she had already registered in anticipation of becoming a maternity patient in two days. Atlantic City Police learned that Wynona Burdette was also known as Mrs. Louise Campbell. She told police she hailed from Oklahoma where Karpis had once served a burglary sentence. Dispatches sent to the Associated Press from Tulsa indicated she had been arrested there in 1932 for the murder of Attorney J. Earl Smith. She had been released on her word to lead the police to "Campbell," but, of course, this was a promise she could not keep.

An X-ray indicated that Dolores Delaney's wound was not serious. According to records of the Associated Press, Delaney came from St. Paul. She and Wynona Burdette were taken to Philadelphia by Department of Justice agents for further questioning.

Seven suitcases were found in the girls' rooms at the Danmor by police. One of the girls told police questioners that they had been in Florida recently, and while there they had seen and talked with Ma and Fred Barker. The girls also said that while in Miami, they had talked with a man identified only as "Duke," and Duke had directed them to the Atlantic City hotel where they were found. He had given them a letter of recommendation, the girls told police, to the proprietors of the Danmor.[17]

Duke was described as an employee of the "Little Club" in Miami and also of the Biscayne Race Track. A report that federal men had asked that Duke be questioned brought the statement from the Miami police that night that they knew nothing of such a request.

In addition to the two women, the proprietors of the Danmor Hotel—Daniel Young and William Moreling—were questioned, as was a black employee of the garage in which the stolen Florida vehicle had been found. When police searched the vehicle, they found a loaded revolver and a loaded sawed-off shotgun. Inside their hotel room, police discovered nine valises filled with clothing.[18]

Clothing became an issue. Karpis was clad in trousers, slippers, and an overcoat while Campbell had on only his underwear and slippers, although he was covered by an overcoat. Police ordered an alarm sent to clothing store proprietors on the chance the two gangsters, out of necessity, might attempt to purchase new clothing. The police learned the identity of the men from their women companions.[19]

Police Captain Sam Wheatley told reporters he did not believe it possible that the two men had been able to get clear of the city. With Mayor Harry Bacharach taking complete charge of the police department, a thorough search was instituted within the city.[20]

The appearance of a light in a house unoccupied for two years sent police and Federal agents on a false trail in their hunt for Karpis. The officers surrounded the house, broke in, and found instead of Public Enemy Number 1, five vagrants. A search of hotels, nightclubs, and city resorts was commenced by a party of twenty-five federal agents.

Although no word was received after the flight of Karpis and Campbell to indicate the direction they were heading, the police believed they would attempt to make New York City or northern New Jersey because of the many hideouts available in the underworlds of those two localities. As a result, the New York Police Department was in frequent communication with Atlantic City and with Department of Justice headquarters in Philadelphia. Police in New York and Philadelphia joined the hunt and "crack" men of the government's criminal hunting force were dispatched to Atlantic City.

Troopers throughout New Jersey, as well as those in other states, were ordered to watch for the fugitives and to be extremely cautious because of the desperate character of the men. Police back-trailed Karpis to Miami, and then to Chicago, from which latter city he had fled when his designation as the new "Public Enemy No.1" served notice on him "that he was marked for the same relentless treatment as befell his predecessors John Dillinger and George "Baby Face" Nelson."[21]

The New York police were told that Karpis and Campbell had probably changed cars and separated. They were also informed that when last seen, the fugitives were riding in a green coach with New Jersey license plates. William S. Cuthbert, Atlantic City director of public safety, blamed the gangsters' escape on lack of proper warning on Karpis' identity:

"If we had been told or had sufficient identification that this was America's Public Enemy No.1 and that he was as tough as he turned out to be, I would have sent the entire police force down there instead of a handful of men as we do in cases involving run-of-the-mines 'tough guys,'" he declared. The call for the arrest of Karpis, police said, did not mention names, although it did warn the fugitives were armed.[22]

John Karpavicz, father of Alvin Karpis, in between stoking coal in the apartment house where he worked as a janitor, talked to reporters about his son. "That boy's day will come soon," he said, having just heard how his son blasted his way out of the Atlantic City police trap. "He gets away with it today but some day he won't."

Karpawicz, a small man, whose brown hair was streaked with gray, bore a strong facial resemblance to his son. He wore a battered, soiled brown hat, a patched sweater, and trousers that were threadbare. His watery blue eyes had difficulty finding things in the gloomy cellar. There were circles under his eyes and he appeared to be quite worn out.

"It don't look like he cares about his life anymore," he added. "It don't look like he cares about anything. He pays no attention to us." He told reporters that he didn't think he wanted anything more to do with his son. He didn't think he could help him and didn't feel that he should. "Look at my hands," he said, holding out a pair, which were black with coal dust. "They are dirty from hard work. There are other hands that are dirty, too, but not from hard work.

"These policemen that chase gangsters like Dillinger. They shoot quick. They have come to talk with me sometimes but I don't know anything about that boy now. They will get him someday. Maybe he could save his life by giving himself up. But he would save it, maybe, just for the electric chair."[23]

Department of Justice agents poured into Atlantic City with submachine guns and tear gas bombs. Their roundup of the reputed kidnappers, with the exception of Karpis was complete, "Shoot first and talk afterwards," was the advice from Chicago where officials thought Karpis might seek a new hideaway.[24]

All radio patrol cars received confidential instructions in the late afternoon, giving descriptions of the car and its occupants, and warning that the fugitives were heavily armed. The alarms also suggested that the gangsters may have picked up additional associates, by saying that the car might contain three men and a woman. The police refused to discuss this possibility, however, or to reveal the source of their information regarding the additional riders in the stolen automobile.[25]

Assistant Chief Inspector John J. Sullivan, in charge of detectives, announced that he had designated an inspector to keep charge of the watch for Karpis and Campbell. Other police officials posted guards at the three Staten Island bridges, the Holland Tunnel, the George Washington Bridge, and the Boston Post Road, the latter because of the possibility that the fugitives might cross from New Jersey by the Yonkers ferry.

While federal, state, and local law forces hotly pursued Karpis and Campbell over eastern Pennsylvania highways, an Allentown, Pennsylvania, doctor was reported to have been kidnapped by the two outlaws. Karpis and Campbell had abandoned the stolen Pontiac they were driving near Quakertown, Pennsylvania, and about midnight on January 20, 1935, they abducted Dr. Horace M. Hunsicker of Allentown.[26]

Dr. Hunsicker reported to Sheriff Roy Kruggel of Medina, Ohio, that he believed the two men were the fugitives, Karpis and Campbell. He said that the two men, armed with machine guns, forced him into the back seat of his car at the point of one of the machine guns. One drove the doctor's car and the other took the wheel of a second vehicle.

Dr. Hunsicker related the men trussed him up with his own belt and a pair of pajamas and drove to Guilford Center, Ohio. Dr. Hunsicker was forced to enter the Guilford Center Grange Hall, where he was bound, gagged, and abandoned. Police Chief T.J. Lucas of Wadsworth said that the physician had told him he was not asked by the fugitives to perform any type of medical treatment. Dr. Hunsicker was ordered not to call authorities until the two men had a good start from the Grange hall.

The physician was able to free himself about 10 P.M., less than an hour after the gangsters had departed, and immediately called the police. The two gunmen made their getaway in the doctor's car; tracks in the snow indicating they had headed west. The car which the outlaws had when they halted Dr. Hunsicker, was abandoned a few miles from Sellersville and they both made their flight in the doctor's car.

Deputy Sheriff Harry Krieger declared that while the physician had not seen a photograph of the two gangsters, it was quite apparent that they were the pair being sought. Meanwhile, Karpis and Campbell fled to Toledo in the doctor's car and later disposed of it by leaving the car at a point near LaSalle, Michigan.[27]

A full force of federal agents and state police officers headed for the Pennsylvania area. The fugitives were trailed into the wild and lonely Haycock Mountain country, forty miles north of Philadelphia and a hundred miles from the scene of their machine gunning escape from the Atlantic City hotel.[28]

Two and a half miles from Quakertown, in Bucks County, on the fringe of the hilly, wooded Haycock area, the green sedan the criminals had stolen in Atlantic City was found by law-enforcement officials. Bullets had ripped its body in the rear and smashed the windshield. Several machine gun shells were found imbedded in the automobile.

With the finding of the shot-ridden vehicle, investigators said three courses lay open to the fugitives. One, considered the most likely even before the doctor told his story, was that they had obtained another car and roared toward Philadelphia and westward, hoping to make good their escape with the aid of one of the heaviest fogs to drop on eastern Pennsylvania in years.

The second possibility they considered was that the pair had taken to the Haycock Mountains to go into hiding, in order that the wounds Campbell suffered in the break from Atlantic City could be treated.

The third possibility, although considered quite remote, was that after purloining another car, they had headed north and west, speeding into the more mountainous regions of Pennsylvania.

In case their immediate destination was Philadelphia, the Bucks County police broadcast an alarm in the afternoon that two men, one identified as Karpis, the other probably Campbell, had been sighted in Doylestown, the county seat, twenty-five miles north of Philadelphia and were traveling fast in the direction of that city.

"Be on the lookout for car containing two men, one of them Alvin Karpis," the alarm said. "Left Doylestown, Pennsylvania, headed for Philadelphia at fast rate of speed. Use caution. These men are armed."

Six Department of Justice men from Atlantic City arrived in Doylestown but were kept fogbound overnight, and unable to continue their search. With two state police investigators, they planned to leave in the morning at dawn when the fog lifted. The federal men said they learned that Karpis had purchased a new suit at a clothing store on the boardwalk in Atlantic City the past Sunday morning. He attempted to pay with a $1,000 bill. Store officials said that Karpis left a small amount of money as a deposit, and promised to return later and pay the balance.

A cordon of officers, bristling with rifles and machine guns was thrown about virtually every road in that part of the state while some officers combed the Haycock Mountain area, believing the fugitives had scurried to cover in the darkness and fog. In addition to the Bucks County police alarm, the head of the state police, Major Lynn Adams, sent a message over the police interstate printer warning all officers of the presence of the criminals in Pennsylvania.

"Important," the message said. "Alvin Karpis has been traced into Pennsylvania. Probably in hiding somewhere in the state. Search your towns for this man. He is desperate. Any squad attempting to apprehend him should be armed with rifles." Along with the message went orders to "shoot to kill."[29]

Belief that Karpis and Campbell might attempt to cross the border and perhaps continue to Montreal, Karpis' old home, led Ontario Provincial police to cover the border from Windsor south to Amherstberg. The trail of the fugitives had been picked up again when Dr. Hunsicker's stolen car was found by authorities near Monroe, Michigan. Federal officers on the American side of the boundary also gave some thought to the fugitives possibly heading for the old Dillinger haunts in Michigan.[30]

Rumors circulated through several states that following their escape from Atlantic City, Karpis and Campbell had shown up at the Casino Club in Toledo, but they received a warning from one of the Angus brothers that the two gunmen were simply too hot to receive assistance from the brothers.[31] Joe Roscoe, a sometimes friend of Campbell, was also suspected of harboring the two men.

Another popular story stated the two fugitives hid out at Edith Barry's House of Prostitution in Toledo. Campbell had acquired a reputation for having visited more than his share of brothels over the years. After completing their escape, Karpis and Campbell did, in fact, ride to Toledo and take refuge in Edith Barry's House of Prostitution. Karpis moved in with Edith Barry and paid special attention to the newspaper and radio reports during his stay.[32]

As far as the general public knew, after the January Atlantic City shootout, Karpis was next seen in August 1935 watching horse races in Saratoga Springs. After he was recognized in Saratoga Springs, Karpis wrote, "[We] pulled out for Hot Springs in a big hurry. We'd already made contacts earlier there . . . Grace Goldstein was my girlfriend there and Freddie went around with one of Grace's hookers, a girl named Connie Morris." (Both Fred Hunter and Connie Morris later stated that Karpis and Hunter first arrived in June, 1935.)

Karpis described Grace as, "a peroxide blonde about thirty-five, and she ran the finest whorehouse in Hot Springs . . . she maintained great connections. The mayor had a big crush on her. She entertained all the top crooks who visited and all the top cops and politicians. Grace was a genuine big leaguer . . . she rented houses and cottages for me . . . when the feds started breathing closer to me, they latched on to Grace. They put her through some rugged times and, for the most part, she stood up to them with a lot of courage."

Reports that were made public shortly after Edward Bremer's release had indicated the kidnappers' hideout was located near Creston, Iowa. Park A. Findley, chief of the Iowa Bureau of Criminal Apprehension, said at the time that he had confidential information to that effect. Investigation, however, by the Department of Justice failed to develop further evidence.

A few days subsequent to the arrest of Doc Barker, special agents learned that the hideout in which Mr. Bremer had been held for twenty-three days was located at Bensenville, Illinois, a suburb northwest of Chicago. Simultaneously with the attack at Oklawaha, Florida, which resulted in the deaths of Fred and Ma Barker, special agents raided the address at 180 May Street, Bensenville.

According to Federal authorities, the building at this address was owned by Herman Baucke and it was found that a former tenant who had occupied a portion of this building in January and February 1934 had moved several months prior to the raid.[33]

On January 19, 1935, Edward Bremer accompanied federal agents to Bensenville and pointed out a frame building two stories high on one side and one story high in the rear. Bremer positively identified this portion of the building, which had formerly been occupied by Harold Alderton as being the house in which he had been held a kidnap victim.

The building, according to the Associated Press, was near a school and two churches. Bremer, kept in the rear and ground floor apartment, had told federal agents that part of the time during his captivity he could hear children playing. This was one of the clues that led authorities to the house on May Street; another being the ringing of church bells.

But once inside the house, it was the wallpaper which presented Bremer with positive identification of the place. His keen memory was successful in identifying the gaudiness of the wallpaper with its varicolored flowers and a design with a wooden fence worked in, adorning the room in which he was held. He also identified the crack in the wallpaper in a corner of the room, the position of the window and height of the sill, the electric light drop, the step between the living room and the bedroom and the broken toilet handle.

It was also found that the bedroom in which Mr. Bremer had been held was situated as had previously been described by him. Bremer had also remembered that when he stood up beside his bed, his head struck a chain hanging from an electric light. It was, he added, eight steps from the bedroom to the bathroom, and he had had to pass through three doors and step up an incline.

The entrance to the house was through the kitchen, as had been related by Mr. Bremer. There was a bedroom adjoining the room in which he was held and the wooden floor in the house answered the description as previously obtained from the victim of the kidnapping. Even trite things such as nail holes in a boarded window had been noticed and remembered.

The banker revealed he was able to fix the descriptions into his mind mostly at mealtime. He ate at a small table and his captors removed his blindfold while he ate, but kept his wrists tied behind his back. They would stand near the back of his chair and reach around his plate, feeding him themselves without showing their faces.

Investigation disclosed that Elmer Farmer, the tavern owner at Bensenville, who had been a close associate of the Karpis-Barker Gang, had secured the use of Alderton's home for the use of the kidnapers at the request of Fred Goetz. It was ascertained that in December 1933, Fred Goetz and Alvin Karpis appeared at Bensenville and examined the hideout. At that time, they agreed to pay Harold Alderton $1,000 for his services in connection with the abduction of Mr. Bremer.

Elmer Farmer was arrested at Bensenville, Illinois, on the morning of January 16, 1935, and confessed that he participated in the conspiracy to kidnap Mr. Bremer. Harold Alderton, an ex-bootlegger, was arrested on January 17, 1935, by special agents at Marion, Indiana and likewise admitted that Mr. Bremer had been held in his home, and that he had received $1,000 for his services in connection with the kidnapping.

Special Agents of the Federal Bureau of Investigation, after learning that Volney Davis and Edna Murray had discontinued their operations in Glasgow, Montana, continued their search to locate these fugitives. Their relentless probing disclosed that Volney Davis and Edna Murray were in association with Jess Doyle and Doris O'Connor in Kansas City.

Volney Davis and Edna Murray in February of 1935 were residing at 3028 Baltimore Avenue, Kansas City, Missouri, under the names of Mr. and Mrs. G. L. Harper. Jess Doyle and his paramour, Doris O'Connor, had left the other members of the Karpis-Barker Gang in St. Paul on January 16, 1934, and together with Eddie and Bessie Green proceeded to Topeka, Kansas.

In May, after a visit to Cardin, Oklahoma, where they spent time with Dors O'Connor's relatives, they moved to Aurora, Illinois, at the request of Edna Murray. They remained in Aurora until June 1934 and then returned to Kansas City, residing at 4112 Locust Street. Prior to determining the exact address of Edna Murray and Volney Davis in Kansas City, special agents ascertained that Davis had stored a Pontiac automobile in a local garage at Kansas City. Agents maintained a surveillance of this car, and Volney Davis was captured at Kansas City, Missouri, on February 4, 1935, and immediately arrangements were made to remove him from Kansas City.

En route to Chicago, Illinois, the airplane in which the agents and their prisoner were traveling in, made a forced landing near Yorkville, Illinois, on the night of February 7, 1935, and during the confusion which resulted, Davis effected his escape. He remained at liberty until he was recaptured at Chicago on June 1, 1935. Davis was questioned concerning a $100 counterfeit bill which was removed from his person subsequent to his capture in Kansas City, Missouri. He claimed that the bill came from Walter "Irish" O'Malley, who was being sought by the Federal Bureau of Investigation in connection with the kidnapping of an Alton, Illinois man.

Davis maintained that he did not pass counterfeit money, but merely carried it with him so that in the event he was arrested by officers of the law, he could tender them the $100 bill in return for his liberty. He believed that he could affect his escape before the officers who had accepted the bribe would discover the bill was counterfeit. Davis, however, never offered the counterfeit bill to the special agents who apprehended him. After his capture, Volney Davis outwardly became penitent, and in a moment of remorse, he penned the following letter to his parents:

"My dear Mother, Father and Sisters: June 3, 1935. At last I am in a position where I can write to you all again. And I am sure glad that I can for it has been awful to be running around over the country and not being able to write to the only ones in this world that really loves me. I am here in jail and have entered a plea of guilty to conspiracy in this case. I guess you have read about it in the papers. I will be sentenced on Friday this week, I don't know what I will get but I expect it will be a life sentence. I guess I will be sent to the government prison out in California, but before I go there I will be held for thirty days in some prison here. But I won't be here long enough time for you to come to see me. But just as soon as I am where you can have time to come to see me I will let you know when and where to come. I have some property and some money I want to turn over to you but if it is so you can I want you to bring Ruby with you as there will be quite a bit of running around and she can do it better than you. I would like to see all of you before I go away for good but it may be impossible as it will cost too much. Tell all the side hello for me and tell the boys to take a lesson from my experience and never touch anything that don't belong to them, for a man can get more enjoyment out of ten dollars he has earned honestly than he can a thousand got dishonestly. I know from sad experience. I am telling you this to tell them because it may do some good and I know my life has been spared for some reason in this world and if I can keep some you boys from going wrong I have accomplished something in this world. I would give anything if I could start over again, for I know I could be successful in business if I was free for I have been fairly successful in business transactions while I have been dodging the law and I know if I had been free to have taken care of them like any other citizen I could have done much better.

"Papa and Mama I don't want you all to feel too bad about this for after all you will know where I am at night when you go to sleep and I won't be in danger of being killed [at] any moment. And I promise if such a thing should happen as I am ever a free man again I will make an honest living regardless of how little I can earn. And I will be a model prisoner wherever I go and for ever length of time I get. I have been treated good here and am well in body. I hope wherever I go that I get work that won't be injurious to my health. Well, I don't know much more to write but I will sure write ever[y] time I get a chance and try to make up for the last time. Tell Uncle

Newt hello and I sure would like to see him. I am going to write a letter to Bertha soon and Irene. I think I know their address, but in case I don't you tell them you heard from me. Be sure to tell me how Beulah is and when you saw her last. I sure do hope she gets well. Guess Mildred is O.K. I hope so. Well, I will close. With all my love to you all, as ever, Volney Davis."[34]

Following the arrest of Volney Davis, Edna Murray, and Jess Doyle sought refuge at Pittsburg, Kansas, where on February 7, 1935, Doyle was located by Special Agents of the Federal Bureau of Investigation. With the cooperation of the Pittsburg Police Department they engaged Doyle in a gun battle. Doyle escaped, but during the day he appeared in Girard, Kansas, where he surrendered to the sheriff.

On this same date, Edna Murray was taken into custody by special agents, together with two individuals who had harbored her, Harry C. Stanley, her brother, and his wife, Mary Stanley. Harry C. Stanley was subsequently convicted on the charge of harboring a fugitive from justice in federal court in the District of Kansas and was sentenced on March 13, 1935, to serve six months in the county jail at Wichita, Kansas, and was also fined $1,000. Mary Stanley, on the same date, was given a five-year suspended sentence on the same charge.

The extensive investigation conducted by the Federal Bureau of Investigation revealed that Alvin Karpis, Doc Barker, Harry Campbell, William Weaver, Fred Goetz, Fred Barker, and Volney Davis were in St. Paul, Minnesota, the morning of Mr. Bremer's abduction, and eyewitnesses stated that five or six men using two automobiles were at the corner of Lexington and Goodrich Avenues at the time the kidnapping took place. Alvin Karpis and Harry Campbell subsequently admitted, after their capture, that they were present the morning when Mr. Bremer was abducted.

It was further ascertained that Mr. Bremer had been transported to the hideout at Bensenville by Alvin Karpis, Harry Campbell, William Weaver, and Doc Barker, who also acted as guards over Bremer while the latter was being held; and that Bryan Bolton, William Harrison, Elmer Farmer and Harold Alderton had taken care of the needs of the guards and their prisoner by supplying them with food, whiskey and running other errands.

"Ma"—The Life and Times of "Ma" Barker and Her Boys

Information was also obtained by the special agents that the guards at the hideout had grown impatient at the delay in the collection of the ransom money and that considerable liquor had been consumed, especially by William Weaver and Harry Campbell. The gangsters had arguments among themselves, and several days before the release of Mr. Bremer, one member of the gang was ordered to leave the hideout. This member was William Weaver, who had become tired of his cramped quarters and the delay in the payment of the ransom money, as a result of which he spent too much time strolling up and down the alley adjacent to the hideout. The rest of the gang feared detection should one of their members be observed outside of the hideout.

Doc Barker endeavored to enliven the days by imitating the voice of a Mexican and, if possible, also to lead Mr. Bremer to believe that a foreigner was one of his guards. Karpis studied maps and made charts at the hideout; possibly compiling getaway routes possibly for some future crime, or a chart which would be used in returning Mr. Bremer to Rochester, Minnesota. The gang kept machine guns in the hideout to be used in the event law enforcement agencies discovered where Mr. Bremer was held.

That same February 7th, Frank Dixon, administrator of the estate of Fred Barker, wrote the Bureau a letter reporting that George Barker had been divorced from Kate Barker for several years, and since the divorce, he had lived in fear of his life. George was afraid not only of Kate Barker but their own sons as well and he blamed Ma for the criminal lives and activities of the boys.

According to Dixon, George Barker never discussed his family with anyone and he never mentioned the boys unless it was in reference to when they all were children. Upon several occasions George had barred his windows and doors with heavy timbers, fearing that during the night, the boys might come in and kill him.[35]

In St. Paul, Minnesota on May 4, 1934, an indictment had charged Arthur R. Barker, Alvin Karpis, John J. McLaughlin, Sr., John J. McLaughlin, Jr., William E. Vidler, Phillip J. Delaney, "Slim," "Izzy," Frankie Wright, John Roe and Richard Roe with conspiracy to kidnap Mr. Bremer and transport him from St. Paul, Minnesota, to the State of Illinois. The Federal Grand Jury completed their investigation of the case in January 1935.

More than a half dozen witnesses, headed by Edward Bremer, had gone before the jury, and a half dozen more were heard on the final day. Among those who had appeared before the grand jury was Mrs. Florence Humphrey, saleswoman at the Grand-Silver department store. She identified Karpis from pictures as the man who bought three flashlights from her and sought to have red lenses in them. Because her store did not stock red lenses, she directed him to another store.[36]

Also appearing before the jury were four "mystery" witnesses, all residents of Bensenville, Illinois, where Department of Justice agents had found the hideout in which Bremer was held. These men "put the finger" on members of the Barker-Karpis Gang as the ones who were at and about the hideout at various times during the kidnapping.

Other witnesses heard at the afternoon session of the grand jury included Adolph Bremer Jr., brother of the kidnap victim; Walter Magee, St. Paul contractor and friend of the victim, who acted as go-between and ransom deliveryman; an official of the American National Bank, who aided in making up the ransom and copying the numbers of the bills; and Werner Hanni, former agent in charge of the St. Paul office of the Department of Justice. Hanni had been transferred to Omaha since the kidnapping.

George F. Sullivan, Harold Nathan, and other federal men declined to disclose the identities of five mystery witnesses, four of whom appeared before the grand jury. The quintet had not been served with subpoenas through the United States Marshal's office in St. Paul. Sullivan did tell the press that the death penalty could not be invoked in the Bremer case because that portion of the law citing the death penalty in cases where kidnap victims were harmed was adopted as an amendment May 1934, after the Bremer abduction. Only in kidnap cases subsequent to passage of the amendment could the death penalty be invoked and only at the discretion of a jury.

While the grand jury was in session, Arthur "Doc" Barker was held under heavy guard in the Ramsey County Jail. Deputy United States Marshal

"MA"—THE LIFE AND TIMES OF "MA" BARKER AND HER BOYS

Stephen Picha received telegraphic orders from Washington to furnish three armed guards for the jail to supplement the sheriff's force on duty. Also a system of floodlights had been installed around the jail to illuminate it brightly on the outside during hours of darkness to prevent jailbreaks.[37]

Due to the results achieved by special agents during the course of the investigation, the Federal Grand Jury at St. Paul, Minnesota, on January 22, 1935, returned indictments superseding the indictment returned on May 4, 1934. The return of the indictments was as secret as the proceedings leading up to them. U. S. District Attorney George F. Sullivan left the grand jury while the jurors voted on the case. Shortly afterwards, George Heisey, Sullivan's assistant, entered the room and remained until the arrival of Judge Gunnar Nordbye.

Ordinarily, when indictments were reported, the court was open to newspapermen and spectators, but at this presentation everyone but grand jurors were barred at Heisey's request. Heisey recommended bail for the various defendants named and bench warrants for those not in custody. These were approved by Judge Nordbye.

One of the new indictments charged Arthur R. Barker, Alvin Karpis, Volney Davis, Harry Campbell, Elmer Farmer, Harold Alderton, William Weaver, Harry Sawyer, William J. Harrison, Bryan Bolton, John Doe, and Richard Roe with the kidnapping of Mr. Bremer and transporting him from St. Paul, Minnesota, to Bensenville, Illinois.

A second indictment was also returned on this date, naming in addition to those previously indicted, Dr. Joseph P. Moran, Oliver A. Berg, John J. McLaughlin, Edna Murray, Myrtle Eaton, James J. Wilson, Jess Doyle, William E. Vidler, Phillip J. Delaney and one "Whitey," who was later determined to be Bruno Austin. This indictment charged the individuals named with conspiring with each other and with Fred Goetz, Fred Barker, Russell Gibson, and Kate Barker to kidnap and transport in interstate commerce Edward George Bremer.

Through the purported confession of Byron Bolton on January 24th that he and five others perpetrated Chicago's ghastliest crime—the St. Valentine's Day Massacre—in 1929, federal officials felt they had enough evidence to pin the seven murders on Al Capone. This, if successful, it was announced, would take Capone from Alcatraz where he was serving eleven years for income tax invasion and deliver him to the electric chair. Bolton, arrested January 10th at 3920 Pine Grove Avenue, in the Federal raid that brought death to Russell Gibson, named the seven killers.[38]

On February 9, 1935, the Springfield Leader and Press printed a bigger than life editorial from the Associated Press, entitled, "'Ma' Barker Turned from Apologies for Lawless Sons to Crime Career." The article began: "Kate 'Ma' Barker, who died at the business end of a machine gun as the reputed 'brains of her brood,' spent her early years apologizing to the law for her crime-stained young. When Arthur 'Doc' Barker, one of the four sons born to her, goes to trial in St. Paul, Minnesota, charged with kidnapping Edward G. Bremer, Commercial State Bank president, 'Ma' Barker will not be there to plead for him as she did when he was a youngster. . . . And all because 'Ma' at some time in her life decided to trade pleas and apologies for a 'chopper.' Perhaps discouraged by the persistence of her boys, 'Ma' Barker joined them."[39]

On April 15, 1935, the trial of Arthur R. Barker, Oliver A. Berg, Elmer Farmer, Harold Alderton, Jess Doyle, Edna Murray, Phillip Delaney, "Boss" McLaughlin, William Vidler, James Wilson, and Bryan Bolton commenced in room 317 of the Federal Courts Building in St. Paul, before Federal Judge M. M. Joyce. This two-tiered courtroom, the largest of four, would become the site of many infamous gangster trials during the 1930s, and some of the FBI's most notorious criminals were tried in the courtroom. FBI G-Men, armed with Thompson sub-machine guns, kept guard in the upper balconies to ward off any courtroom escape attempts or ambushes.[40]

Located just down the hall from this room was the original "Detention Room," and the Butler Room, Courtroom 326, with its English Tudor–style of decoration showcasing ornate marble and decorative plaster work, cathedral arches and marble fireplace.

The Sanborn Room or Courtroom 408 with its beautiful stained-glass ceiling window, formidable raised judge's bench, white marble window wall, and intricately sculpted plaster designs was located on the fourth floor.

One of the most elegant rooms in the building, the Chief Justice Room, originally used as a law library before being converted into a courtroom in 1927, with its carved mahogany woodwork, marble fireplace, and enormous stained glass ceiling dome was also located on the fourth floor. The building had been constructed in 1894.[41]

At 10:30 A.M., the first load of defendants was brought into the courtroom, seated behind their respective counsel. They were Alderton, Farmer, Barker, Berg, Doyle, and Bolton. Before they were ushered in, Judge M. M. Joyce questioned talisman, excusing seven. Four of the men were charged with the actual kidnapping of Bremer—Arthur "Doc" Barker; Harold E. Alderton, and Elmer Farmer, both of Bensenville, Illinois; and Bryan Bolton of Chicago.[42]

Those charged with conspiracy were Mrs. Edna Murray, the "kissing" bandit; Jess Doyle, Kansas City; Oliver A. Berg, convict at the Joliet, Illinois, Penitentiary; and Bruno "Whitie" Austin, Edward A. Vidler, Philip J. Delaney, James J. Wilson, and John J. McLaughlin, all from Chicago. Ten of the twenty-two people indicted for the crime were still at large at the time, including gang co-leader Alvin Karpis.

Killings, bank raids, and kidnappings—the monetary loot estimated in excess of a half million dollars—were charged to the Barker-Karpis Gang by federal authorities. The government claimed to have information linking the mob with at least six killings, in addition to data reportedly connecting the mobsters with the $100,000 kidnapping of William Hamm, for which the Touhy Gang was tried and acquitted.

Crimes attributed to the Barker-Karpis Gang by federal authorities included: Holdup of the Third Northwestern National Bank, Minneapolis, $112,000 loot and three persons, including two patrolmen killed; slaying near Webster, Wisconsin, of Arthur W. Dunlop, stepfather of Barker and second husband of Kate "Ma" Barker; South St. Paul payroll robbery, $30,000 loot, one policeman slain and another seriously wounded; robbery of the Union State Bank, Amery, Wisconsin, of $46,000; holdup of federal reserve messengers in Chicago, no loot, policeman killed; robbery St. Paul Railway Express Agency of $80,000; holdup First National Bank of Brainerd,

Minnesota, $32,000; robbery National Bank & Trust Company, Sioux Falls, South Dakota, $50,000; holdup First National Bank, Mason City, Iowa, $52,000. A machine gun stolen from a police car during the South St. Paul robbery was found in Doc Barker's apartment at the time of his arrest.

Bryan Bolton at the beginning of the trial entered a plea of guilty, but sentence was deferred as to him until August 25, 1936, when he was sentenced to serve three years in prison for his complicity in the kidnapping. The government, after the selection of the jury, began the introduction of evidence with Mr. Bremer as the first witness, who related the details of his kidnapping. Thereafter during the course of the trial, Alvin Karpis was identified as the purchaser of the flashlights.

Over strenuous objections of defense counsel, the gasoline can, which bore the fingerprint of Doc Barker, was introduced into evidence. An employee of the Technical Laboratory of the Federal Bureau of Investigation qualified as an expert witness and in simple language which was capable of being understood by everyone, explained briefly the science of fingerprinting and declared that the possibility of the fingerprint found on the gasoline can being that of anyone other than Doc Barker would only be one chance in several billion. He declared emphatically that the possibility of there being a duplication of fingerprints was so remote as to be out of the question entirely.[43]

On cross-examination, the defense counsel, obviously untutored in the science of fingerprinting, made no effort to get at the real questions involved in the fingerprint evidence, but made every effort to seize upon the ridiculous in an effort to confuse the minds of the jurors. These questions were capably explained by the witnesses and no question was left in the minds of the jurors as to the true identity of the fingerprint. Doc Barker sat through the proceedings in utter silence, glaring as the witnesses who took the stand against him. The sharp criminal eyes of Doc Barker, however, had no effect on the witnesses.

Meanwhile, on May 1st, a graying, mild mannered George Barker was ill back in Webb City—worn out and penniless from his futile fight to save his sons and wife who had abandoned him for crime. "His family was just too much for him," Dick Dixon, Barker's employer at a tourist camp divulged to reporters. Barker, past sixty years old, lay in Dixon's home suffering from a heart ailment. When approached by newspapermen, the elder Barker refused to discuss the activities that brought death to his son Fred and wife Kate. Nor would he talk about his legal efforts to obtain the $18,000 found in Fred's possession after he and Ma died, "guns in hand," trying to shoot it out with federal agents at Lake Oklawaha, Florida, January 16th.[44]

Through his attorney, George Barker had laid claim to fourteen $1,000 bills; five diamonds listed at $1,500; about $500 in bills of various denominations; an expensive automobile; and valuable, miscellaneous articles. Federal agents said they had found a money sack containing ten of the $1,000 bills and Fred was wearing a money belt with the remaining four. Barker's lawyer pointedly contended that none of the money paid for ransom in the Edward G. Bremer kidnapping case a year ago was in thousand dollar bills.

At the conclusion of the government's case against Doc Barker on May 6, 1935, the charges against Jess Doyle and Edna Murray were dismissed. Jess Doyle was later returned to the State of Nebraska, where he entered a plea of guilty at Fairbury on a charge that he participated in the robbery of the Fairbury National Bank on April 4, 1933.

Doyle made a full confession linking the Barker-Karpis Gang to the Kansas City Station Massacre in June 1933; the Edward G. Bremer kidnapping, in which $200,000 in ransom was paid; the raid on the Minneapolis Third Northwestern National Bank, in which two police officers and a St. Paul motorist were slain; and robbery of the First National Bank of Fairbury, Nebraska on April 4, 1933.[45]

Federal agents had known for a number of months that the gang was responsible for the Fairbury robbery, but were not sure which members of the gang were involved. There was also some doubt to the number of bandits engaged in the Nebraska holdup. Several Fairbury witnesses claimed there were six robbers, but according to information obtained by federal agents, there were seven.

Doyle stated in his confession that he did not appear at the scene of the robbery but was stationed with a car at the outskirts of Fairbury where the loot was transferred to his car, he going in one direction and the rest of the gang in another. In his confession, Doyle exonerated Leonard Hankins, then serving a life term in the Minnesota Penitentiary at Stillwater for alleged complicity in the Bremer kidnapping. Doyle was subsequently sentenced to serve ten years in the Nebraska State Penitentiary for his crimes.

One member of the gang, Earl Christman, died from being shot by Deputy Sheriff W. S. Davidson, according to the confession of Edna Murray. She also told federal agents that there were seven men, not six, who left Chicago for Fairbury. Following the robbery, they were to assemble at a hideout, but with Christman mortally wounded, their plans were in limbo.

After Mrs. Christman learned of the death of her husband, she was paid a sum of money which she did not think was sufficient. Edna Murray related the gang found out later that Mrs. Christman made a confession to federal agents. The widow of Frank Nash gave the same story as Edna Murray during her confession to Federal agents.

Edna Murray was returned to the Missouri State Penitentiary at Jefferson City, Missouri, to complete the remainder of her twenty-five-year sentence for highway robbery and she received an additional two-year sentence on the charge of escaping from that institution.[46]

Bruno Austin on May 6, 1935, was discharged from custody on the order of the court, but only to be rearrested in Chicago and on October 11, 1935, he was convicted of murder and sentenced to serve life imprisonment in the Illinois State Penitentiary.

During the course of the trial, Elmer Farmer on May 13, 1935, entered a plea of guilty to the conspiracy indictment and on June 7, 1935, was sentenced to serve twenty-five years imprisonment. Doc Barker had no defense to offer and did not take the stand in his own behalf. The trial of the defendants who had not been dismissed or otherwise disposed of was concluded on May 16, 1935, and the jury began its deliberations. The money-changers during the course of presenting their defense had contended they did not know the money exchanged by them was Bremer ransom money and they nervously awaited the return of the jury.

On May 17, 1935, the jury returned a verdict of guilty as to Arthur R. Barker, Oliver A. Berg, James J. Wilson, John J. McLaughlin, Sr., and

Harold Alderton, and upon this same date, Doc Barker and Oliver A. Berg were sentenced to life imprisonment. Vidler and Delaney were acquitted.

On June 7, 1935 Harold Alderton received a sentence of twenty years imprisonment. McLaughlin and Wilson were sentenced to serve five years each; McLaughlin died a few months later in the United States Penitentiary at Leavenworth, Kansas. Oliver A. Berg, after his conviction and sentence, was returned to the Illinois State Penitentiary to complete his sentence and a federal detainer was filed against him. Elmer Farmer, Harold Alderton, and Arthur R. Barker were temporarily detained at the United States Penitentiary, Leavenworth, Kansas, and later were removed to the United States Penitentiary at Alcatraz. James J. Wilson was ordered to serve his sentence at the United States Industrial Reformatory at Chillicothe, Ohio, but he was later transferred to the Northeastern Penitentiary at Lewisburg, Pennsylvania.

After the arrest of Volney Davis in Chicago on June 1, 1935, he was moved to St. Paul, where on June 3, 1935, he entered a plea of guilty to the indictment charging him with conspiracy to kidnap Mr. Bremer and was immediately sentenced to serve life imprisonment. Davis likewise was temporarily detained at the United State Penitentiary, Leavenworth, Kansas, and subsequently transferred to the United States Penitentiary at Alcatraz. He died in 1978.

Notes

[1] J. Edgar Hoover, *The FBI in Action*.
[2] *St. Paul Pioneer Press*, January 21, 1935.
[3] *St. Paul Pioneer Press*, January 20, 1935.
[4] Ibid.
[5] Alvin Karpis with Bill Trent, *The Alvin Karpis Story*, pp. 80-83.
[6] *Springfield Daily News*, January 21, 1935; *St. Paul Pioneer Press*, January 21, 1935.
[7] Ibid.
[8] *New York Times*, January 21, 1935.
[9] United States Bureau of Investigation, Report of Special Agent D. P. Sullivan, Chicago, Illinois, February 17, 1936; Paul Maccabee St. Paul Gangster History,

1981-1995, Research Files, Minnesota Historical Society.
[10] *Springfield Daily News*, January 21, 1935.
[11] *St. Paul Pioneer Press*, January 21, 1935.
[12] Alvin Karpis with Bill Trent, *The Alvin Karpis Story*.
[13] *St. Paul Pioneer Press*, January 21, 1935.
[14] *Chicago Herald and Examiner*, January 21, 1935; *Springfield Daily News*, January 21, 1935.
[15] *St. Paul Pioneer Press*, January 21, 1935.
[16] Doris Lockerman (Rogers), Melvin Purvis's FBI Secretary, Interview 5/2003 by Joshua Welsh.
[17] *St. Paul Pioneer Press*, January 21, 1935.
[18] Doris Lockerman (Rogers), Melvin Purvis's FBI Secretary, Interview 5/2003 by Joshua Welsh.
[19] *Springfield Leader and Press*, January 21, 1935.
[20] *St. Paul Pioneer Press*, January 21, 1935.
[21] Ibid.
[22] Ibid.
[23] *St. Paul Pioneer Press*, January 21, 1935.
[24] Springfield Leader and Press, January 21, 1935.
[25] Doris Lockerman (Rogers), Melvin Purvis's FBI Secretary, Interview 5/2003 by Joshua Welsh.
[26] *St. Paul Pioneer Press*, January 22, 1935.
[27] FBI Files, RCS:TD I.C.#7-576, November 19, 1936, The Kidnaping of Edward George Bremer, St. Paul, Minnesota, History and Early Association of the Karpis-Barker Gang Prior to the Abduction of Mr. Bremer.
[28] *St. Paul Pioneer Press*, January 22, 1935.
[29] Ibid.
[30] *St. Paul Pioneer Press*, January 23, 1935.
[31] United States Bureau of Investigation, Report of Special Agent D. P. Sullivan, Chicago, Illinois, February 17, 1936; Paul Maccabee St. Paul Gangster History, 1981-1995, Research Files, Minnesota Historical Society.
[32] Ibid; Alvin Karpis with Bill Trent, *The Alvin Karpis Story*.
[33] *Chicago Herald and Examiner*, January 21, 1935; *St. Paul Pioneer Press*, January 21, 1935.
[34] FBI Files, RCS:TD I.C.#7-576, November 19, 1936, The Kidnaping of Edward George Bremer, St. Paul, Minnesota, History and Early Association of the Karpis-Barker Gang Prior to the Abduction of Mr. Bremer.
[35] Federal Bureau of Investigation Freedom of Information and Privacy Acts, Subject: Kate Barker "Ma," File Number 7-5768695.
[36] *St. Paul Pioneer Press*, January 22, 1935.
[37] *St. Paul Pioneer Press*, January 23, 1935.

[38] *Chicago Herald and Examiner*, January 24, 1935.
[39] *Springfield Leader and Press*, February 9, 1935.
[40] Landmark Center, Old Federal Courts brochure.
[41] H. F. Koeper, Historic St. Paul Buildings, St. Paul, St. Paul City Planning Board, 1964, p. 21.
[42] *Mankato Free Press*, April 15, 1935.
[43] FBI Files, RCS:TD I.C.#7-576, November 19, 1936, The Kidnaping of Edward George Bremer, St. Paul, Minnesota, History and Early Association of the Karpis-Barker Gang Prior to the Abduction of Mr. Bremer.
[44] *Mankato Free Press*, May 1, 1935.
[45] *Fairbury Journal*, April 4, 1935.
[46] FBI Files, RCS:TD I.C.#7-576, November 19, 1936, The Kidnaping of Edward George Bremer, St. Paul, Minnesota, History and Early Association of the Karpis-Barker Gang Prior to the Abduction of Mr. Bremer.

Chapter Eleven

The End of an Era

You've read the story of Jesse James
of how he lived and died.
If you're still in need;
of something to read,
here's the story of Bonnie and Clyde.

Now Bonnie and Clyde are the Barrow Gang
I'm sure you all have read.
how they rob and steal;
and those who squeal,
are usually found dying or dead.

There's lots of untruths to these write-ups;
they're not as ruthless as that.
their nature is raw;
they hate all the law,
the stool pidgeons, spotters and rats.

They call them cold-blooded killers
they say they are heartless and mean.
But I say this with pride
that I once knew Clyde,
when he was honest and upright and clean.

"Ma"—The Life and Times of "Ma" Barker and Her Boys

*But the law fooled around;
kept taking him down,
and locking him up in a cell.
Till he said to me;
"I'll never be free,
so I'll meet a few of them in hell"*

*The road was so dimly lighted
there were no highway signs to guide.
But they made up their minds;
if all roads were blind,
they wouldn't give up till they died.*

*The road gets dimmer and dimmer
sometimes you can hardly see.
But it's fight man to man
and do all you can,
for they know they can never be free.*

*From heart-break some people have suffered
from weariness some people have died.
But take it all in all;
our troubles are small,
till we get like Bonnie and Clyde.*

*If a policeman is killed in Dallas
and they have no clue or guide.
If they can't find a fiend,
they just wipe their slate clean
and hang it on Bonnie and Clyde.*

*There's two crimes committed in America
not accredited to the Barrow mob.
They had no hand;
in the kidnap demand,
nor the Kansas City Depot job.*

*A newsboy once said to his buddy;
"I wish old Clyde would get jumped.
In these awfull hard times;*

"Ma"—The Life and Times of "Ma" Barker and Her Boys

> we'd make a few dimes,
> if five or six cops would get bumped"
>
> The police haven't got the report yet
> but Clyde called me up today
> He said, "Don't start any fights;
> we aren't working nights,
> we're joining the NRA."
>
> From Irving to West Dallas viaduct
> is known as the Great Divide.
> Where the women are kin;
> and the men are men,
> and they won't "stool"
> on Bonnie and Clyde.
>
> If they try to act like citizens
> and rent them a nice little flat.
> About the third night;
> they're invited to fight,
> by a sub-gun's rat-tat-tat.
>
> They don't think they're too smart or desperate
> they know that the law always wins.
> They've been shot at before;
> but they do not ignore,
> that death is the wages of sin.
>
> Some day they'll go down together
> they'll bury them side by side.
> To few it'll be grief,
> to the law a relief
> but it's death for Bonnie and Clyde.
>
> —Bonnie Parker, "The Trail's End"[1]

fter the arrest of Wynona Burdette and Dolores Delaney at Atlantic City, New Jersey, they were temporarily removed to Philadelphia, Pennsylvania, where a son was born to Dolores Delaney. These

women were subsequently removed to Miami, Florida, where on March 25, 1935, they entered pleas of guilty in the federal court to the charges of harboring a fugitive from justice, and misprision of a felony and on that same date each was sentenced to serve a five year term in the United States Detention Farm, Milan, Michigan. Mr. and Mrs. John Karpavicz, father and mother of Alvin Karpis, took custody of the son of Dolores Delaney, who was christened Raymond Alvin Karpavicz.

In May, *Every Week Magazine* published an article, "Bad News for Uncle Sam's Female Public Enemies," focusing on the convictions of well known gang women such as Dolores Delaney, Wynona Burdette, and, of course, Ma Barker. According to this piece, women criminals were learning that they could no longer expect privileged status on account of their sex. The old chivalrous idea of pulling punches was out, for the law had finally gotten tough as evidenced by the five-year sentences doled out to Alvin Karpis' two girlfriends.[2]

The investigation continued by the Federal Bureau of Investigation to locate the remaining fugitives in this case, and on May 3, 1936, Harry

The end of Bonnie & Clyde. (Photo courtesy of Rick Mattix)

Sawyer was apprehended by special agents at Pass Christian, Mississippi, by a deputy sheriff and a Mississippi State Highway officer cooperating with the agents in the apprehension. Sawyer, after the ransom negotiations in Miami, Florida, and Havana, Cuba, had joined his wife and together they had proceeded to the Mississippi town, where Harry Sawyer was operating a drinking and gambling joint for black people. This created suspicion in the minds of the white citizens in this Southern state and ultimately led to the identification and apprehension of Sawyer.

This was not the first arrest which Harry Sawyer had experienced, as the records of the Federal Bureau of Investigation show that on December 12, 1914, Sawyer was arrested on charges of breaking and entering the offices of the Standard Oil Company, in Lincoln, Nebraska. On April 23, 1915, he entered a plea of guilty and the court ordered him released on parole for a period of two years and he was subsequently dismissed from parole on September 25, 1917. Sawyer was again arrested on September 11, 1918, in St. Paul, on charges of attempted grand larceny and was subsequently fined $100.00. He was again arrested on January 2, 1920, on charges of robbery and was later turned over to the police department at Lincoln, Nebraska, on charges of jumping a bond, after being arrested for auto theft. He was subsequently released under a $1,000 bond, which was later forfeited.

After the arrest of Harry Sawyer at Pass Christian, Mississippi, he was immediately removed to St. Paul, where he was committed to the Ramsey County Jail in default of $100,000 bond, to await trial on charges of kidnapping Mr. Bremer.

William Weaver and Myrtle Eaton had successfully eluded the company of other members of the Karpis-Barker Gang and had continued to enjoy their small chicken farm at Allandale, Florida, to which place they had fled after leaving Grand Forest Beach, Ohio. On Sunday morning, September 1, 1935, the Allandale house was surrounded by Agents of the Federal Bureau of Investigation.

Weaver left the house early on this morning to get his Sunday newspapers and was confronted by special agents who took him into custody. Immediately thereafter, Myrtle Eaton was arrested in the house in which was found several firearms, including various small firearms and two shotguns. Special agents also found that Weaver and Myrtle Eaton had in their custody a small boy who was known to the neighbors as Bobbie Osborne. The fugitives had obtained custody of this child from its mother and they were residing at Allandale, Florida, as Mr. and Mrs. J. W. Osborne, posing as respectable citizens. Immediately after their capture, Myrtle Eaton and William Weaver were removed to St. Paul, and committed to the Ramsey County Jail in default of bond.

Therese Carmichael . . . witness against Cassius McDonald. (Author's collection)

On November 27, 1935 a new indictment was returned by the Federal Grand Jury at St. Paul, and in addition to those individuals who had been previously indicted, Cassius McDonald was included as a defendant in the conspiracy. McDonald was arrested by special agents at Detroit, Michigan, on September 26, 1935, after conclusive evidence had been obtained that McDonald exchanged the ransom money in Havana, Cuba, with full knowledge that it was the Bremer ransom money.

A second trial in the Bremer case was begun at St. Paul in federal court on January 6, 1936 and the defendants at this time who faced the bar of justice were William Weaver, Harry Sawyer, and Cassius McDonald. Harry Sawyer was confident of acquittal, but admitted on the witness stand that he had harbored and associated with members of the Karpis-Barker Gang for a number of years. William Weaver likewise denied his guilt and contended that he was being prosecuted only because he had associated with members of the Karpis-Barker Gang.

Cassius McDonald endeavored to persuade the jury that he did not know the money exchanged in Cuba was the Bremer ransom money. The evidence was clear to the jury and after a two weeks' trial, which concluded on January 24, 1936, a verdict of guilty was returned against all three defendants.

On that same date, William Weaver and Harry Sawyer were sentenced to serve life imprisonment and after being incarcerated in the United States Penitentiary at Leavenworth, Kansas, were transferred to Alcatraz. The sentence of Cassius McDonald was deferred to serve fifteen years in a federal penitentiary but he, too, was soon transferred to Alcatraz.

The conspiracy indictment which was pending against Myrtle Eaton was dismissed at St. Paul, and on February 26, 1936, she was indicted at Tampa, Florida, charged with harboring William Weaver. She denied her guilt, but on June 3, 1936 at Jacksonville, Florida, Myrtle Eaton was found guilty by jury. On June 10, 1936, she was sentenced to serve six months in jail and pay a fine of $1,000.00.

After the deaths of Fred Barker, Ma Barker, and Russell Gibson and the apprehension of other members of the Karpis-Barker Gang, Karpis and

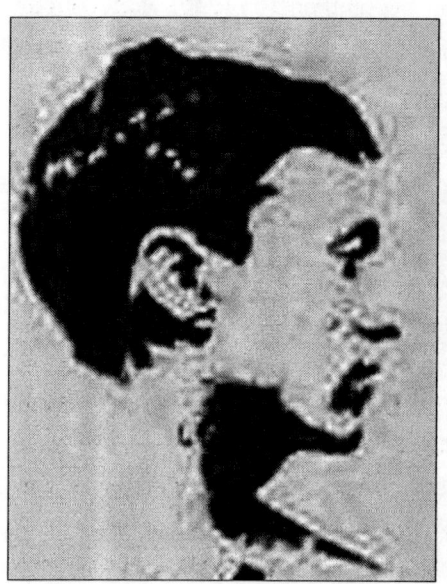

Fred Hunter. (Courtesy FBI files)

Campbell in January of 1935 found the ranks of the once powerful mob depleted of gunmen who could assist in further depredations, which were considered necessary for the fugitives' existence. After their return to Toledo, Ohio, in January of 1935, Karpis and Campbell were afforded protection and shelter by the members of the underworld with who they had been in contact during the more prosperous days of the gang immediately subsequent to the abduction of Mr. Bremer and for several months thereafter. They likewise renewed their contacts in Cleveland, Ohio, from which place they had so hurriedly departed in September of 1934.

Special Agents of the Federal Bureau of Investigation continued the investigation to locate the remaining fugitives and it was learned that one of the first recruits secured by Karpis and Campbell was Fred Hunter, of Leavittsburg, Ohio. It is not definitely known in what manner Hunter first became acquainted with Karpis and Campbell, but it appears that the acquaintanceship was made through mutual friends at the Harvard Club in Newburgh Heights, Ohio, who sent Karpis to the Hollyhock Night Club in Warren, Ohio, in March, 1935, where he met Hunter.

Fred Hunter, an ex-convict, was born October 13, 1899, at Warren, Ohio, and was one of six children in the family. Hunter had four brothers and one sister. The father of the family, George Hunter, made an unsuccessful effort to raise his children to be law-abiding citizens. Fred Hunter's mother died in 1910 and while the father worked daily as a blacksmith and boilermaker, at least three of his sons began careers of crime. Fred Hunter, as Fred John Henderson, was first arrested by the police department, Toledo, Ohio, on June 3, 1920, for carrying a concealed weapon and in lieu of paying a $200 fine and costs he was committed to the Lucas County Jail, Toledo, Ohio. On October 28, 1922, Hunter was arrested by the police department at Akron, Ohio, as a fugitive from justice from Warren, Ohio. He was thereafter convicted for larceny and possession of dynamite and on April 17, 1933, was received at the State Penitentiary, Columbus, Ohio, to serve an indeterminate sentence of three to twenty-seven years.

William Hunter, another son of George Hunter, began his criminal career on July 31, 1919, when he burglarized a hardware store at Warren,

Ohio, and stole goods and merchandise valued at fifty dollars. He pleaded guilty to this charge; was committed to the State Reformatory at Mansfield, Ohio. William Hunter thereafter was received at the State Penitentiary, Columbus, Ohio, on June 2, 1926, to serve a one to fifteen year sentence for burglary and larceny. On April 26, 1932, William Hunter was fined $150 and costs at Warren, Ohio, for receiving and concealing stolen property. In lieu of paying this fine he served time in the County Jail at Warren, Ohio. On December 19, 1934, Hunter was received at the United States Penitentiary, Atlanta, Georgia, to serve two years for violation of the Internal Revenue Act.

Another brother, Albert, has also served a sentence at the Ohio State Reformatory, Mansfield, Ohio, for burglary.

Fred Hunter prior to the time he became associated with Karpis and Campbell, worked sporadically as a welder, but his main occupation and interest was gambling, and to some extent, in selling gambling paraphernalia. He was also a devotee of cockfighting.

This meeting, according to FBI files, probably occurred in January 1935 at Warren, Ohio, soon after the Atlantic City shootout. Karpis and Campbell told Hunter they were referred to him by a friend who said Hunter could find them a place to stay . . . Hunter said he was going to Hot Springs, Arkansas, and "would look the place over to see if the town was cool." In June of 1935, Hunter and Karpis traveled from Warren to Hot Springs where they located a place to stay.

Fred Hunter was afflicted with a noticeable speech stutter, which, strangely enough, disappeared during the high tension of a robbery. In his later years, whenever he saw a police car, friends recalled, he would repeat excitedly, "there's one of them—oh boy-oh, boy-oh, boy-oh, boy."

Karpis and Campbell returned to the southwest for a second recruit by the name of John Brock, who came highly recommended due to his extensive criminal record which began on January 16, 1919, when he was received at the state reformatory, Granite, Oklahoma, to serve a term of three years for grand larceny. The records of the Federal Bureau of Investigation reveal that Brock's second arrest occurred on July 15, 1922, when he was arrested by the sheriff's office at Hutchinson, Kansas, for investigation.

He was next arrested on October 1, 1922, as J. C. Creighton by the Sheriff's Office at Enid, Oklahoma, at which place he was arrested for investigation. Brock also was arrested on suspicion by the sheriff's office at Pawnee, Oklahoma as J.D. Adams on May 17, 1923. On January 19, 1930, as John Brock he was arrested as a vagrant by the police department at Tucson, Arizona, and served twenty days in the city jail.

He was likewise arrested as a vagrant by the police department at Tulsa, Oklahoma, on March 12, 1931, and fined nineteen dollars and costs. On October 18, 1931, he was received at the state penitentiary, McAlester, Oklahoma, to serve five years after committing an assault with intent to kill. During the time Brock was confined in the Oklahoma State Penitentiary, he became acquainted with three of the criminals who later became prominent members of the Karpis-Barker Gang—Doc Barker, Volney Davis and William Weaver.

In March of 1935 Karpis and Campbell proceeded to Tulsa, Oklahoma, where they contacted George "Burrhead" Keady, well known associate of thieves and harborer of criminals. Campbell had previously associated with Keady at the time Campbell was characterized as an oil field petty thief and was committing crimes with Glen Leroy Wright and Jimmie Lawson, who later became well-known criminals in the Southwest. This was prior to the time that Campbell graduated to "big time" crime.

Keady recommended Brock to Karpis and Campbell as a man of ability and the introduction of Brock to them was consumated on a highway near Tulsa, Oklahoma, and Brock agreed to pull a job with Karpis and Campbell. Brock was given instructions to meet Karpis and Campbell in Toledo, from which place Brock was sent to the Harvard Club in Cleveland on an errand for Alvin Karpis. He later rejoined his new associates in Toledo and plans were formulated for another crime.

In April of 1935, Karpis and Campbell disappeared for several days, leaving Brock in Cleveland. He became apprehensive that some misfortune had befallen them and returned to his home at Tulsa, Oklahoma.

Meanwhile, the FBI wasn't letting up on their hunt for the two fugitives, and instead of hiding and keeping low key, Alvin Karpis was still planning robberies. Hoover recalled this phase as "perhaps the most amazing sequence in the whole fantastic case."

On April 24, 1935, a mail truck was robbed at Warren, Ohio, by three heavily armed men and $72,000 in loot, composed of currency and bonds, was obtained by the bandits. Thereafter, two well-known criminals, George Sargent and Anthony Labrizzetta, were identified as two of the participants in the robbery of the mail truck. Sargent and Labrizzetta denied their guilt, but were brought to trial.

The jury convicted them after deliberating ten minutes. Each was sentenced to serve twenty-five years in a federal penitentiary. The court granted Sargent and Labrizzetta a new trial, but they were again convicted at their second trial. Subsequent investigation disclosed that the two convicted men were innocent of the crime and that Karpis and Campbell were the guilty parties.

In July, Alvin Karpis, Public Enemy No. 1, threatened the life of G-Man J. Edgar Hoover in a letter he sent him from Ohio. Hoover declined to comment on the threat except to say that the Barker-Karpis outfit "was one of the most dangerous mobs in the country."[3]

Believing that new angles to the Bremer kidnapping case had been uncovered, authorities on August 26th requested that the Federal Grand Jury be requested to extend the time of the conspiracy to the abduction from May 1, 1935, to January 1, 1936. It was believed the government would seek indictments of additional alleged participants in the kidnapping conspiracy. The grand jury would have to return a new indictment in order to extend the time of the conspiracy, but, in doing so, it would contain additional names to the twenty-six indicted previously.[4]

Karpis and Campbell, with new capital, planned new crimes and through Burrhead Keady, sought to re-establish the Karpis-Barker gang. Following the mail robbery, they returned to Tulsa, Oklahoma, and again contacted Keady and Brock. On September 5, 1935, Keady proceeded to the Oklahoma State Penitentiary and met a half-breed Indian by the name of Sam Coker at the prison gates, who on that date was paroled from the institution where he had been serving a thirty year sentence for bank robbery.

Karpis and Campbell allegedly supplied the funds necessary to secure the release of Coker from the penitentiary. Coker was first received at the Oklahoma State Penitentiary on Mary 17, 1924, to serve a thirty year sentence for bank robbery and he received his first parole from that institution on January 11, 1931, and within a few weeks was returned to the institution as a parole violator. He escaped on February 24, 1931. On May 9, 1931, he was arrested by the police department at Saint Joseph, Missouri, for investigation and on the 10th of the following month he was arrested by the police department at Tulsa, Oklahoma, as a fugitive from the state penitentiary. This arrest occurred at the time Fred Barker and Alvin Karpis were arrested at Tulsa, Oklahoma, on June 10, 1931, charged with a jewel burglary. Coker was not as fortunate as Karpis and Fred Barker, as after this arrest he was returned to Okmulgee, Oklahoma, to await trial for the jewel theft.[5]

Although he was not prosecuted for that crime, he was returned to the Oklahoma State Penitentiary on June 19, 1931, to complete his sentence for bank robbery. Coker remained confined in the institution until September 5, 1935, when he was again released on parole. Coker proceeded with Keady to the latter's home in Tulsa, Oklahoma, and the two of them began celebrating Coker's good fortune by consuming considerable quantities of liquor, and two or three weeks thereafter, Coker proceeded to Toledo and joined Karpis and Campbell.

About the first of November 1935, Fred Hunter returned to Tulsa, Oklahoma, and solicited the aid of John Brock in a new criminal venture which was being planned. Brock agreed to participate in the crime and with Hunter traveled by train from Tulsa, Oklahoma, to Cleveland, Ohio, arriving there on or about November 4, 1935. At Cleveland, Hunter and Brock parted; Hunter proceeding to Youngstown, Ohio, while Brock went to Toledo and registered in a local hotel. However, the following day he was joined at the latter place by Fred Hunter and the two of them proceeded to the Toledo hideout of Karpis and Campbell—Edith Barry's house of prostitution.

On the afternoon of November 7, 1935, Erie Train No. 422, which was en route from Detroit, Michigan to Pittsburgh, Pennsylvania, made its regular stop at Garrettsville, Ohio. Nobody was on the platform except for news dealer, Earl Davis, who had come for newspapers. To Davis' horror, he was suddenly surrounded by five men armed with two machine guns, a shotgun and automatic pistols, who ordered him to leave the area.[6]

During the course of the robbery, the train crew was intimidated. One of the robbers fired a shot into the mail car and three mail clerks quickly came out with their hands up. The robbers immediately forced engineer Charles Shull and fireman P.O. Leuschner out of the locomotive just as several persons showed up at the station. The newcomers were lined up against the wall and the bandits began shooting into the air; one of the bullets striking one of the clerks, Orlin Workman.

Some of the bandits entered the mail car and began throwing mail pouches from the doorway. One of the captives, a postman, was forced to carry seven pouches to their car. As they pulled away with $34,000 in currency and several thousand dollars in securities from the United States mail, one of the passengers jotted down their license number.

After special agents received information concerning the "Wild West" manner in which the robbery was perpetrated, the possibility that Karpis and Campbell were responsible for this crime was considered and an investigation resulted in the identification of the fugitives wanted in the Bremer kidnapping as being two of the participants in the holdup of the mail train. Special agents further learned by their investigation that after the robbery, Karpis, Campbell, Hunter, Brock, and the fifth member of the bandit gang known as "Sam" [Coker], retreated to a garage in Port Clinton, Ohio, operated by one John Zetzer, an ex-convict. Here the loot was divided and the gang separated, with Campbell and Sam going to Toledo, Ohio.

Karpis, Brock and Hunter made elaborate plans for a getaway. The former methods used by modern bandits in driving long distances in a fast automobile after the commission of a crime were too slow for Karpis, Hunter, and Brock, so arrangements had been made through Zetzer, a pilot, for the use of an airplane. Early on the morning of November 6, 1935, the three mail train bandits boarded an airplane near Port Clinton, Ohio, and with Zetzer as the pilot, flew to Hot Springs, Arkansas. Karpis and Hunter remained at Hot Springs while Brock returned to his home in Tulsa, Oklahoma.

During the course of the investigation conducted by special agents, it was learned that on October 19, 1935, Thomas J. Shaw had gone to the Universal Motor Company in Akron, Ohio, for the purpose of buying a Ford automobile for cash and after making preliminary arrangements for the purchase of this car, Shaw proceeded to the vicinity of the Portage Hotel, where he was arrested as a suspicious person.

Approximately three hours later a local gambler called at the Akron Police Department and arranged for the release of Shaw on bond. Thereafter, on October 25, 1935, under the name of Carl Baker, the individual who had previously been arrested as Thomas J. Shaw purchased from the Knowles Brown Motor Company, 1440 West 25th Street, Cleveland, a Plymouth sedan. The eyewitnesses to the Garretsville mail robbery obtained the license number of the automobile used by the bandits at that time and through this it was learned that the Plymouth sedan which had been purchased by Carl Baker was the car used in the robbery.

At the time Thomas J. Shaw was arrested by the police department at Akron, Ohio, his fingerprints were forwarded to the Federal Bureau of Investigation and they were identified as being identical with Milton Latt, who on November 2, 1930, had been arrested by the police department at Wichita, Kansas, for vagrancy. The record further disclosed that Latt had been arrested for investigation by the police department at Coffeyville, Kansas on February 10, 1931, and on September 3, 1932; that he also had been again arrested by the police department at Coffeyville, Kansas, on November 6, 1935. On November 7, 1935, the date of the mail robbery at Garrettsville, Ohio, Latt was confined in the County Jail at Yates Center, Kansas on a charge of robbery, for which he was not prosecuted. Prior to this time the Federal Bureau of Investigation had information that Milton Latt was an associate of Harry Campbell and that Latt had also been employed as a "shiller" at the Harvard Club at Newburgh Heights, Ohio, where members of the gang frequently spent their time.

After Campbell returned to Toledo from Port Clinton, Ohio, he continued for the next several months to spend the majority of his time in Toledo. Campbell found refuge with Clara and Ed McGraw at a rooming house operated by them at 2011 1/2 Adams Street. He also frequented the many taverns located in the vicinity of his place of refuge.

A short time after Karpis and Campbell returned to Toledo subsequent to their escape from Atlantic City, New Jersey, Campbell met a girl by the name of Gertrude Billiter at the McGraw rooming house and thereafter, on May 19, 1935, Campbell, under the name of Clarence C. Miller, married Gertrude at Bowling Green, Ohio. Campbell, with his wife, frequented a tavern known as the Goulet's Grill, located at 2130 1/2 Monroe Street, Toledo. Campbell also had as a companion at Goulet's Grill and other taverns in the Toledo area, the sheriff of Lucas County, James O'Reilly.

After the robbery of the mail train at Garrettsville, Ohio, Campbell returned to his outlaw cronies. Sam Coker, at the time of the robbery of the train was ill in a hospital in Toledo, which prevented him from being a participant in that crime. He, however, continued his association with Campbell at Toledo after the successful consummation of that robbery while Campbell was spending his time in Toledo.

In late 1935, agents were ordered to inform J. Edgar Hoover if they located Karpis, for the FBI head had said he wanted to get involved in the case personally. His first opportunity came in March 1936 when agents tracked Karpis and Hunter to Hot Springs, Arkansas, where the criminals were enjoying the pleasures of the health resort. But before Hoover and his men could make their raid on the two fugitives, they found Karpis and Hunter had already fled after being tipped off by local police officers.[7]

Karpis also made a trip to Corpus Christi, Texas, where he engaged in his favorite pastime of fishing in the Gulf of Mexico. He also made a trip to the west coast of Florida for a similar purpose. Karpis after his retreat to Hot Springs also made infrequent trips to Cleveland, Toledo and Canton.

In early April, Karpis rented an apartment on Canal Street in New Orleans from the owner and manager, Mrs. J.B. Mayer. Of course, he gave her an alias: Ed O'Hara. Through the investigative efforts of Special Agents of the Federal Bureau of Investigation, it was determined that Alvin Karpis, with Fred Hunter, and his woman, Connie Morris, were located in Apartment 1 at 3343 Canal Street, New Orleans, where Karpis and Hunter maintained a residence. Hoover and some of his top agents, including Clyde Tolson and Louis Nichols, immediately flew to New Orleans to make the arrest.

The apartment building in which Karpis and the others were located was surrounded by special agents at approximately 5:30 P.M. on May 1, 1936, and as the special agents were about to enter the fugitive's apartment building, Karpis and Hunter emerged, with the intention of entering a Plymouth coupe, which was parked in front of the building. Special agents commanded Karpis and Hunter to surrender and they complied peacefully. Upon searching Karpis and finding no weapons, agent Melvin Purvis allegedly asked him where his gun was. He replied, "Home, and ain't that a hell of a place for it?"

The FBI's version of the capture claimed that Hoover and another agent approached the car, confronted the two suspects, and made the arrests. Karpis stated, however, that after he and Hunter were disarmed and arrested, only then did Hoover and another agent appear at the scene. According to Karpis, Hoover came running around the corner on cue to tell the already detained Public Enemy Number One that he was under arrest. Karpis recalled: "I noticed someone peeping around the corner of a building. Several agents begin shouting . . . 'It's OK! Come on Chief! We got him! You can come out now!'" At that time J. Edgar Hoover emerged and took the official credit for the arrest. The G-Men found, despite their careful preparations, that they'd forgotten to bring handcuffs, so one of the agents took off his necktie and tied Karpis' hands with it.[8]

Mrs. Mayer said after the arrest, "He was such a nice, quiet little man. He is just a boy. I can't imagine such a slim fellow being as bad as they say he is."

Special Agent Earl Connelley, who had been the main FBI "operating boss" throughout most of the Karpis manhunt and arrest, penned a summary report of these activities dated May 18, 1936—seventeen days subsequent to the capture:

". . . At the New Orleans office all men to participate in this raid were fully advised as to the activities of all persons involved in the raid, and a diagram of the premises and immediate vicinity was prepared on the blackboard for their full information . . . the general plan of raiding the house was briefly as follows:

"Special Agent Tollett was to remain at the observation point in the vacant house across the parkway, and Special Agent Bowman was to leave the observation house and join the two squads, which were to take and maintain the rear of these premises, this rear raiding squad to consist of the following:

"Assistant Director Mr. Clyde Tolson and Agents Baldwin, Glavin, McNulty, Neal, Peyronnin. This squad was divided with one group to be established at the rear end of the house on the backside; one group at the front end of the house on the backside. Agents Toulme, Bain, Heavrin and Lunsford to be established, two men in an automobile on the far corner of Canal and Jeff Davis Parkway; two agents in a car to be established on the corner directly across Canal Street on the corner of Jeff Davis Parkway—these two cars to be in such position as to be able to take up the pursuit, should the subjects escape from the house and try to leave in an automobile.

"The two rear groups or squads were to maintain their positions to prevent the escape of the subjects from either the front of the house or the back side of the house, and to withhold their fire until directed by the raiding squad, which was to enter from the front unless, of course, some individual in escaping had cleared the house and it was necessary to pursue him.

"Special Agent in Charge D.W. Magee was to be established across the street from the house at a drug store, to be available at the telephone, in order to advise the New Orleans police, should any shooting occur, and in particular to request police officers to keep traffic cleared, this being a very heavily traveled thoroughfare, both as to Canal Street and Jeff Davis Parkway.

"To raid the place if necessary, and to control the possible exit of subjects from the front of this house, either through the garage to the rear, or the windows or doors facing on Jeff Davis Parkway, Mr. J. Edgar Hoover, Director, Special Agents In Charge E.J. Connelley and Dwight Brantley, and Agents C.O. Hurt, and W.L. Buchanan were to take care of the raiding of the house and the entering of the house, if necessary, and the actual taking into custody of the individuals if they submitted to arrest. It was planned to have the five above indicated agents immediately move into position to take the place when the raiding squad at the rear of the house signaled that they were definitely in location.

Clyde Tolson. (Courtesy FBI files)

"Agent J.V. Blake, as the squads moved into position, was to enter the second floor apartment of Mr. R. J. Reid, in order to block anyone who might leave from the rear of the Karpis apartment, and try to go up the stairs into the upstairs apartments. At the approximate time all the agents moved into position, and just prior to the signal that they were ready for a move, Agent C.O. Hurt and Special Agent In Charge E.J. Connelley were established on the opposite corner of Canal and Jeff Davis Parkway, followed by a car occupied by Mr. J. Edgar Hoover, Agent W.L. Buchanan, and Special Agent in Charge Dwight Brantley, subjects Karpis and Hunter came out of the apartment and started to enter the Plymouth coupe, and Agent Hurt and this Agent immediately crossed Canal Street, and blocked their car into the sidewalk, covering them at the same time as we left our car, and Mr. Hoover, together with Agents Brantley and Buchanan, immediately moved across Canal Street to block their car in at the rear and also cover these individuals with their guns, at the same time that Agent Hurt and myself covered them."[9]

FBI Director J. Edgar Hoover later wrote: ". . . Karpis, the prototype of the cold and ruthless killer, had sworn he would not be taken alive. We did not expect to take him easily and we planned the raid carefully. It was approximately five-fifteen o'clock in the afternoon of May 1, 1936. Four assistants and I were to enter the front door. The other squads were deployed in the rear and on both sides of the building. The signal for action was about to be given but it had to be delayed when a man on a horse moved leisurely into the lane beside the through traffic.

"We waited, eager to avoid attention, until he had passed on down the street and then moved forward. As we did so, two men stepped from the doorway and walked briskly down the steps. We recognized Alvin Karpis. Again our timing was thrown off. As the fugitives walked toward their car, a small boy on a bicycle scooted between the pair and our vantage place. Fearful that the child would be caught in the crossfire if any shooting started, we moved out and hurried forward, demanding their surrender as the two men were entering the car.

"The last thing in the world that Alvin Karpis expected to see was the head G-man and a squad of what he had called 'sissy' agents! The tough hoodlum turned ashen. His expression was a curious mixture of amazement and fright. Neither he nor his shaking companion made an effort to resist. There was no gunplay. Like their entire breed, their courage was the kind derived from getting the drop on their victim. It oozed away when they were on the other end of the gun. We placed Karpis, who told me that he never thought the bureau would take him alive and his companion under arrest . . ."[10]

J. Edgar Hoover 1895-1972. (Courtesy Library of Congress)

Hoover had never before participated in any arrests, and because of this, he was criticized by many congressional leaders. During the hearings of the Senate Appropriations Committee, Senator Kenneth McKellar questioned Hoover about his qualifications and investigative experience, and whether he had ever made an arrest. The director admitted he had never made an arrest but only because the power to do so was not granted him until 1934.[11]

There was no love lost between Hoover and Karpis. Because Karpis had threatened his life in retaliation for the killing of Ma Barker, and to silence his critics, Hoover wanted to be in on the capture. The fact that Hoover's statement on the capture belittled Karpis' courage, as well as intelligence, indicated he was gloating over his victory.

Subsequent to the apprehension of Karpis, it was learned he had maintained an apartment at 3300 Saint Charles Street, New Orleans, and it was further learned that the raid on the apartment on Canal Street was timely, as Karpis claimed he was making preparations to go on another fishing trip. A search of the Plymouth coupe and the apartment in which Karpis and Hunter had rented revealed that they had been prepared to resist arrest if the opportunity was presented, as there were found a rifle, two .45 caliber automatic pistols and a .3_0 caliber pistol. Later, a Terraplane coupe, which had been used by Karpis, was located and it was found to contain a .222 caliber rifle, a .22 caliber automatic pistol and a .45 Colt automatic pistol.[12]

Karpis' former wife, Dorothy, told the *Tulsa World* the day after his capture that the gangster "had made his bed and he'll have to sleep in it." She said she had lived with Karpis for less than five weeks after the two were married in September 1931 and that she had not seen him since. Her big desire, she said, was that reporters leave her alone.[13]

After the capture of Karpis, he was immediately removed to St. Paul, Minnesota, and committed to the Ramsey County Jail in default of one half-million dollar bond to await trial. Arriving in Minnesota, Karpis was described as being "straw-hatted, coatless, manacled, a bewildered bellhop in appearance—returning to his summer playground." One of those accompanying him was G-Man J. Edgar Hoover—"stern-visaged, jutting-jawed, fierce haired—a Roman conquering hero of modern times, demonstrating to the world, and congressional inquisitors in particular, that the division of investigation, United States Department of Justice, always get its man."[14]

Hoover led the way as Karpis was surrounded by a veritable arsenal of quick-firing small arms manned by federal agents. For hours, armies of federal men, newspaper reporters, and photographers had waited for the flight bringing Public Enemy Number 1 from Kansas City, as storms ripped across the central states delaying flight after flight.

Finally the huge dual-motored plane, which they were waiting for, roared over the field. Within minutes, the fourteen-passenger Douglas "skyliner" landed smoothly. The huge doors of the hangar of the 109th aero squadron, Minnesota National Guard, slid open and a crew of militiamen under the direction of Major Ray S. Miller took care of the mechanical end of the reception.

Travelers aboard two commercial transport planes were startled at the reception they received: thronging newsmen, cameras in hand; racing automobiles bristling with firearms; and airport attendants delaying normal activities. Chief Agent Clinton W. Stein, in charge of the agents, took no chances, keeping fifteen men surrounding Karpis.

"It was the biggest plane I'd ever seen at that time," recalled former *St. Paul Daily News* Reporter Nate Bomberg. "Gigantic! It pulled up to the administration building and finally the doors opened and down the ramp came a flock of FBI agents led by J. Edgar Hoover and Karpis. And Karpis was wrapped in leg irons and arm irons and he was irons all over. Mr. Hoover was holding the irons and led Karpis to a waiting car. They got him in the car and whisked him off to the Federal Building."[15]

Later that day, J. Edgar Hoover, sitting in a comfortable chair at the St. Paul offices of the Division of Investigations, Department of Justice, discussed the government's war on crime, and in particular, Public Enemy Number One, Alvin Karpis: "The man who said he would never be captured alive folded up like the yellow rat he is, and the rest of gangdom is, at heart. Stammering, stuttering, shaking as though he had palsy, the man whom you newspapermen bestowed the title of 'Public Enemy No. 1' quit cold as all the others have.

"Ma"—The Life and Times of "Ma" Barker and Her Boys

"Who will replace him as Public Enemy Number One? We, we don't rank the yellow rats. It is you newspapermen who do that for us. But if you want to know whom I rank as Public Enemy No. 1 today, it is old man politics. Karpis may have been co-leader of the now extinct Barker-Karpis Gang, but the fugitive Harry Campbell is the man with the brains.

"Karpis reminds me of Dillinger and George 'Machine Gun' Kelly. They talked a lot but each had to follow the master mind of their respective chief aides. Dillinger had his John Hamilton, Kelly his Harvey Bailey, and Karpis his Campbell. We're still after Campbell and eventually we'll get him."[16]

Fred Hunter was committed to the federal jail at New Orleans to await prosecution on several charges. The investigation was continued by special agents at Toledo, Ohio, for the purpose of locating Harry Campbell, and it was learned that he, under the name of G. Miller, was residing in Apartment 1, at 2132 Monroe Street, Toledo. It was further ascertained that Campbell was known in the vicinity as Robert or Bob Miller.

At daybreak on May 7, 1936, special agents conducted a raid on this apartment and there apprehended Harry Campbell. A search of the apartment revealed that Campbell had concealed under a pillow a .45 caliber Colt automatic pistol which he did not have an opportunity to use.

About 11:50 A.M., Campbell arrived at St. Paul's Holman Municipal Airport in the custody of Special Agent in Charge E.J. Connelley and Special Agents C.E. Smith and T.M. Birch. The prisoner was met at the airport by Special Agent in Charge C.W. Stein and Special Agents J.E. Brennan, R.T. Noonan, S.K. McKee, J.V. Anderson, S.W. Hardy, G.A. Paulson, F.C. Guerrero, and R.C. Suran. He was immediately taken to the St. Paul Bureau Office for questioning.

Following interrogation, Campbell was committed to the Ramsey County Jail in default of $200,000 bond, to await the disposition of his case. Bureau agents continued questioning Campbell on May 7th, 8th, 9th, 10th, and 11th, and elicited only information concerning his association with members of the Barker-Karpis Gang. The prisoner vehemently denied any participation in the Bremer kidnapping, or that he received any of the ransom money for his release.

"Ma"—The Life and Times of "Ma" Barker and Her Boys

Campbell maintained that his association with persons connected to the case commenced in September 1933. He added that he had met Wynona Burdette four or five years ago in Tulsa, Oklahoma, prior to the time that she became the wife of Eldon Stanborough, but his relationship with her did not begin until after she had left her husband.

He talked freely of his friendship with Fred Barker, Arthur Barker, and Volney Davis and related they had met in grade school. When shown photographs of the trio, he said the pictures represented who they were supposed to be. When asked about his own education, he informed them he had quit school in his junior year.

Campbell insisted his principal associate in 1932 was Glen LeRoy Wright. During this time he was acquainted with Jimmie Lawson, a local hood, but they had never become friends and he denied that he had ever pulled any jobs with Lawson. He then contradicted himself by saying that during that year 1932, he and Wynona Burdette, Glen LeRoy Wright, and Jimmie Lawson lived together on a farm near Joplin, Missouri, with two men he knew only as "Dutch" and "Shorty." He claimed he had been set up by a "fink" who gave police his whereabouts at the farm. Although a police raid was conducted, no arrests were made.

That same year, he admitted, he and Wynona had taken trips to Hot Springs, Arkansas; Berryville, Arkansas; Tulsa, Oklahoma; and Casper, Wyoming, although he could not remember the dates. He said that just prior to his leaving Oklahoma for Chicago in 1933, he and Wynona visited a farm at Mannford, Oklahoma, owned by a man known only as the "Old Bachelor." He denied knowing anyone named either "Speedy" and Ruth, although, he said, he once had heard of someone with the moniker, "Speedy Quick."

From Mannford, he and Wynona went to the home of his sister, Mrs. Myrtle McNeil in Wichita Falls, Texas, and there he left Wynona, and returned to the home of his parents in Tulsa. He denied that at any time he had received a letter from Fred Barker requesting him to come to Hammond, Indiana, although about September 1933, he borrowed some money from a man he refused to identify and went to Hammond where he met Fred and Doc Barker at a hotel, the name of which he could not remember.

In Hammond he met Willie Harrison, who owned a saloon not far from the hotel. He had not been in the city very long when he was joined by Wynona Burdette. Fred and Doc, as well as Alvin Karpis, were living in Chicago, and he and Wynona stayed with them, although, of course, he could not remember the name of the apartments. He later stated that Karpis was not present in Chicago, and that while he had seen him in Tulsa, he didn't meet him until he came to Hammond.

Campbell said he had not journeyed to Hammond to commit a kidnapping, and that shortly after Wynona arrived, the couple drove to Reno, Nevada in a borrowed car. He could not recall the name of the owner of the automobile. Initially, he said they did not stop in St. Paul on the way to Reno, but afterwards said they may have stopped there to visit Bill Weaver and Myrtle Eaton.

He did tell them that in Reno he hung out with Doc Barker, Fred Barker, Volney Davis, Alvin Karpis, Edna Murray, Dolores Delaney, and Paula Harmon. It came as no surprise to his interrogators when he said he could not remember the address where he and Wynona lived, or the addresses of any of his friends. One of the agents mentioned the Highland Apartments at 234 West Liberty Street, and he agreed that must have been where they had resided.

Although he could not remember the dates, he told investigators that he and Wynona, as well as all the others, drove to St. Paul just prior to the Bremer abduction and that he and his lady stayed at Bill Weaver's place for a short while. After a few days, the couple rented an apartment at the Capitol Apartments on St. Peter Street during the latter part of 1933 and early 1934.

When asked if he had associated with Fred Goetz, Campbell could not remember. He did recall, however, that he had temporarily left Wynona at the Capitol Apartments and caught a bus to Chicago. He was quite sure he was a passenger on the bus the day of the Bremer kidnapping. After Wynona joined him in Chicago, they went on to Toledo where he claimed he met Russell Gibson, Jimmy Wilson, and Dr. Joseph Moran. He admitted that Dr. Moran had operated on his fingertips but denied the doctor altering his facial appearance through an operation.

On May 12th, special agents took Campbell to the county jail where he was allowed to talk privately with Alvin Karpis. In the presence of agents, Karpis afterwards told Campbell that the two of them would be better off by entering a plea of guilty. Campbell agreed to plead guilty but said he would not make any statement regarding the case.

United States Attorney George Sullivan appeared at the St. Paul Bureau Office and Campbell reiterated that he wished to plead guilty. On that same day, May 12th, Campbell openly admitted that he had been one of the kidnappers of Edward Bremer, that he was in one of the cars which blocked Bremer's automobile on the corner of Lexington and Goodrich, and that he had assisted with taking him from St. Paul to Bensenville, Illinois, where he had acted as a guard at the hideout while Bremer was confined there.

Campbell also confessed that he had been one of the men, who had freed Bremer at Rochester, Minnesota. He stated, however, that he would furnish no information regarding his accomplices but did admit that he had received $6,000 of his share of $15,000 for his role in the abduction. He did not elect to stand trial for the kidnapping of Mr. Bremer and on May 12, 1936, he entered a plea of guilty at St. Paul, and on the same date was sentenced to life imprisonment in the United States Penitentiary at Leavenworth, Kansas, "or any other institution designated by the Attorney General."[17]

On the same morning, Sam Coker was taken into custody by special agents in a private home a few blocks from where Harry Campbell had been residing. Coker was returned to the Oklahoma State Penitentiary at McAlester, Oklahoma on May 9, 1936, to complete his unexpired term for bank robbery.

Fred Hunter, after being indicted at New Orleans on May 27, 1936, entered a plea of guilty to the charge of harboring Alvin Karpis and was sentenced to two years in the United States Penitentiary at Atlanta, Georgia.

The widow of Frank Nash, who was slain in the Kansas City Massacre in 1933, took the stand as a government witness on July 16, 1936, in the trial of John (Jack) Peifer on a charge of participating in the William Hamm kidnapping. Mrs. Nash, also known as Mrs. Frances Miller, of

Aurora, Minnesota, was the first prosecution witness and described how she, her late husband, and their young daughter visited Peifer's nightclub in St. Paul and Harry Sawyer's farm six miles north of St. Paul. At the farm, she met Peifer and several members of the Barker-Karpis Gang, including Alvin Karpis, Arthur "Doc" Barker, and Freddie Barker.[18]

Mrs. Nash slowly answered questions put to her by United States District Attorney George F. Sullivan, heading the prosecution. She related that on her many trips from Aurora to St. Paul, where she also visited the kidnapper gang's alleged headquarters, she was accompanied by her husband and her six year old child.

Miss Belle Borne of South Bend, a Mankato suburb, testifying as a government witness, revealed the activities of certain members of the Barker-Karpis Gang following the $100,000 kidnapping of St. Paul brewer, William Hamm, Jr., on June 15, 1933.[19]

Mrs. Borne, who admitted on the stand she lived with confessed kidnapper Charles "Big Fitz" Fitzgerald told of going to the cottage of slain gangster Freddie Barker at Long Lake, Illinois, near Chicago, where the government contended the ransom money was split up. She said she had met and lived with Charles Fitzgerald for six years, part of the time in several Chicago apartment houses. She identified a photograph of Fred Barker, whom she said she knew as "Mr. Anderson" at that time.

On her visit with Fitzgerald to the lake cottage, she testified she saw "Anderson" and his girlfriend, Paula Harmon. Asked by George Sullivan if she saw any other persons there, she mentioned a woman named "Edna" and "another man." The woman named Edna was, of course, Edna "Rabbits" Murray, known as "the kissing bandit," who also was scheduled to take the stand as one of the government's principal witnesses.

Edmund C. Bartholmey, ex-postmaster at Bensenville, Illinois, took the stand as another government witness and began a recitation of details leading up to the negotiations to use his home as a hideout. The day before, the second day of his trial, he had pleaded guilty to kidnapping charges.[20]

Testifying as a government witness at the Peifer trial, confessed kidnapper, Byron Bolton said a St. Paul policeman "was to get $25,000" when the arrangements for the abduction of William Hamm were being discussed by the Barker-Karpis Gang. Bolton, relating a conversation he had with Fred Goetz, alias George Ziegler, at a Bald Eagle Lake cottage, testified:

"Ziegler told me he had met the policeman who was going to give them the information. It was a man on the kidnap detail and he instructed Ziegler that it took only two minutes to check a telephone call and that he should be very careful when making telephone calls. Ziegler told me Peifer would relay the news to Ziegler."[21]

When District Attorney Sullivan asked if anything had been said about money, Bolton replied, "The policeman was to get $25,000." Sullivan then inquired whether there had been any mention of the police, to which Bolton told him there was not. Sullivan asked when the next time was that he saw Ziegler again at the cottage and Bolton told him it was the following morning, June 14, 1933, the day before Hamm was kidnapped.

On the same day, Gus Barfus, commissioner of public safety, announced Thomas Brown, former chief of police and current head of the police auto theft division, had been suspended. "There have been rumors of the association of the police department with St. Paul kidnappings for some time," Barfus said. "They have been checked with federal officials who were not in a position to divulge information. Mr. Brown's name has been mentioned unfavorably in this trial [of Jack Peifer] in Federal court on charges in connection with the William Hamm Jr., kidnapping."

On July 27, 1936, Alvin Karpis entered a plea of guilty to the indictment charging him with the kidnapping of William A. Hamm, Jr. and he received a life sentence. Karpis and Campbell were temporarily committed to the United States Penitentiary, Leavenworth, Kansas, and on August 3, 1936, were transferred to the island prison at Alcatraz, California.

During the course of the investigation to apprehend the various members of the Karpis-Barker Gang, special agents learned that William J. Harrison, who had been closely associated with the mob, had unwittingly communicated to associates of the gang certain information which should not have been divulged. Using a ruse, Harrison on the night of January 6, 1935, was lured by some of his companions to an abandoned barn in the vicinity of Ontarioville, Illinois. When he entered the barn, in the hope of affecting his mission, he was shot to death by several of his erstwhile associates. His body was then soaked with gasoline, placed in an appropriate position and the barn set on fire. The structure was completely demolished.

On January 6, 1935, the charred outline of an apparently unidentified body of a human being was observed in the smoldering embers. The Sheriff's Office at Wheaton, Illinois, made a search for identifying items left at the scene of the crime and an Elgin wrist watch and a gold linked bracelet were found beside the body. There was also found what remained of a pair of octagon shaped eyeglasses. In addition, a five gallon gasoline can and a crank for a Model "A" Ford automobile were found. Federal Bureau of Investigation ascertained definitely that Harrison had been murdered by certain of his companions and that his body had been burned in an old barn to prevent identification. Special agents secured from the Sheriff's Office at Wheaton, Illinois, pertinent data concerning the wrist watch which had been found near the corpse. Systematic inquiry in the vicinity of Hammond, Indiana and Calumet City, Illinois, where Harrison had spent considerable time, disclosed that on August 21, 1933, Harrison had a wrist watch repaired by a jeweler friend in Hammond. The jeweler had scratched his repair number, C-833, on the inside of the case and this entry appeared on the case of the Elgin watch which had been found next to the unidentified corpse at Ontarioville on January 6, 1936.

The finding of the body of William J. Harrison gave significance to the letter which had been found at Oklawaha, Florida, written by Doc Barker to his brother Fred in which it was stated, "I took care of that business for you Boys it was done Just as good as if you had did it yourself."

Notes

[1] One of several poems written by Bonnie Parker.
[2] Katharine A. Kellock, "Bad News for Uncle Sam's Female Public Enemies," *Every Week Magazine*, May 1935; FBI Agent E. Scheidt to Agent Clegg dated May 1, 1935, Federal Bureau of Investigation Freedom of Information and Privacy

Acts, Subject: Kate Barker "Ma," File Number 62-35637.

[3] *Mankato Free Press*, August 20, 1935.

[4] *Mankato Free Press*, August 26, 1935.

[5] FBI Agent E. Scheidt to Agent Clegg dated May 1, 1935, Federal Bureau of Investigation reedom of Information and Privacy Acts, Subject: Kate Barker "Ma," File Number 62-35637.

[6] Miriam Allen deFord, *The Real Ma Barker*, pp. 64, 81.

[7] Athan G. Theoharis, editor, *THE FBI A Comprehensive Guide from J. Edgar Hoover to The X-Files*, pp. 56-57.

[8] National Archives, Bruno, California.

[9] FBI "New Orleans" Barker-Karpis File #7-15 FOIPA #445856.

[10] "The Toughest Mob We Ever Cracked" by J.Edgar Hoover with Ken Jones, from The FBI In Action. Originally published as a magazine article.

[11] Athan G. Theoharis, editor, *THE FBI A Comprehensive Guide from J. Edgar Hoover to The X-Files*, pp. 56-57.

[12] FBI Files, RCS:TD I.C.#7-576, November 19, 1936, The Kidnaping of Edward George Bremer, St. Paul, Minnesota, History and Early Association of the Karpis-Barker Gang Prior to the Abduction of Mr. Bremer.

[13] *Tulsa World*, May 2, 1936.

[14] *St. Paul Daily News*, May 2, 1936.

[15] Nate Bomberg, "The Day Karpis Returned," Capitol, *The St. Paul Pioneer Press & Dispatch Sunday Magazine*, March 28, 1971, pp. 6, 10.

[16] *St. Paul Daily News*, May 2, 1936.

[17] United States Bureau of Investigation, Report of Special Agent D. P. Sullivan, Chicago, Illinois, February 17, 1936; Paul Maccabee St. Paul Gangster History, 1981-1995, Research Files, Minnesota Historical Society.

[18] *Mankato Free Press*, July 16, 1936.

[19] *Mankato Free Press*, July 17, 1936.

[20] *Mankato Free Press*, July 16, 1936.

[21] *Mankato Free Press*, July 17, 1936.

Chapter Twelve

The Great Escape

"If I had my way we would have the legislature authorize construction of a separate building for the criminal insane at the state prison under charge of expert psychiatrists."
—Louis Foley, Chairman State Board of Control[1]

On April 20, 1936, St. Paul police announced they were holding a Mankato area woman in the Ramsey County Jail as a material witness in the William Hamm kidnapping case. Officers of the State Bureau of Criminal Apprehension, however, would not reveal her name or her exact connection with the case, but she was believed to be a key witness in the kidnapping case.[2]

The federal grand jury was meeting the following day to be asked to indict seven persons in the Hamm case. Shackled and under heavy guard, Charles "Big Fitz" Fitzgerald, accused of being one of the principals in the $100,000 kidnapping of Hamm, was brought to St. Paul by train from Los Angeles. Fitzgerald, the government charged, was the man who clasped Hamm's hand on June 15, 1933, and said "Hello, Mr. Hamm," while two accomplices seized and forced him into an automobile a block from the Theodore Hamm Brewing Company.

Taken to the offices of the Federal Bureau of Investigation by a squad of agents who accompanied him, Fitzgerald, alleged bank robber, was grilled concerning the abduction as United States District Attorney George F. Sullivan prepared his case against the seven men.

Questioned also in the Federal Bureau of Investigation offices were John (Jack) Peifer, St. Paul gambler and owner of the Hollyhocks nightclub, and Edmund C. Bartholmey, forty-two-year-old Bensenville, Illinois, postmaster. E. J. Connelley of Cincinnati, in charge of special agents who had been heading the investigation into the Hamm and Edward G. Bremer kidnappings, arrived in St. Paul earlier that day.

District Attorney Sullivan was seeking indictments against Alvin Karpis, public enemy No. 1 at large; Arthur "Doc" Barker, serving a life term in Alcatraz for the Bremer abduction; Elmer Farmer, Bensenville tavern proprietor who was then serving a twenty year sentence in Leavenworth; and Bryan (Byron) Bolton, who had pleaded guilty as a kidnap conspirator in the Bremer case; in addition to Peifer, Bartholmey, and Fitzgerald.

Peifer, as "the fingerman," was accused of keeping the gangsters informed of the activities of the police and aided in hatching the kidnap plot. Bartholmey, whose home was identified by Hamm as the "hideout," where he was held four days, received only a small fee, federal authorities reported. Bartholmey's home was only two blocks from the place in which Bremer was kept for twenty-one days. Authorities announced that the trial of anyone indicted wouldn't take place until the fall term of court, federal agents preferring to wait, hoping that Karpis would be arrested and tried simultaneously.

The following day, Mrs. Belle Borne, also known as Belle Norse, Isabelle Borne, and Nellie Anderson of South Bend, three miles west of Mankato, was still held as a material witness as the federal grand jury convened in St. Paul. Mrs. Borne was known to be a close friend of Charles Fitzgerald, held in connection with the kidnapping.[3]

Edmund C. Bartholmey, according to the Associated Press, waived immunity and stood ready to appear before a special federal grand jury which had convened that very day. William Hamm, Jr., was the first witness before the grand jury and he had already identified Bartholmey's home in Bensenville as the place where he was kept prisoner for four days.

Awaiting also to be called were William W. Dunn, "contact man" who delivered the $100,000 ransom preceding Hamm's release; Bryan Bolton, who was the government's principal witness in the trials of a group of Bremer defendants; and Daniel Rush and Albert Miller, both of St. Paul, who saw Hamm seized near the brewery. Both men had testified in the trial of Roger Touhy and three others, previously acquitted for the Hamm kidnapping, but they did not identify anyone.

Three material witnesses were held and questioned concerning the movements of Fitzgerald and Peifer. In addition to Belle Borne, Morris Roisner, St. Paul, liquor store proprietor, and Sam Tanaka, Japanese cutler for Peifer at Hollyhocks, were detained. Roisner, however, was released later that day.

Another witness that Tuesday was Henry K. Maihori, Minneapolis, a Japanese cook, whom federal agents claimed was employed in 1933 by Alvin Karpis at a cottage operated by the fugitive and occasionally by other members of the Barker-Karpis Gang at a lake north of the Twin Cities. Maihori reportedly told federal operatives of the comings and goings of the gang in 1933.[4]

The testimony of Belle Borne concluded two days of presenting evidence to the grand jury. Mrs. Borne, well known in Mankato, testified that she had lived with Charles Fitzgerald, Los Angeles convict, in Chicago and other cities. Belle testified attired in a red dress and carrying a broken arm in a sling. She was released on $2,000 bond. Bail of $100,000 each was set for Peifer, Bartholmey, and Fitzgerald, pending their arrival in federal court.[5]

Meanwhile, Harold Stassen, Dakota County attorney, said he would seek indictments from the county grand jury against Karpis, Fitzgerald, Doc Barker, and two unidentified men on charges of first degree murder in connection with the killing of a patrolman in a $30,000 payroll holdup in South St. Paul three years earlier.

Archie M. Cary, Minneapolis attorney, was in St. Paul that same day, preparing an application to be filed in federal court seeking a reduction in the $100,000 bail demanded by the government for the release of Jack Peifer. Cary told the press that preparation of the application could take several hours. He indicated that if the reduction was not permitted, Peifer probably could still come up with the $100,000 bail amount.

Indictment of Belle Borne was seen as a possibility on April 24th as two "mystery witnesses," a man and a woman, were brought to the Department of Justice office in St. Paul for questioning. The pair, closely guarded by three federal agents as they were brought into the federal building in St. Paul, was regarded as acquaintances of Charles Fitzgerald. A. R. Pfau, Jr. and A. R. Pfau III, attorneys, had been in St. Paul since the past Tuesday as representatives of Belle Borne.[6]

Meanwhile, Larry DeVol, serving his life term in the penitentiary, was having psychiatric problems and was being considered for a transfer to the state asylum. DeVol's skirmishes with the law had transformed him into a big time hood, capable of breaking out of any jail, several years earlier, beginning, perhaps, with the 1930 Severs Hotel murders.

Late in the evening of April 26, 1930, Lee Jones, the manager of the elegant Severs Hotel in Muskogee, Oklahoma, received a call from a hysterical guest named Powell Seeley, seventy-three, reporting a robbery in an adjoining room. Jones and the hotel's engineer, V.S. Sullivan, scurried to the eighth floor to investigate. Upon entering the adjacent room (#819), they spotted two still figures lying on the floor in a large pool of blood just inside the door. After a closer look, the bellboy proclaimed that both men were dead.[7]

Both victims had obviously suffered bullet wounds to the head and body. The room's walls were reportedly spattered with bloodstains. Lying nearby on a bed was an individual with a washrag stuffed in his mouth, his hands tightly bound with some sort of twine or rope. Other than having a large red welt on his right cheek, he appeared unharmed. Jones kneeled down untying the man's hands while ordering the bellboy to call the police. The man who had been bound and gagged, was John Wike, fifty-five, from Connecticut; the gunshot victims, George and David Smith, ages sixty-two and sixty.

The first solid break in the case came on May 15th, when a contingent of Muskogee policemen led by Police Lieutenant Marsh Corgan raided a flophouse near the KATY rail yards in hopes of capturing several persons suspected of robbing the main office of the Griffin Food Company at gunpoint earlier in the week. The raid yielded the arrest of a pair of thugs identified as Pat MacDonald and R.L. Benton.

MacDonald broke easily under interrogation, admitting his participation in the robbery, naming Benton and a habitual criminal named Jimmy Creighton as his partners in the heist. Of even more interest to the police was that Benton matched the description of one of the Severs Hotel murder suspects. Authorities ordered the mug shot of the third man, Jimmy Creighton, from the Oklahoma State Penitentiary where he had served time.

R. L. Benton turned out to be an alias for none other than the notorious Larry Devol. Known to his friends and enemies alike by his nickname, "the Chopper," Devol was described by police as a walking nightmare. Growing up fatherless on the tough streets of Tulsa and in the Osage oil fields where his mother was employed as a nurse, Devol had quickly evolved into a hard-core juvenile delinquent. He had first been incarcerated at the age of nine in a boy's reformatory. He later served time in prisons in Kansas and Oklahoma. In 1929, at the age of twenty-three, he and the infamous Alvin Karpis, of the "Ma"Barker-Karpis Gang escaped from the Kansas State Prison in Lansing. After committing about a two-dozen burglaries in five states, the pair was captured in March of 1930 in Kansas City, Missouri, but Devol was allowed to post a $1000 release bond. He immediately jumped bail, and headed back to Oklahoma for a rendezvous with his baby brother Clarence and Jimmy Creighton in his hometown of Tulsa.

The third suspect in the killings, Jimmy Creighton, who was still at large, had served three terms in Oklahoma prisons and was currently wanted on a robbery, kidnapping, and attempted murder charge in Hastings, Nebraska. Muskogee County authorities issued a warrant for Creighton's arrest for suspicion of armed robbery. When questioned, Devol and MacDonald both denied the murder charge, stating they had been staying at the Weiser Hotel in nearby Haskell on the night of the robbery. Neither man could be prodded into telling what they were doing in Haskell, but emphatically claimed they had not stepped foot in Muskogee that entire week.

A few days after the raid, Sheriff Fred Hamilton made a trip by plane to Connecticut in order to re-interview Seeley and Wike. When Wike was shown a photo of Larry Devol, he positively identified him as one of his attackers. Overjoyed with this encouraging development, the lawman asked Wike to accompany him back to Oklahoma to officially identify the suspect in person. The prim and proper Wike agreed to his proposal.

Soon after the pair's arrival, Wike was escorted to the Muskogee County Jail where he picked DeVol out of a lineup, positively identifying him as one of the murderers. The painter at the hotel, who had witnessed the pair of unsavory characters on the back stairwell, also identified him as one of the men he had seen, and upon studying the prison mug-shot of Jimmy Creighton, stated, "That's the other guy."

The other two witnesses, Severs' Night Manager, Lee Jones, and the cook did not recognize either Devol or Creighton, although Jones thought MacDonald bore a resemblance to one of the individuals he had seen loitering in the hotel's lobby on the night of the murders. When police questioned the manager of the hotel in Haskell, he identified both MacDonald and Devol as ex-boarders at his establishment, but stated the two men had moved from their digs the day before the Muskogee murders.

On the evening of July 25th, MacDonald broke out of the run-down, dilapidated county jail. A massive manhunt was quickly instituted but the fugitive slipped through the net. A week later, Larry Devol jimmied the lock on his cell door and strolled out of the front door of the same jail.

In the months following his escape, "the Chopper" drifted throughout the Midwest burglarizing an assortment of businesses for his daily bread. In September 1930, he helped rob a bank in Ottumwa, Iowa, with a group of bandits including George "Machine Gun" Kelly, Tommy Holden, Jimmy Keating, Harvey Bailey, Verne Miller, and Fred Barker. In the early morning hours of November 17th, he shot and killed a Kirksville, Missouri policeman named John Rose and severely wounded his partner with a .45 caliber handgun when they attempted to question him regarding a gas-station robbery. Marshal Rose, sixty, had been in law enforcement for eighteen years and was survived by his wife and six children.[8]

"Ma"—The Life and Times of "Ma" Barker and Her Boys

On May 16, 1931, the second suspect, Jimmy Creighton, was arrested in Joplin, Missouri. Apparently, he had split with his partners and rented an apartment with an old pal, Freddie Barker, who had recently been released from the Kansas State Prison. Barker, who had a long criminal record, was also a known member of the notorious Barker-Karpis Gang of Tulsa.

At a little before midnight on May 15th, Creighton, who had been out drinking and carousing in nearby Webb City, accidentally bumped into twenty-seven-year-old Coyne Hatten on a crowded sidewalk in front of a drugstore. According to witnesses, Hatten turned to Creighton and asked him if he was "Looking for trouble." Creighton whipped out a Colt .45 automatic pistol, and pumped three steel-jacketed rounds into Hatten, who was dead before he hit the sidewalk. Creighton was arrested later that night at his apartment in Joplin, passed out from the effects of strong drink.

After the Kirksville shooting, Larry Devol fled to Omaha, Nebraska, where the local mob employed him as a paid assassin. After spending several months there, he was involved in at least three homicides, Devol traveled to St. Paul, Minnesota, rejoining the Barker-Karpis Gang as a "Triggerman."

Over the next eighteen months, the gang robbed at least seven banks in five states. On December 16, 1932, they hit the Third Northwestern Bank of Minneapolis for $115,000 in cash and bonds. The gang killed two policemen and a bystander while making their escape. Devol was captured on December 21st at a St. Paul apartment house and charged with murder. He was sentenced to life in prison, and shortly after his arrival at the state penitentiary, Warden John J. Sullivan referred to him as "probably the most cold-blooded man that ever entered the prison. I have not the slightest doubt but that he would take any chance to make a break, and would not hesitate to kill anyone that might stand between him and freedom." Restricted to detention, he assured his fellow inmates that he "had friends on the outside and would get out regardless of the warden, his deputy or any of his God damn guards."[9]

After DeVol claimed that prison guards were attempting to shoot poison gas into his cell, he was judged as severely unhinged and promptly shipped to the Minnesota Hospital for the Criminally Insane. DeVol did not remain in the hospital long, and on June 7, 1936, he led himself and fifteen other prisoners in a mass escape.[10] Larry Devol had a natural talent for escaping from prisons, jails, and hospitals and, one way or another, managed to free himself.

"My old pal Lawrence DeVol once got himself sprung for a mere fifty dollars dropped into a jailer's pocket," recalled Alvin Karpis years later. "It was in the winter of 1930 in a little Oklahoma town called Ponca City after he'd been nabbed on a burglary charge."[11]

At the insane asylum in St. Peter, DeVol made the first hostile move in the overpowering of five guards, according to Bert Hokanson, one of the guards on duty. About a half hour before the usual 7:30 P.M. bedtime, the first warning came when Hokanson heard a shuffling of feet behind him. He turned, to find DeVol close behind him, holding a knife against his throat. "Keep quiet—don't move!" DeVol commanded.[12]

Lucky for Hokanson, he followed DeVol's orders. Had he committed one wrong move, his captor would not have hesitated to kill him, as evidenced by Alvin Karpis' later writings: "I still looked up to DeVol and always let him be the leader. But something about him was beginning to shake me up a little. For instance, there was the incident in the drugstore in Perry, Oklahoma. He was on his own, without me, and he told me that after he'd broken into the store, he heard somebody out in the alley at the bank calling to him to come out with his hands up. Well, according to DeVol, instead of looking for a way to sneak out, he burst into the alley blasting with his .45 automatic. And he left one guy lying on the ground with blood spurting out of a hole in his neck. DeVol figured he caught the fellow in the jugular vein, and he had a real gleam in his eye when he told the story."[13]

As DeVol made his break from St. Peter, the inmates participating in the break pounced on Hokanson and the other four guards—George Fay, Hans Hansor, Roy Sampson, and Norbert Steeple. Unarmed, the guards had been seated in a semi-circle watching the seventy-five prisoners. The escapees, armed with table and chair legs, quickly over-powered the guards and were ordered by DeVol to "put them into the pipe room!" Later, just as

DeVol slid out the window, he had the guards locked in a sound-proofed cell where unruly prisoners were kept.[14]

"I thought we would smother," Hokanson said later, relating the experience of the five guards locked in the tiny room in which fire hoses were kept and through which steam pipes ran. "We were in the dark for a time but finally managed to find a light. Then we heard a scraping at the door. I felt sure they were coming back to kill us, but instead, they opened the door and whispered to us to come out, one at a time.

"It was like a nightmare. I thought they were going to kill us. I was the first one out. DeVol was at the window, ready to slide out. He told them to put us in one of the sound proof cell blocks. Then he disappeared."[15]

Once DeVol was gone, several of the patients not involved in the break, who had been warned to stand back, went into action. They were quickly overpowered, however, and two of them were locked in another cell. "After that," Hokanson said, "it was like a real war. Chairs were flying all around."

When released from the cell, the first thought of Hokanson and the other four guards was to join the hunt. "I'm willing to meet any of them," Hokanson said. "Now I'll have an even chance. I didn't have that when DeVol had a knife at my throat."

Hokanson, a guard in the criminal building of the insane asylum since 1919, had had previous experiences with escaping prisoners. In September 1922, several inmates armed with guns and knives that had been smuggled in, attempted to escape. Shooting as they came, they tried to break out the front gate but were repulsed. Hokanson was one of the guards who had stood them off.

"That was different," Hokanson said. "When bullets are flying, you've got a chance, but with a knife at your throat, you're helpless."

Hokanson was on duty at the institution when three men escaped through a tunnel in 1927. They were caught several days later and returned to their cells.

The men who escaped with DeVol were William "Pat" O'Neil; Ben Drussell; Tom DeLargo, alias Halloway; Adolph Walwort; Tony T. Smith;

George Tremont; Wilbert Jorissen; Donald Reeder; Walter M. Hornstein; Frank Gibson; Percy Kenosha; Albert Soroko; William Lammi; David Rhoades; and Lawrence Leonard Gunderson.

Devol, convicted killer of two Minneapolis police officers, engineered the break and was credited with being the "brains" behind it. According to a written confession by bank robber Jess Doyle, who was serving a term in the Nebraska State Penitentiary, DeVol had been the machine gunner of the Barker-Karpis Gang that mowed down Patrolmen Ira Evans and Leo Gorski during the Third Northwestern National Bank robbery in Minneapolis. DeVol had pleaded guilty to first degree murder of the patrolmen.

Doyle stated that DeVol had "taken the rap" for the Minnesota charge rather than be returned to Missouri where he was also wanted for murder and would face capital punishment. According to Doyle's confession, Leonard Hankins, convicted on a charge of killing the two Minneapolis officers, was innocent and had no connection with the crime.

While he was held in Stillwater Prison for three years, Devol was not permitted by Warden John J. Sullivan to mingle with other convicts and was not assigned to any work. Warden Sullivan regarded him as one of the most desperate characters in the institution and ordered that all of his meals be served him in his cell.

Alvin Karpis later recalled that DeVol always remained cool and calm in any situation. Following the shootout at the Third Northwestern National Bank in Minneapolis, the gang knew there would be a big investigation and making themselves scarce seemed the wisest and only option available. Karpis wrote: "Finally, it was agreed that everybody should blow town for a couple of months. 'Well,' DeVol said, 'my bags are in the Chrysler and I've got a half-gallon jug of gin and orange juice and I'm ready to roll. DeVol didn't take this thing as seriously as the others. Actually, he had killed so many cops that this was just another incident to him."[16]

Bank robbers and killers were among the other fifteen escapees who fled the insane asylum with DeVol. Walter M. Hornstein, twenty-four, had confessed to the killing of Patrolman Fred Nolan in St. Cloud on April 29,

1934. The bandit claimed that the gun was fired accidentally when the patrolman ordered him to hand it over. Witnesses, however, said that the assailant walked up behind the officer and fired. He was admitted December 27, 1935, on a second degree murder charge.[17]

Frank Gibson, thirty-eight, known as "Slim" and Tex McFarland, was the confessed slayer of H. N. Peterson, cashier of the Citizens' State Bank of Wheelock, North Dakota. Peterson was killed November 12, 1926, in a bank holdup. Gibson also confessed with Jack Northrup, who was serving a life term in Stillwater Prison, to the slaying of Frank Dahlin, marshal of Isanti, Minnesota in December 1927.

Gibson had been arrested with Northrup and five others on May 9th during a gunfight in Elk River. Gibson escaped being charged with the murder of Peterson in Wheelock, North Dakota, by confessing to the slaying of the Isanti marshal. He was sentenced to life imprisonment by Judge E. A. Giddings of Anoka on May 14, 1927, and was moved to the asylum in St. Peter on September 8, 1931.

Gibson told authorities at the time the sentence was imposed that he had previously served jail terms in Bismarck and Fargo, North Dakota, and that in 1914 he had participated in a $33,000 bank holdup in a Kansas town. Gibson's record pointed out that he was "part Negro."

Tom DeLargo, twenty-four, had been convicted of a robbery charge in Ramsey County and was admitted to the asylum on February 2, 1934. Adolph Walworth, thirty-five, had been admitted August 30, 1932, following his conviction on a first degree grand larceny charge in Hennepin County. Tony T. Smith, thirty-six, was listed as "very crazy, delusional." He came from Ramsey County where he had been charged with first degree robbery. Wilbert Jorissen, twenty-three, came from Carver County on a first degree robbery charge, being admitted May 25, 1933. Donald Reader, twenty-seven, residence unknown, had originally come from Missouri. He had been involved in a bank holdup. Percy Kenosha, twenty, listed as an "Indian," was from Wisconsin but gave his residence as Minneapolis.

Albert "Scarface" Soroko, forty, sentenced to life imprisonment for the murder in the first degree of Peter Hoffman during a Minneapolis theatre holdup on November 22, 1930, was a native Russian. He was committed from Hennepin County on July 17, 1935. William Lammi, a truck driver, was sent to the institution from St. Louis County on a charge of using an automobile without the owner's permission. George Tremont, thirty-one, was regarded by authorities as being "very delusional," and Lawrence Leonard Gunderson, thirty-five, a Minneapolis laborer, was reputed to be a "dangerous person."

The sixteen inmates escaped by breaking out a bar on a second floor porch with a table leg, then sliding to the ground by means of a fire hose. Timing their flight perfectly, they avoided an armed guard as the scaled the ten-foot wall surrounding the criminal ward.

Seven or eight of the inmates headed by DeVol, or "Barton" as he was listed on the asylum records, forced Freda Marske, 319 East Main Street, Mankato, to get out of her car, a 1929 Pontiac coupe. She and a friend, Walter Huettl, also of Mankato, were sitting in the car after visiting an inmate at the hospital. The escapees quickly piled into the coupe and sped across the asylum grounds and out the main gate.

"The leader of the men who came over the wall," Miss Marske related, "picked up a club and came toward me shouting, 'We'll show them we're not crazy! We want this car!'

"I saw them climb over the wall," she said. "They ran like deer when they got away and scattered in all directions, while a group of seven or eight ran toward my car. I got out and screamed for help. Four of the men jumped inside my car, two climbed onto the fenders and another caught the spare tire and was dragged quite a distance before he got on."[18]

Two of the men, William "Pat" O'Neil and Ben Drussell, were recaptured before they left the asylum grounds. George Tremont, thirty-one, was quickly apprehended early in the morning at New Ulm while sitting on a bench on Main Street. Chief of Police Anton Groebner of New Ulm stated that Tremont wore no hat or coat and that his shoes and trousers were soaking wet up to the knees. He was arrested because of his strange appearance and he offered no resistance.

Just before noon, two more of the fugitives were captured in St. James—Tom DeLargo, twenty-four, alias Halloway, committed from Ramsey

County on a robbery charge in February 1935, and with DeVol branded as one of the ringleaders in the break, and David Rhoades, thirty-three, committed from Minneapolis.

DeLargo and Rhoades were captured shortly after Watonwan County Sheriff J. C. Bermel received a report from a country store nine miles north of St. James that "two suspicious looking men were trying to hook a ride." Fearing the men would escape if he wasted time assembling a posse Sheriff Bermel got into his car and rushed to the scene.

As he approached the store, he observed a farmer hauling some barley on a trailer attached to an automobile. He asked the farmer to give the two men a lift on his trailer, asserting he would follow them until they reached town. "It worked out just as I planned," Sheriff Bermel told the press. "The two men got a ride on the trailer. Meanwhile a posse had been assembled in town. When we reached St. James, the two men, apparently suspicious they were being watched, jumped off the trailer and started to run.

"But there were some fast runners in that posse. They chased them and captured them after a long foot race. They were brought to the city jail but they refused to give their names or any other information. From their actions I am quite certain they are escaped inmates."

All through the night, sheriffs, guards, police officers, and highway patrolmen cruised the roads in the vicinity of St. Peter and Mankato, particularly the two river roads between the two cities, along which hiding places were innumerable. No trace of the stolen car was found during this search.

The search for the remainder of the fugitives was directed by Sheriff John A. Johnson of Nicollet County; Dr. George H. Freeman, superintendent of the hospital; William Conley, in charge of a Detachment of State Bureau of Criminal Apprehension Agents; and Emerson Hopp, St. Peter attorney, former government agent who resigned months earlier from the Federal Bureau of Investigation.

Participating in the search were thirty-five members of a machine gun company of the 205th Infantry, called out by Governor Floyd B. Olson, when word of the break was sent to his country home at Gull Lake, 200 miles north of St. Peter. With the first break of daylight in the morning, these thirty-five National Guardsmen from St. Peter and more than a hundred officers began a search of the Minnesota River bottoms. The guardsmen searched until seven A.M. and then were recalled. They were sent out again in the afternoon, however, to continue the search in "the dense jungles along the river." Because the Minnesota River skirted the asylum and the dense woods provided ready cover, authorities concentrated their search in this section of the river flats.

Sheriff John A. Johnson was notified that afternoon that some hunting lodges on Swan Lake where guns might have been stored had been looted. Johnson attributed the break-ins to the fleeing inmates from the asylum who he believed had secured firearms. With the escapees armed and dangerous, panic set in across the countryside as farmers and townspeople protected their homes with strong latches and firearms. Local residents spent an anxious night after they had been warned by authorities that the fleeing criminals might resort to extreme violence to obtain food, clothing, and transportation. Many farmers carried rifles as they worked their fields.

At noon, the first report of a home being molested came in, thus strengthening the belief in some quarters that most of the convicts had headed into the woods along the river. P. S. Culhane, a Belgrade Township farmer, told authorities that two men had attempted to break into his house. He immediately telephoned the police but the pair had disappeared before North Mankato Chief of Police H. J. Quimby and a posse arrived.

Farmers along the river bottoms were particularly alert, but most believed the criminals, pestered by hunger and swamp mosquitoes would show up that night, risking capture to obtain supplies. Mankato police and highway patrolmen were fired upon twice by frightened farmers mistaking them for the criminals. Highways and side roads, meanwhile, bristled with armed volunteers engaged in the manhunt.

Members of the State Board of Control met in St. Paul that morning to discuss the need for greater safeguards at the St. Peter asylum. Board members indicated to the press that an investigation into the mass escape would be launched as soon as the roundup was completed. Following the brief meeting, Chairman Louis G. Foley left for St. Peter where he conferred with Dr. George H. Freeman, superintendent of the institution.

Officials and police officers considered the possibility of the escape being made with the aid of outsiders. A guard reported that he had ordered a suspicious looking man off the grounds Saturday when the man persisted in asking questions about the criminal ward. So thoroughly had the break been planned by DeVol and his lieutenants that the participants had even made a map of the entire second floor from which they made their escape. Following the break, a large sheet of paper was found in the ward showing the arrangement of the second floor rooms and indicating every door and window. Dr. Ralph Rossen, assistant superintendent of the asylum, stated that an inmate had informed him the break had originally been set for Friday night but that DeVol insisted they wait a couple nights.

With the arrest of the seventh "escaped criminal lunatic" on June 9th, William Lammi, St. Louis County auto thief, at Oshawa, nine of the inmates were still at large, while the anxiety of southern Minnesota residents spread into northern Iowa. Three of the most dangerous fugitives headed towards the Ozark Mountains in Missouri and two others were believed cornered in the woods near Norwood, Minnesota.[19]

The dangerous trio headed for the Ozarks were Larry DeVol alias Barton; Albert "Scarface" Soroko; and Donald Reeder. Abandoning the coupe from which they made their escape from the asylum, on the Iowa-Minnesota border in East Chain Township, Martin County, the fugitives made their way to Armstrong, Iowa. The desperadoes broke into two garages on the main street of Armstrong and appropriated a tan colored Chevrolet with Emmett County license plates, a hacksaw, and a sledge hammer.

Farmers in the area loaded their guns and stayed up all night. House, garage, and barn doors were all locked and barricaded. Armed men from Fairmont guarded seventy young girls in a camp on an Iowa lake, nine miles west of where the car had been purloined.

Melvin Passolt, superintendent of the state crime bureau, reported that the garage raid was carried out by "professionals" and the maneuvers of DeVol and his two accomplices "dovetailed" with proposed plans related by some of the captured "lunatics." The glass from the broken window in the Armstrong garage was sent to the Iowa Department of Justice, Bureau of Identification, for fingerprint analysis. Classification numbers of the three fugitives were also dispatched to the same department by Passolt.

Forced into a ditch after an automobile chase marked by gunfire, Wilbert Jorissen and Adolph Walworth, meanwhile, fled into the heavy woods near Norwood, east of Glencoe, Minnesota. Jorissen, the more dangerous of the two, had been committed to the asylum following a "torture" robbery, and had been convicted of torturing Phillip and Theodore Sons, elderly Carver County farmers.

The pair was first spied in Waconia inside the rear of the Kusserow Hardware Store, which they had broken into by Patrolman Ed Redde. They already had abandoned a stolen automobile in Jordan, and when seen by Redde, they rushed to another car two blocks away, which they also appropriated. Patrolman Redde gave chase, but when they succeeded in getting away in the automobile, with the ignition key in place, the officer summoned Game Warden Albert Schutz and Elwell Broberg, a farmer.

Schutz, Broberg, and Redde, after communicating with Sheriff Frank Trende of Chaska, took up the trail of the fugitives. Near Bongards Station, ten miles west of Chaska and three miles east of Norwood, the pursuers caught up with the two "lunatics." Schutz fired a number of shots and the escapees plunged into a ditch and fled into the woods. Additional assistance was summoned by Superintendent Passolt, who assigned several men to the scene.

State Highway Patrolmen, under special orders of Chief John P. Arnoldy, were told to be on the lookout for the fugitives along the 12,000 miles of state and secondary roads in Minnesota. Peace officers warned bank, garage, and hardware store proprietors to take extra precautions against any invasion of their businesses by "the crazy men." Police also kept an eye on the home of Jorissen's sister, who resided in Norwood, believing her residence could be the intended destination of the escapees.

A half a dozen automobiles, according to Chief Arnoldy, had been stolen since the asylum break in the area within a radius of seventy-five miles of St. Peter. Although it was probable that some of the cars had been purloined by others not involved in the getaway, the license numbers were flashed to the one hundred highway patrolmen.

Lawrence L. Gunderson was captured in Belle Plaine that day, becoming the sixth of sixteen escapees to be returned to the asylum. After DeLargo and Rhoades had been captured earlier, they told Superintendent George Freeman that the carefully planned flight had been engineered by DeVol. What they called the "lunatic car" zigzagged southward, they said, purposely to avoid a direct course.

According to the two recaptured prisoners, it had been the goal of DeVol, Soroko, and Reeder to hit a series of Iowa towns where they hoped to raid National Guard armories for weapons. Once they had acquired firearms, they planned to hold up banks and stores. Passolt, Johnson, and Freeman concluded the break had been planned for months ahead. Frequent reports from the State Bureau of Criminal Apprehension Network of Radio Stations, kept officers up to date on the manhunt, rated the greatest in southern Minnesota history.

Alarmed citizens kept Mankato busy all night with a barrage of telephone calls reporting suspicious characters lurking behind trees and in dark alleys. Every call was investigated, however, on the possibility that some of the "madmen" might be hiding in the city.

Asylum authorities revealed that they had considered locking up the three ringleaders just prior to the escape. Dr. George H. Freeman, superintendent, reported to the State Board of Control that a tip on the escape plot had reached officials, but they felt that since the plan had been discovered, there was no need for any further precautions.

"There have been from time to time plots to escape which never materialized, possibly because we succeeded in separating out the ringleaders and secluding them for the time being," Dr. Freeman told the Board of Control. "These situations at the institution had been talked over with special regard for plans being made for escape, and it was felt that it might possibly be wise to seclude Barton [DeVol], DeLargo, and Walworth but it was felt these inmates knew the superintendent had been consulted regarding plotting and it was thought best to delay the lockup for a day or so. There was nothing to indicate the plot was to be carried out into effect immediately."[20]

Louis G. Foley, chairman of the State Board of Control, informed the group it was "possible" some of the sixteen men who had escaped feigned insanity in order to be transferred from Stillwater Prison to the insane asylum where it would be easier to escape.

Because of the mass escape, members of the Board of Control planned to ask the legislature to authorize construction of a separate criminal asylum building within the walls of the state penitentiary. Board members said that the new building might require an expenditure of $200,000 and that possibly use could be made of an unexpended 1932 appropriation of $260,000 allotted for a new cell block at the Stillwater Penitentiary. The new cellblock had never been built because Warden J.J. Sullivan objected to it until absolutely necessary because it would detract from the recreation grounds.

Meanwhile, the theft of the automobile, sledge hammer, and a hacksaw in the Armstrong garage led Glen Schmidt, Iowa bureau chief to tell the press that, "It apparently looks like they're in Iowa now." Armstrong was twenty-five miles southwest of Elmore, Minnesota ,where the fugitives earlier had abandoned an automobile.

Schmidt ordered all cities with an armory to post a guard because Minnesota authorities had informed him that one of the captured fugitives said Lawrence DeVol, "demented Barker-Karpis gangster," planned to raid Iowa armories in search of weapons. "I've also warned all Iowa officers not to take any chances if they come across DeVol and his two companions" Schmidt said.

A man who resembled thirty-six-year-old bank robber and "escaped lunatic" from the St. Peter Asylum, Tony Smith, was arrested in Minneapolis later that day. He said he was Albert Miller, thirty-five, of Albert Lea, Minnesota. The suspect had a heavy growth of beard and was wearing clothes similar to those given out at the institution.

"I'm glad I wasn't kidnapped," Freda Marske, whose car had been commandeered at the asylum by the escapees, told reporters on June 9th. Miss Marske told police she had left her camera, coat, and a purse containing last week's pay in the car when she was forced from it by Larry Devol, who brandished a club at her. Tom DeLargo was wearing Miss Marske's coat when he was apprehended in St. James with David Rhoades on June 8th.

Police Officer Cal Palmer was a big, jovial man with a ready smile. He had been an Enid Policeman for two years, coming from Fairview, where he was a Major County Deputy Sheriff. It had been a hot July in 1936, and Officer Palmer wasn't feeling very well. He had returned to duty at 4:00 P.M. that day, following a short vacation, and Officer Bert Utsler offered to work for him. Palmer declined, saying he thought he would feel better after the sun went down. The heat had been bothering him.[21]

Officer Cal Palmer. (Author's collection)

Around 11:00 P.M., July 8th, one month after the asylum escape, Jim O'Neal, a former police officer who was operating the German Village beer parlor at the corner of Broadway and Grand, noticed a man come in and take a seat in a front booth. O'Neal had been tipped off earlier that his bar was going to be robbed, so he was keeping an eye on his customers. The man ordered a beer and a few moments later, motioned for two girls outside the bar to join him. O'Neal kept an eye on the man for a while and finally, feeling that he recognized the man from pictures he had seen, decided to call police to check him out. A few minutes later, Palmer and his partner, Officer Ralph Knarr, entered the bar. After talking to O'Neal for a minute, they approached the booth where the man was seated.

Palmer made contact with the man and stated, "Come, and go with us." The youthful stranger paled and asked Palmer if he could finish his beer, adding, "I think I know what you want me for." Palmer agreed. He finished the stein of beer while officers waited, then sat it down on the table, and with the same movement, brought up a gun which had been in the booth next to him, and started firing.[22]

Palmer fell first, hit with three bullets, the fatal one going into his heart and killing him instantly. Knarr then fell, hit four times. Another subject was also hit in the leg by a stray bullet. The killer then ran out the side door of the bar to the north. He ran into the alley next to the Broadway Tower and raced up the alley towards Randolph Street, pursued by the Night Chief Lelon Coyle and Officers Ted Roberts, Phil Sawyer, Earle Moore, and Carl Bundren.[23]

Near the Max and Rex Cafe at the end of the alley, DeVol came upon a parked car occupied by Fred Caldwell and Dr. L.D. Huff. He climbed into the rear seat of the car and told Caldwell, "You're driving me. Get going quick". Caldwell put the car in gear and began moving forward when he saw the officers coming towards him with guns pointing at the car. Easing down into the seat, he and Huff opened the doors of the car and dropped out, leaving the man in the car.

Pointing towards the car, Caldwell directed officers to the man sitting in the back seat. Officers began firing at the car, while the killer jumped out and hid behind it. Police officers fired nine shots at the car, one of which hit the murderer in the head, apparently killing him instantly, but not before he had shot off one of Coyle's fingers.

The killer was later identified as Lawrence DeVol, triggerman of the Karpis-Barker Gang, recently broken up when the Barkers were killed in a shoot-out with federal police, according to Desk Sergeant Harold Woolwine. DeVol had supposedly killed three other policemen before the altercation in Enid. A young woman with DeVol during the shootout in Enid said she had met him only the night before and was released by officers.[24]

Shortly after the shooting, police arrested a man who gave the name of Donald Reeder. He told police he was DeVol's companion; that they had escaped together from the asylum in St. Peter on June 7th, and that they had robbed a bank in Turon, Kansas, several days earlier.

From his jail cell, Reeder told a newspaperman how he and DeVol had lived off the profits from robberies in Kansas and Oklahoma, amassing

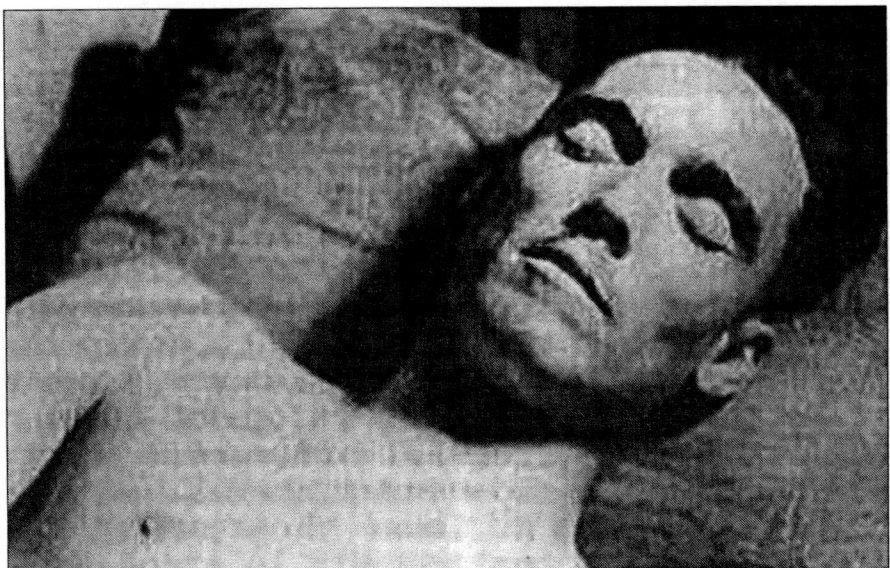

Lawrence Devol after his death at the hand of police officers. (Author's collection)

funds with which to make their escape to Mexico and freedom. The three of them, he said, had come to Oklahoma only recently and Albert Soroko had been killed.

For his present plight, Reeder blamed unemployment. "I couldn't take it—there was no work to do," he said. "But I'd work for a nickel a day now just to be a free man."

Reeder also said that he initially had decided to commit a single crime to obtain money for his family. He said he made off with $3,000 in robbing a bank in Luverne, Minnesota, but four months later in 1931, he was arrested and sentenced to life in Stillwater Prison. Unable to escape, he said he feigned insanity and was sent to the asylum in St. Peter earlier in the year. There, he lamented, he fell in with the ringleaders of the escape plot.

Reeder related five of them had escaped together, but two of them were captured, but DeVol, Soroko, and him, continued their flight, which led them to Iowa, through South Dakota, Nebraska, Kansas, and later Oklahoma. With the death of DeVol and recapture of Reeder, only one escapee remained at large.

Meanwhile, Frank Stone, assistant director of the Kansas State Highway Patrol, announced that two patrolmen, Joe Anderson and Hugh S. Edwards, were on their way to Enid to return Reeder to St. Peter. Stone said the suspect and his slain companion, DeVol, matched descriptions of the two men who had robbed banks in Attica, Little River, and Turon, Kansas, recently.

The day after the shooting, police headquarters in Enid was quiet. Palmer's funeral was held July 10th, in the chapel at Henninger-Allen Funeral Home. More than 500 people attended the funeral. He was buried with honors in Memorial Park Cemetery in Enid. Palmer, thirty-eight years old, left a wife and two sons. Officer Ralph Knarr recovered from his wounds and went on to become Chief of Police in Enid from 1943 until 1956.

On July 8th, federal authorities in St. Paul announced that money found in a safety deposit box in a Waukegan, Illinois, bank was not part of the original ransom notes paid for the release of William Hamm, but it was believed to have belonged to Charles Fitzgerald, who admitted participation in the brewer's kidnapping, and Mrs. Belle Borne of Mankato.[25]

Instead of $6,000 as reportedly found, authorities said they understood the box contained $8,000, including several one thousand dollar bills, drawn on the Federal Reserve Bank of Atlanta, Georgia. In previous trials of defendants linked with the $200,000 Bremer kidnapping, it was brought out Bremer ransom notes were exchanged in Cuba for $1,000 notes from the Atlanta Federal Reserve Bank.

Thomas Newman, attorney for Fitzgerald, contended a "large part" of the money belonged to Belle Borne who was at liberty on bond as a material witness in the Hamm kidnapping. Fitzgerald told Newman Mrs. Borne turned the money over to a friend for deposit in a safety deposit box in the Waukegan First National Bank. Both Mrs. Borne and Fitzgerald contended the money was not obtained through exchange of "hot" money.

A $5,500 portion of the $100,000 ransom paid kidnappers for the release of William Hamm, Jr., was later returned to him under a ruling by Circuit Judge Ralph J. Dady. The money was part of $8,000 found in a safety deposit box in the First National Bank. Mrs. John Vioski, in whose name the box was held, told police she had been given the money for safe-keeping by Mrs. Belle Borne, friend of kidnapper Charles J. Fitzgerald. Lawyers in the case permitted Mrs. Borne and Thomas J. Newman, Minneapolis, attorney for Fitzgerald, to share the balance of $2,500.[26]

On September 3, 1936, Chief Jailer E.J. Clewett of the Ramsey County Jail in St. Paul talked with reporters about the various big name criminals who had been incarcerated there. Clewett related that "many a sophisticated eye must have blinked" the day Volney Davis tacked a letter on the jail's white porcelain walls. In the juvenile department of the steel and concrete jail hung a typewritten copy addressed to his parents, saying in part:

"Don't feel too bad about it because you will know where I am at night and won't be in danger of getting killed. Tell the boys [his younger brothers] to take a lesson from my experience and never touch anything that don't belong to them. A man can get more enjoyment out of a dollar he has earned honestly than he can $1,000 got dishonestly. I know from sad experience."[27]

Davis' sad experience had gotten him a life sentence in Alcatraz Penitentiary for being a Barker-Karpis Gang member when the gang kidnapped Edward Bremer for a $200,000 ransom. He was only one of more than a score of the toughest criminals in the country housed in the Ramsey County Jail. This jail, according to Jailer Clewett, held probably more outlaws of the "public enemy" variety, and certainly more kidnappers, than any other institution of its kind in the United States, save federal penitentiaries. Davis, however, was the only one to leave a tangible reminder of his stay. Of the Karpises, Barkers, Sawyers, and Touhys—only a memory remains.

Clewett said that looking back over the past few years the only thing they all had in common was an innocent habit—all were gum chewers. Doc Barker, who was given life for his role in the Bremer kidnapping, was perhaps the most avid gum chewer of them all. He chewed gum in jail and in court, and while being sentenced, the even grinding motion of his jaws on a cud of gum never ceased.

"They were all nice fellows—in jail," recollected Jailer Clewett. "They tried to make the best of it. They knew of course they wouldn't get anywhere by being tough."

Barker talked about baseball and hunting and fishing with the jailers. Karpis, "Old Creepy," was nervous. He paced his narrow cell in solitary and sometimes would chat about hunting in the South. He used to like to travel fast at night in automobiles, he confessed to jailers. Neither talked about their cases, although Barker once remarked to a jailer he would like to have five minutes alone in the same cell with Byron Bolton, who talked on the witness stand.

Of the lot, former nightclub proprietor, Jack Peifer, took his sentence the hardest. He swallowed poison soon after his sentence and died. He was the second outlaw of notoriety to commit suicide in the Ramsey County Jail. Willie Sharkey was the first. He hanged himself in 1933 with his necktie after being acquitted of the William Hamm kidnapping.

Notes

[1] *Mankato Free Press*, June 9, 1936.
[2] *Mankato Free Press*, April 20, 1936.
[3] *Mankato Free Press*, April 21, 1936.
[4] *Mankato Free Press*, April 22, 1936.
[5] *Mankato Free Press*, April 23, 1936.
[6] *Mankato Free Press*, April 24, 1936.
[7] R. D. Morgan, "The Severs Hotel Murder Mystery," Internet.
[8] The Officer Down Memorial Page, Inc.
[9] Paul A. Sevareid, *The People's Lawyer: The Life of Eugene A. Rerat*, Minneapolis, Ross and Haines, 1963.
[10] *Mankato Free Press*, June 8, 1936.
[11] Alvin Karpis with Bill Trent, *The Alvin Karpis Story*, p. 93.
[12] *Mankato Free Press*, June 8, 1936.
[13] Alvin Karpis with Bill Trent, *The Alvin Karpis Story*, pp. 35-36.
[14] *Mankato Free Press*, June 8, 1936.
[15] Ibid.
[16] Alvin Karpis with Bill Trent, *The Alvin Karpis Story*, p. 66.
[17] *Mankato Free Press*, June 8, 1936.
[18] Ibid.
[19] *Mankato Free Press*, June 9, 1936.
[20] Ibid.
[21] Enid, Oklahoma Police Department Memorial Files.

[22] *Mankato Free Press*, July 8, 1936.
[23] Enid, Oklahoma Police Department Memorial Files; *Mankato Free Press*, July 8, 1936.
[24] *Mankato Free Press*, July 8, 1936.
[25] Ibid.
[26] *Mankato Free Press*, December 18, 1936.
[27] *Mankato Free Press*, September 3, 1936.

Chapter Thirteen

The Rock

"This Island is chiefly composed of irregularly stratified sandstone covered with a thin coating of bird guano. . . . The stone is full of seams in all directions which render it unfit for any building purpose & probably difficult to quarry . . . The island has no beach & but two or three points where small boats can land."

—Lt. William Warner, U.S. Topographical Engineer[1]

The name Alcatraz is derived from the Spanish "Alcatraces." In 1775, the Spanish Explorer Juan Manuel de Ayala was the first to sail into what is now known as San Francisco Bay—his expedition mapped the bay and named one of the three islands Alcatraces. Over time, the name was Anglicized to Alcatraz. While the exact meaning is still debated, Alcatraz is usually defined as meaning "pelican" or "strange bird."[2]

In 1850, a presidential order set aside the island for possible use as a United States military reservation. The California Gold Rush, the resulting boom in the growth of San Francisco, and the need to protect San Francisco Bay, led the U.S. Army to build a Citadel, or fortress, at the top of the island in the early 1850s. The Army also made plans to install more than 100 cannons on the island, making Alcatraz the most heavily fortified military site

"Ma"—The Life and Times of "Ma" Barker and Her Boys

The Rock—Alcatraz. (Author's collection)

on the West Coast. Together with Fort Point and Lime Point, Alcatraz formed a "triangle of defense" designed to protect the entrance to the bay. The island was also the site of the first operational lighthouse on the West Coast of the United States.

By the late 1850s, the first military prisoners were being housed on the island. While the defensive necessity of Alcatraz diminished over time (the island never fired its guns in battle), its role as a prison would continue for more than 100 years. In 1909, the Army tore down the Citadel, leaving its basement level to serve as the foundation for a new military prison. From 1909 through 1911, the military prisoners on Alcatraz built the new prison, which was designated the Pacific Branch, U.S. Disciplinary Barracks for the U.S. Army. It was this prison building that later became famous as "The Rock."

The U.S. Army used the island for more than eighty years—from 1850 until 1933, when the island was transferred to the U.S. Department of Justice for use by the Federal Bureau of Prisons. The federal government had decided to open a maximum-security, minimum-privilege penitentiary to deal with the most incorrigible inmates in federal prisons, and to show the law-abiding public that the federal government was serious about stopping the rampant crime of the 1920s and 1930s.

USP Alcatraz was not the "America's Devil's Island" that many books and movies portray. The average population was only about 260-275 (the prison never once reached its capacity of 336—at any given time,

Alcatraz held less than one percent of the total federal prison population). Many prisoners actually considered the living conditions (for instance, always one man to a cell) at Alcatraz to be better than other federal prisons, and several inmates actually requested a transfer to Alcatraz.

Attorney General Homer Cummings' plan to ship all the most notorious criminals in the country to Alcatraz turned the prison into a who's-who of the decades most wanted; a gang more dangerous than any mob on the street. The inmates sequestered at "the Rock" included such dangerous gangsters as Al Capone; George "Machine-Gun" Kelly; Volney Davis; Harry Campbell; Albert Bates; a Dillinger cohort named Bobby Sherrington; John Paul Chase from "Baby Face" Nelson's gang; Harvey Bailey; train robber Roy Gardner; Charles "Limpy" Cleaver; San Francisco counterfeiter, John Stadig; the "Wyoming Bad Man," Mack Smith; Alvin Karpis, and Doc Barker.[3]

Alcatraz was, of course, home to Al Capone for slightly under four and a half years. Transferred from USP Atlanta in August of 1934, Capone was among the first "official" shipment of prisoners to be received. His arrival generated bigger headlines than the opening of the institution, giving birth

Alvin Karpis. (Courtesy of FBI files)

to the endless myth of Alcatraz. The most difficult aspect of Capone's management in Alcatraz was his constant contact with family members who took up residence at a nearby hotel. Through this channel of communication, Capone continued to run his organization in Chicago. He also worked at corrupting officers and enlisting fellow prisoners as personal servants. Influence and privilege were lost at Alcatraz where Capone was assigned menial jobs and treated in accordance with others. In failing health due to syphilis, he was transferred to FCI Terminal Island in January of 1939, and then on to USP Lewisburg, released from there in November of that same year.[4]

Arriving on the second "official" shipment to Alcatraz in September of 1934 was George "Machine Gun" Kelly. Involved first in bootlegging, he was apprehended and sentenced to Leavenworth. At the conclusion of a three-year stay, Kelly emerged from prison in touch with some of America's best bank robbers, and immediately pursued a new line of work. From lucrative bank jobs, he advanced to kidnapping in 1933, holding for ransom a wealthy Oklahoma oil magnate. His capture resulted in the first Lindbergh Law trial and it was a courtroom sensation. Kelly was given a life sentence and returned to USP Leavenworth, within months being transferred to Alcatraz. He was considered a model prisoner by the officers with whom he came in contact, causing some questions regarding his transfer to the more secure institution. After seventeen years on Alcatraz, Kelly suffered a mild heart attack and was returned again to Leavenworth in 1951. Within months of being paroled in 1954, a final attack ended his life at the age of fifty-nine.

While several well-known criminals did time on Alcatraz, most of the 1,576 prisoners incarcerated there were not well-known gangsters, but prisoners who refused to conform to the rules and regulations at other federal institutions, and were considered violent and dangerous, or escape risks. Alcatraz served as the prison system's prison—if a man did not behave at another institution, he could be sent to Alcatraz, where the highly structured, monotonous daily routine was designed to teach an inmate to follow rules and regulations.

At Alcatraz, a prisoner had four givens: food, clothing, shelter, and medical care. Everything else was a privilege that had to be earned. Some privileges a prisoner could earn included working, corresponding with and having visits from family members, access to the prison library, and recreational activities such as painting and music. Once prison officials felt a man no longer posed a threat and could follow the rules (usually after an average of five years on Alcatraz), he could then be transferred back to another federal prison to finish his sentence and be released.

There were, however, prisoners who decided not to wait for a transfer to another prison. Over the twenty-nine years (1934-1963) that the federal prison operated, thirty-six men (including two who tried to escape twice) were involved in fourteen separate escape attempts. Of these, twenty-three were caught, six were shot and killed during their escape, and two drowned. Two of the men who were caught were later executed in the gas chamber at the California State Prison at San Quentin for their role in the death of a correctional officer during the famous May 2-4, 1946, "Battle of Alcatraz" escape attempt.

The first attempted escape from the Rock since it became a Federal prison was by Dutch Bowers, killed trying to climb a wire fence. Ted Cole and Ralph Roe reached the water and disappeared. No trace of them has been found. That was in December, 1937. In May 1938, three convicts broke from a prison shop and reached the roof. Guard Royal Cline and Convict Thomas Limerick were slain.[5]

Whether or not anyone succeeded in escaping from Alcatraz depends on the definition of "successful escape." Is it getting out of the cell-house, reaching the water, making it to land, or reaching land and not getting caught? Officially, no one ever succeeded in escaping from Alcatraz, although to this day there are five prisoners listed as "missing and presumed drowned."

Arthur "Doc" Barker was not in Alcatraz long before he decided he wasn't going to spend the rest of his life there. Among the inmates he befriended was Henri Young, a prisoner who managed to get both the guards and his fellow prisoners mad at him, despite his intentions to the contrary. The twenty-three-year-old Young had compiled a prison record in both Washington and Montana before he was sent to Alcatraz. He and his two confederates robbed a federally-insured bank in Lind, Washington, bagging $406. Though they had taken the precaution of locking the cashier in the bank vault, they failed to maintain their stolen car, and as they drove away, a tire blew out and they were captured.⁶

The crime spree which had ended for Young in a Spokane federal court room had had other victims. Young kept to himself the secret that he'd shot and killed an Everett, Washington, baker during a hold-up. Shortly after his arrival on the Rock in 1935, he became acquainted with some other "new fish" besides Doc Barker—Dale Stamphill, Rufus Franklin, and the man he would kill, Rufus McCain. Prison officers identified Young as a leader in the general strikes of the late 1930s. He certainly agitated on behalf of the strike leadership; in 1936, for example, he left his work station in the kitchen after dumping several boxes of vegetables on the basement floor.

Young was repeatedly in trouble with authorities for petty violations of the prison code and for more serious infractions. He was punished for talking at meals, passing contraband currency, sabotage, fighting, possession of contraband, disobedience, and creating disturbances. Young spent a short time in the Alcatraz dungeons after the 1937 strike (as did many other Alcatraz convicts) before being returned to the D-Block Isolation Unit.

Early on the morning of January 13, 1939, Doc Barker, Henri Young, Rufus McCain, William Martin, and Dale Stamphill tried to beat the Rock's natural walls. The five men defeated the prison's security, first, by sawing their way through the iron slats of their D-Block isolation cells. Then they

Henri Young. (Courtesy of National Archives)

used a small, handmade pressure jack to break the tool-proof bars on the outer windows. Preparing for the break took several weeks and the convicts did most of the work during the morning and evening meals when guards were busy with the general population.

At 4 A.M., an Alcatraz guard checked through his cell block. He discovered that five men had sawed out, and gone over the wall. He telephoned the switchboard and operators roused guards, and called the police on the mainland. The distress siren wailed. Prison searchlights made tiny pools of light in the dense fog and police boats, muffled in the woolly night, crept around the island, and could locate none of the convicts.[7]

When a thick winter fog moved in, the men made their way to the tiny pocket beach beneath the Road Tower, eluding the officer guarding the outside of the cell block. Here they started to build driftwood rafts. The noise of the fog horn drowned out the alert which had been sounded when a guard discovered their escape about half an hour after they left the Cell House.

At 4:47 A.M. two shadows were spotted on the rocky, gate side of the Rock. "Halt!" shouted a guard. The shadows ran, and slipped over the rocks. There were two shots and both came down. At 4:55 A.M. another was found and by 5:35 A.M. the other two had been located, shivering in the bay's icy water.

A prison launch had surprised the convicts. Young and McCain immediately surrendered. Barker and Stamphill ran into the fog. Prison guards on the beach and on the hill above opened fire and both men were hit. Barker died later that day of his wounds. Dale Stamphill, another kidnapper, was shot in both legs and with a major artery severed, was in a critical condition as prison officials continued to profess wonder at the manner in which the men got out of their cells. Stamphill, serving a life sentence, remained in critical condition. Cut and bruised by rocks and possibly suffering other injuries, William Martin, a post office robber, also was taken to the hospital. Rufus McCain, serving ninety-nine years for kidnapping, and Henri Young, national bank robber, surrendered as they saw their comrades fall.[8]

Henri Young later described the escape attempt: "My heart was in my mouth. I felt strange, nervous, like a man in a dream. On the beach we hurriedly threw together a makeshift raft, tying the lumber we had gathered, with the sheets we carried. We stripped and made bundles of our clothes and put them on the raft. We swam out, pushing the raft before us. Thirty yards out, McCain called a halt. He said that the raft was weak, in danger of falling apart. He insisted on going back for more lumber to strengthen our raft."[9]

There was no evidence that they had had any help from the outside and there were no boats found in the vicinity of the island.[10]

On January 14, 1939, FBI Director, J. Edgar Hoover penned the following letter to prison officials at Alcatraz regarding the escape attempt: "Mr. Pieper called at this time to report developments in the investigation of the escape from Alcatraz. . . .I informed Pieper that this is a very bad spot and that some weeks ago he made a report on the situation, stating that he could not see the guard on the gun gallery and that the man on the gun gallery could not see him, and that those particular cells were not visible to the man who is supposed to see them from the gun gallery. . . .

"As for the administration angle of the prison, Mr. Pieper stated that at the top is the warden who stands by himself and will not listen to anyone. Then there is Deputy Warden Miller who has his own clique. Miller seems to be a tough, hard-boiled prison official who can't get along with the men. Miller appears to tell the warden just about what he wants to tell him, and any other information he covers up, he merely answers the questions which the warden puts to him. The men employed in the prison appear to have been making reports on the things which seem wrong to them and every time they make a report to Miller he takes it as a personal criticism instead of something constructive, with the result that the men have gotten to the point where they no longer make any reports. Mr. Pieper stated, of course, that the morale of the prison is pretty bad.

"I advised Pieper that the situation in the Isolation Section almost makes that section a country club. The D-Cell Block is the place where the prisoners want to be. They have the best ventilation there, they have reading material and they are the best cells. I also told Mr. Pieper that the administrative officers at the prison appear to bargain with the prisoners, allowing them to be in whatever cell they desire or next to someone they want to be near, just as long as the prisoners behave. I was told there is absolutely no discipline; that when a guard in the cell block tries to discipline a prisoner he reports to the deputy warden who doesn't back the guard up, with the result that the prisoners, when the guard returns to the cell block, just laugh at him. . . .

"Mr. Pieper stated that he understands they thoroughly searched the kitchen last night but found nothing of value there, but they did find a meter box saw in the print shop and also a putty knife with a saw blade on one end of it. These two articles were concealed in the print shop. . . ."[11]

That same day Hoover sent a very lengthy memorandum to the United States Attorney General which he termed his "Preliminary Report." In his report, he discussed prison count checks made at night, in which there were three—midnight, 3:00 A.M., and 6:00 A.M. About 3:30 A.M., one man was found missing from Cell Block D, which was the Isolation Ward, from where the three men attempted their escape.

San Francisco police were notified at 4:14 A.M. and the police boat D. A. White sped to the island. Coast Guard cutters joined it. Ashore soldiers at the Presidio patrolled the beach in the event the men were carried in by the swiftly swirling tides. Fifteen police radio cars cruised back and forth along the water's edge.[12]

In all, five men were discovered missing, the FBI was alerted, and at 4:10 A.M., Barker and Stamphill were spotted on the shore. William Martin, one of the five men who attempted to escape and was captured, said he was saved from drowning by Deputy Warden Miller. Martin told prison authorities that all five men who attempted to break out had worked on their own individual cells night and day, and when they were finished, the saw blades were thrown into the lavatories on the island.

The heavy bar on the outside of the wall windows, and through which the prisoners escaped could not be sawed, but they pried it loose with a homemade "screw-jack." The saw blades that were kept and carried on the prisoners went through prison inspection glued inside musical instruments believed to be mouth harps. Copper would not show up on the mechanical devices used in the prison so the prisoners turned to making copper knives.

Junior Officer C. Y. Hurst, in charge of the cell house where the prisoners made their escape, later stated: "No unusual noise occurred during this time. I made a regular watch call at 3:30 A.M., and started checking B Block. Approximately one minute after I started this check I heard a slight noise such as a steam radiator or a steam kettle in the kitchen makes. The noise was not unusual and was not repeated so I could make no investigation other than the regular check I was making at the time."[13]

Henry W. Weinhold, lieutenant in charge of the morning watch was making his rounds that morning, and when he arrived at the Dock Tower, he was told he was wanted on the telephone. When Officer Hurst heard his voice on the phone, he reported that a prisoner was out of his cell in D Isolation. Hurst caught up to Weinhold, and when the pair went to D Isolation, they found five prisoners missing. Weinhold telephoned Assistant Warden Miller at home and reported the escape and was told to have the alarms, siren and whistle, sounded.

Clifford E. Ditmer, junior officer, reported: "On hearing the siren sounded early on the morning of January 13, 1939, I came as soon as possible to the Administration Building, met the associate warden and he told me to draw a gun and see if I could locate the prisoners. I was finally sent down to the road near the Road Tower. I was looking along the beach but it was rather foggy when I first got down there and you could not see the water, but the wind came in and the fog drifted out and I saw a couple of white shapes moving to the water, so I hollered to them to stop. I knew they were men by the way they were moving. They did not stop, and I fired five shots into the water, between them and the water. They continued to go towards the water, so I aimed directly at the men and fired nine shots and when I finished firing the last shot they were both down, so I quit firing. There were others firing. I heard firing on both sides of me but it was dark and I do not know who did the shooting."[14]

The prisoners had planned to escape on a crude raft they had constructed after getting down to the shore, as there was an abundance of lumber, not only from driftwood, but lumber being used by civilian workers making improvements to the sewage and water supply problems encountered at Alcatraz.

Barker and Stamphill were sighted first on the shore of the island at a point approximately midway on the Golden Gate side. The Coast Guard launch and the Alcatraz launch turned their lights on that side, and when the two prisoners were spotted, they were ordered to halt. When they did not, they were fired upon with a .45 automatic and Thompson submachine guns.

Barker's left femur was broken by a bullet which entered the thigh about the middle of the outer surface and emerged a little lower on the inner surface of the thigh. Another bullet entered the neck in the back below the right ear, and emerged from the inner angle of the right eye. When Doc Barker was apprehended, he said to one of the guards, "I am crazy as hell—I should never have tried it."

John P. Oberto, chief engineer water equipment at the prison, was awakened by the siren and hurried to the dock tower and started the boat. He and his assistant, Mr. Rebholtz, started around the east side of the island without the search light playing on the beach. Oberto steered the boat while Rebholtz operated the search light and the radio. As they got just a little around the seawall on the east end of the island, they saw something on the beach that looked unusual. Some officers on shore fired a couple shots and two men jumped out with their hands up.

Oberto and Rebholtz continued along the beach while circling the island. When they reached a cove near the incinerator, they saw two men huddled on the beach. Firing a couple warning shots, they noticed that the men lying there were badly wounded. Other guards reached the injured escapees, who were taken ashore and taken away in the bus.

While prison authorities sought solutions of how Doc Barker and his accomplices were able to saw their way out of Alcatraz cells, P.F. Reed, former convict, told the press that despite all precautions, dozens of saws were circulated among the prison colony. Doc Barker was slain in his attempt to escape, but only after he had escaped from the cell block. A coroner's jury met and urged that drastic improvement of the guard system was needed at once.[15]

One of the many myths about Alcatraz is that it was impossible to survive a swim from the island to the mainland because of sharks. In fact, there are no "man-eating" sharks in San Francisco Bay, only small bottom-feeding sharks. The main obstacles were the cold temperature (averaging 50-55 degrees Fahrenheit), the strong currents, and the distance to shore (at least 1-1/4 miles). Prior to the federal institution opening in 1934, a teenage girl swam to the island to prove it was possible.[16]

Doc Barker died of his wounds at 5:45 P.M. His body was brought to San Francisco in the penitentiary cutter more than an hour later and was turned over to Coroner T.B.W. Leland. About 10 people were at the dock when guards carried the body on a blood-stained stretcher from the launch to the ambulance. One of the guards remarked: "Well, he's a lot better off now where he is than where he was."[17]

The body was soon brought to the W. C. Lasswell Mortuary. Services were set for the following week unless Barkers aged father came forth to claim the body. The mortician, who had the government contract for burying unclaimed bodies, said "simple but respectful services" would be held.[18]

Prison grapevine and a portable, electric eye—the old underground method of convict communication and the newest scientific device—were centers of interest as efforts continued to solve the mysteries behind that Friday's attempted break from Alcatraz Island. While investigation continued of the manner in which five convicts obtained saws, cut bars in their individual cells and pried apart bars in a corridor window without being detected, plans were being made for a Coroner's inquest in the death of Arthur "Doc" Barker, killed in the attempt. The inquest was tentatively set for the coming Thursday.

Warden James A. Johnston announced that Dale Stamphill, who was also shot while the five men were building a driftwood raft on the shores of the island, was still in a serious condition. Barker, one of the island's most notorious convicts, was shot almost between the eyes. The bullet smashed against the bridge of his nose, glanced through the right eye and came out near the right ear, an autopsy by Dr. Sherman Leland showed. Another bullet struck his left thigh Coroner T.B.W. Leland said he was awaiting a report from Johnston before making final plans for the inquest.

Stating normalcy at the prison had been resumed, Warden Johnston announced the "magnetic detector" or portable electric eye was being used in investigating the attempted escape. The device was intended to show any bits of hidden metal in clothes or cells. Although the inquiry has not yet revealed anything definite, the warden said it was expected the full story would be developed eventually in a "fragmentary fashion." Possibility that the five might have expected outside aid caused guard cutters to make careful study of all craft in bay yacht harbors. Officials said they were not overlooking a possibility that quick apprehension of the men may have thwarted would be confederates.

Other sources revealed officials were relying considerably on the prison grapevine for news as to how the break was prepared and accomplished. The warden explained that the five men had sawed the lower ends of bars in each of their cells and then pulled the bars apart. They gathered in the cell block corridor shortly before 4 A.M. while a guard found their cells empty and sounded the alarm. They were discovered on a small beach of the island by the searchlights of boats and the prison. Rifles were trained on them and the two who refused to surrender were shot.[19]

The attempted break brought Federal Prisons Director James V. Bennett speeding westward from Washington to make a thorough inquiry. The short-lived flight of the quintet meant they had broken out of five separate cells. Warden James A. Johnston said they had been locked in for the night and the break came about 4 A.M. Bars of the cells were not sawed, prison sources declared, but bars of an outside window had been sawed and pried apart. The cell doors were electrically controlled and the entire cell block, guarded by most intricate devices, had been considered "escape proof."[20]

Bennett left Washington by train and planned to board a plane at Chicago. He said prison officials had "no idea" where they convicts obtained the saw or saws. Every prisoner's clothing, shoes, bedding and cell, he said, was to be subjected to the closest examination.

Its impregnable reputation tottering, Alcatraz Prison, began preparing for Federal Prisons Director James V. Bennett. While guards on "the

Rock" continued a search for the mysterious saws which the convicts used to rip through the "file proof" bars of five cells, the investigation of the escape was expected to be intensified with Bennett on the scene. Bennett, whose offices were in Washington, D.C., had planned a trip to Alcatraz for some time, Warden James A. Johnston said, but decided on the immediate visit because of the escape attempt, at the request of the warden. Johnston said he believed Bennett would make his headquarters on the prison island throughout his stay.[21]

An exhaustive examination was slated for the modern "fool proof" escape preventive devices specially arranged by prison authorities for Alcatraz when it was made the penitentiary for the federal government's most dangerous "cons." The five prisoners, who were found on the shore of the island building a drift wood raft to carry them to possible freedom, had sawed their way from cells electrically controlled and supposedly visited every thirty minutes by guards.

Of greatest concern to authorities was how the convicts obtained the saws and stripped the bars in the five separate cells without detection. Constant searches were carried on by guards, aided by photo-electric eyes, to detect the presence of metal objects on the men or in their cells. All prisoners and cells on the island had been closely examined since Friday without the disclosure of any of the instruments used in the escape attempt.

Coroner Leland said an inquest on Barker's death would probably be held the following Thursday. Subpoenas for the inquest would include one for the slain convict's father, George Barker of Joplin, Missouri. Subpoenas might be issued, it was said, for one or more of the four survivors of the break—Dale Stamphill, who was shot in both legs; Henry Young, Rufus McCain and William Martin.[22]

Alcatraz' highly publicized impregnability was largely a matter of the water around it, as it was revealed in a "debunking" session before Coroner T.B.W. Leland. For the Rock's assistant warden, Edward J. Miller, appearing as sole witness at the inquest into the death of Arthur "Doc" Barker, killed in an escape attempt on January 13th, admitted the water was a "great help."[23]

Doc Barker was buried on January 17th in a Government-owned cemetery plot south of San Francisco while prison officials tried to unravel the mystery of how he had led an attempted break from "impregnable" Alcatraz. Six dry-eyed mourners—the prison chaplain, a prison clerk and four pallbearers from an undertaking parlor were the only persons present at the brief services. All were paid to stand beside the grave as Barker was buried.[24]

Federal Director of Prisons James V. Bennett arrived at Alcatraz Island from Washington, D.C., and immediately began direction of an investigation of Friday's attempted convict break in which the notorious Arthur "Doc" Barker was shot to death. Boarding a motor launch at the water front upon arrival of the ferry boat connecting with his train, Bennett hastened to "the Rock" and immediately went into conference with Warden James A. Johnston and Associate Warden Edward J. Miller.[25]

Bennett, stirred by the shattering of the prison's reputation for impregnability because the five inmates had been able to cut their way out of supposedly escape-proof cells, was determined to find the answer to the mystery. He spent his first night investigating all phases of the attempted break and planned to continue his investigation on the island the following day.

"We have found nothing here today," he said, "to cause us to lose any confidence in the prison personnel or to make us feel that any change should be made in prison policies. No saws have been found and we are not sure that saws were use to sever bars in the attempted escape. Bars could not have been severed by the use of thin strips of metal and abrasives."

He added that satisfaction with present policies did not mean that "we are not going to continue to check up continuously to discover any conditions which might need improvement or correction. It does not mean that we are not going to continue to perfect apparatus to prevent escapes. "The Department of Justice has never called Alcatraz 'escape proof,' although I believe thus far it has been virtually escape proof."

Bennett planned to question the four survivors of the attempted break—Dale Stamphill, reported improving in the prison hospital from two bullet wounds; Rufus McCain, bank robber and kidnapper; Henri Young, bank robber; and William Martin, post office robber. During previous questioning of these men by prison officials they were said to have remained secretive.

Any doubt that saws were used to cut the bars of the five Alcatraz convicts who attempted a break for freedom was set at rest last night following a second day of on-the-scene investigation led by Director Bennett. He had previously entertained the possibility that other instruments had been employed—such as banjo string and valve grinding compound, piano wire or watch springs, or any thin strips of metal and abrasives.[26]

Bennett, who had been scheduled to return the previous night to Washington, D.C., decided to remain at least another day. Much of his time the preceding day was spent in questioning prisoners in an effort to learn how wide-spread was advance information regarding the escape plot. He was endeavoring also to learn how the escape saws were obtained and to find others believed hidden in the prison. The saws used by the plotters were believed to have been cast into the bay when the fleeing men reached the island shore.[27]

Reiterating his personal inquiry had disclosed no reason for anything approaching a "shakeup," Bennett announced that if further investigation by himself and Warden James A. Johnston indicated a need for change in the methods of handling prisoners or supervision, these changes would be made. The prison, he mentioned, housed the country's most cunning and nerviest escape artists who had plenty of time to think up ways of getting out. "And when they go through our first line of defenses, we have to rebuild them," he said. "That is what we are doing."

Federal Prison Director James V. Bennett that night completed his immediate investigation of the escape attempt by five Alcatraz island penitentiary prisoners and left to look over conditions at Terminal Island, the new federal prison off San Pedro. He planned to proceed to Washington, D.C. where he would enlist the services of engineers in an effort to make Alcatraz and Terminal islands as more nearly escape proof as science could possibly make them.

In forcing their way from their cells, the Alcatraz desperadoes used some sort of powerful jack, probably prison made, Bennett told reporters. This jack wrenched and tore the bars apart. It was believed also to have been used in breaking the bars on a first floor cell block corridor, through which the prisoners dropped eight feet to another floor and made their way to the island beach. No trace of the hack saws, which may also have been used, had been found.

The so-called electric eye system, which detected metal hidden in clothing, was found to work only about sixty per cent of the time. But three guards, two in gun galleries and one on the floor were on duty in the cell block when Barker and four companions made their break. "Possibly" they might have been asleep, but they definitely "were not alert."

The flat, soft-iron bars of the five adjoining cells could be cut with a two-inch length of hacksaw blade. The sawing had been done during a "long period of time" and not discovered, despite examinations by guards experienced in the ways of escape tries. The "foolproof" steel bars of the outside windows were forced with something heavier than a crowbar, despite the Rock's reported eternal vigilance.

When the five convicts made their way from the cellblock, there wasn't a searchlight on the island strong enough to pierce the fog. But two guards patrolled the shoreline, passing any given point about once every half hour.

Miller's reputation-blasting testimony brought the following verdict from the jury: "We, the jury, find that the said Arthur R. Barker met his death attempting to escape from Alcatraz Prison from gunshot wounds inflicted by guards unknown. From the evidence at hand, we the jury, believe this escape was made possible by the failure of the system for guarding prisoners now in use at Alcatraz Prison, and we recommend a drastic improvement by those in authority.

"Further, that a more efficient system be adopted for illumination of shore and waters immediately surrounding the prison; and that the citizens of San Francisco unite in an effort to have a more suitable location chosen for imprisonment of the type of desperadoes at present housed at Alcatraz."[28]

Miller had recounted how a guard had found one cell vacant and turned in the alarm. Three of the convicts surrendered at the water's edge. Barker and Dale Stamphill refused to halt and were shot, Barker fatally. Questioned by Leland on whether the guards were asleep, Miller admitted it was "possible," but said they were required to report by telephone every half hour. He said, in his opinion, the prison was "well-manned."

Miller testified no saws had been found, no trace of filings or any material which might have been used to smear the sawed bars to conceal the progress of work on the iron. Neither was the instrument used to force the "tool-proof" outside bars found. Coroner Leland's report showed that except for bullet wounds in the head and leg, Barker was "well nourished and well developed."

United States Attorney Frank J. Hennessy asked that the record of Barker, a pal of Alvin Karpis, Midwest desperado and participant in the $200,000 Bremer kidnapping, be introduced into evidence. On the Barker record of transfer in 1935 from Leavenworth to Alcatraz was this notation: "To break up prison gangs."

In closing his case, Leland said of Alcatraz: "We don't like it and we don't want it. The citizens of San Francisco resent Alcatraz, and criminals of that type should be placed elsewhere. However, as long as it is here, and not a beautiful park as I'd like to have it, we can but hope it will be open for inspection by the public."[29]

Hennessy said he did not consider the prison a "blot on San Francisco," and added proximity to a big city is better for a prison because law enforcement agencies are well organized in such areas.

Two years later, Henri Young talked of the day on which Rufus McCain, kidnapper and robber, was fatally stabbed in the tailor shop at Alcatraz Prison. For that slaying, Henri Young was charged with murder and was being tried before Federal Judge Roche . . . Young was asked to tell about the years preceding the murder of McCain . . . A plan by eight men to escape was hatched. Among the eight were McCain and Young.

"McCain held a great deal of animosity toward me," said Young. "He wanted to use the wives of the guards as shields in the break, but I wouldn't do it. I obstructed the plan. I told McCain freedom wasn't everything, but he wouldn't listen." . . . Five men broke out of their cells on January 13, 1939. They were on the beach. They got separated. "We were supposed to be one for all and all for one," said Young. "Like the three musketeers," added Hennessy.

"On the beach McCain said, 'They're going to kill us. Let's run to the houses. They won't shoot us there.' Then the boat came around, and the flashlight struck us. Officers began shooting. He told McCain and me to come to him. He had two pistols. McCain begged him not to shoot him. They took us back to our cells." . . .[30]

On March 21, 1963, USP Alcatraz closed after twenty-nine years of operation because the institution was too expensive to continue operating. An estimated $3-5 million was needed just for restoration and maintenance work to keep the prison open. That figure did not include daily operating costs. Alcatraz was nearly three times more expensive to operate than any other federal prison. The major expense was caused by the physical isolation of the island—the exact reason islands have been used as prisons throughout history. This isolation meant that everything—food, supplies, water, and fuel had to be brought to Alcatraz by boat. For example, the island had no source of fresh water, so nearly one million gallons of water had to be barged to the island each week. The federal government found that it was more cost-effective to build a new institution than to keep Alcatraz open.[31]

Alvin Karpis spent more time in Alcatraz, (twenty-six years), than any other prisoner. He arrived within a few months of its opening and stayed until a few months before it closed, when he was transferred to another federal prison, McNeil Island, in the fall of 1962. Karpis himself reported that he lived in fear during his first days at Alcatraz, so firmly had it been impressed on him by the guards that one stepped out of line at the risk of one's life. He reported later (some say that it never happened like he said it did) that, when he arrived, guards lined the catwalks outside of Building 64 and their families gawked at him from the apartment windows. As he boarded a truck, one little boy shouted "Daddy kill Public Enemy Number One and collect the reward!"

Two prisoners, including his former partner Volney Davis and a white slaver and corrupt police officer named Anderson, showed their toughness to the other prisoners by beating him up. Unlike his former partner Arthur "Doc" Barker, Karpis was a survivor. He would outlive Hoover and see freedom one day.

He quickly learned that work was a privilege. Those who did not work had to spend the entire day, except for meal times, in their cells. They could not earn money to buy magazines, bridge tutors, musical instruments, art supplies, and other pleasures. They could not accrue extra "good time" days which would be deducted from their sentence.

When Karpis first arrived, he found that the industries were the only place the prisoners were allowed to talk to each other. Though they were not supposed to discuss anything other than their jobs, civilian shop foremen often looked the other way as the men quietly socialized.

Each day, the workers lined up in the walled recreation yard next to the Cell House. Queue by queue, they walked down the steep flight of stairs to the industries. The long, white New Industries Building sat atop a landfill. Alcatraz used to have a dent here called Pirate's Cove which the Army found inconvenient and, so, it was buried under tons of gravel quarried off the Rock's summit.

The Bureau of Prisons built the New Industries in the 1940s after several escape attempts from the older Model Industries Building, the square building sitting on the island's westernmost tip. Guards posted in watch towers could not see what was happening on the ocean face of the Model Industries Building. The first prisoners to attempt to escape here were Theodore Cole and Ralph Roe. These two men sawed through the bars in a workroom, climbed out, and ran down to the Bay. They got in the water—some say carrying five gallon cans for flotation—and disappeared into the fog. Though San Francisco newspapers and national tabloids reported sightings of the pair for years, a 1967 FBI report concluded that the men had drowned in the undertow and were dragged out to sea by the tide.

The Model Industries Building was also the scene of the Rock's most celebrated murder. Rufus McCain was working in the tailor shop in

"Ma"—The Life and Times of "Ma" Barker and Her Boys

December 1940 when he was stabbed by Henri Young, his former confederate in the 1939 escape attempt at Barker Beach. Young used a sharpened planer knife which he claimed he had found hidden at his station in the furniture or "Model" shop. A sensational trial followed.[32]

In the early years at Alcatraz, Karpis' cell mates were criminals such as Al Capone, Doc Barker, and "Machine-Gun" Kelly. At McNeil Island, he spent another seven years (total of thirty-three years in prison), where a young inmate named Charles Manson persuaded the old gangster to teach him how to play guitar.[33]

Karpis later wrote about Manson in his memoirs, *On the Rock: Twenty-five Years at Alcatraz*: "This kid approaches me to request music lessons. He wants to learn guitar and become a music star. 'Little Charlie' is so lazy and shiftless, I doubt if he'll put the time required to learn. The youngster has been in institutions all of his life—first orphanages, then reformatories, and finally federal prison. His mother, a prostitute, was never around to look after him. I decide it's time someone did something for him, and to my surprise, he learns quickly. He has a pleasant voice and a pleasing personality, although he's unusually meek and mild for a convict. He never has a harsh word to say and is never involved in even an argument."

After Manson had actually become somewhat proficient on the guitar, he asked Karpis for help in getting a job playing in Las Vegas as Karpis had contacts with nightclub and casino owners there. Manson even told him he would be bigger than the Beatles, but in the end Karpis decided to leave Manson on his own regarding his music career. Manson was moved to a Los Angeles facility in 1967, which proved to be one of the most ominous prison transfers ever. Later Karpis added "The history of crime in the United States might have been considerably altered if 'Little Charlie' had been given the opportunity to find fame and fortune in the music industry. He later became the infamous Charles Manson."

But back on "the Rock" before he was transferred to McNeil Island, Karpis spent his time mostly in the prison bakery—when he wasn't fighting with other inmates, participating in strikes, or creating disturbances. By all accounts, he was an excellent baker (he'd worked in bakeries a bit before he opted for crime as a career).³⁴ Guards and prisoners said he made great bread. Karpis often volunteered to work extra time on holidays, preparing the meals. He also often enjoyed the beer which other kitchen crew convicts prepared using the yeast he provided.

When Karpis arrived at Alcatraz in August 1936, a few days before his twenty-eighth birthday, he caught his first glimpse of Al Capone and was shocked by the changes time and disease had made. Number 85 seemed to Karpis, "a pale, shrunken figure" although "calm and controlled." Because of Capone's condition, he did not feel that he was equipped well enough to survive the drudgery of Alcatraz.³⁵

The very first Sunday that Karpis appeared in the recreation yard an inmate approached him and whispered, "My name is Frank Del Bono. Al would like to talk to you. He knows a lot of people you know. He'd like to talk with you if it won't put any heat on you."³⁶

Karpis, however, did not commit immediately as he wanted to find out first how the other prisoners regarded Capone. Everything he heard about Capone was good and the only ones that hated him, according to Karpis, were "mostly scum, white trash" He told Del Bono he would talk to Al anytime.

The rule of silence between prisoners had been relaxed a bit but conversation nonetheless was a hard won rarity. During their initial meeting in the recreation yard, their backs against the cell-house wall, Capone asked him if he needed any money. Karpis replied that he was fine and everyone was taken care of. Capone noticed that Karpis played a fair guitar and talked him into joining the prison band.

They talked the next two Sundays with their heads draped over a music stand, pretending they were discussing a score. Karpis was the first of the new arrivals to keep Capone posted on underworld activities outside the prison. While another prisoner served as lookout, Capone and Karpis one day had a lengthy conversation in the shower room.³⁷

Capone immediately voiced his concern over the welfare of his successor, Frank Nitti. Capone knew that Nitti had been shot during a violent altercation with the law and wanted to know why a detective had shot and wounded him. Karpis told him he had seen Nitti several months after the shooting in Benton Harbor, Michigan, where many of Capone's men had their summer cottages. Karpis had been staying at the house of the former mayor of Cicero, and when he spoke with Nitti on the beach, he learned the detective was named Walter Lang. Despite Nitti taking the bullet in his neck, he seemed fully recovered. Nitti also confided in Karpis that the lawmen had shot him over some kind of personal grudge going back many years.

Capone changed the subject and asked Karpis if he knew what the reason was behind the killing of Willie "Three-Fingers" White, who had once been in the Capone organization. "Whenever someone in your outfit is killed," related Karpis, "you guys always claim he was caught talking to the FBI. Sure enough!" He went on to say that White had been seen talking with Melvin Purvis, head of the FBI's Chicago office. Although Karpis thought he knew who had killed White, he kept it to himself and the clandestine conference ended before the guards discovered it.

Alvin Karpis got along with most everyone at Alcatraz, but Fformer Public Enemy Number One was not, however, a friend to the guards. Karpis joined other prisoners during the 1937 General Strike and was accused, in 1953, of "propositioning an officer" and acting as a leader in a rebellion against Warden E.B. Swope.

Bad feelings between Swope and Karpis began three years earlier when the state of Missouri, in response to a routine inquiry by the Alcatraz administrative staff, began proceedings to charge Karpis with the 1933 murder of a West Plains sheriff. Karpis, who insisted that Freddie Barker and Donald Phoenix had committed the crime, evaded the detainer by forcing the prosecution to concede that it had no eyewitness to the crime. The court dismissed the charge against him for good. The convict suspected that Swope had illegally solicited the detainer and tried to move to get the Warden indicted. Swope's notorious abrasiveness did not help the situation, but there is no reason to suspect that he was out to get Karpis at the time. For his part, the warden erroneously believed that Karpis fomented the strikes against him and had him placed in solitary.

Alcatraz, "Old Creepy" insisted, had not reformed him. He did, eventually, win his freedom, but from McNeil Island Penitentiary where the

E.B. Swope's Conduct Report at the Penitentiary, 1937-1953

"4-23-1937: FIGHTING WITH #271 - Davis. This inmate was fighting with Davis, near the rear gate at 2:15 P.M., this date. Report #2008. [undeciph.] Little. Action: To be placed in solitary confinement on restricted diet and to forfeit all privileges until further orders. E.J. Miller, Deputy Warden.

4-27-1937: Removed from solitary confinement to regular cell and work assignment, all privileges restored, effective this date. E.J. Miller, Deputy Warden.

6-8-1937: FIGHTING WITH ANDERSON-#340, IN LAUNDRY. This inmate had a fight with inmate Anderson; I had to use force to separate them. Report #580 I.B. Faulk. Action: To be placed in solitary confinement on restricted diet and to be reduced to third grade. Would not say what the fighting was about, just a fight, agitating other men to fight. E.J. Miller, Deputy Warden.

6-14-1937: Removed from solitary confinement to regular cell and continued in 3rd grade. E.J. Miller, Deputy Warden.

9-4-1937: RETURNED TO FIRST GRADE, EFFECTIVE THIS DATE. E.J. Miller, Deputy Warden.

9-23-1937: PARTICIPATING IN STRIKE AND REFUSING TO WORK. This man claims that he is not on strike and is willing to work at his own assignment, not on the assignment of an inmate on strike. Report #758, E.J. Miller, Deputy Warden. Action: To be placed in isolation on restricted diet and to forfeit all privileges until further orders. (This man was warned but refused to return to work) E.J. Miller, Deputy Warden.

9-30-1937: Upon his promise to abide by all regulations in the future this man was removed to regular cell and work assignment with continued loss of all privileges and with understanding that no industrial good time would be granted in his case, for the month of September, 1937. E.J. Miller, Deputy Warden.

10-10-1937: ALL PRIVILEGES ARE RESTORED, EFFECTIVE THIS DATE. E.J. Miller, Deputy Warden.

3-28-1938: CONTRABAND IN CELL. When searching this man's cell, found a small knife hid in his mattress. This knife appeared to be an old paring knife. Report #571, E.J. Miller, Associate Warden. Action: Placed in solitary confinement on restricted diet and to forfeit all privileges until further orders.

Said that the knife did not belong to him and that he was framed. E.J. Miller, Deputy Warden.

4-2-1938: Removed to regular cell and work assignment, with continued loss of all privileges until further orders. E.J. Miller, Associate Warden.

4-9-1938: Mail privileges only restored, effective this date. E.J. Miller, Associate Warden.

5-8-1938: ALL PRIVILEGES [indeciph.], EFFECTIVE THIS DATE. E.J. Miller, Associate Warden.

5-20-1938: ALL PRIVILEGES ARE RESTORED, EFFECTIVE THIS DATE. E.J. Miller, Associate.

4-26-1939: FIGHTING WITH #137 BATES. About 8:30 A.M. this inmate was turned out of his cell to work along with inmate #137-Bates. When they got to the west end of "C" cell block, they started to fight. Officer Daly and myself separated them; neither one seemed to be the aggressor. Report #2660, O.F. Boyd, JR. OFFICER. Action: Prisoner stated that he had not been able to get along with Bates for sometime and had wanted to get out of the Library. He said he was the aggressor in the fight. TO BE PLACED IN SOLITARY CONFINEMENT ON RESTRICTED DIET AND TO FORFEIT ALL PRIVILEGES UNTIL FURTHER ORDERS. E.C. Schilder, Associate Warden.

4-29-1939: Removed from solitary to regular cell and work assignment with continued loss of all privileges until further orders. E.J. Millere, Associate Warden.

5-7-1939: MAIL & SHOW PRIVILEGES RESTORED THIS DATE. E.J. Miller, Associate.

5-15-1939: ALL PRIVILEGES RESTORED, EFFECTIVE THIS DATE.

8-21-1939: [indeciph.] IN MESS-HALL AND INSOLENCE TO OFFICER. This man talked all during Sunday evening meal. Then he [indeciph.] I told him he must discontinue talking, he said "Go fuck yourself" and then laughed as he left the mess-hall. Report [indeciph], Jr. Officer. REPORT: Said he did not use profane talk to officer but said "you bet" admitted he talked in dining room and did laugh as he left the mess-hall. FORFEIT ALL PRIVILEGES UNTIL FURTHER ORDERS. E.J. Miller, Associate Warden.

[?] 1939: REFUSING TO WORK. This man refused to work, choosing instead to strike with eight other men. Report #[indeciph.] by [indeciph.] Jr. Officer. ACTION:- Said if other men refused to work, he was not going to work. To be placed in solitary confinement on restricted diet and to forfeit all privileges until further orders. E.J. Miller, Associate Warden.

9-[?]-1939: Removed to regular cell and work assignment with the continued loss of all privileges. E.J. Miller, Associate Warden.

9-15-1939: [indeciph.]

1-29-1942: This afternoon I noticed that this inmate appeared to be in somewhat of a stupor and was unsteady on his feet. Although I did not actually see him drinking, there is no doubt in my mind that he was under the influence of some concoction of an inebrious nature. Report by S.P. Ozaklewitz, Sr. Officer. ACTION: Stated he did not have anything to drink and that he did not act funny that he knew of. Forfeit 30 days of privileges; sentence suspended on future behavior. E.J. Miller, Associate Warden.

3-29-1942: While working in the kitchen this P.M., this man was acting in an unnatural condition, apparently under influence of some home-made concoction. Report by C.B. Stewart, Jr. Officer. ACTION: This man seemed to be under influence of some kind of brew. Admitted that he had made and drank some kind of mixture but stated he was not under the weather or even drunk. Would not say what he had made the mixture out of—just talked wildly. Placed in solitary, restricted diet; examined by Dr. Patterson and found to have drank some kind of brew, but alright to be disciplined.

4-2-1942: Removed to regular cell and work assignment.

4-30-1942: REFUSED TO WORK IN THE LAUNDRY AS ASSIGNED. Mat Shop closed due to lack of material. When assigned to work in the laundry this man refused. Report by Captain Weinhold. ACTION: Would make no excuses and simply stated he was not going to work in the laundry. Placed in solitary confinement, restricted diet; case recommended for good time trial board. E.J. Miller, Associate Warden.

[indeciph]: [indeciph.].

[indeciph]: Removed from Solitary to regular cell [indeciph.].

[indeciph]: All privileges restored this date. [indeciph.] Assoc.Warden.

3-18[?]-1952: REFUSAL TO RETURN TO CULINARY ASSIGNMENT. Culinary inmates were removed from the kitchen on afternoon of March [?] during reorganization of this unit. All inmates assigned there were interviewed subsequently, to learn if they would return to duty under new regulations, etc. Karpis stated he believes we are punishing inmates in culinary unit because of a few screw balls that mess up the details. He believes that cooks, dismachine workers and bakers should be provided with a bath before they return to cellhouse in the evening. He has enough of culinary unit and would not go back to work under the rules read to him. Karpawicz is undoubtedly one of the ring leaders in opposition to orderly [indeciph.] and regulations in operating the culinary unit. N.F. Stucker, Assoc. W. ACTION: PLACED IN T.U. UNTIL FURTHER ORDERS FOR REFUSAL TO WORK IN CULINARY UNIT. REMOVED FROM MERITORIOUS COMPENSATION AS OF Mar. 1, 1952. WARDEN, Approved. N.F. Stucker, Associate W. Classification Comm recommend above action.

    3-18-1952: to T.U.

    4-15-1952: MUTINOUS PARTICIPATION IN GROUP RESISTANCE TO DULY CONSTITUTED AUTHORITY. This inmate refused to return to his assigned job in the Culinary Unit. He insists on participating in a prolonged group resistance to established policy for operation of the Culinary Unit. P.H. Bergen, Captain. ACTION: CONTINUE IN "OPEN FRONT" S.T.U. STATUS ON REST. DIET AND LOSSOF ALL PRIVILEGES UNTIL SUCH TIME HE DECIDES TO RETURN TO WORK. REFERRED FOR GOOD TIME TRIAL, HOWEVER IS SERVING A LIFE SENTENCE WITH NO STAT. GOOD TIME.

    5-1-1952: 4-[?]-52 off restrictions.

    5-18-1953: PROPOSITIONING AN OFFICER. On Sunday 5-17-53, while I was in west end of cell house, Karpawicz-325 stopped on way to recreation yard and asked if he could talk to me. He stated that he had talked it over with some of the "old timers" and was acting as spokesman for them. He said they were interested in seeing that the men returned to work in the shops. He also stated that some of the inmates might lose some good time if the work stoppage continued. He felt sure that if some assurance was given that no good time would be taken and as he put it, "nobody holding the bag." and if the inmates in the Treatment Unit were returned to the regular population, the inmates would go back to work in the shops. E. Rychner, Acting Captain. TO S.T.U., CLOSED FRONT CELL, BULL, DIST. Agitator, active in organizing resistance, etc. L. Delmore Assoc.[38]

warden, who Karpis called his friend, put the aging robber in charge of a special house outside the prison walls for young offenders. Paul Madigan, third warden of Alcatraz and warden of McNeil Island during the 1960s, got the credit for making an honest man of Karpis. When the last surviving member of the Barker Gang applied for parole, many former guards and citizens with contacts in the prison, wrote letters urging his release.

On December 10, 1948, the Alcatraz Classification Committee had this to say of Public Enemy Number One: "During the time this inmate has been at Alcatraz, he has been assigned to the Culinary Department for approximately eight years, three years and eight months of which he served as a baker, and two years as a cook. He is efficient in these trades; and while assigned as kitchen clerk, he helps the bakers and cooks when the necessity arises. In his efforts to improve himself, he has become proficient as a clerk by studying and practicing at the job while assigned to the print shop. At present he is keeping abreast of late developments in cooking and baking by studying these trades in his cell at night and consulting with cooks, bakers and stewards on the job, and by practicing when he can, or when cooks or bakers need assistance on their jobs.

"He is a leader among the inmates and has their respect. He intends to follow baking after release and will no doubt be put in a key position in that trade. His conduct is very good, his last report for misconduct being on 3/31/45 for becoming intoxicated. He, on numerous occasions, has stayed in the kitchen during rest periods to work at tasks he felt he could see through to a satisfactory conclusion by applying extra efforts, and gets much satisfaction from doing so. This happened, for instance, again on Thanksgiving day when he passed up a recreation period to help out on the table set-up and in helping dish up food in the kitchen. This also happens on each weekend when he makes ice cream for Sunday or helps the bakers with their extra products for Sunday. He also cheerfully helps a porter mop the floor, a pot-washer wash pots, or the garbage man dispose of the garbage. This last happens daily.

"Recently a baker who was ill received two days of idle status, and subject voluntarily worked in his place. Typical of the resourcefulness generally displayed by subject, he suggested cupcakes be changed to layer cake, which could better be made in the short period before meal time, caused by the illness of the regular baker. He works with the least supervision as he knows what to do and proceeds in a capable manner. His work can be depended on to be first-class. Subject takes excellent care of the equipment in the Culinary Department. Because of his understanding of the tasks to be performed, he is often called upon to instruct other inmates; and when giving these instructions, he is careful to see that the man learning the job understands the correct usage of the machines employed. For instance, when showing another inmate how to mix a small batch of dough on the cake mixer, he is careful to see that the proper gear is used to avoid strain on the machine.

"It recently came to the attention of the officials of the institution that because of some dissatisfaction which had arisen in the Culinary Department, an attempt was made at sabotaging the fruit cake prepared for the Christmas holidays, and that this attempt was foiled solely by the conscientiousness of this inmate. Exact details of this incident are difficult to elicit inasmuch as if it should be generally known among the inmate body as to the part played by subject in this incident, it would jeopardize subject's welfare at this institution, perhaps moreso than at any other Institution in the Service. However, it is felt that he should be commended for this act, and it is mentioned for whatever value the Committee feels it merits."[39]

The Committee, however, decided not to recommend Karpis for meritorious good time "in view of the fact that he is serving a life sentence and such recommendation would be only an idle gesture as good time does not shorten a life sentence."

George E. Barker died in April 1941 at age seventy-sixe, in Joplin, Missouri. He too, was buried at Maybelle (Welch) Cemetery, near Welch, Oklahoma.[40]

Echoes of the many gun battles fought by notorious members of the Barker Gang resounded in Tulsa on March 22, 1949, when news was received from Denver that Lloyd Barker, the last of the Oklahoma outlaw gang, had been killed there by a shotgun blast. Denver police charged Lloyd's death to his wife Jean, thirty-seven, who cut him down as he attempted to unlock the door of their home. She told officers she feared he would kill her and her children. She pleaded innocent by reason of insanity.[41]

The Denver FBI Bureau received the following letter from national headquarters on April 15, 1949: "Newspaper dispatches reflect that Lloyd Barker, last survivor of the Barker boys, was killed by his wife on March 18, 1949, in Denver. For record purposes, it is requested that you conduct appropriate inquiry to determine the outcome of charges against Mrs. [Jennie] Barker and also to secure the facts concerning Barker's life in Denver subsequent to his release from prison. This information should be furnished the Bureau by letter marked 'Research.' Any inquiries should be made in such a manner as not to elicit press inquiries, and should be casually secured through local authorities."[42]

The SAC Director at Denver wrote J. Edgar Hoover back on May 12, 1949:

"Reference is made to Bureau letter dated April 15, 1949, requesting that appropriate inquiry be conducted to determine the outcome of charges against Mrs. Barker for killing her husband Lloyd Barker. It is also requested that the facts concerning Barker's life in Denver subsequent to his release from prison be secured. The following information was obtained by SA James W. Lail from Sheriff Homer Mayberry and Deputy District Attorney General George Fischer at Brighton, Colorado:

"Jennie Barker shot and killed her husband Lloyd "Red" Barker at their home, 3426 West 73rd Avenue, Westminster, Colorado, on March 18, 1949. She was arrested the same date and placed in the Adams County Jail in Brighton, Colorado, where she readily confessed to the shooting, claiming she was afraid of him, he having threatened her life on numerous occasions. On March 21, 1949, she was tried by Jury in the District Court at Brighton and entered a plea of 'not guilty by reason of insanity at the time and since.' Upon the testimony of two competent doctors she was sentenced to life in the Colorado State Insane Asylum at Pueblo, Colorado, where she was confined on April 9, 1949.

"The only background information concerning Barker as known to Mayberry and Fischer is that he has been employed for several years at the

Denargo Grill at the Denargo Market, Denver, and was, at the time of his death the assistant manager of the Grill. He has reportedly been living with Jennie as a common law wife for approximately seven or eight years, having two children by her. He was legally married to her at Brighton, Colorado, in February 1949. Jennie had two children by a previous marriage.

"Jennie is described as born February 20, 1912, at New York City, U. S., five feet two inches, ninty-two pounds, blue eyes, brown hair, fair complexion. No further inquiries have been made in this matter in view of the Bureau instructions that the inquiries should be made through local authorities and in such a manner as not to elicit press inquiries. If the Bureau should desire that additional information regarding Barker's life be obtained this information could probably be secured through local newspaper contacts.

"Deputy District Attorney George Fischer, Brighton, Colorado, also advised that Jennie Barker's lawyer, L.E.F. Talkington, Denver, Colorado, told him he has been well acquainted with Lloyd Baker for many years. Talkington is the individual who originally advised the Adams County authorities in Brighton that Lloyd "Red" Barker was one of the notorious 'Barker Boys' and son of 'Ma' Barker. Mr. Talkington is supposedly aware of the activities of Barker since his release from prison. He is not being contacted at this time, however, in view of the Bureau investigations contained in the reference letter."[43]

Lloyd's brothers had all died before him: Herman in the 1920; Fred, who with his mother had been killed in the 1935 Florida gun battle; and Arthur or "Doc," who was slain by a prison guard while trying to escape from Alcatraz in 1939. "That's the finish of the Barker Gang," a law officer told the press. "Never again will a police department have to face their bullets."[44]

In June 1962, Alvin Karpis was considered for parole after he filed a new application for a deportation [to Canada] parole, but was turned down. One year earlier, he had filed a similar application, which was also considered and rejected by the Federal Parole Board.[45]

Alvin Karpis was released from prison in 1969 and, because he had never been given official immigrant status in the USA, he was deported to the country of his birth, Canada. In Canada he wrote the first book about his criminal career, *Public Enemy Number One: The Alvin Karpis Story*, with a Montreal reporter, Bill Trent. The book was published in 1971.

Within a few years, Alvin Karpis retired to an apartment at Torremolinus, Spain where the weather was pleasant year round and he could live frugally on his limited budget. He passed away there in 1979.[46] The *Chicago Sun-Times* reported:

"Gangster Alvin Karpis apparently died of natural causes police said, contradicting earlier reports that he had committed suicide by taking an overdose of sleeping pills. Karpis, triggerman for the notorious Ma Barker Gang that terrorized the Midwest with blazing machine guns in the 1930s was found dead Tuesday at his home on Spain's Coastal Del Sol. He was seventy-one."[47]

In spite of all they accomplished in their criminal endeavors, the public enemies, according to the FBI, were hardly geniuses. For example, the Karpis-Barker Gang once seized a hand truck, "stacked with bulging sacks" and heavily guarded, outside the Federal Reserve Building in Chicago. The gang got away—only to discover they had stolen not money but bags of mail. In contrast, knocking off a bank appeared to be child's play. The "public enemies" raced about the country, stealing wads of cash from banks, renting apartments, buying cars, picking up women and having a good time between jobs. They were protected by a network of supporters and hangers-on (and sometimes corrupt officials). Their insatiable greed—and their inability to stop robbing and killing—led to their own destruction.[48]

Perhaps St. Paul Reporter Nate Bomberg's explanation of why the gangster era ended abruptly is as good as any: "It was the kidnappings, not the Dunlop killing that brought everything to a head in the cleanup of St. Paul. After William Hamm and Edward Bremer were kidnapped the other fat boys started to get scared. Pressure was put on Washington. When the fat and rich get hurt, that's when you get action out of public officials."[49]

Minnesota Poet Roger Brezina apparently agreed with Bomberg's explanation when he penned his poem:

"Ma"—The Life and Times of "Ma" Barker and Her Boys

"Ma Barker Comes of Age"

Simplistic Ozark miners earned
Their livelihood as minimal,
And therein grew poor, little Kate
Whose hero was a criminal.

Her family scratched for vegetables
Around their shack and hunted game.
God-fearing till she married, she
Avowed to make herself a name.

Her husband, George D. Barker, worked
The mines to dig out zinc and lead,
But little did he know, his sons
Would use the lead to shoot men dead.

Ma ruled her roost with iron fists
And foremost in the things she taught
Of pious ways and thievery:
The greatest wrong was getting caught.

They were the Barker-Karpis Gang
And ruthless public enemies—
Marauders, robbers, murderers—
But cared for Ma most tenderly.

Thus ends the story of the "Bloody Barkers"—one of the most notorious gangs in American history—and with them, an era when machine guns talked faster than law and order.

"Ma"—The Life and Times of "Ma" Barker and Her Boys

Notes

[1] National Park Service.
[2] Federal Bureau of Prisons, United States Department of Justice Records.
[3] Laurence Bergreen, *Capone The Man and the Era*, New York, Simon & Schuster, 1994, pp. 540-541.
[4] Alcatraz Island, U. S. Penitentiary, National Park Records.
[5] *San Francisco Chronicle*, January 14, 1939.
[6] Alcatraz History—Prisoner Henri Young, National Archives, San Bruno, California.
[7] *San Francisco Chronicle*, January 15, 1939.
[8] *San Francisco Chronicle*, January 14, 1939; *Fairbury Journal*, January 19, 1939.
[9] Alcatraz History—Prisoner Henri Young, National Archives, San Bruno, California.
[10] FBI Files #76-4175, Arthur Barker, Escaped Federal Prisoner (Death of).
[11] Ibid.
[12] *San Francisco Chronicle*, January 14, 1939.
[13] FBI Files #76-4175, Arthur Barker, Escaped Federal Prisoner (Death of).
[14] Ibid.
[15] *Chicago Herald & Examiner*, January 31, 1939; *San Francisco Chronicle* January 18, 1939; Washington Star, January 25, 1939.
[16] Federal Bureau of Prisons, United States Department of Justice Records.
[17] *San Francisco Chronicle*, January 14, 1939.
[18] *San Francisco News*, January 14, 1939.
[19] *San Francisco Chronicle*, January 15, 1939.
[20] *San Francisco Chronicle*, January 14, 1939.
[21] *San Francisco Chronicle*, January 15, 1939 and January 16, 1939.
[22] *San Francisco Chronicle*, January 18, 1939.
[23] *San Francisco Chronicle*, January 20, 1939.
[24] *Chicago Daily News*, January 18, 1939.
[25] *San Francisco Chronicle*, January 17, 1939.
[26] *San Francisco Chronicle*, January 18, 1939.
[27] *San Francisco Chronicle*, January 19, 1939.
[28] *San Francisco Chronicle*, January 25, 1939.
[29] Ibid.
[30] *San Francisco Chronicle*, April 29, 1941
[31] Federal Bureau of Prisons, United States Department of Justice Records.
[32] Alcatraz History—Prisoner Henri Young, National Archives, San Bruno, California.
[33] Robert Livesey, "Information About Alvin Karpis," Little Red Schoolhouse, Inc., website. Livesey co-authored the book *On the Rock: Twenty-Five Years in*

Alcatraz with Alvin Karpis.
[34] Alcatraz History—Prisoner: Alvin "Creepy" Karpis (#325-AZ).
[35] Laurence Bergreen, *Capone The Man and the Era*, New York, Simon & Schuster, 1994, pp. 554-555.
[36] John Kobler, *Capone The Life and World of Al Capone*, New York, G. P. Putnam's Sons, 1971, p. 375.
[37] Laurence Bergreen, *Capone The Man and the Era*, pp. 555-556.
[38] Warden Johnston's Notebook, United States Penitentiary, Alcatraz, California Prisoner Records, Name: KARPAWICZ, Alvin No. 325-AZ, Conduct Report.
[39] Alcatraz Classification Records, National Archives, Bruno California.
[40] "Ma Barker," Lawrence County Historical Society Bulletin, Number 120, July 1991.
[41] *The Evening Star*, Washington, D.C., March 22, 1949; *Tulsa Tribune*, March 22, 1949.
[42] FBI Files Freedom of Information Act.
[43] FBI Files, Lloyd Barker, Death of, File Number 62-89785.
[44] *Tulsa Tribune*, March 22, 1949; FBI Files Freedom of Information Act.
[45] *St. Paul Dispatch*, March 23, 1962.
[46] *Lincoln Journal*, August 29, 1979.
[47] *Chicago Sun-Times*, August 30, 1979.
[48] *Seattle Times*, August 29, 2004.
[49] Nate Bomberg, "The Day Karpis Returned," Capitol, *The St. Paul Pioneer Press & Dispatch Sunday Magazine*, March 28, 1971, p. 10.

Bibliograhpy

Books

Alsop, Kenneth, *Hard Travelin'*, New York, New American Library, 1967.
    Attorney General of the United States, 1789-1985, Washington D.C., U.S. Department of Justice, 1985.
Behr, Edward. *Prohibition: Thirteen Years That Changed America*, New York, Arcade Publishing, 1996.
Bergreen, Laurence, *Capone The Man and the Era*, New York, Simon & Schuster, 1994.
Blegen, Theodore C., Minnesota, *A History of the State*, Minneapolis, University of Minnesota Press, 1963.
Bowen, Ezra, ed., *This Fabulous Century*, 6 volumes. New York: Time Life Books, 1969.
Cashman, Dennis Sean, *America in the Twenties and Thirties—The Olympian Age of Franklin Delano Roosevelt*, New York, New York University Press.
Coffey, Thomas M., *The Long Thirst: Prohibition in America: 1920–1933*, New York, W.W. Norton & Company, Inc.
Conley, Robert J, *The Saga of Henry Starr*, New York, Doubleday, 1989.
Cowdery, Ray R., *Capone's Chicago*, Lakeville, MN., Northstar Maschek

Books, 1987.

Dalton, Emmett, *Beyond the Law*, Coffeyville, Coffeyville Historical Society, Reprint of 1918 original.

DeFord, Miriam Allen, *The Real Ma Barker*, New York, Ace Publishing Corporation, 1970.

Edge, L. L., *Run the Cat Roads*, New York, Dembuer Books, 1981

Elliott, David Stewart, *Last Raid of the Daltons*, Coffeyville, Coffeyville Journal, 1892.

Flanagan, John T., *Theodore Hamm in Minnesota: His Family and Brewery*. Minneapolis, Pogo Press 1989.

Gentry, Curt, *J. Edgar Hoover, The Man and the Secrets*, New York, Penguin Books, 1992.

Gerdes, Louise I., editor, *The 1930s*, San Diego, Greenhaven Press, Inc., 2000.

Giradin, G. Russell and Helmer, William J., *Dillinger, The Untold Story*, Bloomington & Indianapolis, Indiana University Press, 1994.

Gish, Anthony, *American Bandits*, Girard, Kansas, Haldeman-Julius Publications, 1934.

Glewwe, Lois A, author and editor, *West St. Paul Centennial 1889-1989. The History of West St. Paul, Minnesota*, West St. Paul, West St. Paul Centennial Book Committee, the Mayor, and City Council, 1989.

Gordon, Alfred Bryce, *King of the Ozarks*, Mount Magazine, Magazine, Arkansas, Alfred Bryce Gordon, 1999.

Harris, Moira F., *The Paws of Refreshment The Story of Hamm Beer Advertising*, St. Paul, Pogo Press, 1990.

Hollatz, Tom, *Gangster Holidays The Lore and Legends of the Bad Guys*, St. Cloud, North Star Press of St. Cloud, Inc., 1989.

Hoover, J. Edgar and Ken Jones, *The FBI In Action*, 1957, New American Library.

Hounschell, Jim, "Ma Barker and Her Viper Brood," *Lawmen and Outlaws, 116 Years in Joplin's History*, published in cooperation with The Fraternal Order of Police Lodge #27, Walsworth Publishing Company, Inc., 1989.

Karpis, Alvin Karpis, Bill Trent, *Public Enemy Number One: The Alvin Karpis Story*, New York, Coward, McCann & Geoghegan, Inc., 1971.

Karpis, Alvin, Bill Trent, *Public Enemy Number One: The Alvin Karpis Story*, Richmond Hill, Ontario, Canada, Pocket Books Canada, 1973.

Kirchner, L. R., *Robbing Banks An American History 1831-1999*, Rockville Centre, New York, Sarpedon Publishing.

Kobler, John, *Capone The Life and World of Al Capone*, New York, G. P. Putnam's Sons, 1971.

Koeper, H. F., *Historic St. Paul Buildings*, St. Paul, St. Paul City Planning Board, 1964.

Kunz, Virginia Brainard, *St. Paul Saga of an American City*, Woodland Hills, California, Windsor Publications, Inc., 1977.

Lamme, Vernon, *Florida Lore Not Found in History Books*, 1973, privately printed.

Louderback, Lew, *The Bad Ones Gangsters of the '30 and Their Molls*, New York, Fawcett Books, 1974.

Maccabee, Paul, *John Dillinger Slept Here*, St. Paul, Minnesota Historical Society Press, 1996.

Mayer, George H., *The Political Career of Floyd B. Olson*, Minneapolis, University of Minnesota Press, 1951.

Miller, Floyd, *Marshal of the Last Frontier*, Garden City, New York, Doubleday & Company, Inc., 1968.

Millett, Larry, *Lost Twin Cities*, St. Paul, Minnesota Historical Society Press.

Nash, Jay Robert, *Bloodletters and Badmen Book 2*, New York, Warner Paperback Company, 1975.

Nash, Jay Robert, *Bloodletters and Badmen Book 3*, New York, Warner Paperback Library, 1975.

Nash, Jay Robert and Offen, Ron, *Dillinger Dead or Alive?* Chicago, Henry Rignery Company, 1970.

Nickel, Steven and Helmer, William J., *Baby Face Nelson Portrait of a Public Enemy*, Nashville, Cumberland House, 2002.

Quimby, Myron J., *The Devil's Emissaries*, South Brunswick & New York, A. S. Barnes and Company, 1969.

Rosheim, David L., *The Other Minneapolis or A History of the Minneapolis Skid Row*, Maquoketa, Andromeda Press, 1978.

Samp, Ardyce, *The Dillinger Robbery of the Security National Bank & Trust Company of Sioux Falls*, Sioux Falls, Rushmore House Publishing, 1992.

Samuelson, Nancy, *Shoot from the Lip, The Lives, Legends and Lies of the Three Guardsmen of Oklahoma and U. S. Marshal Nix*, Eastford, CT., Shooting Star Press, 1998.

Sevareid, Paul A., *The People's Lawyer: The Life of Eugene A. Rerat*, Minneapolis, Ross and Haines, 1963.

Shirley, Glenn and Bud Ledbetter, *The Fourth Guardsman*, Austin, Texas, Eakin Press, 1997.

Shirley, Glenn, *Henry Starr Last of the Real Bad Men*, New York, David McKay Company, Inc., 1965.

Smith, Robert Barr, *Daltons! The Raid on Coffeyville, Kansas*, Norman, University of Oklahoma Press, 1996.

South St. Paul Centennial History, *South St. Paul*, South St. Paul Historical Society, 1987; St. Paul

Stipanovich, Joseph, *City of Lakes An Illustrated History of Minneapolis*, Minneapolis, Windsor Publications, Inc., 1982.

Theoharis, Athan G., editor, *THE FBI A Comprehensive Guide from J. Edgar Hoover to The X-Files*, New York, Checkmark Books, 2000.

Toland, John, *The Dillinger Days*, New York, Da Capo Press, 1995.

True Crime Most Wanted, Alexandria, Virginia, Time-Life Books.

Truman, Harry S., *Harry S. Truman, Memoirs, Volume II, Years of Trial and Hope Garden City*, New York, Doubleday & Company, 1956.

Vadnais, Cynthia E., *Looking Back at White Bear Lake, A Pictorial History of the White Bear Lake Area*, White Bear Lake, Sentinel Printing Company, Inc., 2004.

Walker, Charles Rumford Walker, *American City*, New York, Farrar and Rinehart, Inc., 1937.

"Ma"—The Life and Times of "Ma" Barker and Her Boys

Magazines & Periodicals

Bomberg, Nate., "The Day Karpis Returned," Capitol, *The St. Paul Pioneer Press & Dispatch Sunday Magazine*, March 28, 1971.

Bomberg, Nate, "Veteran Newsman Recalls Hamm, Bremer Kidnaps," *St. Paul Sunday Pioneer Press*, August 6, 1972.

Chapman, Paul M., "A Dartmoor Mystery," *Sherlock Holmes The Detective Magazine*, Issue 43, 2001.

Cordry, Dee, "The Outlaw and Lawmen Map of Oklahoma 1865-1935," Internet.

Cowie, Anne E., "Two Horses and One Buffalo Robe, The Ramsey Count Attorney's Office and Its 150 Years: All the Frailties of Human Nature," *Ramsey County History*, Fall 2000, Volume 35, Number 3.

Curtis, William, "Dateline April 7, 1933 PROHIBITION ENDS!" *Brewery Age*, March/April 1958.

Denney, James, "The Day the Barker Gang Hit Fairbury," *Sunday World-Herald Magazine of the Midlands*, March 30, 1969.

Hrenchir, Tim, "Other 1930s Outlaws Had Topeka Ties," *Topeka Capital-Journal*, date unknown.

Jones, Diana Nelson, "Y2K a Breeze When Compared to Life in 1900 When Our City Had No 'H,'" *Pittsburgh Post-Gazette*, December 31, 1999.

Karpis, Alvin with Trent, Bill, "The Hollihocks, the Green Lantern and Other Pleasure Places of St. Paul," Capitol, *The St. Paul Pioneer Press & Dispatch Sunday Magazine*, March 28, 1971.

Kellock, Katharine A., "Bad News for Uncle Sam's Female Public Enemies," *Every Week Magazine*, May 1935.

Livesey, Robert, "Information About Alvin Karpis," Little Red Schoolhouse, Inc., Web site.

Lovering, Lisa, "We Will Remember," .38 Special Press for police files.

"Ma Barker, Crooks Ran in Her Family," *Pageant Magazine*, December 1959.

"Ma Barker," *Lawrence County Historical Society Bulletin*, Number 120, July 1991.

Millikin, Rick, "Cuba's International Playa Veradero," Travel Lady

Magazine, Internet.

Minneapolis Labor Review, May 11, 1934, Volume 27, No. 403. Official organ of Minneapolis Central Labor Union and Hennepin County, the Minneapolis Building Trades Council, the United Card and Label Council, and the Minnesota Pipe Trades Association.

Morgan, R. D., "The Severs Hotel Murder Mystery," Internet.

Moskowitz, Dara, "Minneapolis Confidential," *City Pages*, Volume 16, Number 775, October 11, 1995.

Outlook Magazine, June 8, 1928.

Poholek, Catherine H., "Prohibition in the 1920s, Thirteen Years that Damaged America," Online, May 6, 1998.

"Public Enemy #1 - John Dillinger," EyeWitness to History, www.eyewitnesstohistory.com (2000).

Riege, Edwin J. (Ed), "The Barker-Karpis Rouges," *Minnesota Police Journal*, August 1991.

Samuelson, Nancy B., "The Passing of Chris Madsen," *Oklahombres Journal*, Volume II, Number 3, Spring 1991.

Samuelson, Nancy B., "Chris Madsen: Soldier, Oklahoma 89'er, and Deputy United States Marshal," *Oklahombres Journal*, Volume IV, Number 4, Summer 1993.

Samuelson, Nancy B., "Bill Doolin was Killed, and Killed, and Killed," *Oklahombres Journal*, Volume VII, Number 3, Spring1996.

Smith, Patterson, "Thomas McDade and the Annals of Murder," *AB Bookman's Weekly*, April 22, 1996

Thorton, Mark, "Policy Analysis: Alcohol Prohibition Was a Failure," July 17, 1991, Online Netscape, April 23, 1998.

Time Magazine, February 20, 1933.

Time Magazine, October 29, 1934.

Tuohy, John William, "The St. Paul Incident, Part 1," *Gambling Magazine*, 1999.

Vogel, Elsie, "In the Early 1900s, FL 'Law and Order' Unfolds," *Forest Lake Times*, May 21, 2003.

Zehnder, Charles G., "Barker/Karpis Gang's $100,000 Stash," *Western*

"Ma"—The Life and Times of "Ma" Barker and Her Boys

Treasures Magazine, June 1970.

Manuscripts, Letters, Reports

FBI Agent E. Scheidt to Agent Clegg dated May 1, 1935, Federal Bureau of Investigation, Freedom of Information and Privacy Acts.

Rick Mattix letter to author dated January 6, 2006.

Rick Mattix letter to author dated January 9, 2006.

"Supervisor" Rosen letter to St. Paul Special Agent K. R. MacIntire, December 29, 1955. Federal Bureau of Investigation Freedom of Information and Privacy Acts, Subject: Kate Barker "Ma," File Number 7-5768695.

United States Bureau of Investigation, Report of Special Agent D. P. Sullivan, Chicago, Illinois, February 17, 1936.

Special Agent C. B. Winstead Memorandum for File, July 25, 1934. Federal Bureau of Investigation

Presentations, Theses

Ted Curtis Smythe, "A History of the Minneapolis Journal, 1878-1939," unpublished thesis.

Newspapers

Beloit Daily News, August 18, 1932; August 19, 1932.
Boston Evening American, October 24, 1931.
Brooklyn Daily Eagle, December 18, 1931.

Casper (Wyoming) *Tribune-Herald*, April 3, 1934.

Cedar Rapids Gazette, June 9, 1934.

Chandler News-Publicist, April 2, 1915.

Chicago Daily News, December 20, 1930; February 27, 1931; January 18, 1939.

Chicago Daily Tribune, June 13, 1931; September 21, 1933; January 31, 1934; February 23, 1934; March 20, 1943.

Chicago Sunday Tribune, April 22, 1934.

Chicago Herald and Examiner, November 30, 1933; May 19, 1934; November 29, 1934; January 21, 1935; January 24, 1935; January 31, 1939.

Chicago Sun-Times, August 30, 1979.

Cleveland Press, March 22, 1932

Dallas Morning News, July 25, 1933; April 2, 1934; May 24, 1934; January 17, 1935.

Des Moines Tribune, March 14, 1934.

East Liverpool (Ohio) *Review*, October 22, 1934.

Fairbury Journal, April 6, 1933; April 13, 1933; April 20, 1933; April 4, 1935; January 19, 1939.

Fairbury Journal News, April 23, 2004.

Fairbury News, April 4, 1933.

Flandreau Herald, September 7, 1932.

Forest Lake Times, May 21, 2003.

Jackson Daily News, September 26, 1933.

(Jacksonville) *Florida Times-Union*, January 17, 1935;

Joplin News Herald, September 30, 1935; October 1, 1935.

Lincoln Journal, August 29, 1979.

Los Angeles Herald Express, Night Edition, June 17, 1933; November 27, 1933; July 23, 1934.

Mankato Free Press, September 1, 1932; September 2, 1932; September 23, 1932; December 17, 1932; December 20, 1932; December 21, 1932; December 22, 1932; December 23, 1932; December 27, 1932; December 29, 1932; December 30, 1932; June 24, 1933; September 11, 1933; September 13, 1933; April 15, 1935; May 1, 1935; April 20,

1936; April 21, 1936; April 22, 1936; April 23, 1936; April 24, 1936; June 8, 1936; June 9, 1936; July 8, 1936; . September 3, 1936; December 18, 1936.

Minneapolis Journal, March 9, 1929; October 30, 1929; September 4, 1930; February 25, 1931; April 10, 1931; April 24, 1932; July 24, 1932; August 3, 1932; October 31, 1932; November 3, 1932; November 10, 1932; December 17, 1932; December 18, 1932; December 19, 1932; December 20, 1932; May 16, 1934; May 17, 1934; May 21, 1934; May 24, 1934; July 21, 1934.

Minneapolis Tribune, December 5, 1928.

Moody County Enterprise, September 8, 1932; March 15, 1934.

Mount Vernon, (MO.) Fountain & Journal, September 22, 1892

New York Daily Mirror, May 13, 1932.

New York Daily News, February 9, 1931.

New York Evening Graphic, May 4, 1932.

New York Times, January 19, 1934; February 9, 1934; January 17, 1935; January 21, 1935.

New York World Telegram, March 3, 1934.

Oklahoma News, November 1936

Pittsburgh Post-Gazette, December 31, 1999.

Redwood Gazette, September 29, 1932.

St. Joseph Daily Gazette, April 5, 1882.

St. Paul Daily News, April 23, 1934; May 2, 1936..

St. Paul Dispatch, April 25, 1927; March 3, 1931; March 16, 1932; June 17, 1933; August 30, 1933; January 18, 1934; February 8, 1934; March 23, 1962.

St. Paul Pioneer Press, December 25, 1887; December 17, 1932; December 19, 1932; December 20, 1932; December 21, 1932; December 22, 1932; August 31, 1933; January 20, 1934; January 21, 1934; January 22, 1934; January 23, 1934; January 24, 1934; April 1, 1934; April 24, 1934; April 28, 1934; August 24, 1934; January 17, 1935; January 18, 1935; January 19, 1935; January 20, 1935; January 21, 1935; January 22, 1935; January 23, 1935.August 6, 1972.

San Francisco Chronicle, January 14, 1939; January 15, 1939; January 16, 1939; January 17, 1939; January 18, 1939; January 19, 1939; January 20, 1939; January 25, 1939; April 29, 1941.

San Francisco News, January 14, 1939.

Seattle Times, August 29, 2004.

(Sioux Falls) *Daily Argus Leader*, March 6, 1934.

South St. Paul Reporter, August 31, 1933.

Springfield Daily News, January 17, 1935; January 18, 1935; January 19, 1935; January 21, 1935.

Springfield Leader and Press, January 9, 1935;.January 16, 1935; January 17, 1935; January 21, 1935.

Topeka Capital-Journal, date unknown.

Tulsa Tribune, March 22, 1949.

Tulsa World, December 30, 1926; August 20, 1932; January 17, 1935; May 2, 1936.

(Wahpeton) *Richland County Farmer-Globe*, October 4, 1932; October 7, 1932.

Washington Star, January 25, 1939; March 22, 1949.

(Xenia, Ohio) *Evening Gazette*, July 23, 1934

Interviews

Paul Maccabee, Crime Historian & author of *John Dillinger Slept Here*, Interview, March 18, 2003 on Verne Miller by Brian Bull.

Mrs. Sally Koether telephone interview with author February 7, 1999.

Doris Lockerman (Rogers), Melvin Purvis's FBI Secretary, Interview May, 2003 by Joshua Welsh.

Cathy Prachar interview with author March 16, 1983, Plymouth, Minnesota.

Alston Purvis interview conducted by Brian Bull, April 29, 2003.

Mrs. Frances Siftar interview with author February 22, 1999.

Ray Terrill, autobiographical interview as told to Meredith Williams, "I

Tried Crime." Series, Oklahoma News, five consecutive weeks, November 1936.

Public Documents and Records

Alcatraz Classification Records, National Archives, Bruno California.
Alcatraz History—Prisoner: Alvin "Creepy" Karpis (#325-AZ)
Alcatraz History—Prisoner Henri Young, National Archives, San Bruno, California.
lcatraz Island, U. S. Penitentiary, National Park Records.
Cherokee Nation Cultural Resource Center Archives, Tahlequah, Oklahoma.
Davis v. State, 227 P. 848, 27 Okl.Cr. 319, Oklahoma Court of Criminal Appeals.
Enid, Oklahoma Police Department Memorial Files.
Federal Reserve Bank of Minneapolis Archives.
Federal Bureau of Investigation History Archives. United States Department of Justice.
Federal Bureau of Investigation Files, Freedom of Information Act, File #76-4175, Arthur Barker, Escaped Federal Prisoner (Death of).
Federal Bureau of Investigation Files, Freedom of Information Act, Lloyd Barker, Death of, File Number 62-89785.
Federal Bureau of Investigation Files, Freedom of Information Act, Charles "Pretty Boy" Floyd Summary.
Federal Bureau of Investigation Freedom of Information and Privacy Acts, Subject: Herman Barker, (Death of), File Number 26-9961.
Federal Bureau of Investigation Freedom of Information and Privacy Acts, Subject: Kate Barker "Ma," File Number 7-5768695.
FBI Files, RCS:TD I.C.#7-576, November 19, 1936, The Kidnaping of Edward George Bremer, St. Paul, Minnesota, History and Early Association of the Karpis-Barker Gang Prior to the Abduction of Mr.

Bremer; Federal Bureau of Investigation Freedom of Information and Privacy Acts, Subject: Kate Barker "Ma," File Number 7-5768695, Memorandum Re: Kate Barker, August 19, 1955.

Federal Bureau of Investigation Files, Freedom of Information Act, File #32-16384, Alvin Karpis and Fred Barker.

Freedom of Information and Privacy Acts, Subject: John Dillinger, File Number 62-29777-1.

Federal Bureau of Investigation Files, Freedom of Information Act, Melvin H. Purvis, File Number 67-7489.

Federal Bureau of Investigation General Archives.

Federal Bureau of Investigation Headline Archives 7489.

Federal Bureau of Investigation, "New Orleans" Barker-Karpis File #7-15 FOIPA #445856.

Federal Bureau of Prisons, United States Department of Justice Records.

Carl Fredrickson Family Archives, Document #19.

Kansas Department of Corrections.

Landmark Center, Old Federal Courts brochure.

Laramie County, Wyoming Sheriff's Department Records.

Lawrence County Courthouse Archives, Mt. Vernon, Missouri, Book F, Marriage License of George and Kate Barker.

Lee P. Loomis Archive of Mason City History, First National Bank Robbery, Mason City Public Library.

Maccabee, Paul, St. Paul Gangster History, 1981-1995, Research Files, Minnesota Historical Society, St. Paul, Minnesota.

MPD Federation, Police Officers Federation of Minneapolis Archives.

Nathan Boone Homestead State Historic Site, Missouri Department of Natural Resources Archives.

National Archives, Bruno, California.

National Park Service.

The Officer Down Memorial Page, Inc.

Okmulgee, Oklahoma Police Department Archives.

Parole Report by U.S. Attorney for 49369-L (Charles Fitzgerald), no date (1936?); Whelan, Parole report for Edmund C. Bartholmey, August 1,

1936 (cross-filed in Charles Fitzgerald file).

Poulsen, Ellen, "Don't Call Us Molls: Women of the John Dillinger Gang," The Alderson Federal Correctional Facility Archives.

South Dakota Public Broadcasting.

U.S. Penitentiary Leavenworth, Kansas, Admission Summary for #46928 (Arthur Barker), June 3, 1935

Warden Johnston's Notebook, United States Penitentiary, Alcatraz, California PrisonerRecords, Name: KARPAWICZ, Alvin No. 325-AZ, Conduct Report.

Memoirs and letters of former Agent, Charles Winstead, Red River Historical Museum,

Sherman, Texas.